Forgotten People: Poverty, Risk and Social Security in Indonesia

Verhandelingen van het Koninklijk Instituut voor Taal-, Land- en Volkenkunde

VOLUME 296

Power and Place in Southeast Asia

VOLUME 6

The titles published in this series are listed at *brill.com/vki*

Forgotten People: Poverty, Risk and Social Security in Indonesia

The Case of the Madurese

By

Gerben Nooteboom

BRILL

LEIDEN | BOSTON

KITLV

The realization of this publication was made possible by the support of KITLV (Royal Netherlands Institute of Southeast Asian and Caribbean Studies).

Cover illustration: Brickmaking enterprise (*serobong*) of Madurese migrants in East Kalimantan (photo by author).

Library of Congress Cataloging-in-Publication Data

Nooteboom, Gerben, 1970-
Forgotten people : poverty, risk and social security in Indonesia : the case of the Madurese / by Gerben Nooteboom.
pages cm -- (Verhandelingen van het Koninklijk Instituut voor Taal-, Land- en Volkenkunde ; 296/6)
Includes bibliographical references and index.
ISBN 978-90-04-28250-6 (hardback : alk. paper) -- ISBN 978-90-04-28298-8 (e-book) 1. Poor--Indonesia. 2. Peasants--Indonesia--Java--Economic conditions. 3. Madurese (Indonesian people)--Indonesia--Kalimantan Timur--Economic conditions. I. Title. II. Series: Verhandelingen van het Koninklijk Instituut voor Taal-, Land- en Volkenkunde ; 296/6.
HC450.P6N66 2015
305.5'6909598--dc23

2014035814

This publication has been typeset in the multilingual 'Brill' typeface. With over 5,100 characters covering Latin, IPA, Greek, and Cyrillic, this typeface is especially suitable for use in the humanities.
For more information, please see www.brill.com/brill-typeface.

ISSN 1572-1892
ISBN 978-90-04-28250-6 (hardback)
ISBN 978-90-04-28298-8 (e-book)

This book is printed on acid-free paper.

FSC www.fsc.org MIX Paper from responsible sources FSC® C109576

Printed by Printforce, the Netherlands

Contents

Acknowledgements

This book is based on long periods of fieldwork in East Java and East Kalimantan and takes a broad perspective integrating theoretical issues related to peasants, inequality and individual agency. It combines the study of poverty, risk and insecurity with classic and contemporary debates in rural sociology, anthropology and development studies. I often think how fortunate I have been to study at Wageningen University in the early 1990s, to continue my PhD at Radboud University, Nijmegen during the early 2000s and to work as lecturer and researcher at the University of Amsterdam (UvA) from 2006 onwards as this has offered me networks and ideas sufficiently broad and theoretically deep and challenging to integrate and combine all these aspects.

During the fieldwork and the writing of this book, I am especially grateful to a few people who inspired me, guided me and made this study possible in one way or another. I remember Frans Hüsken, who unfortunately passed away far too early, as the person who enabled me to conduct this study in the first place. He challenged me to dive deep into historical debates on agrarian change and rural development, and stimulated me to study the lives of 'forgotten people' in the rural Indonesia of today. How much I would have loved to show him the final result. I would also like to thank Huub de Jonge for pointing me towards the Madurese in the first place. We both share love and respect for the Madurese in the new Indonesia. I also thank Ben White and Franz and Keebet von Benda-Beckmann, who, from a distance, have been very influential in this study, both academically and also personally. I owe thanks to Mario Rutten and John McCarthy for critically and constructively reading parts of the final manuscript and to the department of sociology and anthropology of the University of Amsterdam who enabled me to finish this book during busy teaching schedules.

I cannot possibly mention all by name. Among those I will mention are colleagues, friends and PhD fellows at the Department of Anthropology and Development studies in Nijmegen: Catrien Notermans, Edwin de Jong and Oane Visser who read and commented on earlier drafts of chapters and papers and my close colleagues at the University of Amsterdam: Laurens Bakker, Leo Douw, Tina Harris, Barak Kalir, Willem van Schendel, Roanne van Voorst and especially Rosanne Rutten who was never tired of discussing agrarian questions in Southeast Asia today.

I thank the Royal Dutch Academy of Sciences (KNAW) for sponsoring the first part of the research dealing with East Java, the University of Nijmegen for paying a large part of the costs of the second part of the fieldwork in East Kalimantan, as well as the Moving Matters (Momat) research group at the

University of Amsterdam, the Amsterdam Institute of Social Science Research (AISSR), as well as The Netherlands Organisation for Scientific Research (NWO) and NWO-Wotro, Science for Global Development for covering some of the travel costs. In Indonesia, I want to thank the Indonesian Institute of Sciences (LIPI) for supporting the work in the field, the Population and Policy Study Centre (PSPK) and the department of Anthropology of the Gadjah Mada University, Yogyakarta for all their support and facilities, both at home and abroad and the University of Mulawarman, Samarinda.

I am grateful to the book series editors Gerry van Klinken and Ed Aspinall for reading previous versions of this book and I thank the two anonymous reviewers for their serious and helpful comments. I believe their inputs have improved the book greatly. I also thank Giles Stacey for correcting and editing this book.

A special thank you goes to my friends and colleagues in several research projects for their friendship, trust and helpful comments. Particularly, Hotze Lont, Juliette Koning, Ratna Saptari, Ruli Marianti, Pande Made Kutanegara, Pujo Semedi, Andreas Susanto, Edwin de Jong, Laurens Bakker and also many others who have become friends as much as colleagues.

Most important, I would like to thank Jolanda, my wife, and Aron, Ellis and Thimo, our children, for always being supportive and cheerful and for joining me during several long research periods in the field. Jolanda, you have sacrificed a lot and supported me doing fieldwork in a great way. As a family, our lives became shaped by and entangled with Indonesia and I believe, in the end, it has enriched us all.

In the research areas, special thanks go to *Pak* Eko, *Bu* Sumrati Eko, *Mas* Abdurahman and *Mas* Taufiq who were great assistants and who developed into clever, flexible and creative fieldworkers from whom I learnt more about fieldwork than books could ever teach. Without you, this book would not be as it is now. When we said goodbye, I felt I was leaving behind more than just friends and colleagues. I hope you will never lose your eagerness and curiosity, and continue to wonder about the world you live in. Besides them, I thank *Pak* Bambang Suwito and *Pak* Asis Efendi in East Java and *Pak Haji* Yusuf and *Pak* Holik in East Kalimantan for their hospitality, company and for facilitating me whenever needed.

Above all, I want to thank all those Madurese friends, neighbours, villagers and migrants for accepting me and my family. It was an honour and privilege to work, learn and live with you. I thank all of you who patiently explained the simplest things to me over and over again, who answered silly and sometimes sensitive questions and recalled stories, figures, events and feelings, sometimes entrusting me with experiences that were never intended to be told. It is for you, and by you, that this book is in the first place written.

List of Maps, Tables, Figures and Illustrations

Maps

Tables

Figures

Illustrations

CHAPTER 1

Introduction

In the last two decades, major changes have taken place in the livelihoods of Indonesian people. Some groups in society have experienced major improvements in living conditions, benefitting from steady economic growth of about 6.5% annually (Burke and Resosudarmo 2012:301), while other groups have missed the boat and face economic stagnation, social exclusion, political underrepresentation, dispossession of land and growing inequality (Alatas et al. 2012, Hall et al. 2011, McCarthy et al. 2012, Nooteboom 2008:43). This inequality is often based on class and ethnicity and includes spatial dimensions such as inequalities between cities and rural areas and between regions (Mishra et al. 2009, Suryadarma et al. 2006). A significant group of people who seem to have largely missed out in the new Indonesia are the Madurese[1] (Stenross 2011:27–29).

Although the national economy has almost doubled since 2000,[2] a large proportion of the Indonesian people still live in poverty and face daily difficulties in making ends meet. According to a 2012 World Bank Country Report: 'Out of a population of 234 million, more than 32 million Indonesians currently live below the poverty line and approximately half of all households remain clustered around the national poverty line set at [a very low] 200,262 rupiahs per

1 Throughout this book, the term 'Madurese' simply refers to Madurese-speaking people. Among them, there are many differences regarding area of origin, self-identification and official representation. Madurese themselves make more refined qualifications regarding region of origin and language use, and their self-identification might differ from those imposed by outsiders. Madurese from Madura, for instance, do not always regard Madurese from mainland East Java as Madurese.

The Madurese originally came from the densely populated and resource-poor island of Madura. Since the 17th and 18th centuries Cribb 2000:33, 52, large groups of Madurese have moved to eastern parts of mainland Java (including Surabaya, Malang, Pasuruan, Sitobondo, Bondowoso and parts of Jember, Banyuwangi and Lumayang). See: Cribb 2000:52; Stenross 2011:24; Tennekens 1963:310. They also live on the Bawean and Kangean islands. Nowadays, they can be found in all the major cities of Indonesia and in rural West and Central Kalimantan Husson 1997a with major concentrations in Pontianak, Sambas and the large cities of East Kalimantan, Balikpapan and Samarinda.

2 The country's gross national income per capita has steadily risen from $2,200 in 2000 to $3,720 in 2009, and it continues to grow at rates above 6 – 6.5% annually (www.worldbank .org country overview, accessed February 2013).

month ($22)'.[3] This poverty consists of 'old' patterns and 'new' forms of poverty.

Poverty in Indonesia is not as static as the World Bank and BPS (National Board of Statistics) figures of persistent poverty might suggest. Some of the poor have lived in abject poverty all their lives, others have only recently fallen into poverty, while others have managed to climb the social ladder. Key elements are social relations offering support and protection, but surprisingly little is known about the meaning and scope of these relations today (Hüsken and Koning 2006:8). The existence or absence of social ties and relationships of care, support and social security make a great difference to the ultimate consequence of poverty on people's lives. Today, poverty in Indonesia is diverse and dynamic and, consequently, social relations of support and protection that provide social security are worthy of a more detailed study.

In this book, this persistent and yet dynamic nature of poverty will be explored in detail. The book aims at understanding the unstable, vulnerable and dynamic livelihoods of poor, Madurese people living on the margins of a nation in flux. It is based on extensive fieldwork in a village in Bondowoso, East Java, and among migrants in Samarinda, East Kalimantan, between 1998 and 2010. To maximize contrast in the case studies, the first selected location is an upland village (Krajan[4]) in rural Bondowoso, East Java, and the second is the urban Samarinda in East Kalimantan (see Map 1). In East Java, the population of Krajan speak Madurese and moved there long ago, whereas the Madurese migrants in East Kalimantan are relatively recent arrivals. While livelihoods and social relationships are reasonably established in East Java, the livelihoods of Madurese migrants in East Kalimantan are both dynamic and precarious. The book will use these two case studies of Madurese livelihoods outside Madura as a window to study the universal theme of poverty, social security and risk in Indonesia. The cases contrast the relatively stable setting of a rural society in East Java with the vagaries of migrant life in the bustling city of Samarinda and, at the same time, they are linked through the study of one ethnic group.

Although the case studies in this book deal with people living in small areas, namely the village of Krajan, close to the Argopuro Mountain in East Java, and those people working and living in the brick kilns, stone quarries, plantations and slums of Samarinda, East Kalimantan, it develops an approach which aims

3 www.worldbank.org country overview Indonesia (accessed February 2013). Exact figures differ depending on the kind of poverty line used. In January 2014, Kompas speaks of 28,55 million people in Indonesia who live below the very low BPS poverty line (Kompas, Special Supplement Indonesia Satu, Wednesday January 8, 2014: A-D).

4 Most of the names of places and people in this study are pseudonyms.

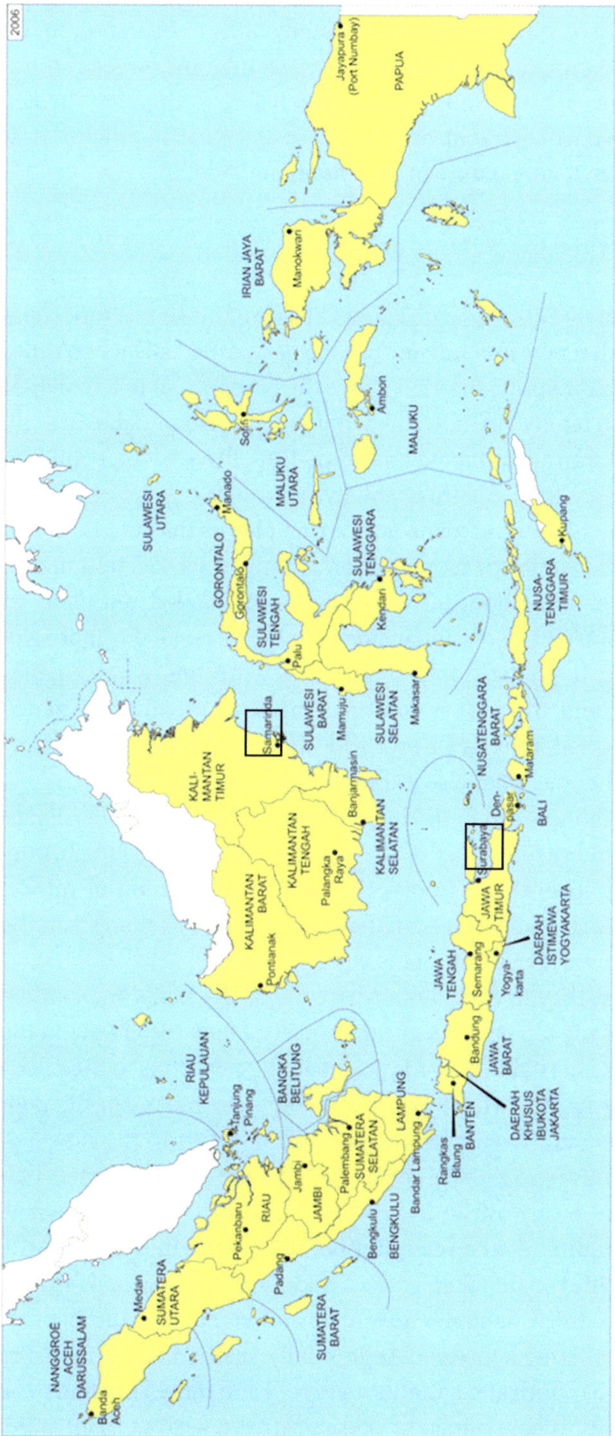

MAP 1 *Map of Indonesia. Research locations*
SOURCE: CRIBB 2010, DIGITAL ATLAS.

to go beyond the study of small localities. The study aims to overcome static images of poverty and simplified distinctions between migrant survival strategies and village support systems in isolated areas. Before addressing the key themes of this book, we will first look at the Satrawi and Patik families in East Java and illustrate the dynamic nature of poverty in more detail.

Fallen from affluence: the Satrawi family

It is hard to estimate Satrawi's age. I guess he is around sixty. Work starts to become a burden now and income hard to gain, especially when times are tough. Mr (*Pak*) Satrawi married about thirty years ago to a daughter of a relatively rich family but, nowadays, not much of these riches are left. They had six children and adopted a seventh. Now, three of their children are married, one has died and three still live at home.

'Nowadays, my household owns only a tiny plot of infertile land, not enough to feed the family for more than two months' Satrawi tells me. 'In the past, however, we belonged to the better-off'. Faded remnants of woodcarvings above the doors and inside their house recall this more glorious past. Today, the house looks shabby and worn-out, windowpanes have been sold, and the roof is in urgent need of repair. 'Our match (*jodoh*) was not good, they say. I probably should not have married my wife', Satrawi sighs, 'but what else did we do wrong?'

In front of his house, and in the houses of neighbours and old friends, I was gradually told the full story of the Satrawi family. It is a long history of a family going from riches to rags through a combination of misfortune, sheer bad luck and perhaps an inability to read the changes in the social and economic fabric of Krajan society.

After marriage, they inherited many rice fields, dry fields and cattle – they were part of the top echelon of rural society. Many recall how, in the past, Satrawi was charitable towards poor people, gave alms to the needy and staged huge parties where everybody felt welcome, even his poor neighbours. Gradually, twenty years ago, decline set in in the house of Satrawi. The rituals (*selamatan*) performed to commemorate their parents' deaths were costly, cattle were sold and land had to be pawned. Their second daughter died a year after her marriage while giving birth, leaving a grandchild to be taken care of and more costly rituals to perform. Ami, their third daughter divorced and remarried three times within six years, costing a fortune. Additionally, she had to be treated in hospital for over a month and so cattle were sold and more land had to be pawned. They had to cover most of these costs themselves as gifts and support from relatives and neighbours were insufficient.

Notwithstanding dwindling resources, Mrs (*Bu*) Satrawi continued to spend money freely on 'expensive' food such as meat, chicken, noodles, coffee and sugar. She was known for her collection of *sarong* and 'her children looked like princesses', as people say in the neighbourhood. She kept up her lifestyle even when the family income was far too low to finance all her luxurious expenditures. The pawned rice fields had to be sold, and more land had to be pawned in order to obtain credit to keep up appearances and to meet the demands of the ritual exchange economy (organizing large *selamatan* and giving expensive presents). They still hoped to recover from their misfortune but, as their main resources such as cattle and land had gone, household income fell drastically making it impossible to repay debts and regain the pawned lands.

In 1997, at the onset of the economic crisis, their situation was dire. They had fallen into the lowest stratum of the village. During the economic crisis at the end of the millennium and the subsequent rapid inflation, Satrawi's cash income dropped yet further and he could no longer buy items such as fish, eggs, noodles, coffee, sugar or cigarette wrapping paper. He had to use the dried leaves of maize cobs to roll his own cigarettes. Every time I met him, he smiled happily, but his face looked older and more tired. If I asked him how he was, the answer was always the same: *'Biasa, biasa saja, kerja terus* [...] *Alhamdulillah saya masih makan'*, ('The same, the same, we just work on [...] Thank God, I can still eat').

Nevertheless, Satrawi was still invited to weddings, praying groups and *selamatan,* often as a special guest or as a prayer leader (freeing him from the obligation to contribute financially). He is known as a good and respectable man, a good prayer leader, as one who never complains and is always ready to join mutual help and cooperative labour activities. He does not try to keep up appearances now that he is poor. By knowing his place, he is accepted by everyone. 'His wife is different. She still has difficulties in adjusting to lower living standards and rejects work such as helping with kitchen activities in the houses of rich people', *Bu* Maryami, a neighbour, commented. 'She never learnt to work. Still today, she cannot do dirty work and instead calls her daughter to do it. *Bu* Satrawi is still so haughty. People here do not want to help her'.

Although the cash income of the household decreased substantially and prices tripled in the course of the crisis years, Satrawi's family did not slide much further down. Their own resources were completely used up, but friends and neighbouring landowners continued to offer work regularly. By working their fields, Satrawi earned some stable income in kind (rice and maize). They also helped his family out with some small loans, free meals and invitations to religious parties and *selamatan* where food is served and can be taken home. Also, Satrawi's fourth son, Saleh, married into a richer family who owned rice fields and were also active in house construction. 'I hope Saleh will be able to support himself, and maybe us, in the future', Satrawi said.

Upwardly mobile: Patik

The story of one of Satrawi's neighbours, the Patik family, forms quite a contrast. The house of Pak Patik is made from solid bricks and stands on a hill a hundred metres above the crowded and dirty neighbourhood where Satrawi lives. While the family of Satrawi was falling from relative wealth to poverty over the course of a dozen years, in the same period the Patik family moved from rags to riches. Once, Patik and his wife worked for the Satrawi family, but now Satrawi works for the Patik family.

Pak Patik, a cattle trader, is a self-made man, and he is proud of this. He likes to wear good shirts and jeans, and often wraps an expensive Madurese sarong over his shoulders, making his tall figure even more imposing. When Patik enters a house, he enters slowly and with dignity. He says he is not even afraid of the village head, and that one day he will run for village head himself. However, when sitting in the same room as Bagenda, the village head, he is noticeably silent. Other villagers all agree that the story of Patik is a fine one, and that he is very clever, perhaps too clever, in accumulating wealth.

In the past, he was one of the former friends and frequent visitors to Satrawi's *selematan* and, just after his marriage, he worked as a poor labourer in Satrawi's fields. Nowadays, as a rich man, he seems to have forgotten the former generosity of the Satrawi family. Patik's children played in Satrawi's house and were given sweets and snacks, but now they order him around when working in the fields and only pay him a little respect because of his age. However, their father is said to be worse. 'Patik has no heart', villagers say. Even if he has ready money in his pocket, he does not lend money to less fortunate villagers such as Satrawi. 'Those people don't know how to deal with money', Patik says, 'I will not give them money, because they only know how to spend it. They should take better care of their own money'. Saleh, the son of Satrawi, put it differently: 'If I ask for help or money, there is none to be had they say, but, if I am in need and want to sell a cow, or if I need to pawn a piece of land, definitely there is money'. Indeed, half of the five hectares of land that Patik has acquired over the last fifteen years was once the property of *pak* Satrawi, his former patron and protector who is now a labourer on his own land.

> In Patik's perception, he acquired his wealth on his own merits. At least that is what he likes his visitors to believe. However, people say that, in fact, it was his wife who did most of the work in managing the lands, controlling the household budget and building up a large network of labourers through exchanging gifts with neighbours and friends in the village. She comes from a relatively well-off family but only inherited a small area of rice field because her father used almost all of his land, cattle and money to finance his pilgrimage to Mecca. According to neighbours, she used to work terribly hard, and for years did not ask for anything for herself being determined to regain the 'lost' family property. She became famous for saying: 'Don't spend, save the money to buy a calf first'. Although thrifty, neighbours generally respect her, and all mention her kindness. She secretly offers free meals to poor children from the neighbourhood on a regular basis and is willing to provide small incidental loans (in the form of cash, rice or maize) to the wives of their labourers. Besides this, labourers praise the food she serves for being tasty. 'There you get real coffee, and plenty of sugar in it', they say, 'she is not like her husband, who is even too greedy to buy cigarettes for his workers'. Without her, probably no-one would have been willing to work for Patik and so she helped him build his wealth.
>
> In Patik's view, he, and he alone, can take care of their family wealth, and he even tries to check all his wife's expenditure. Others are not entitled to his support 'because nobody has helped me in the past'. He once said, 'Why should I help someone who should be able to take care of themselves?' Only if people are struck by disaster is he willing to support them, he says. 'He doesn't notice common people. In the past he was poorer than I am, but now he only thinks about money, not about us'. Patik says himself that he doesn't want to have too many social relations. 'Having too many friends is an expensive business'.

What went wrong with the Satrawi family? Was it simply bad luck with the family hit by a series of misfortunes? Clearly, they made poor choices in maintaining a high level of consumption and by failing to accumulate as household resources dwindled. They also clung too long to their previous elite status and sold productive assets such as land and cattle to maintain this status. They kept on investing in social relations through expensive rituals, helping out and gift giving even when they were impoverished. Maybe they backed the wrong horse by clinging on too long to old village values of sharing and mutual help and expected more help in return when times got tough. When confronted with a series of misfortunes and becoming impoverished, little came back from all the past investments.

Were all the investments in social relationships unsuccessful? During and after the crisis, they clutched to their last straw: the once large network of neighbours and friends. Where other villagers and returning migrants had difficulties in finding work, they remained part of a social network which offered access to work, small loans and irregular distribution of food. Slowly, with help from children and relatives, the family has recovered to the level of 'poor but decent' in recent years. Until today, however, they have not regained their former lands.

For the Patik family, social relations are also important, but perceived as 'expensive'. For them, social obligations are a barrier to social mobility, but also needed to mobilize labour. They strategically juggle between opportunities and obligations. While the thriftiness of Patik is resented, his wife is praised for being good, and she maintains good relations so as to able to mobilize loyal workers. The case of the Patik family also shows that social relations might be less relevant for social climbers, as their maintenance might hamper accumulation, while they do does not protect against falling into poverty. Here, the double meaning of social relationships comes to the fore; they can be useful and protecting, as well as exploitative and a means to control people. Social relations have multiple meanings for different people in different periods of time.

These examples show that the lives and living conditions of poor people are not stable, should not be taken for granted and can change quickly. Poverty and affluence are not fixed categories, and neither are friendships and other social ties. Wealth can diminish over time, and friends and relatives can disappear or turn out to be unreliable partners. Sometimes minor events or misfortunes are sufficient to trigger the downfall of a family while others receive support and are able to cope with the difficulties. Conversely, with some luck, hard work and favourable conditions, some Madurese manage to rise above others and establish a stronger livelihood or better support relationships. How should one capture these differences among socioeconomic classes, events and trajectories?

Key Themes of the Book

The examples also show that people seldom bring about major changes in their livelihoods on their own. Households consist of men, women, children and often elderly parents. Even if these members have conflicting interests, they eat together, work together, pool resources and care, and support one another. As a household, and sometimes as individuals, members exchange gifts, cooperate or compete, and claim or provide support to other households and individuals in times of need. Establishing and maintaining good relationships with others is of crucial importance in enhancing and maintaining a living but, at the same time, others can also be a major source of insecurity. It is precisely the ways in which poor people handle insecurities, both alone and together, and the dilemmas associated with exchange and support that form the core of this study.

This book thus has a larger story to tell. It is about the difficulties that people face in making a living, and about the ways in which they try to safeguard their livelihoods when times get hard. More than anything, it sets out to understand the everyday responses of people when they are confronted with misfortunes, hazards and major and minor crises in their lives. It describes the multiple ways in which people try to secure their livelihoods over time, directly through their own efforts or indirectly through support from others. Such actions vary greatly between people of different socioeconomic backgrounds, occupations, age and gender. Central to this book is the idea that people follow diverse trajectories guided by individual and cultural preferences that are shaped within structural boundaries, which I call styles. It offers an alternative to poverty studies focussed primarily on incomes and assets as well as to structural approaches which emphasise structural inequalities and the adverse consequences of capitalism and globalisation. This book searches for new conceptual ways to deal with diversity and agency, and aims to integrate both the strategic and structural dimensions of making a living and securing support at a daily basis. How should one capture these differences between socioeconomic classes, events and trajectories, and how can we develop a dynamic understanding of livelihood insecurity and poverty in Indonesia?

Many of the people who are described in this book can be called poor – living below or close to the official Indonesian poverty line – and are living in a more-or-less continuous state of insecurity. Poor people however do not stand alone, but search out and receive – directly or indirectly – support from others. Moreover, they are not always 'frozen' below or close to the poverty line since poorer and richer periods alternate as a result of seasonal fluctuations in income, lifecycles and alternating periods of misfortune and relative prosperity. Clearly, the poor I describe are not living in isolation, but need and use other individuals and institutions to secure their living, to access resources, to gather wealth and status and to provide support in times of need.

The book aims to find the middle road between studies focussing on the agency, capability and opportunities of the poor and critical approaches which emphasise structural inequality, adverse incorporations into the capitalist system and the adverse effects of structural power differences.[5] First, it highlights the material basis of poverty by studing the resource base and livelihoods of peasants and migrants and the diversity found within the livelihoods and the reportoires of mutual help and social assistance. Second, it describes the different combinations people make in linking their livelihoods to mutual relationships of support, social security arrangements and institutions of mutual help to show opportunities for social protection and room to manoeuvre for poor people living under adverse conditions. And third, I analysis the intricate interplay of structure and agency, individual survival and social protection. This approach differs from conventional approaches that insufficiently take into account the capabilities and agency of poor people living under conditions of coercion and which are oftend one-sided in the emphasis on social exclusion and vulnerability. This book uncovers patterns and trajectories in the ways people try to obtain and maintain this access both individually and collectively within constraining and enabling structures. Before we study these issues in detail, key concepts of livelihood, social security, risk and insecurity will be discussed.

Livelihood

The livelihood approach, developed by DFID (the British Department for International Development) and still influential among human geographers, rural sociologists and development economists, takes the above-described dynamics of poverty into account (Bebington 1999, Chambers and Conway 1992, Scoones 2009:171).[6] The livelihood framework offers a good way to start to capture poverty as multidimensional. Moreover, it acknowledges the strategic and creative choices people make in dealing with poverty. Livelihood studies not only focus on the ownership of assets and structural constraints in society, but also on the actual and potential ways to access resources. As Frank Ellis put

5 Such as for instance Hall et. al. (2011), Tania Murray Li (2007, 2014).

6 Livelihood studies and intervention programmes have never been very popular within Indonesian policy circles. This might have to do with the participatory nature of most livelihood programmes – participatory development planning is not a strong point in Indonesian policy – or with the fact that applying a livelihood approach implies recognition of the capabilities and capacities of local people – a feature which has often been ignored. The Indonesian state-led anti-poverty programmes can be better characterised as welfare policies. Hüsken and Koning (2006:4).

it: 'a livelihood comprises the assets (natural, physical, human, financial and social capital), the activities, and the access to these (mediated by institutions and social relations) that together determine the living gained by the individual or household' (Ellis 2000:10).[7] A livelihood thus includes assets, entitlements, individual characteristics, relationships and activities.

A livelihood is not something temporal, but embedded in social, economic and political relationships which stretch over time. Chambers and Conway (1992: 8) define, in their classic conceptualization, a sustainable livelihood as follows: 'a livelihood comprises the capabilities, assets (including both material and social resources) and activities required for a means of living. A livelihood is sustainable when it can cope with, and recover from, stresses and shocks and maintain or enhance its capabilities and assets both now and in the future, while not undermining the natural resource base'.

Over the years, livelihood studies have received criticism for generally failing to integrate regional, global–local and state-power connections. Most livelihood studies have been unable to analyse the social, structural and cultural embeddedness of action (Scoones 2009:174). In livelihood studies, being somewhat preoccupied by people's and households' strategies, there is an inherent risk of too narrow a focus on the actions and strategies of a group of poor people. One of the consequences of adopting a livelihood perspective is that a fairly positive image of poverty is created. In its focus on capabilities, it fits well with recent development approaches that put 'rational' individuals and their actions to the fore. This explains its appeal in neoliberal policies, and partly explains its popularity.

A livelihood perspective can be blind to the structural causes of poverty, such as unequal power relationships and unequal access to resources. It also fails to explain why some poor people are better able to climb out of poverty than others, and why some are better protected against shocks and stresses than others. This can be addressed by paying close attention to the notion of embeddedness and the social relationships which offer potential access to resources and social assistance in times of need. It is helpful to add a social security perspective to livelihood studies that takes power differences and structural inequalities into account.

---

7 See also on livelihood: Akram-Lodhi and Borras 2007; Bebington 1999; De Haan and Zoomers 2005; Farrington, Carney, Ashley and Turton 1999; Kaag, Brons, De Bruijn, De Haan, Nooteboom, Van Berkel, Van Dijk and Zoomers 2004; Moser and Norton 2001; Scoones and Wolmer 2003.

Social Security

A central aspect for poor people confronted with misfortune is access to social security. This security can be either provided by the state or locally organized. In Indonesia, the state has been relatively weak in providing social welfare to its people, but discussions and attempts to establish systems of social welfare, such as national health insurance, labour benefits and anti-poverty schemes, regularly surface. Some nationwide schemes have been established, but these are far from effective. Social welfare remains ad hoc and selective in its concentration on disasters and poverty alleviation programmes, and sensitive to political priorities during election times. Over the past three decades, pension schemes, social protection programmes and health insurance have become available to greater numbers of the Indonesian population including civil servants, military personnel and private sector actors rich enough to buy private social security bonds. Within the last decade, increasingly, the poor are also reached through several government programmes. These include subsidized rice (Raskin), free health cards (Jamkesmas), cash transfers for poor students (BSM), conditional cash transfers (PKH) and a temporary unconditional cash transfer (BLT) (WorldBank 2012b:12). However, it has been shown that at best, only half of the targeted people in extreme poverty have been reached by 'at least one of these programmes' (WorldBank 2012b:47). Overall, full coverage is still a long way off. Moreover, for the majority of the Indonesian population, the government tends to add to their insecurity rather than to their security through the risk of eviction, legal insecurity and direct or indirect processes of dispossession (Aspinall and van Klinken 2011, Collins 2007, Ford and Lyons 2006, Hall et al. 2011, Hüsken and Koning 2006, Von Benda-Beckmann and Von Benda-Beckmann 1998, Wilson 2011).

This does not mean that the people studied here do not do anything to organize their own welfare. On the contrary, they do so constantly, and they often do this in a social way by involving relatives, neighbours and friends, and also, as many studies show, political leaders (Collins 2007, Hüsken and Koning 2006, Kreager and Schröder-Butterfill 2005, Marcus and Asmorowati 2006, Suryahadi and Sumarto 2003, Von Benda-Beckmann et al. 1994). Often this does not concern general social security but the security of life, health, a social position and access to resources. In Chapter 4, some key mechanisms in this respect will be evaluated.

Since the 1988 and 1994 classic studies of Von Benda-Beckmann et al. on insecurity and locally organized social security, the study of local forms of welfare provision and social security has increased. This approach investigates welfare organized by people themselves, or provided by village, ethnic or religious institutions, NGOs and charity organizations. These local forms of support are not embedded in state regulations and legislation, are generally not formalized in explicit rules and regulations, are context-specific, are restricted to small areas and are mainly organized by local people. This will be explained in more detail below.

Throughout the book, when I refer to social security I am including self-organized or locally organized social security. As such, by 'social security' I am referring to all the ways in which individual people, households and communities protect their livelihoods in a social way and are protected socially against the shocks and stresses that threaten its continuity and stability. This includes both established institutions, norms and structures of mutual help as well as individual strategies to obtain support from others such as the everyday tactics for improvement and protection of individual people. Adopting such a definition results in this book focusing primarily on non-state, people's and locally-organized forms of social security,[8] often referred to using terms such as 'informal', or 'traditional', social security.[9]

Whereas strategies for survival, access and the maintenance of access (by risk avoidance, diversification and insurance) are central in livelihood studies, social security studies are much more oriented towards support, protection, collectives and welfare provisions, and consider the embeddedness and vulnerability of livelihoods. Naturally, the focus tends to be on national schemes, coverage, policies and legislation. However, a social security approach that

8 In the late 1980s and 1990s, the study of local forms of social security gained momentum, including studies by: Ahmad, Dreze and Hills 1991; Biezeveld 2002; De Bruijn and Van Dijk 1994; Hirtz 1995; Leliveld 1994; Platteau 1991; Van Ginneken 1999; Von Benda-Beckmann, Von Benda-Beckmann, Casino, Hirtz, Woodman and Zacher 1988; Von Benda-Beckmann, Von Benda-Beckmann and Marks 1994.

9 The use of terms such as traditional, indigenous or informal social security is problematic due to misleading connotations and suggestions of false dichotomies. For a discussion on these dichotomies, such as formal – informal and traditional – modern, see: Hüsken and Koning 2006; Midgley 1994; Von Benda-Beckmann 1990, Von Benda-Beckmann, Casino, Hirtz, Woodman and Zacher 1988; Von Benda-Beckmann, Von Benda-Beckmann and Marks 1994. If a distinction needs to be made between state-organised social security and other forms of social security, I prefer the term local social security for the latter to stress its heterogeneity and embeddedness in local communities, the specific socioeconomic landscapes and the cultural repertoires. This does not mean that the state is absent in those communities but that old and new forms of social security are intermingled and that state programmes are modified and negotiated at the local level. Different forms of social security can all be relevant for people at the same time. Throughout this book, when I speak of social security I refer to all forms of local as well as state-organised social security.

claims to take the priorities and considerations of local people into account cannot do without having an understanding of the strategies of individuals and households and an emphasis on their ways of accessing resources.

In this book, I combine the study of poor livelihoods with a social security perspective. Such a perspective builds upon and augments previous livelihood studies by combining two perspectives: attention to actors' and households' strategies within the enabling and constraining landscape of social security opportunities, inequalities and limitations, and the role of social relations. I define livelihood security as follows: livelihood security covers the – often local – provision of care, support and welfare to individuals and groups through social and/or individual means. This provision can be achieved either by individual, social and collective strategies, or by arrangements and institutions that offer access to care, insurance and general wellbeing to individuals, households and specific categories of people. Both strategies for achieving social security, and the mechanisms that provide support, are often intermingled and simultaneous, and therefore inseparable. Moreover, they are diverse and not uniform for all people.

A secure livelihood can thus be achieved in various ways, differently organized for different people, and subject to changes over time. It includes institutional and arranged social protection against shocks and stresses that occur when conditions change and major contingencies arise. It addresses unequal access and changing strategies and the networks of support to be mobilized. If people or households are confronted with shocks and stresses, then how many ways they have to access support matters, rather than their wealth or poverty as such. Although all layers of society are confronted with occasional and periodic uncertainties, it is particularly the poorer sections that face the greatest problems when fate hits them. To thoroughly analyse the lives of poor people on the margins of Indonesian society, livelihood and social security studies need to be integrated.

The core question is what underpins local forms of social security, and are they, or have they ever been, able to protect people in times of need? Moreover, what happens when networks stretch over place and time? In any society, the crux of social security boils down to a few basic questions for the people involved: how can they get direct or indirect access to resources to secure basic needs, how can they themselves directly or indirectly protect, secure and maintain this access (and their livelihood in general) and through what mechanisms and processes are people excluded from benefit of access to resources. Such questions are relational since survival necessarily involves other people (with the possible exception of Robinson Crusoe, but even he had a Friday). They are also stretched over time through relationships of kinship, shared descent, language and friendship. These networks consist of partners, household members, relatives, the neighbourhood, the community, the state and state bodies, and possibly larger social groups or associations, all of whom can offer and/or expect to receive care. While they may be supportive and protective, they may also demand support, be exploitative or even threaten survival.

Poverty and Economic Growth in Indonesia

The impressive economic growth of Indonesia during recent decades has enabled many rural people to find pathways out of poverty. Nevertheless, very large numbers remain poor and vulnerable. According to the World Bank, about 32 million people live below the national poverty line in Indonesia and almost half of all households remain highly vulnerable (2012a:6). Seventy per cent of these poor live in rural areas.[10] The basis for these developments was laid during the New Order years. Indonesian development during the New Order, and its aftermath, contained several key aspects: rural development, poverty eradication and social welfare development through healthcare and education, modernization, infrastructural development and industrial policy.

In the mid-1990s, it was believed that Indonesia would become one of the economic 'miracles' in Asia, able to sustain high growth levels and be successful in eradicating poverty. In 1996, for instance, the Australian economist Hal Hill wrote an optimistic book on the modernization and development of the Indonesian economy: 'The Indonesian Economy since 1966: Asia's Emerging Giant'. His analysis of the Indonesian economy included a core section on agricultural developments in which he states that the New Order (*Orde Baru*) regime had been successful in creating rural development and improving rural people's livelihoods. However, this growth was not seen by all and during the same period inequality grew.

Ironically, a year after the publication of this book, Indonesia faced a severe economic crisis, and economic development slowed for many years.

10 According to the World Bank 2012 report on Protecting Poor and Vulnerable Households in Indonesia: 'Declining poverty, however, partially masks a high degree of vulnerability: much of Indonesia's population is clustered just above the 2011 poverty line of Rp 233,000 per month (about US$27 at 2011 nominal exchange rates). Around 24% of Indonesians live below the official near-poor line of 1.2 times the poverty line while 38% of the population lives below 1.5 times the poverty line and is almost equally vulnerable. Even relatively small shocks to these vulnerable households can be enough to push them into poverty' World Bank (2012a:7). Moreover, inequlities are rising. See also the special edition added to Kompas January 8 2014 for a recent overview of Indonesian poverty statistics.

Notwithstanding this setback in Indonesia's economic development in the late 1990s, impressive changes have taken place on the economic, social, cultural and demographic levels in recent decades. For example, population growth has decreased, education and basic healthcare have improved, economic growth has increased and large numbers of the rural population have migrated to the large cities. These, and other, developments have led to higher life expectancy, widespread commercialization, industrialization and globalization.

Economic development during the New Order regime also brought about a gradual shift of focus to the urban areas, and the urban problems of unemployment and poverty. The New Order government's attention to the rural areas materialized in a series of rural development programmes, such as the Green Revolution programme,[11] education for all, the 'Colt Revolution',[12] road construction projects, electrification and the development of small-scale industries. Between 1975 and 1997, the living conditions in rural areas of Indonesia in general improved significantly and mobility became possible. Moreover, after this period, welfare support by the state increased, as did access to higher education. At the same time, in most areas, the pressure on rural resources also continued to increase, and the negative consequences of decreasing fertility and the migration of many (often landless) villagers to the cities in search of work became apparent. New Order policies created rapid agricultural development and increased rural incomes, but they also put a strain on employment. While agricultural production increased, inequality grew, and employment opportunities for landless villagers decreased so rapidly that growing numbers of young villagers left to work in the cities.[13] This process has only increased in recent years, with smallholders having experienced dispossession of their lands and reduced access to arable land (Hall et al. 2011). As a result, domestic migration, both rural to urban and rural to rural, has massively increased. Once people arrive in the cities or in settlement areas, success is far from guaranteed. There are simply too few jobs being created in the new and growing economic sectors (Li 2009:78), and land has become increasingly difficult to get. Transnational migration to Malaysia or to the Gulf States (mostly women to the latter) is much more profitable. However, for many poor families, these

11 Many studies exist on the social and economic consequences of the Green Revolution: Collier 1981; Hart, Turton and White 1989; Hüsken 1988; Hüsken 1989; Hüsken 1988; Hüsken 1999; Hüsken and Kemp 1992; Hüsken and White 1989; Wiradi 1984.

12 The 'Colt' was a popular motorized vehicle and its name became synonymous with the improvement of roads and infrastructure which boosted mobility and migration opportunities.

13 See: Breman 2000; Edmunson 1994; Hart, Turton and White 1989; White 2000; White and Wiradi 1989.

better labour opportunities are beyond reach or fail to yield the expected returns (De Regt and Moors 2008). Migration is also not free from risks, and migrants sometimes end up in countries or circumstances which were not foreseen (Ford and Lyons 2011, Ford and Lyons 2007).[14]

The situations outlined above show that, in the middle and longer terms, the quest to create and maintain secure livelihoods will remain important for large numbers of Indonesians and therefore deserves continuing attention. Social protection is needed, both to address the vulnerability of the poor (through social assistance) and the risk of becoming poor (through social insurance). In Indonesia, various factors hamper state responses, and there remain large holes in the state-provided social safety nets (Alatas et al. 2012, WorldBank 2012b). Problems include widespread under-delivery of assistance and inadequate targeting of poor populations. Social protection efforts are also fragmented across a range of different agencies with resulting coordination and integration problems (World Bank 2012).[15] Since blanket coverage is not achieved, the poor in Indonesia need to organize their own social security.

All of these abovementioned processes and welfare incentives have touched upon and changed Madurese lives and have helped many Madurese in rural areas to survive and to maintain some basic level of living. With rural livelihoods being transformed in recent decades, smallholders must intensify their own production and diversify livelihoods, or move out of farming altogether. In the absence of supporting rural policies for such transitions, the risk of poverty and vulnerability follow and may create significant pockets of disadvantaged rural households (McCarthy et al. 2012). Madurese are often among those to be found in these 'pockets'.

Risk

Over the last two decades, the group of people under study here, the Madurese, seem gradually to have lost what seemed a relatively favourable, or at least a

14 For instance, a number of Indonesian citizens are held in (mainly Saudi Arabian) prisons without trial or contact with their families or compatriots Nooteboom and Bakker (2013).

15 These facts are not widely acknowledged among government officials. Romantic images of homogeneous villages prevail at the government level. This is not only the heritage of the major scholars who have studied Java, but also the heritage of political and cultural norms in society. These romantic ideas about the village where life is good and harmonious, the place where the good life is, are to be found in many countries in Southeast Asia Barlocco (2010).

relatively well protected, position in society. It is not that they have been impoverished but more that other groups in society are doing better – at least when it comes to education, income, health and political participation. Except for some individuals who have been able to establish thriving businesses or to achieve good education, the majority of the Madurese have remained in sectors of the economy which have not experienced much economic growth, or they have remained where they were a generation ago.

During the Suharto years, rural, Islamic and Java-based sections of the population were relatively privileged. The rural Javanese and Madurese benefitted directly from state programmes of rural investment, including in rural infrastructure, rural anti-poverty programmes, education and community development programmes, and indirectly through transmigration[16] schemes and systematic attempts to create national citizens through the curtailment of local ethnic groups through forced migration and resettlement as part of Suharto's territorial policies (Bertrand 2004:58, Peluso 2006, Peluso and Harwell 2001:84,105). However, most Madurese did not migrate to the cities, but migrated to outer islands or to Malaysia to work as rural or unskilled labourers. This is not without risk as the following story of the Holik family shows.

Tied up in debts: Holik

While the members of the Satrawi and Patik families have stayed in rural East Java, many young families moved away in search of greener pastures. Kalimantan is one of the main destinations for poor, unskilled migrants from Madura and East Java. Among them was the Holik family who, in early 2004, suddenly decided to accept a cash offer from one of the *mandor* (recruiters, foremen) who roamed the villages in search of cheap labourers to work in the oil palm plantations of Kalimantan, in stone quarries and in brickmaking kilns. In return for a cash sum of Rp 1.5 million (125 Euro), which they used to pay off their long standing debt from their marriage, they followed the recruiter to the outskirts of Samarinda, East Kalimantan, to work in a brick kiln owned by a Madurese from rural Bangkalan, Madura. 'I had heard that work in the plantations was hot and heavy. So I thought that working in a brick kiln would be easier', Holik told me. He also hoped to be able to send money home to repay his father's debts who pawned his cattle and the family land to cover debts

16 Organised schemes to transport poor, landless villagers from Java and Bali to sparsely populated or empty areas in Sumatra, Kalimantan and Sulawesi. For a historical overview and problems see: Elmhirst 1999; Evers and Gerke 1992; Harjono 1988.

> from unsuccessful tobacco trading. 'The work in the kiln would enable us to stay together as a family', Holik said, 'I talked with my wife, and within two hours we decided to go'.
>
> After arrival, the family soon found out they had been cheated. 'The gift of Rp 1.5 million turned out to be a loan and was added to the costs of the trip to Kalimantan (Rp 2 million), the *mandor's* premium of Rp 1 million and the living costs incurred during the first months after arrival. We did not know how to make bricks fast enough and our debts only increased during the first months'. The Holik family, unable to read nor write, did not receive any salary or any information about their total debts. They worked day and night to pay off their debt to the owner of the brick kiln. Daily necessities such as rice, cooking oil, soap, tea and cigarettes were provided by the kiln owner, but again added to the debt. According to the kiln owner, the debt was still not paid off at the end of 2004.
>
> I regularly visited them at their brick kiln. After a year, and still deep in debt, they had been unable to send back money to their parents in East Java. Increasingly, they felt unhappy and mistreated, and thought about ways to get away and return to East Java. 'Better poor without land in Bondowoso, than labouring day and night for money which we cannot hold'. The kiln owner forced them to work faster and faster and became angry when they asked for payment. He told them time after time that they were still indebted. 'I cannot check it', said Holik, 'I do not keep any records of expenses and I only know the number of bricks we've made in a week. I think he is cheating us and I want to go home'. In 2005, they finally received Rp 1 million as a loan, to buy clothes and necessities for the festivities of *Idhul Fitri*. The day after, I received a text message in the middle of the night, that they were heading to the harbour to catch the first ship home. They had decided to walk away and return to their village, after one and a half years of labouring in Kalimantan and with no money to take home.

Many studies on social security in rural societies deal with a range of institutions and mechanisms for support and assistance that exist to protect villagers from the consequences of adversities. Poor people are assumed to be risk averse and to optimize security, and rarely is it mentioned that social relations can also be exploitative. Recently, the focus has shifted to risk and resilience studies (Hilhorst and Bankhoff 2004) with livelihoods seen as at risk (Blaikie et al. 1994). Implicitly, most of these studies appear to start from the assumption that people prefer security above insecurity, and that social relationships and village institutions are oriented towards enhancing some form of social security rather than disrupting it. In this book, I intend to draw a more nuanced picture by taking a closer look at Madurese who are involved in ambiguous practices, which are either risk reducing or risk increasing, and thus endangering as much as enhancing livelihood security. Some even explicitly increase risk-taking practices as described in Chapter 5.

The Holik story above shows that migration can be very risky, although in this instance they were unaware of the risks. In other cases, poor people deliberately take risks, as in the example of Wahyudi, an uncle of Holik, who went to Kalimantan six months later.

> In Bondowoso, Wahyudi is known as a daredevil, drinker, gang leader and gambler. After running into trouble due to an affair with a married woman and being threatened with murder (*carok*), he ran off to Kalimantan to work in one of the stone quarries at Lempake, northeast of Samarinda. Soon, once he found out how difficult the work was and how hard is was to earn money, he started organizing night-time gambling and drinking parties at the market. He made good money with this but, at one of these parties, a fight broke out between two competing gangs. The police came and Wahyudi was beaten up and imprisoned. I was not able to visit him there and after his claimed release from prison nobody could tell me where he went. According to one informant, he had died from pneumonia and general weakness.

Risk, vulnerability and security have become an important and emerging field of study. Although a highly interdisciplinary field, three basic schools or traditions can be distinguished in risk and disaster studies: a psychological school, looking into the different perceptions and decisions people make during disasters, and two that address livelihood risks – one focussed on the material conditions which explain vulnerability, and one that integrates social and cultural elements to understand risk. The first of these three is more focussed on individual characteristics and psychological coping strategies, while the second looks at the circumstances, conditions and physical differences that can be mapped and is a field largely dominated by geographers. Both tend to be technocratic, focus on resilience, homogenise the poor, have difficulties in capturing the diversity in responses to risks and disasters, are largely insensitive to deliberate risk taking and are generally blind to the reasons why people make different choices. The third tradition aims to understand the social, cultural and political embeddedness of risk. It is this third debate to which this book contributes.

Rural development economists generally point to the fact that poor farmers adopt a diversified portfolio of income-earning activities, accepting lower returns for the benefit of avoiding and spreading risks. Such assumptions on the nature of poor people's behaviour are also prevalent and influential in anthropology.[17] The risk aversion assumption is widespread in development theory, and seems to be even more dominant than the assumption that farmers are profit maximizing. Ellis (2000: 61) for instance notes that: 'The amelioration of risk helps to explain much observed livelihood behaviour in rural areas of developing countries, including the economic strategies of occupational diversification and migration, and supporting social strategies of maintaining an extensive network of kinship ties'.

The assumption that peasants in Southeast Asia are risk-averse has been criticized from several angles, but still retains a powerful hold among policy-makers. Poor people, and not only peasants, are assumed to be able to take risks only after 'liberalization', the removal of certain barriers and restrictions such as monopolies, cultural barriers, poverty and political repression. Such studies usually address risk-taking related to agriculture, innovation and income activities. They often blame the structure of a society for preventing poor people from taking risks, and suggest that risk-taking is only possible if there is a basis of security, a well-prepared subsistence floor and a financial infrastructure accessible to all villagers. This fits neatly in neoliberal ideas which produce policies to enable people to engage in risks (Rankin 2001, Shakya and Rankin 2008). In practice, these conditions seldom exist and therefore such an understanding of risk-taking means that, in such societies, only the rich will be able to take risks. These assumptions only partly hold. Often, insufficient attention is given to those cultural and normative decisions of people which are not directly related to farming or work but do affect their occupational strategies and the risks taken in other parts of life, such as in gambling, spontaneous migration and partaking in illegal activities.

Some relevant examples of risk-taking by poor people can be found in older studies of farmers who were engaged in commercial vegetable farming in the Philippines and Indonesia. Lewis (1992) described the excessive ecological and financial risk-taking by Philippine mountain peasants in vegetable production in Northern Luzon. 'Buguias residents became professional risk-takers; their agricultural endeavor, as they perceive it, is now one of continual gambling [betting]' (Lewis 1992:131). He distinguishes various production strategies by

17 One example is the so-called moral economy approach Scott (1976) although this has been criticized from a rational actor perspective Popkin (1979), leading to what is generally known as the Scott-Popkin debate. For a description of this debate, see among others: Feeny 1983; Keyes 1983; Platteau 1991.

peasants, some of whom were opposed to the more conservative strategies. 'Other gardeners deliberately choose risk, gambling [betting] on the chance of a windfall. Precarious strategies include planting a crop during its season of maximum hazards, or sowing a dry field at the first rain, in hope that more will soon follow' (Lewis 1992:136). These farmers indeed seem to prefer risk to security: '[...] the Bugias farmers have never shied away from the risks so entailed. Indeed, many have welcomed them, pinning their hopes not so much on steady income, as on a jackpot. Their belief that the flow of luck is largely controllable promotes this attitude; the new economic realities only affirm traditional ideology on this score'. (Lewis 1992:138). Hefner (1990) described similar practices in Indonesia, and their social, cultural and political embeddedness in vegetable production in Tengger in East Java. Bankoff showed in his studies in the Philippines how risk perceptions are often culturally informed (Bankoff 2009). The majority of risk studies are dominated by structural approaches to risk, by vulnerability mapping and by cultural perceptions (Wisner et al. 2012), and there is a need for a detailed, well-informed inquiry into the diversity of individual and collective reasons for engaging in risk. We need to understand why some poor people actively engage in risky lifestyles – an under-researched aspect to date.

During fieldwork, I became increasingly dissatisfied with the view that peasants and migrants shun risks and prefer stability and security. I observed that nearly all villagers and migrants sometimes took risks, and that some of them deliberately and constantly sought risks (see Chapters 5 and 8). Some take huge risks, even though this behaviour may endanger security and the long-term continuity of their households' livelihoods. How can we understand such 'excessive' risk taking in regard to mainstream society given the abovementioned assumptions, and how does studying the various forms of risk-taking help in understanding poverty and livelihoods?

By describing and analysing risk taking in an ethnographic way, I want to show that deliberate risk-taking cannot simply be labelled deviant behaviour. It represents an attractive way of living for some people who search for alternatives to norms of decency and conformity. They deliberately forego investments in social security and reciprocal relationships. Further, studying these practices helps to explore the contours of risk protection and risk-taking, even of those people living close to subsistence. It hints at the structural underestimation of diversity and the human agency of people living on the margins of society in their daily quest for provision and support and their strategies to achieve security.

Filling the Gap: Bridging the Dichotomies of Provision Versus Strategy Approaches

In the above sections on livelihood, on social security and on risk, two theoretical standpoints vie for position. On the one hand, we see attention given to local people who employ livelihood strategies, take risks and strategically organize their own social security. The other perspective focuses on structural inequalities and views social security as something that needs to be provided by outside agencies or the state, and risk as something that people need to be protected from. As such, it is either communal institutions and organized structures, based on long-term bonds of reciprocity or state intervention, which provide support in times of need, or it is individuals designing strategies to cover their own risks through maximizing profit, and only sharing among a small groups of social equals, plus some stubborn individuals who take 'irresponsible risks'. However, these positions are not mutually exclusive.

Rather than initially opting for one of these two perspectives as the more valid, they should both be 'tested' and integrated in specific research settings. In my fieldwork in Krajan and East Kalimantan, I set out to ascertain the role of communal institutions in providing social security, and what room individuals have, and use, to achieve such security. Moreover, I go beyond the 'either/or' and the 'both/and' questions by building upon Giddens' concept of agency which integrates individual and structural dimensions. Below, this is related to the often divergent ways in which people manage their social security.

A good starting point is to acknowledge that both locally organized institutions and people's strategies are by nature diverse: 'people survive by doing many different things, rather than just one thing or a few things' (Ellis 2000:ix). Further, they do not do this in a social vacuum since social and familial constraints do apply, and not only what people do, but their capacity to change what they do, is influenced by their social and institutional context (Ellis 2000:8–9) and, one may add, by personal choices and characteristics. Returning to the story of local social security, and the diversity of strategies and opportunities one can observe in this field, it pays to look back to common patterns of protection, coping and security strategies. People do not randomly invest in reciprocal relationships, or opportunities for social security, but establish specific and meaningful combinations reflecting their orientations, perceptions and assessments, as well as their capabilities and resources.

Not every combination is open to all. Wealthy people can heavily rely on their own resources and networks, while their less fortunate neighbours must heavily invest in mutual support and care in order to be eligible for social security when they, in turn, are in need. These combinations can also be gender-specific since men and women can have different orientations and resources. Often, women are much more concerned with household food security and livelihood protection than their husbands. At the household level, these differences may be smoothed out as many activities require the involvement of both husband and wife, and social relations are a matter for the whole household.

At the local level, therefore, there can be a large heterogeneity in strategies and arrangements for social security that stem from the differentiated responses of actors to the ecological, economic, political and social insecurities that they face and the resources to which they have, or can mobilize, access. In this heterogeneity, one can distinguish patterns or pathways or, as I prefer to call them, 'styles' of social security. Styles are coherent patterns that reflect the strategic and habitual decisions people make.

Research Strategy: Combining Structural and Agency Perspectives into Styles

The concept of style I take loosely from the work of Van der Ploeg and Bolhuis (1985) and of Van der Ploeg (Van der Ploeg 1990, 1999, Van der Ploeg 2008) who use the concept of farming styles to analyse patterns of farming strategies in Peru, Italy and the Netherlands. Van der Ploeg argues that the heterogeneity in contemporary agrarian societies can be explained by the wide range of differential responses made by farmers to the political, social, economic and environmental problems they face, and that these reflect their ideas about solutions, 'good' farming and the desired future of the farming enterprise. In the late 1990s, his styles framework provided a basis for a powerful critique on the hegemonistic policies of European governments and banks to stimulate farmers to engage in capital-intensive farming in the Netherlands and Italy. In a similar vein, I studied the livelihood styles of Madurese in Indonesia which occur mainly as blind spots beyond the attention of the state. More recently, the approach has been improved by De Jong (2013) to analyse livelihood diversity in Toraja and Van Voorst (2014) in a context of vulnerability to disasters in Jakarta. Especially, the study of Van Voorst shows convincingly how the style concept is able to capture and analyse diversity in responses to floods and explain why some people and households are more vulnerable than others.

Like Van der Ploeg's farming styles, the styles of Van Voorst are also based on emic categorizations of farmers, and are empirically validated by analysing farmers' orientations towards markets and the level of intensification and extensification in their use of labour and technology. In his view, 'a style of farming is a valid structure of relations between producers, objects of labour, and means of production. It is the outcome of a particular labour process guided by certain options, structured in a specific way by a corresponding "logic," and conditioned by particular social relations of production. Through the farm labour process both the social relations of production and the style of farming are reproduced' (Van der Ploeg 1990).

In an analogous fashion, I see livelihood and social security styles as distinguishable patterns of orientations and actions regarding the range of means (labour, capital, social relations and the market) to address risk and security within a livelihood. As such, these patterns are structured by an internal logic and conditioned by social, economic and personal characteristics of the people involved. Again following Van der Ploeg, I see these styles as emic social constructions based on the various ways people manage their livelihood and mix risks and social support options. In the research areas, for instance names are used such as thrifty, sociable and business oriented to indicate the different values behind and activities of people. Styles are not the same as strategies in the sense that they are strategically designed by individuals. People do not follow a style, but have a style of organizing their livelihood and social security. These styles are made tactically as well as representing habitually reproduced patterns of dealing with livelihood insecurity and risks in daily life.

Applying the concept of style in poverty studies has the advantage that it includes the structural, individual and the 'habitual' dimensions of social action (such as the concept of *habitus* introduced by Bourdieu (1980) can bridge the dichotomy between structural and individual dimensions as the concept entails agency in mutual interplay with structure).[18] It also helps to identify pathways out of poverty and to capture the diversity in responses to poverty and vulnerability. Style operates as an interface between long-term

18 The habitual everyday responses on risk and insecurity are analytically not the same as 'habitus' such as defined by Bourdieu which has a more structural dimension. '*Habitus* refers to the views and preferences held by individuals, which are molded within specific contexts of nationality, ethnicity, gender, age and class' Dahles and Bras (1999). Bourdieu (1989:13) explains *habitus* as the internal, 'embodied' dispositions which are drawn in individuals as durable schemes of observation and interpretation which bring action into being. In his understanding, *habitus* remains structural. It is the result of institutionalising the social and the objective field structures in separate bodies, and generates, as a practical matrix of practices, the determinants for the reproduction of these structures. Such an understanding of the concept of habitus does not leave much analytical space for the capacity to make a diference, the creativity to play with different repertoires in a style and to reproduce it in a creative way.

practices and institutions on the one hand, and individual strategic choices on the other. People have a certain style because of past experiences, because they like it, were raised in a particular fashion, share a cultural repertoire or because circumstances force them into a style. When conditions change, people can turn to new, and probably more advantageous, ways of organizing their livelihood and social security. However, for social and economic reasons, such a shift of style is not always that easy since styles carry a history and a legacy: if one has been strongly involved in profit maximizing and has made individual arrangements for social security, it will be well-nigh impossible to suddenly switch to a style based on strong ties with neighbours, relatives or patrons. There is, nevertheless, room for gradual shifts if one moves out of tight networks, or if one's economic position dramatically changes. A style perspective offers a possibility to link livelihood strategy approaches as well as structural analysis and welfare state perspectives in one analytical frame.

A focus on how people shape their lives and how they form and reproduce their orientations on life requires a view from below, or in the words of Benda-Beckmann et al. (1994) an 'underall perspective'. Such an approach seeks to understand the lifeworlds of people through the close and intimate study of the actors' points of view as well as their strategies and constraints. This book is based on detailed anthropological fieldwork and puts people at the centre. By its nature, this is a holistic approach. It includes an analysis of the embeddedness of social action and includes the study of the social and economic context, structures of cultural domination within and through which people think, form opinions, act and give meaning to their actions. Olivier de Sardan, influenced by Bourdieu, speaks of understanding the 'entangled social logic', an approach 'centred on the analysis of the embeddedness of social logic' (Olivier de Sardan 2005:11).

Methodological Approach

I carried out research in the village of Krajan in 1998 and 1999. I collected in-depth data on village livelihoods, wealth and poverty, perceptions of threats and insecurities, coping strategies, labour and migration, and on the role of the local government. The research in East Java took place primarily in one village but this does not mean that the research area was confined to the village of Krajan. In the research, I have tried to study the relationships of Madurese with the outside world, not only those living within specific boundaries. Neighbouring villages were taken into account when it came to trade, exchange, family relations and access to resources. Since then, migrants have been followed and studied in for instance the harbour of Surabaya, on Pelni ships to Kalimantan, and in urban and rural Bangkalan on Madura. I accompanied Krajan villagers when they went back to their religious teachers at the Islamic boarding school (*pesantren*) and leaders who went to government meetings or to informal encounters with military or police officials in town. Moreover, I followed migrants to Denpasar and Bali, and to Ijen in East Java, and met semi-resident villagers there. I also visited villagers living in other parts of East Java, and tried to recover the migration histories of villagers who worked in Kalimantan, Sulawesi and Malaysia. However, all my case studies of families and the main survey were carried out within the village since I needed to study families on a daily basis, something that would not be possible in a larger area.

In Samarinda, I carried out research in several periods between 2003 and 2009. Both in Samarinda and in Krajan, I used a number of qualitative research methodologies including life histories, participant observation and semi-structured interviews. I also conducted extensive surveys. In these surveys, I concentrated on six major themes: household and family composition; expenditure and consumption; property and income; adversities and people's perceptions of them; engagement in mutual help, giving or receiving support; and debts and saving. Although the questions were predetermined, I used the list in a rather flexible way, sometimes changing the sequence or the formulation of the questions depending on the interview process and the quality of the conversation, allowing me to go deeper into subjects when needed. The majority of the survey interviews were carried out with an assistant, Pak Eko in Java and *mas* Taufiq in East Kalimantan. They translated complex questions and answers as required, and often reassured people and explained the purpose of the survey. We developed a close working relationship and found ways to encourage informants to elaborate on relevant stories, examples, experiences and sensitive topics. Most of these interviews lasted three to four hours and often ended in being offered a meal at the house. In most cases, both wife and husband were present. Wherever possible, questions were addressed to the household member who knew most about the topic, often the mother of the family.

In total we interviewed 100 families in Krajan, each on two occasions, and 300 families in Kalimantan once. In both locations, a dozen families were studied in greater depth and followed on daily and important events. The purpose of this detailed study of a limited number of families and individuals was not only to see how they coped with adversities in life, but also to identify the daily and small ways they employed in making a livelihood. These families were studied using the extended case study method (Van Velsen 1967) which provides a framework for studying networks, activities, labour relations, conflicts, insecurities, norms and practices in a coherent and interrelated way. An extended case study is the study of an event, phenomenon or, as here, a household with all its members, activities and interrelationships through time. An extended case study makes it possible to study the changes, dynamics and problems of coping with insecurity in actual daily life. It also provided the opportunity to link strategies and arrangements for social security to changes in the wider social, economic, political and environmental context. 'The extended case method applies reflexive science to ethnography in order to extract the general from the unique, to move from the "micro" to the "macro," to connect the present to the past in anticipation of the future' (Burawoy 2009:21).

Last but not least, I also studied these families from a three-generational perspective, and made genealogies to document changes and to gain insights into family histories and kinship relationships (Den Ouden 1989). Historical information was gathered by studying secondary sources such as historical records and maps, and by interviewing various family members, both young and old, about the past.

In dealing with such a multiplicity of topics and personal experiences, I used different levels of inquiry to come to a rich as possible picture, focussing on subjects and events, and on individuals, households, families and social networks. I started by studying general perceptions of livelihood, poverty, risks and insecurities, coping strategies, economic activities, labour relations and village values of support and, later, the focus shifted towards people and households. In addition to the wide and integrated scope of this study, the specific normative dimensions of social security also created methodological difficulties. What people say they would do, does not always coincide with what actually happens. In helping or not, the social actions of villagers are the critical issue, not norms and values. In adopting that stance, my fieldwork has been focussed on observation and analysis of actual support (or the lack of) rather than norms and values.

My position as an insider/outsider enabled me to visit and participate in most activities in the neighbourhood. I also participated as far as possible in forms of mutual help and, especially in the dry season, the numerous mutual help parties and housebuilding activities. While participating, I could observe the rules of the game, the people present and those absent, gift giving, food sharing and gambling. While working in the fields with others, I could ask numerous questions about details, reasons and the past, while it simultaneously enhanced my acceptance as a member of the community. I also visited many poor people, widows and handicapped, to unravel the support for these vulnerable and weak groups, their orientations and their strategies. Finally, I tried, by making frequent visits to a few selected families, to observe the daily, minor ways of support and subsistence.

In East Kalimantan, I followed similar lines of enquiry. Long informal talks with neighbours and during long nights at the brick kiln formed a crucial source of additional information to the systematic data collected in the surveys and from the many semi-structured interviews. In this way, I gathered subjective accounts of insecurity, cooperation and survival, all contributing to my search for and understanding of support and subsistence in the village. Moreover, by participating in as many activities as possible, by using intuition and by visiting people at different times of the day, I had opportunities to discover aspects of village life I could never have imagined in advance. Many of these I stumbled upon by accident, while other opportunities were more-or-less deliberately created.

A Note on Language

In both Krajan and Samarinda, most Madurese are bilingual, able to speak both Indonesian and Madurese. In Krajan, about half of the male population and a quarter of the women were able to speak Indonesian fluently. Most of the men and the majority of the women could speak some Indonesian but about a quarter, mostly elderly and women above 50, could not (see Map 2). Communicating with those who were not fluent in Indonesian was sometimes difficult, and in those cases I had to ask for help from bystanders or assistants. In casual village life, there were always people willing to explain what was going on when I did not understand something. Sometimes these translations were explanations in themselves, and the comparison between explanations given by different people enhanced my understanding of local terms or reference and frames of meaning and interpretation. After a year, I had acquired some fluency in Madurese. In Samarinda, everybody was able to speak Indonesian well.

Forgotten People: Madurese in Indonesia

In Indonesia, the Madurese officially constitute the fourth largest ethnic group, after the Javanese, Sundanese and Malay.[19] In general, they constitute a diverse

19 Since 2000, the Madurese have been officially ranked as Indonesia's fourth largest ethnic group with 6,771,727 people, 3.37% of all citizens BPS 2001; Suryadinata, Arifin and Ananta 2003:7. Other estimates suggest much higher numbers of Madurese and rank them the

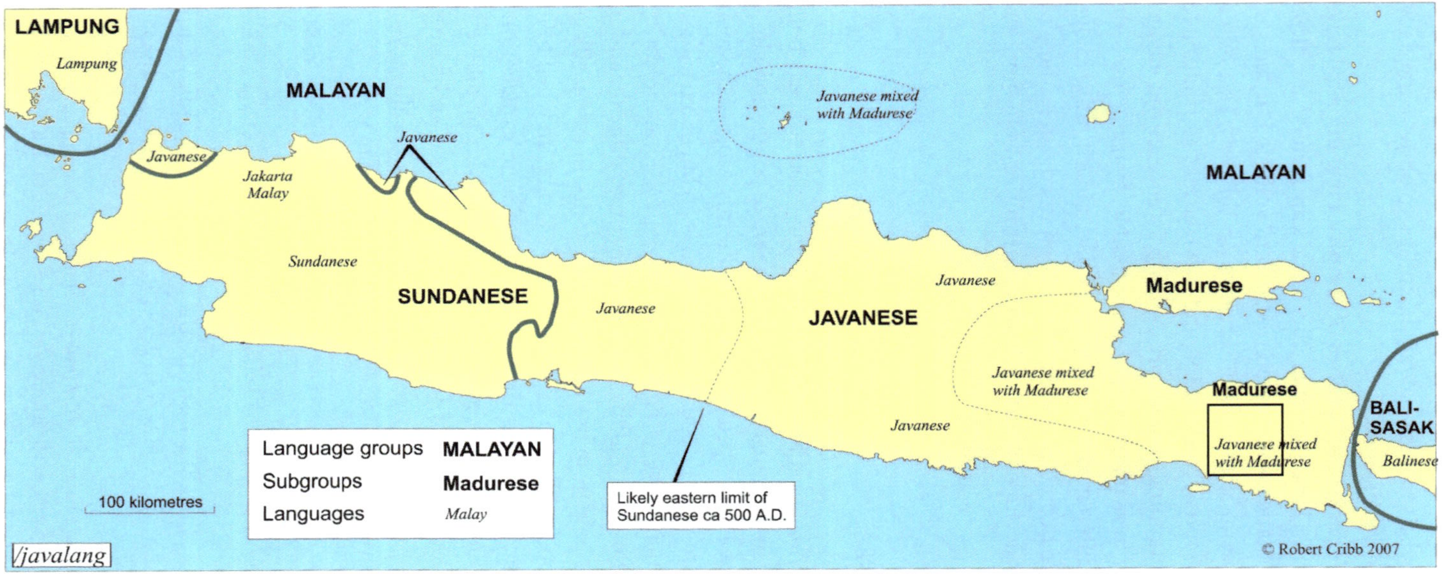

MAP 2 *Madurese speaking areas in Indonesia*
SOURCE: CRIBB 2010, DIGITAL ATLAS.

group of farmers, traders, migrants, labourers and entrepreneurs (De Jonge 1995). They have not been intensively studied[20] and, as a group, are underrepresented in Indonesian politics, government bureaucracies, the educational system, the media and in popular culture. Stenross (2011:1) notes: 'Although one of the main ethnic groups of the archipelago, the Madurese are arguably the least understood and, in recent times, the most controversial'. Since colonial times, Madurese men have been known for their touchiness, suspicion, temperament, hot temper, fierceness, vengefulness, combativeness and violence (De Jonge 1995:13). Besides this, many sexual stereotypes exist as the men are said to be macho and promiscuous, and the women to be good providers of sexual pleasures. The most well-known feature of Madurese violence is revenge killing (*carok*), committed when a man's honour is insulted. Among the main reasons for *carok* are (rumours of) someone having had a sexual affair with a wife or daughter. *Carok* is still regularly committed (Latief Wiyata 2002). In contrast to the many negative stereotypes of Madurese in Indonesia, researchers often report Madurese as being hospitable, friendly, open, direct, sociable, reliable and loyal (Bouvier 2002:14,32, De Jonge and Nooteboom 2006:460, Retsikas 2007, Stenross 2011:xxv, Van Dijk et al. 1995:3).

Although some very rich Madurese entrepreneurs can be found in East Java, Jakarta and East Kalimantan, and Madurese being popularly seen as being able to prosper even under difficult circumstances – yet another powerful stereotype – the Madurese are in general relatively poorly educated and often on low wages as most occupy the lower echelons of society and the majority live in marginal and unfertile areas. Madurese traders, migrants and labourers can be found in many places ranging from cities and towns in Sumatra, Kalimantan, Sulawesi, Java, Bali and Lombok to as far away as Singapore and Malaysia. They are well known as sellers of *sate*, traders in second-hand items and recycled goods, construction workers, rural labourers on large agro-industrial estates such as for palm oil, rubber and coffee, and as seasonal sugar-cane workers. They often occupy, and sometimes monopolize, niche markets, such as in selling *sate*, fruit and vegetables in a communal way where members come almost

third largest ethnic group Husson (1997a:77); Stenross (2011:18–19). Less than one-third of Madurese live on Madura.

20 Notable exceptions include: Bouvier, De Jonge and Smith 2006; Bouvier and Smith 2006; De Jonge 1995; Husson 1997a; Husson 1997b; De Jonge and Nooteboom 2006; Kuntowijoyo 1980; Latief Wiyata 2002; Mansurnoor 1990; Niehof 1985; Niehof, Jordaan and Santoso 2005; Smith 1997; Smith 2011; Stenross 2011; Van Dijk, De Jonge and Touwen-Bouwsma 1995. There was an upsurge in Madura studies in the 1980s and 1990s, largely as a result of the Dutch Indonesian Madura Research Project.

exclusively from one area. Here, the *sate* sellers mostly originate from Bangkalan, West Madura, and the brick-makers in East Kalimantan who come from Geger village, Tanah Merah, Madura.

Such stereotypes are constantly reproduced in daily life and serve as social and psychological barriers for many Madurese in establishing themselves as a trader, entrepreneur or farmer in other areas of Indonesia. Moreover, they have been officially excluded from transmigration programmes because of their bad image.[21] Nevertheless, in the slipstream of transmigration programmes, they have settled and started businesses in Kalimantan, albeit restricted to economic niches considered too dirty, dangerous or rough for many outsiders. Nowadays, millions of Madurese live outside Madura (Stenross 2011:24) and explanations offered for this 'will to survive' or 'will to succeed' range from push factors related to poverty and overpopulation on the island of Madura and in adjacent areas of East Java to the existence of a 'migration ethic' (Husson 1997b). How did the Madurese actually become involved in this migration and can a historical pattern be distinguished?

For centuries, Madurese have been known as brave soldiers, strong and reliable labourers and as vigorous migrants travelling to many places in the Malay world. In modern history, this migration has been more significant than other, better-known, diasporas such as the Bugis and the Minangkabau (Husson 1997a:98, Stenross 2011:23). There are indications that as far back as the thirteenth century inhabitants of Madura travelled and settled in Java as serfs and rural labourers (Husson 1997a:80–81). From the 16th to the 19th centuries, Madurese soldiers, recruited by Javanese and colonial forces of the Dutch East Indies Company (VOC), were a feared force and a crucial instrument in the power play of kings and rulers (Husson 1997a:81–84). Many of them were rewarded with land in East Java for their military services.

Since the 17th century, large numbers of Madurese have moved to the mainland of Java and especially to its north coast and its eastern part (Cribb 2000:52, Nooteboom 2003:78, Tennekens 1963). Husson (1997: 85) quotes Van Nes (1832) who writes that already by 1832 the residence of Pasuruan (on the mainland of Java) had a population of 170,049 Javanese and 92,463 Madurese. This migration increased in the late 19th and throughout the twentieth centuries when many Madurese labourers were sought for work in the plantations in Malang and Besuki district and in the growing factories of Surabaya (Nawiyanto 2003:36–39). Elson (1984: 4), quoted in Stenross (2011: 23), notes a Madurese population seven times larger than the Javanese for the residence of Besuki.

21 Personal communication: officers Department of Transmigration (Depnekartrans), 2005.

After the age of plantations, this migration continued. In the population census of 1930, 14% of all people born on Madura were living in other parts of the archipelago (Cribb 2000:54). According to some sources, the population on the island of Madura even declined in the period between 1940 and 1950 due to outmigration (Husson 1997:89). Major factors in this mass migration, which continues to the current day, are the infertility of the island of Madura, a lack of natural resources and labour opportunities, overpopulation and the widespread belief that only by migration (*merantau*) can economic success be achieved.

Since 2000, the Madurese have been officially ranked as Indonesia's fourth largest ethnic group with 6,771,727 people, 3.37% of all citizens (BPS 2001, Suryadinata et al. 2003:7). 92.8% of the Madurese live in East Java where they comprise 18.1% of the provincial population. There have been Madurese diaspora of all sorts, mainly to Kalimantan which is relatively near and has offered many opportunities for unskilled labourers. According to official data collected in 2000 (BPS 2001), about 4.92% of counted citizens in Kalimantan were self-identified as Madurese (5.5% in West Kalimantan, 3.5% in Central Kalimantan, 1.22% in South Kalimantan and 1.24% in East Kalimantan). These figures are based on ethnic self-definition of residents and do not include temporary workers or those who wish to avoid calling themselves Madurese. The real figures for the number of Madurese in Kalimantan are thought to be much higher.

To date, little is known about the current everyday livelihoods of Madurese in the areas where they are mainly concentrated outside Madura, that is on mainland East Java and in parts of Kalimantan, except for Stenross' 2011 book on seafaring Madurese.

Why the Madurese?

The book describes and analyses Madurese lifestyles in making a living in both Java and Kalimantan. The Madurese make an interesting study given their high levels of poverty, their close networks of kinship and ethnicity, their image as troublemakers and violators of the law, their lack of political capital on both regional and national scales – especially after the fall of Suharto – and their recurrent exposure to violence and ethnic conflict in migration areas. From a state perspective, they are neither indigenous – and thus able to claim special benefits as an indigenous people – nor dominant or privileged, and thus also unable to benefit from close proximity to the state or developmental resources. Although they are officially the fourth largest ethnic group, after the Javanese, Sundanese and Malay, they are a kind of forgotten people of Indonesia, often invisible, poorly represented at higher governmental levels and squeezed between Java and the rest. In recent decades, there has been little research on this ethnic group.[22]

In this book, by looking at Madurese, I look into the margins of the Indonesian developmental state and pay attention to the creation of new inequalities within a nation in flux. The impact and experience of the two major developments in Indonesia, rural development and poverty eradication, as well as the preservation and exploitation of local traditions such as mutual help are explored through the eyes of local Madurese people. Often forgotten as a group, and neglected as citizens by a largely ignorant state, this study shows the intricacies, insecurities and ambiguities of these, frequently poor, people making a living through turbulent times in Indonesia.

Research Locations

The book divides into two parts. The first deals with rural communities in East Java and offers an in-depth case study of a rural Madurese community in Bondowoso, East Java. Madurese migration to that area has been ongoing for generations and, today, many migrants to Kalimantan depart from here. It offers a relatively stable and confined location to study the core themes of livelihood, social security and risk. The second part of the book deals with an area in Kalimantan where Madurese migrants go to try and make a better living. Sometimes families stay connected but, more often, migration means disconnectedness and severed ties with the home community. Both parts of the book come together in the study of the livelihoods of people on the margins of Indonesian society, their quest for livelihood security and the parallels in the constitution and reproduction of poverty, inequality, social security and risk.

In the first part of the book, Madurese life on Java is studied in detail by studying Krajan, an upland village in East Java. In the second part, people from this village and from similar villages, both on Java and Madura, are followed into Borneo and East Kalimantan. The book starts with a historical chapter on

22 Nowadays, very few scholars work on this ethnic group and they are seldom studied in Indonesian academia except for a wave of attention during the outbreaks of violence following the fall of Suharto. Notable exceptions are: Bouvier and Smith 2006; De Jonge and Nooteboom 2006; Retsikas 2007; Smith 2011; Stenross 2011. During the process of regime change and decentralisation, the Madurese have disappeared from the larger picture and have received only negative attention during the outbreaks of violence in West and Central Kalimantan between 1999 and 2003.

Java in the late 1990s and analyses the inequalities in access to resources, welfare schemes and leadership at the village level, as well as risk-taking practices and active participation in dangerous styles of living. It follows these people for more than a decade in their search for money and a livelihood, through both failure and pleasure. The successes and failures of individual people, as well as their insecurities, worries, jealousies and dreams surface through intimate encounters and detailed descriptions of events.

In the second part of the book, the locations of these Madurese migrants and settlers in Kalimantan are analysed in more detail. Some of the villagers could be traced to East Kalimantan's brickmaking and plantation industries, but the story mostly deals with other Madurese with similar backgrounds who struggle to make a living in a hostile and insecure environment. The focus in Kalimantan is no longer purely rural, and looks to three sectors of economic activity: the construction sector, the brickmaking sector and the agricultural sector. Within these sectors, the livelihood activities of Madurese are described and analysed as practices embedded in larger contexts of political change and economic insecurity. Risk-taking practices such as speculation, gambling and engagement in criminal activities, as well as threats and interpretations of violence, will be discussed in detail.

Krajan, a Village in Upland Java

Krajan is situated on the slopes of Mount Argopuro between 800 and 1,200 metres above sea level (see Map 3). The area is fairly infertile and dry. Except for some small plots of rice fields, the landscape is dominated by tobacco and maize grown on dry lands (*tegal*). Since the road was asphalted in the 1990s, Krajan is easiest reached from the direction of Bondowoso. After the junction on the main road towards Besuki, a small asphalted road heads uphill towards Krajan. It follows a ridge of the mountain and is very winding and, in some places, quite steep. In good weather, the road is covered in rice, maize, coffee beans and bamboo strips laid out to dry.

Before reaching Krajan, the road passes through five large hamlets, separated by tegal fields and sometimes lush plots of *sawah*. Just before reaching Krajan's welcome gate, an asphalted side road goes down to the rice growing village of Ardisaeng. The first hamlets of Krajan, Mengkuara and Pakuarah can be spotted somewhat later as green islands of bamboo bushes down the hill to the right. The houses are built in small clusters around a central courtyard (*tanèan*) along the road, similarly to village housing patterns seen on Madura (Smith 2011:145–150). The houses are made of wood or bamboo plaid and covered with terracotta roof tiles and, typically, one *tanèan* consists of one or two conjugal units. After a few more bends and another steep climb, the houses of

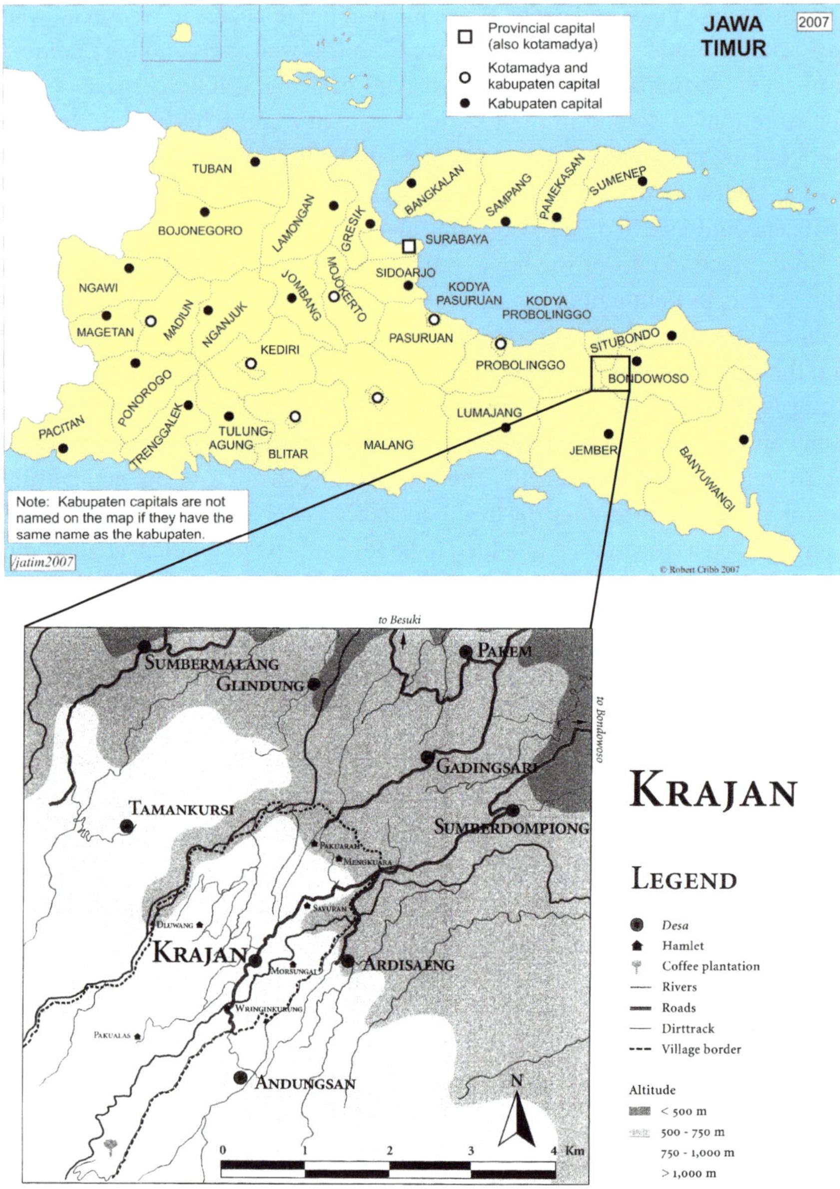

MAP 3 *Research location I: Krajan, a village in Bondowoso district, East Java*
SOURCE: MAP EAST JAVA: CRIBB 2010, DIGITAL ATLAS. MAP OF KRAJAN: AUTHOR.

Sayuran can be seen on a small hill to the left. Closer to the road, on the right, are situated a mosque, a shop, two coffee stalls and some stone houses. After another kilometre, passing more scattered and clustered dwellings, Krajan's village office is reached. It lies along a flat stretch of the road, away from the larger hamlets of Krajan. Around the village office, one sees a dozen houses (some made of bricks), a shop and a coffee stall, including the houses of the village head, his mother and his sister. Here the dirt road towards Dluwang starts. This was improved with World Bank money between 1998 and 2000, as part of social safety programmes and rural infrastructural schemes, but is still impassable in cars. By this part of the road, there is little motorized traffic but many people walk along the road carrying cattle fodder, fuelwood, rice or maize. Besides income from agriculture, small trade and home industries, such as the production of brooms and bamboo baskets (*besek*), and occasional government projects such as road construction and repairing irrigation canals, there are few other income earning opportunities.

Desa Krajan is situated in the middle of the poor and fairly infertile mountainous area between Bondowoso and Besuki. The village is demarcated to the northwest by the deep ravine of the Dluwang River which forms a natural border with the Besuki sub-district, and to the southeast by a gentle ravine covered with sawah belonging to the villages of Ardisaeng and Andungsari. Krajan itself does not have much sawah as irrigation in the higher areas is problematic. With its rugged terrain, the village has always been much more isolated than most of the lowland villages on Java. It was only in 1994 that the village road to Krajan was asphalted and irregular, but daily, transport to Bondowoso or Besuki became available by pickup trucks. Krajan is far from the large urban centres of Java. The nearest city is Jember at a distance of 60 kilometres, and few villagers have ever been there.

The village of Krajan receives slightly more rainfall than the other villages in the region due to its high altitude but it has few irrigation opportunities and sawah is scarce. The major crops include maize, tobacco and rice. Besides this, cattle raising is important. Given that land is scarce and not very fertile, yields tend to be insecure compared to villages in lowland Java. Krajan is a relatively poor village but is doing slightly better than many other villages in the area which have even fewer resources, less fertile soils and less rain. Only the neighbouring villages of Ardisaeng (with its sawah-covered valley) and Andungsari (with lower population pressure, easier access to the state forest and a coffee plantation) have higher average incomes.

In the village, access to resources is unequally distributed. About one-third of the population can be called rich, while two-thirds have difficulties in making ends meet. The 9% richest families own 53% of all village sawah and 37%

of all tegal in the village. Fifty-one per cent of the village population is landless or virtually landless. In the next chapter, these differences will be described and analysed in more detail. These differences in wealth are visible in consumption styles. Eating white rice, vegetables from the market and meat or fresh fish are clear indicators of a high social status, along with the ownership of brick houses, motorbikes, television and radio sets, jeans, mobile phones and expensive *sarong*. Distinctions between social classes are especially visible in the smoking habits of men, and the cigarettes provided at praying sessions and celebrations.

In 1997, Krajan numbered about 3,400 inhabitants of which 48% were male and the rest female, spread among 880 households of which 150 were female-headed.[23] This number has since declined to below 3,000 as a result of migration and declining fertility. The majority of the villagers are engaged in farming, supplemented with one or more other income-generating activities such as trade, handicraft production and house construction. Unlike many Javanese villages, migration rates to urban areas and to other countries are relatively low. Krajan migration is mostly rural to rural, and Krajan people who migrate permanently, in as far as it is possible to trace them, mostly go to Kalimantan and end up in low paid jobs such as waged workers in oil palm plantations, road construction or the brick industry, or as petty traders. As a result of these poor migration livelihoods – see Part II of this book for a detailed description – remittances are rarely sent and do not form a significant source of income for most households. In addition, there are village members who do not wish to migrate to far away areas and who look for temporary jobs in the area such as harvesting coffee in Bondowoso, Banyuwangi and Jember, in sugar cane production, or as a brick maker. Some sell brooms and cheap artefacts in Bali. Typically, these jobs are very low paid, lower than those found by those who migrate to Kalimantan. Very few people have good contacts in urban areas and are able to mobilize and organize groups of workers. Villagers often expressed a reluctance to leave when they own or care for cattle. The background and logic behind these choices will be described in detail in Chapter 4 when I analyse the styles of making a living.

23 Most of the female-headed households are headed by 'widows' (*janda*). *Janda* are women without men, and can be divorced, unmarried or left alone by the departure or death of their husband. Widows who are living with children and are being cared for are often not counted as individual households. The large number of female-headed households can partly be explained by absent men working in Kalimantan.

Madurese in Samarinda, East Kalimantan

Samarinda (see Map 4) is a medium sized city with 726,223 inhabitants in 2010.[24] It is the capital of East Kalimatan province and lies inland on the Mahakam River, about 50 kilometres from the sea. It consists of three parts, Samarinda upstream (*ulu*), downstream (*ilir*) north of the Mahakam River, and Samarinda across (*seberang*) which lies to the west of the river. The two sides of the city are connected by a bridge. As a provincial city, it contains most of the important governmental offices and police headquarters. Economically, it has always been overshadowed by Balikpapan, the major oil, gas and mining city in East Kalimantan. In the past, up to the mid-1990s, Samarinda was booming due to the logging industry and the large number of sawmills along the Mahakam River. Now it is a major governmental city and a hub for coal mining and oil palm development in the massive hinterland of the Mahakam River.

Most Madurese in Samarinda have not been very successful economically and remain poor. They are poorly educated, but are known for being hard workers and reliable guards. This means that they are in demand in sectors where hard physical labour is required, such as in transport and construction, and as security guards. Many porters in the harbour and at the markets are Madurese, as are many road workers, construction workers, garbage collectors, stone-cutters and brick makers. Others work as security guards or carpenters and a few as owners of repair shops and hairdressers. The banana trade and the *sate* sector are dominated by Madurese, as are most of the canteens on the main university campus. In general, one can say that Madurese migrants occupy the lower strata of East Kalimantan society.

It is widely claimed that Madurese migrants in Kalimantan tend to spatially isolate themselves from other groups (Peluso and Harwell 2001: 103). In this, however, they do not differ from other ethnic groups who also prefer to live close together. In East Kalimantan, Madurese do tend to settle in close proximity to each other, often in groups related to occupation and village of origin. In Samarinda, they live in the old quarters close to the harbour and the city markets. Clusters of brick makers from rural Bangkalan can be found on the outskirts of the city on otherwise unused land. Temporary labourers engaged on roadworks and building sites mostly originate from eastern Java and Sampang in Madura. And they tend to live in barracks or deserted houses scattered throughout the city. Migrants who stay for longer sometimes live in mixed communities and interact with other ethnic groups such as the Javanese, Banjarese, Kutai Malay and Butonese. However, relationships between

24 BPS Indonesia (Indonesian Statistical Office) http://dds.bps.go.id/hasilSP2010/kaltim/6400.pdf (last accessed April 2012).

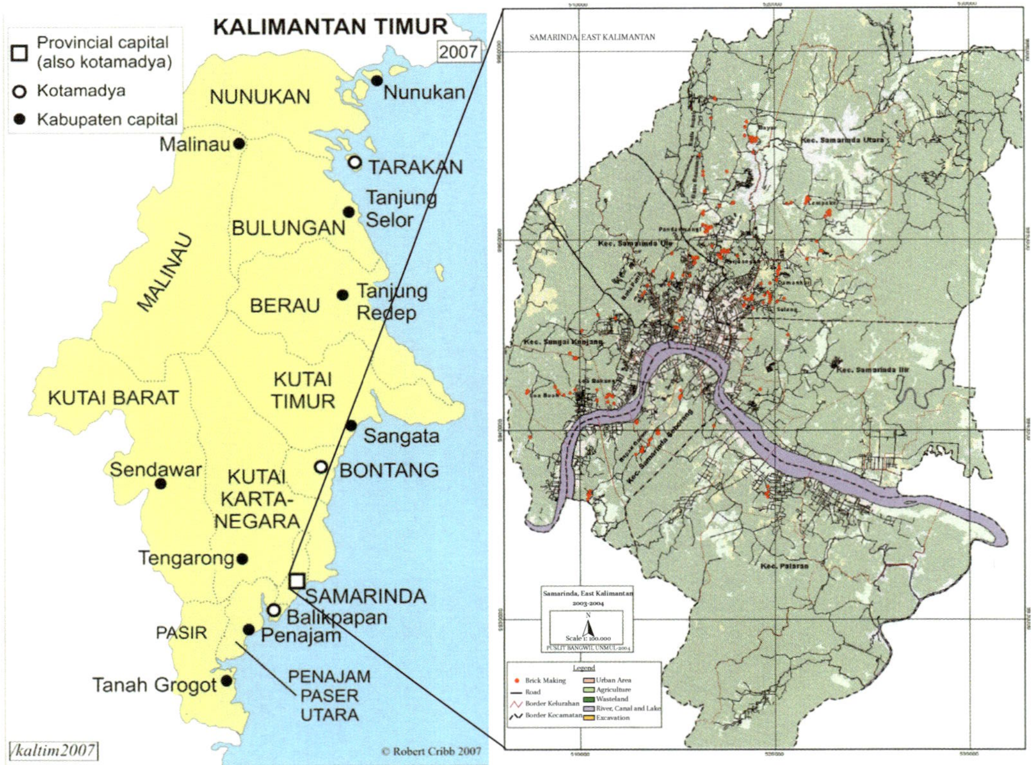

MAP 4 *Research location II: East Kalimantan and Samarinda*

SOURCE: MAP EAST KALIMANTAN: CRIBB 2010, DIGITAL ATLAS. MAP SAMARINDA: MADE FOR THIS STUDY BY PUSLITBANGWIL UNMUL 2004, MULAWARMAN UNIVERSITY, SAMARINDA, EAST KALIMANTAN

Madurese and Bugis, the second largest ethnic group in East Kalimantan, have long been tense. Traditionally, contacts with the indigenous Dayak, are relatively cordial, although they also became tense following the violent attacks on Madurese by Dayaks in West and Central Kalimantan between 1999 and 2003.

During the colonial era, most Madurese in this province were employed as unskilled labourers on plantations and in the mining and oil industries around Balikpapan.[25] This situation remained largely unchanged until the late 1970s since when migrants have mainly been engaged in road construction, the recycling business (scrap metal and tyres), petty trade, brickmaking, logging, and the building and transportation sectors. Some have become very successful, acquiring heavy machinery and large trucks. A small number have also been involved in illegal activities.

The Madurese in Samarinda live simply, save money to invest, marry young and work together. They also provide accommodation for newly arriving migrants – who are often relatives or people from their villages – and help them to find work. They are not attracted by education and the few Madurese in East Kalimantan who have graduated from university face difficulties in finding suitable jobs. As a result, there are almost no Madurese in the government bureaucracy or in the higher ranks of the police in East Kalimantan. According to Hendro (2001:72), 'the majority can neither read nor write', with illiteracy rates of 40 to 50% for male workers and even higher for women. Madurese parents often keep their children away from school to help them in making a living. Religious knowledge is however highly appreciated and several Madurese *pesantren*, religious boarding schools, have been founded in East Kalimantan. Well-to-do Madurese often send their children to *pesantren* in Madura and Eastern Java. Some have made the hajj. The various groups of Madurese speak different dialects, follow different religious leaders (*kiai*) and emphasize different cultural traits. For instance, Sumenep Madurese are said to be more refined than those from Pamakasan, whereas those from Sampang are generally perceived – and perceive themselves – as being the least refined of all, and as being troublemakers and unreliable.

In the following chapters, I first turn to East Java, after which I will return to East Kalimatan in Chapter 6.

---

25 During the Japanese occupation, an unknown number of forced labourers (*romushas*) were 'recruited' from Madura to work on plantations and infrastructural projects in Kalimantan.

PART 1

East Java

CHAPTER 2

A Baseline of Desire

Rural Livelihoods, Inequality and Social Mobility

The examples in the introduction show that the lives and living conditions of people are not stable, cannot be taken for granted and can change quickly. Over the course of one generation, some families have fallen from relative wealth to sheer poverty, while others were able to escape from poverty. Class alone does not determine one's future. Poverty and affluence are not fixed categories, and neither are friendships and other social ties.

To understand this fluidity, we need to study the interrelationships between agrarian structure, opportunities and bad luck, and individual and collective choices. The above-mentioned cases and questions reflect people in the relatively small world of the village. However, the lives of the villagers are not confined to the village: villagers are part of, and live within, a wider regional and national context. Villages are not isolated communities but interknit with the outside world through politics, the media, networks of kin, migration, trade and religion.

In this chapter, we look at the structural conditions of rural society in East Java, the baseline from which migrants depart. It first looks at the village of Krajan, the history of Madurese settlement in East Java and at the basic agrarian structure of Madurese East Java. We look at three aspects: rural livelihoods; access to resources; and inequality. Before doing so, we look at the history of Madurese migration to Krajan.

Madurese Migration to East Java – a Short History

The area between Besuki, Bondowoso and Jember was inhabited long before the official founding of Krajan, but these populations disappeared as a result of long periods of warfare prior to 1700. There is archaeological evidence that the areas west and south of Jember were densely populated before and during the 16th century (Cribb 2000:43). These populations were almost entirely wiped out before Madurese settlers repopulated the areas.

In the mid-slope area around Krajan, there are also signs of earlier habitation. In the village itself, as in other places on the north slope of Mount Argopuro, graves, tombstones and holy places (*keramat*) are to found that originate from before the 17th century, and which recall a more prosperous past. Archaeological remnants of Hindu settlements and holy places have been found three kilometres north of Krajan and at the northern end of the Argopuro mountain (Gennep 1895, Veth 1903). In the village, many stories circulate of people who have found jewellery, pottery and other valuables in and around these old places. Some of the *keramat* are still in use as burial places, mosques have been built on others and some can be spotted as mounds or graveyards in the fields or have simply been demolished by villagers in search of valuables or wishing to extend their fields.[1]

Although Madura had Muslim rulers since 1527 (Ricklefs 1991:39), mainland East Java was under Hindu rule in the 16th century. Pasuruan was the only significant Islamic power in the Eastern Salient during the 16th century. There were numerous wars on the extreme southeast coast of Java during the 16th century between Pasuruan and Blambangan. In 1600–1601, the town of Blambangan was conquered by Pasuruan fighters (Ricklefs 1991:39–40). The area of Bondowoso – situated between these kingdoms – oscillated between Hindu and Pasuruan rule, and every now and then passing armies must have destroyed houses, fields and crops with resulting depopulation.[2]

In 1614, Sultan Agung of Mataram assaulted much of Java's northern coast, the Eastern Salient and Pasuruan; and again raided Pasuruan in 1616 and 1617 during the Trunojoyo revolt. In 1624, Sultan Agung subdued Madura. One of the strategies of Sultan Agung was to weaken the enemy through forced migration of large populations and the destruction of crops, food reserves and livestock in the area under attack (Ricklefs 1991:43).

These wars in the Eastern Salient led to huge devastation, starvation and epidemics in the area where Jember and Bondowoso are now situated. VOC reports from 1625 (quoted in Ricklefs, 1991: 44) claim that two-thirds of the population died in some of the conflict areas. In 1633, more raids took place in the Eastern Salient including against Blambangan and Panarukan, which again led to huge devastation. After crushing the resistance of Pasuruan, Panarukan and Blambangan, the Eastern Salient remained the scene of several conflicts between Mataram and Balinese rulers until the end of the 17th century. By the beginning of the 18th century, none or only a few of the original people who had inhabited the areas around Pasurauan, Panarukan and Blambangan were left.[3] The area was ripe for resettlement, and often undertaken by people from

1 These *keramat* and artefacts from graves are believed to possess magical powers and curses and only daredevils are inclined to open graves and demolish burial mounds (after giving a *selamatan* and lengthy fasting).

2 See for an overview: Cribb 2000:86–92.

3 They had died as a result of killings, starvation, deportation or epidemics caused by the wars between the kingdoms of Bali and Mataram. Passing armies of both central Javanese and

Madura. The VOC left the rule of these coastal areas of East Java to the Sultans of Sumenep, reflecting the already firm relationships between these areas.[4] Such strong links with east Madura remain until the current day.

After 1740, the influence of the VOC continued to grow on the north coast of Java, and several trading ports and fortifications were established.[5] Slowly, the Dutch imposed a firm hegemony over this part of Java, peace was restored and the population again increased, mostly with Madurese people from the Sumenep area following the already established ties. The VOC offered the empty lands of East Java to those Madurese soldiers who had fought for them.

Thus, Madurese migration into the interior of the Eastern uplands first started in the coastal area of Besuki after 1700. A century later, the whole northern coastal zone of *residentie* Besuki, and some of the inlands were almost completely, albeit still sparsely, populated by Madurese. After 1768, when the VOC seized full control over the region, migration to Besuki from the overpopulated, dry and infertile island of Madura was actively encouraged by both Dutch and Madurese rulers, and more settlers started to move into the mainland of East Java (Tennekens 1963).[6] A few decades later, the area was sufficiently important to link it to Daendeals' Great Mail Road (*Jalan Raya Pos*). The trunk road connecting Besuki and Panarukan with the rest of Java further added to the economic possibilities of the area. With the boom in agricultural commodity production in the second half of the 19th century, more Madurese came as settlers and labourers. Population pressure on the fertile coastline of Besuki was building at the end of the 19th century, increasing the size of towns and cities on the north coast including Pasuruan, Probolinggo, Besuki and Panarukan, and new land was needed (Suhartono, 1993; Tennekens, 1963:327).

Balinese – East Javanese origin had ruined the land between these kingdoms. As a result, the area of Bondowoso and Jember was virtually uninhabited at the beginning of the 18th century except for the areas around Besuki, Panarukan and Banyuwangi where new migrants – probably from Madura – had settled Tennekens (1967:323). It is also likely that some of the original Hindu communities survived in the higher mountains, as Hefner Hefner (1990:57) describes for the Tengger area. In the cities and towns of the north coast, the influence of traders and rulers from Madura increased.

4 For an elaborate account of rule, trade, commercialisation and global connections see: Kwee Hui Kian's (2006) well documented book on the political economy of Java's Northeast coast, c. 1740–1800.

5 In 1743, Mataram seceded the Eastern Salient to VOC rule, but it would not be until 1767–68 that they defeated the 'Surapati rebellion' in the area Cribb (2000:92).

6 See also Kumar (1979) in Hefner (1990:8) 'After winning control of the region in 1743, the Dutch made up for the shortage of population by encouraging migration from the impoverished island of Madura (Kumar 1979)'.

Populating the Uplands: Madurese Migrants Coming to Krajan

Now, two hundred years later, the contrast with the emptiness of the past is striking. Not a single patch of land in the area is unused. Population pressure is high and all land, even the poor pieces, are cultivated or occupied. Over 40% of the population does not own any land, and livelihood opportunities outside agriculture are few. The population in the rural areas near Besuki, Bondowoso, Situbondo and Jember is predominantly Madurese, and most people in the cities also belong to this ethnic group or are of mixed descent (Retsikas 2007:188).

The early Madurese immigration into the hinterlands of Besuki, Panarukan and Bondowoso created a basis for these later waves of upland settlements. Initially, migrants moved to the lowland areas in East Java where sawah could be established (Palte 1989:18). However, early in the 18th century they were settling in the mountainous areas north and northeast of Besuki. It was this wave of migrants that populated the lower areas of Wringin, Pakem and Bondowoso in the second half of the 18th century. Although Madurese is the mother tongue of all villagers today, it is not certain that the first inhabitants of the upslope regions were all of Madurese descent.[7]

Boomgaard draws attention to the fact that the widespread cultivation of maize in this period, especially in the Eastern Salient, enabled the uplands and semi-permanent dry agricultural land to be populated (Boomgaard 1999:64).[8] According to Hefner, it was the introduction of compulsory cultivation, especially of coffee, on upland 'wastelands', which led to migration to the uplands

7 There were probably some of the original people still living; remnants of Hindu populations who had fled from wars and the hegemony of new kingdoms or Muslim rule, or people who had fled from the coastal areas. It is possible that in the Argopuro area a similar development took place as in Tengger where Hindus had fled to mountainous areas and survived. Here, the original populations have merged with the Madurese migrants. Boomgaard (1999: 65) comments: 'It is possible that the introduction of maize enabled similar migratory movements elsewhere to successfully establish themselves as "mountaineers," thus constituting "heathen" upland "tribes" (*masyarakat terasing* in modern Indonesian parlance), who preferred to live at a distance from coastal Muslim-Malay sultanates, the European and Chinese trading settlements, and the risk of epidemics. This, by the way, was much to the regret of the Dutch colonial administration who always attempted to get the mountain-dwellers to come and live in the coastal areas, and to make them grow "wet rice"'. See also Hefner (1990:9–10) who describes the flight of Hindu Javanese to Bali and the Tengger mountains in East Java (The Tengger volcano and its Hindu population are about 50 kilometres from Mount Argopuro).

8 The availability of a new food crop, maize – which grows well to altitudes over 1,500 metres – enabled settlers to continue to spread higher up the mountains.

in the nearby Tengger area: 'From 1830 to 1850, therefore, all territory between 600 and 1,200 meters above sea level was stripped of its jungle and transformed into one vast coffee stand. At first, the cultivated expanse was punctuated by only occasional native settlements. Soon, however, land-hungry migrants poured into the highlands' (Hefner 1990:10). Both these perspectives, the food availability thesis and the commercialisation thesis, could be correct. In the area around Krajan, both developments took place simultaneously on the lower and middle range slopes of Mount Argopuro.

Tennekes (1963) shows that the lower Krajan area was certainly populated between 1800 and 1845, if not earlier. A map of the Dutch Indies (Melvill van Carnbée and Versteeg 1853–1862) notes Krajan as an independent *desa* in 1856[9] and also shows extensive coffee plantations.

Due to the limited possibilities for further settling, the relatively poor soil fertility and better opportunities on the Bondowoso and Jember plains, the focus of migrants coming from Madura shifted from Besuki and Panarukan to the more distant fertile areas of Bondowoso, Jember, Banyuwnagi and Lumajang. Moreover, the establishment of coffee, tea, rubber and kina plantations, and later tobacco production, attracted new waves of migrants to these areas from the end of the 19th century onwards. The age of plantations thus constituted a second wave of Madurese migrants to mainland East Java, most notably to the plantation districts of Jember, Banyuwangi, Lumajang and Bondowoso.

Another explanation for the early population of higher areas such as Krajan is the desire of villagers to escape the pressures of local rulers, Islamic sultanates and colonial rule which became especially severe after the introduction of the *cultuurstelsel* in 1830 (Boomgaard 1999, Hefner 1990). Villagers wanting to escape from the pressures of the *cultuurstelsel* and *corvée* services (*heerendiensten*) in the lower areas could settle in the Krajan area, clear forest and 'live undisturbed by the colonial government on their semi-permanent swiddens' (Boomgaard 1999:65). Scott calls these processes nonstate options, state evasion and state prevention (Scott 2009:179, 328). Similarly, Li (1999:26) notes 'fleeing debts and excessive *corvée* demands, people frequently moved off in search of less oppressive conditions with another master, or autonomy (often temporary) on a forest frontier'. Soon, however, the obligation to plant coffee on their lands thwarted their urge for freedom. The Krajan frontier offered labour opportunities, shelter and relative freedom for those who fled from the pressures of the *cultuurstelsel*, and statute labour in the Besuki area where the enforced sugar cane cultivation increased population pressures.

9 This atlas, including the maps of East Java, was published in 1856.

Prior to 1932, free access to the uphill forest of Krajan was still possible, despite the 1870 Agrarian Law and later regulations that restricted customary rights on waste and forest land. Until the 1930s, in upland Java, villagers continued to clear forests and construct terraces for farming and so slowly encroached into the upland areas (Hefner 1990:51). Oral histories in Krajan confirm opportunities to clear land for fields far into the twentieth century.[10] In the 1930s, these practices came to an abrupt end due to stronger colonial water-control programmes to fight erosion, flooding and droughts that inhibited shifting cultivation at these altitudes and the further expansion into the mountains.

The population in Krajan continued to grow from this period onwards, and the pressure on the land increased. It was no longer possible to extend the total areal of land and newcomers and villagers who had no access to land had to look for some other livelihood. Land was divided among children, production became intensified, sawah were constructed and some families lost their land to richer villagers. Since the 1930s, the trend of diversification in land ownership has reversed, slowly leading to large inequalities in land ownership.

By the 1960s, agriculture in Indonesia was in crisis. Agricultural production had stagnated, no more peasants could be absorbed and tensions increased. Communists proclaiming land reform gained increasing influence *vis-à-vis* religious and landed elites. Starvation was becoming a natural event in rural areas and Krajan villagers recalled stories of hardship.

The final years of Sukarno were marked by hyperinflation, infrastructural decline, falling rice production and the flight of foreign capital. Not much is known of the Madurese in Krajan during this period except that the population continued to grow while migration opportunities to urban areas were limited. Geertz (1963) has been among the most influential writers about this period. He sketched an image of rural Java as stuffed with labour and under pressure due to continuous population growth. The sawah ecosystem was able to absorb large numbers of workers through intensification made possible by a shared poverty ethic. Although total production rose, the production per head of population decreased. This could therefore not be accurately called evolution (or development), and Geertz coined the term involution.

His book has been tremendously influential in rural development thinking in East and southeast Asia and served as a basis for persisting ideas on village social security and harmony (see Hüsken and Koning 2006:18–21) that are still influential today. According to Geertz, it was not a class of landlords opposed to rural proletariats (landless serfs) that was formed as a result of population

10 Villagers in that area told me stories of their parents and grandparents about clearing their fields to start farming.

pressure and commercialisation but a rural society which remained relatively egalitarian; and he argues that 'native institutions maintained a comparatively high degree of social and economic homogeneity by dividing the economic pie into a steadily increasing number of minute pieces'.

From In-Migration to Out-Migration

The conviction arose in Krajan that nothing would improve by staying in the village and, from this time onwards, the first villagers set out in search of land or work. First to the nearby plantation areas, but soon to the newly opened agricultural areas in West Kalimantan. Very few of these migrants ever returned, and villagers today hardly remember names and families as poor connections and infrastructure at the time made communication almost impossible. In many parts of Java, the hardship of village life proved a fertile ground for communism and the call for land reform became louder and louder. The PKI, the communist party, had its base in the rural areas, with East Java as a stronghold. In the early 1960s, they tried to outflank their urban rivals by mobilising the countryside and pushing an agenda of land reform.

The years 1965 and 1966 mark the government inspired campaign against the PKI. As far back as the guerrilla war against the Dutch, several Krajan villagers had been sympathetic to communism. Most of them were either secular small farmers or landless occupants from Pakuarah, the upslope hamlets of Pakualas and Wringinkurung and in the neighbouring upslope areas of Andungsari. These PKI supporters were the obvious targets for vengeance from the military and the strongly anti-communist religious groups from outside the village. In the region around Krajan, some were killed, many were arrested, others abducted never to return and most were ostracized and marginalized. As communism is still a delicate subject today, villagers were reluctant to talk about this part of the history of East Java. However, older people from Bondowoso showed me some of the places where bodies were dumped.[11] The exact numbers of those killed in Indonesia are not known, but some estimates mention one million people, most of whom were living in East Java (Cribb 1990, Ricklefs 1991).

---

11 One of the places where, according to eyewitnesses, thousands of bodies were disposed is Arak Arak on the road between Besuki and Bondowoso. Arak Arak is a steep rock just below the road, and bodies could be thrown over without being seen from anywhere else due to the dense teak forest below. Other spots where bodies have been dumped are limestone caves around Bondowoso, deep wells and a river canyon in the dense forest between Situbondo and Banyuwangi in the Asembagus area. According to eyewitnesses, bodies were dumped from military trucks.

In Krajan, only a few people were killed in this period (1965–1966), and in neighbouring Andungsari only ten. The situation was worse in other villages in lower areas of Bondowoso. The relatively small number of people killed in Krajan was because, while many had communist sympathies, only a few had become active party members. This reflects the general tendency in the area to stay aloof from strong involvement in supra-village affairs. As someone expressed it: 'we have always wanted to stay away from lowland influence and government control as it has never brought us any good'. When the killings in the Bondowoso area started, mostly carried out by the military and by semi-military bands of followers linked to regionally important religious leaders (*kiai*), Krajan stayed on the sidelines. Krajan's village head (from the nationalist party PNI) forbade villagers to join in the killings, and tried to keep his people away from them.

When groups of religious youths from Wringin, Besuki and Situbondo tried to enter Krajan, they were confronted by Krajan villagers and called back by their *kiai*. The Krajan village head had direct negotiations with him. He had drawn attention to the fact that most Krajanese were true followers of this *kiai*, and warned that the Krajan population would not support or tolerate any attempt to kill fellow villagers. Although relatively successful in preventing mass killings, the village head had to eventually pay the price for his opposition when religious leaders gained control over local and regional politics and accused him of having communist sympathies. Eventually, the changing political climate after 1966, and his resistance to the new government, forced the village head to step down.

The stage was set for a new government: The New Order. Besides opening up the economy for foreign investment and introducing measures to bring inflation under control, it also launched new initiatives in agriculture, including programmes for the distribution of fertilizers, pesticides and newly developed modern rice varieties. The programmes expanded after 1973 when international oil prices rose and government revenues swelled. After initial problems, the modernisation process became seen as a success. By the late 1970s, the majority of rice fields in Java were planted with new rice varieties and fertilizer use had become among the highest per hectare in Asia. Yields increased dramatically with annual increases of 3–5%. Indonesia's rice production almost doubled in the 1970s, outstripping population growth.

Many of these developments initially passed Krajan by due to its remote location and small number of rice fields. However, from the 1970s onwards, under the relative stability of the authoritarian New Order regime, the village economy of Krajan did open up: more villagers got jobs inside and outside the local economy, trade increased and irrigation canals were improved and extended.[12] Tobacco became a successful and popular cash crop due to the demands of the *kretek* industry. From this time onwards, village life started to change rapidly and it became possible to obtain the cash necessary for migration. With huge profits from tobacco, land-rich villagers could build brick houses, two new mosques were built, more villagers were able to send their children to secondary school in Bondowoso, some large farmers bought motorcycles – although these could only be used in the dry season on the village's mud roads – and, in the New Order years, twenty to thirty villagers were able to travel to Mecca to make the pilgrimage and achieve the prestigious status of a Haji.

Over the years, with the Krajan population rising, as in most rural populations in Java, the pressure on land increased although very few figures are available for this period. In Java as a whole, average land holdings fell from 0.7 to 0.66 hectares between 1963 and 1973, a process which resulted in 40% of the rural population becoming excluded from land (Hüsken 1988). Between 1924 and 1976, the proportion of 'very poor' in Java grew from 3.4% to 39.8%.[13] Inequality in income distribution dramatically increased over these years. At the same time, the absolute consumption of the lowest 40% did not increase: some informants in Krajan commented that they ate rice with dried fish in the colonial time and, now, they still eat rice and fish. Nothing had changed in their standard of living despite all the development promises by the government. This quote from a newlywed man summarizes the feeling of many youngsters about the possibilities of making a living in Krajan: 'If we want change, we have to move out of here'.

Land and Land Use in Krajan

Numerous researchers from different disciplinary backgrounds have studied agricultural systems on Java. Some from an economic or historical point of view,[14] others are more sociological.[15] In general, these studies have focussed upon the lowlands. Studies of upland agriculture on Java are relatively rare with a few

12 This was desperately needed because deforestation and the poor maintenance of irrigation canals had led to the water supply to far fields diminishing enormously. Nevertheless, the various improvements to irrigation canals during the 1970s, 1980s and 1990s could not prevent some fields becoming dry and being degraded from *sawah* to tegal.

13 Incomes in equivalent kilograms of rice per head of the population (poverty line 240 kg).

14 Boomgaard 1988; Bottema 1995; Van de Koppel and Van Hall 1946–1950; Van der Kolff 1937; Van Schaik 1986.

15 Cederroth 1995; Hartveld 1996; Kanó 1980; Saptari 1995.

notable exceptions such as Hefner (1990) who worked in the nearby Tengger region, Murray-Li et al. (1999) in upland Indonesia, Palte (1989) who wrote about mountainous Central Java, and Wolters (1998) who has been involved in a long-term study of a Central Javanese mountain village. Leunissen (1982) and (Smith 2011), who did research on Madura, produced the only available studies that describe the peculiarities of Madurese dry land agriculture in detail. As my research concerns an East Javanese upland area populated by Madurese, I will at times refer to Hefner's and Palte's analyses and, when relevant, to Leunissen and Smith to consider the peculiarities of Madurese agriculture.

The agricultural system of Krajan does not fit well into any of the systems described in these studies of agriculture on Java and Madura. The agricultural system of Krajan has concurrently the specific characteristics of Madurese agriculture, and a distinctive highlandness that make agricultural systems in uplands so special. As on Madura, it has a long dry season, is poorly irrigated, and mainly oriented towards cattle, maize and subsistence production; with tobacco as the only cash crop offering erratic returns. The altitude and rugged terrain makes the area remote and hard to access, ecologically sensitive to soil erosion and depletion, and it gives its people a sense of stubbornness, independence and distinctiveness, which can be observed in many mountain communities. Its economy is neither purely based on cash crop production of specific upland crops, nor purely commercialized and market-oriented.

Land in Krajan is divided into sawah, tegal, plantation land, government land (*tanah pemerintah/bengkok*) and wasteland (*tanah liar*).[16] Around 75% of all arable land is tegal, 20% belongs to an experimental coffee plantation, while sawah only makes up a meagre 2% to 5%. The coffee plantation is situated in the upper part of Krajan and it extends into the mountain forest of the upper slope of the Argopuro.

Krajan village data on land are unreliable and still based on land survey reports made in the 1930s by colonial surveyors. These surveyors made a distinction

16 The categories of government land and wasteland are locally contested. In general, wastelands are mountainous areas and steep slopes unsuitable for any type of agriculture (except for cutting fodder). According to Bagenda, the village head, wasteland includes land along brooks, roads and rivers, and for this reason belongs to the village officials and especially to him: ignoring all kinds of customary rights and grazing rights of villagers in these areas. During the period 1992–1998, he ordered, several times, trees to be planted in these areas, giving him (according to local law) ownership rights over these trees and the land. Most of the trees planted however 'died'. Farmers can think of numerous accidents leading to trees not surviving. Other wastelands are the forests higher up the mountains. Here village borders are unclear and these wastelands are government land controlled by the Department of Forestry.

between first, second, and third class sawah: based on the productivity of the sawah and the reliability of water. On first class sawah, rice can be produced the whole year round, while third class sawah is only irrigated by small brooks in the dry season and may yield only one crop of rice a year. Today, second and third class sawah are no longer used to produce rice due to a lack of irrigation water. According to official village statistics, Krajan has around 50 hectares of first-class sawah, 4% of the total village acreage of arable land, 25 hectares of second-class sawah, and about the same of third-class sawah. Based on my own observations, today, only about 50 hectares of sawah remain, most of which is of low quality (these fields are split up in hundreds of small pieces and terraces belonging to different families). Comparing the amount of sawah in 1922 with the amount in 1999, the total acreage of sawah has decreased with more than 50%. Due to major deforestation and erosion from the 1930s until the 1960s in upslope areas; small brooks, wells, and old irrigation canals have become dry thus turning formerly first class sawah into second or third class, or even into tegal. New Order irrigation projects tried to reverse this trend and made it possible to irrigate some new areas, mostly owned by village officials. Recently, many of these irrigation canals have decayed again.

Even the best sawah remaining are of a much lower quality than those that are generally found in the Javanese lowlands. Rice yields in Krajan are lower due to the less favourable conditions related to infertile soils, a cooler climate, and less available inputs. In Krajan, good sawah can be planted two times a year with rice. As for most sawah water supply in the dry season is unreliable, one or two crops of maize are often planted after a first crop of rice. Most low quality sawah lie fallow in the dry season, and are only planted with rice when the rainy season is well established and when the rains are most reliable. On these sawah, a crop of maize or tobacco follows the first crop of rice. In general, the quality, taste and price of tobacco produced on sawah are lower than on tegal, although production is higher.

Farmers themselves make more distinctions in soil quality than simply first, second or third class. Soils can be 'cold' or 'hot', 'heavy' or 'light', 'shallow' or 'deep' and 'thirsty' or 'saturated' indicating different grades of fertility, soil texture, construction, temperature, elevation, location, and water-holding capacity. According to older farmers, it is important to 'know' the soil and its character in detail. In some soils, young seedlings can be planted, while in others, seedlings have to be taller. A sawah can be 'sensitive', prone to diseases or '*nakal*' hard to understand/hard to master, sometimes giving good yields but low yields in other years. In some sawah, 'the water source is coming from below' indicating that water wells up in the field and therefore contains fewer nutrients while other sawah can be 'polluted' if the water sources run through a hamlet picking up dirt and nutrients. Understanding these minor, often invisible, qualities is essential for successful tillage. Fertilizing 'warm' or 'polluted' sawah leads to weak rice and empty grains as the soil receives too many nutrients, whereas under-fertilizing a 'cold' field or sawah with a hidden water source or leads to smaller plants and poor yields. The repertoires of local knowledge are important for success in farming on these varying soils.[17] These are based on personal experience, common knowledge and information from older people, and acquired from small-scale experimentation by farmers. Owning, or having access to, the right repertoire of knowledge, is essential for a good harvest. When persons migrate, this knowledge is lost.

Ownership of good sawah in Krajan, as elsewhere in rural Java, is highly valued as it has economic, cultural and social functions. It not only offers food and income security, as good sawah enables its owner to cultivate food crops the whole year round, it also adds status. The ability to grow one's own rice on one's own fields is very important and someone's status is measured primarily according to the number of rice fields they own.

In the past, less than half of the families who own sawah have ever been self-sufficient in rice.[18] Nowadays, only 10% of the families are fully self-supportive in rice. Krajan inhabitants own most of the sawah in Krajan. Sometimes villagers marry and move to a neighbouring village and maintain their sawah in Krajan. Krajan villagers have also bought rice fields in neighbouring Ardisaeng and Andung. Although distances are far to those villages and fields, according to these landowners, it is better to buy sawah in another village than not to have any sawah at all.

The arable lands of Krajan also comprise 800 hectares of tegal. Some pieces are rather large, while others are tiny and carved out on steep slopes. Farmers distinguish dry lands of good, middle and bad quality. These qualifications of good and bad are not always fixed, but depend on the location and the crops farmers want to plant. Tegal is used for growing subsistence as well as cash crops. Although the fertility of Krajan tegal is not very high, sometimes with tobacco huge profits can be made. Depending on the crop, the tegal soils need various labour inputs.

Before the rains start in October or November, the tegal is worked with a simple plough and two oxen. As soon as possible after the first rains – when the

17 See for studies on local farmer's knowledge: Chambers, Pacey and Trupp 1990; Geertz 1983; Richards 1985; Scoones and Thompson 1994; Van der Ploeg 1990; Van der Ploeg 1999; Van der Ploeg 2010.

18 This figure is probably too rosy, as in the past all families mixed their rice with cassava, sweet potato, or maize.

soil is wet enough[19] – the field is ploughed again while maize seeds are thrown into the furrow. Early planting is needed, as the growing period for maize is long (four months or more in upslope Krajan) and the rainy season is short. After the first maize crop, on fertile fields a second maize crop can be planted. On the less fertile fields, tobacco is planted. Tobacco is best planted on shallow, sandy and poor tegal soils as this produces a much better flavour and yields a higher price. It depends on the soil quality, the price of tobacco, maize, fertiliser and the strategic choice of the owner, which crop is planted. A good tobacco harvest provides the opportunity to buy enough maize and rice to survive the long dry period. However, growing tobacco is expensive and bears the risk of total crop failure and thus losses and indebtedness. A second crop of maize will at least offer some additional food, and limit expenses as local maize varieties do not require any inputs. Thus, the agricultural landscape of Krajan serves as the enabling context in which people make livelihood choices.

The ownership of tegal is symbolically less important than that of sawah. If someone is called rich, villagers usually mention only the possessions of sawah. If someone has a lot of sawah, then he or she will generally have a lot of tegal as well because most Krajan farmers prefer a combination of sawah and tegal. Tegal offers the opportunity to grow maize and tobacco in addition to the important rice crop. It can also be pawned in the event of an urgent need of cash, and it changes hands somewhat more readily than sawah.

A frequent leasing or long term pawning of tegal leads to decreasing soil fertility. Pawned tegal is less well cared for than privately-owned land. Soil fertility in the long run can only be guaranteed by applying cow dung or mulch and compost. The availability of dung is limited and carrying dung too far away fields is laborious. Landowners choose to dress their own land first, before caring for their leased land. Often they do not bother about the long-term sustainability of the leased fields because of the fact that they can always be taken back. These differences between leased and owned lands are often visible in the way they are intensively or extensively cultivated.

Another crucial factor in the sustainability of tegal soils lies in the differences among sharecropping systems. If landowners give land out to subcontractors, soil quality is likely to fall. In Krajan, sharecropping maize production is rare, but with tobacco production it is common practise. With maize,

19 Farmers use the length of a hand as an indicator of whether the soil is wet enough. They dig small holes at several places in the field and measure to what extent the rain has entered the soil. If the soil is wet for a hand's length, maize can be planted. As rainfall is sometimes very irregular and localised in Krajan, some fields are planted weeks later than others.

important labour arrangements exist, including working in turns (labour exchange groups and harvest shares), part of a share tenancy relationship where the workers get a one-fifth share of the harvest. Usually, in these arrangements, workers are more concerned with the quality of the work and maintaining soil fertility as they receive a harvest share, not a cash income.

If only a little manure is available, people use it for their home gardens (*pekarangan*). Most houses have at least some gardens with fruit trees and sometimes vegetables. In these gardens, jackfruit, bananas, papaya, coconut, coffee, chillies, cassava and taro are among the most common crops. *Pekarangan* in Krajan are not big and they only contain a few fruit trees. In general, these gardens do not contribute much to household incomes, but in the event of temporary shortages, villagers can fall back on fruits and vegetables produced on them. Moreover, the fruits and vegetables of the home gardens form a significant supplement to the daily diet (Singarimbun and Penny 1973).

The forest above the village is an important resource, especially for poor villagers. Access to the forest is relatively open as with other wastelands, such as roadsides and riverbanks. The forest is used for searching for fodder, firewood, lumber, and small bamboo sticks suitable for making baskets. Poor villagers can earn €1–2[20] a day by carrying firewood or bamboo down from the forest and selling it in hamlets and *desa* lower along the road. One return trip to the forest takes around six to seven hours and, especially in the rainy season, carrying wood is hard work, but up to €4 per day can be made.

Although the government officially owns the forest, and prohibits logging, many villagers cut trees in the forest and sell lumber. At the beginning of the crisis, around 25 people were regularly cutting wood and selling this to fellow villagers or to the village head. The latter was able to sell this wood 'legally' with the help of police friends and government employees in town. He explained it as help: 'I help my "children" [the villagers] to make some profit and make a living'. Clearly, he does not solely intend to help the poor villagers as he has made huge profits on the wood for himself. He did, at least, provide loans to selected villagers if they needed money. These loans could be repaid in wood, and to those working for him he offered protection through his good relationship with the forest police.

As cutting and selling illegally logged wood is very risky, relatively large bribes have to be paid to local officers of the forest department and sometimes also to the police. Around the 1999 national elections, he stopped accepting wood as loan repayments and villagers were forced to find ways of selling the

20 I use Euro's here, as the wages have been changing from Rp 3,000 in 1997 to Rp 15,000 in later years as a result of inflation.

wood themselves. He decided to free his hands so that he could lead the election campaign of the PDI-P, and refused further help to villagers who had problems with the forest police. From that time onwards, only a few villagers had the courage, or network, to continue their forest business. Around 10% of the population uses forest products from time to time, and for 5% of them access to the forest provides their main resource.

To be successful as a logger, at least some relationships with the forest officials are needed. In a small and hilly community such as Krajan, illegal loggers and their products are easy to trace. Lower ranked forest officials who live in Krajan can be offered 'money for petrol or cigarettes', petty bribes. Powerful high officials are more difficult to bribe for ordinary villagers and meeting such an official in the forest can easily become a disaster and lead to imprisonment. Therefore, villagers need protection, and the village head can offer that as he has always maintained good relationships with police and forest officials.

Recently, some farmers and village officials have started with planting trees on the least fertile plots, or upland plots far from the village centre. Besides teak, which always has been planted at wastelands and at borders of plots, new varieties planted are *sengon* and *meranti*.[21] The afforestation might be a sign of structural changes taking place the village: a decline in population pressure on the land and a further exclusion of landless labour out of the village economy. Trees are only be planted by people who own land and on these lands no longer need wage labourers to grow maize and cassava.

Land Transactions

Villagers who have been successful in trade, politics or business eagerly try to buy sawah for reasons of prestige, security, and collateral, even if they could have invested their money more efficiently elsewhere. Sawah is rarely sold and villagers only do so if they have no other choice. Most land transactions happen through pawning of fields. As the price of tegal is much lower than sawah (good tegal costs about one third of good sawah) more people have the possibility to buy or lease a piece of tegal. Tegal is also sold easier to cover costs when people face bankruptcy, gambling debts, urgent needs of money, and sometimes demands from children who beg their parents for a transport van, stock for starting a shop, or a motorcycle.

In 1997, two villagers sold land to buy a pick-up truck to transport goods and villagers to and from town. They were quite successful. In 1998, another family followed their example and sold land as well. During these years, competition on the road between transporters, both from Krajan and outside, increased

---

21 *Meranti* (*Shorea Spp.*), *sengon* (*Albizia falcata*), teak (*jati*) (*Tectona grandis*).

and some of the drivers went bankrupt. In particular, the last family who had sold land faced severe difficulties finally sold the car. Other villagers commented: 'Now you see. Never sell land'.

Sometimes, large plots of land are sold to buy a motorbike for a demanding child. Parents cannot always refuse the demands of children to sell land, even if this would make them the subject of gossip. All villagers agree: selling land on the demand of children, for consumption goods, or even for repairing a house is not good. In practice however, sometimes even sawah is sold to meet these demands. A decade ago, a number of villagers (mostly from Wringinkurung) sold sawah to pay the high school education costs of their children. When most of these children failed to secure a good job – and could not repay the investment – other villagers said they would not follow this example. Few children from Krajan finish high school and only one finished university. Selling land for the education of children is regarded as consumption rather than as an investment and is perceived as not wise.

In contrast to selling land, pawning (*gadai*) is a common practice and a major mechanism for accumulation and dispossession. Villagers in need of cash, pawn land in return for money, cattle, gold or sometimes sugar. The most common way to pawn land is to ask for one or more cows or bulls that can then be sold at the market. This is a public way to transfer the use rights of land as all villagers can witness the transaction: the cows or bulls will be transferred in daylight and exhibited at the house of the pawn giver, and after the transfer at the house of the pawn taker.

When families are confronted with unexpected expenses, as for instance in the case of death or hospitalisation of a family member, pawning land is a fast way to obtain money to cover the costs. The Satrawi family pawned land on several occasions to Patik. When their daughter was in hospital and the doctor's fees had to be paid, Satrawi asked Patik (their patron and neighbour) for a bull of about one year old in return for a piece of sawah. On the first available market day, he took the bull to Bondowoso with Patik who advised and assisted in selling the bull for a good price. After the transaction, Satrawi went directly to the hospital to pay the fees. By pawning his land, he still kept the option of reclaiming it whenever there would be a windfall or an improvement in his financial means. Although Satrawi had intended to pay back an animal as soon as possible, he later had to pawn more land. Now the family has fallen into poverty, even their children might never be able to pay back animals and so return the land to the family. In some cases in Krajan, children were able to get the land of their parents back after more than thirty years.

In general, a *gadai* loan can be repaid in parts, animal by animal, or it can be increased if more cash is needed. This will naturally only happen if the creditor has money or an animal available, and is willing to increase the loan. Often he or she will try to refuse, as he or she already has the use-right and does not earn additional benefits by adding to the price. If the loan is not increased, other people can take over the *gadai* by repaying the loan and by giving additional credit to the owner. This is not very popular as it reflects a severe breach in the relationship between parties but nevertheless, during my stay in Krajan, I witnessed several cases. Satrawi once tried to go to pawn his land for a higher price to *pak* Heri. Heri was willing to provide two cows for the field pawned previously to Patik for one bull. Patik fiercely objected, as a cow was not similar to the bull he had provided, and he did not accept cash as repayment. Finally, the deal with Heri was cancelled. He was not willing to risk his good relationship with the Patik family and their relatives and friends.

If the credit supplier does not want to increase the loan, and the owning party still needs or wants more money, the land can be sold to the creditor. If the creditor cannot, or does not want to buy it, someone else can buy. When selling land, the transaction has to be registered at the village office and at the land administrative office at district level. For powerful people, land transactions with the government, or government related institutions, can be quite profitable. In the last decade, Bagenda has been involved in several of such transactions making nice profits. In the 1960s, the village head (grandfather of Bagenda) asked the government to buy village land to establish *tanah bengkok* and indeed a few patches of sawah were bought. Later, when Bagenda became the village head of Krajan in 1991, he asked the government for more land to be bought. When money was made available to buy sawah, he bought run down, cheap plots of tegal that once had been sawah. These pieces were still registered as first class sawah and Bagenda reported the purchase of first class sawah. He used the surplus money for his own ends. In this way, he both followed the government's request to buy a fixed amount of sawah and made a nice profit. In the village, he led the people believe he received money for tegal, not for sawah. As the lad was bad, he planted trees on them.

Farming for Food: Livestock, Poultry, Crops

Important sources of income are cattle production, maize and rice. With a population of 3,400 people, over 1,500 head of cattle are raised in Krajan. An adult is able to raise only one or two cows on his own because grass has to be cut every day and brought to the shed where the cows are kept. Most of the people who take care of cattle do not own them. They raise cattle of other people and get half of the profit or offspring. Poor villagers, or newlywed couples without cattle, can borrow a cow or bull from others to make a start, if they are considered as reliable, and capable of raising cattle. Generally, cattle owners and caretakers are relatives, neighbours, or friends, and their relationship often has many features of a patron – client bond.[22]

Other livestock such as sheep, goats and horses are relatively unimportant in Krajan. The government has supplied goats a couple of times in its IDT-programmes[23] to help 'backward' villages, but these programmes have been rather ineffective as villagers tried to sell their goats as soon as possible, and village officials took their cut of the benefits. According to villagers, the goats were difficult to keep inside, and then destroyed the crops of neighbours, were noisy, and smelled. Many men and women expressed their disgust of goats and the meat is rarely eaten.[24] Nowadays, widows can be seen every now and then tending goats which they received from a goat programme along the roadside or on harvested fields as goats can eat nearly all crop leftovers. For them, goats can serve as an additional source of income.

Maize is less valued than rice, but it is the crucial staple food-crop in Krajan, guaranteeing most villagers a basic level of subsistence. Madurese are fervent maize eaters. According to Boomgaard (1999: 50) these food habits are very old. Maize is important for food security because it is cheap and it can be stored for long periods and retains a good nutritional value. Maize can be cooked, processed as flour, and eaten as porridge, or baked like pancakes. Young maize cobs are cooked or roasted as a snack.

Local varieties of maize are stored as unpeeled cobs in houses above the fireplace. When needed, the maize is peeled, ground and cooked with rice in the ratio of 1:2. Higher proportions of maize are not appreciated and – according to villagers – difficult to swallow and digest. However, poor people who cannot afford to buy much rice have to mix more maize in with their rice and, accompanied only with vegetables, this results in tasteless and heavy dishes, albeit of good nutritional value.

There are a large number of local maize varieties in Krajan. Farmers distinguish many of these by local names such as *jagung Madura, jagung manis* or *jagung putih*. All of the local varieties belong to the 'pearl-seed' type. Short varieties with cobs between 5 and 10 centimetres in length (Leunissen 1982:74). These varieties need little or no inputs, give only small yields, but are very reliable. Local maize varieties have a good taste, can be stored for long periods and can be grown on every soil type. The growing period of these varieties is long (up to four months) and production is purely intended for the subsistence of

---

22 For a description of these caretaking arrangements for cows and bulls see Chapter 3.

23 IDT means *Inpress Desa Tertinggal*.

24 People often commented: 'We are Madurese, and Madurese people do not like goats, we are only happy with cattle'. Some even refuse to eat cow meat.

the household: it is barely commoditized and seeds are freely exchanged among villagers.

During recent years, new seeds have been introduced by government extension programmes. Hybrid maize varieties need better soils, more fertilizer, more care and work, and the seeds are expensive. They are however, more prone to drought, heavy rains, wind, pests, and bear higher risks as they are more expensive and always need fertiliser. Especially on the higher slopes of the Argopuro, where rains are very unpredictable and heavy winds often occur, the risk of a harvest failure is considerable. Only the somewhat larger farmers decided to try the seeds as they had enough land to takes some risks. They reserved a small part for the new varieties, and planted the rest with old maize varieties.

Basically, there were three types of responses by farmers to these new seeds. The first group carefully applied fertiliser and followed all the instructions on the seed packages aiming at a maximum yield. They spent relatively large amounts on fertilizer and labour. The second group reduced the fertiliser and labour as much as possible and so reduced costs and potential loss in the event of failure. The third group interpreted the instructions of the seed company according to their own needs and circumstances. They selected their best fields with 'warm' soils and applied little fertiliser, but a lot of manure and labour. The first group got the highest yields, while some of the farmers of the second group had the worst yields. Some crops were damaged due to damage by heavy rains and winds. The last group, in general, did not achieve the highest yields, but were the most successful in economic terms. By saving on inputs and investing in locally available techniques and resources, they farmed the most economically and made the best profits.[25]

A smaller proportion of about 20% offered the workers a cash wage instead, thus radically changing the relationship between landowner and labourer. About half of the landowners did not change anything. Both landowners and those taking harvest shares were forced to sell most of the maize because of its lower quality, or exchange it for local varieties. Suddenly, maize had become a commodity in Krajan.

Rice is the favoured staple food in Krajan, but total rice production in Krajan is nowhere near able to meet village demands. Rice prices are relatively high when compared to other staples. Rice has a high economic and cultural exchange value. Rice can be sold, and it can be exchanged for other goods, for services, or for assistance. Rice can be borrowed, used as a gift (*sumbangan*), used as collateral, or invested in a mutual exchange, and it is needed for several religious duties (such as *zakat, selamatan*). Rice is an important commodity in

---

25 Profit calculated as yield minus the costs (in Rp).

Krajan society, and the possession and consumption of rice means a lot to villagers.

In Krajan, two major types of rice varieties are planted, and used mainly for household consumption. The first type includes the old long-stalk and sticky rice varieties. The second type includes the new, high yielding, varieties. These new varieties, introduced since the Green Revolution, have short stalks, a shorter growing season, are more receptive to fertilisers and give higher yields. They are often referred to as 'modern' varieties and were expected to replace 'traditional' varieties completely. The 'new' varieties used in Krajan are now more than thirty years old. Still about one-third of all the rice planted in Krajan is long-stalk varieties. The older varieties are not grown out of tradition, but for economic, ecological, technical and cultural reasons. Growing old varieties attributes more status, they do not require much fertiliser, are risk prone and simply taste better. Also according to some villagers, traditional rice varieties only 'work' in rituals and blessings.

The most commonly planted variety in Krajan at the end of the 1990s and early 2000s is the 'new' IR 64, which is a quite reliable variety offering high yields, but yielding rice of low taste and low quality. In Krajan, IR 64 has been planted since the end of the 1970s. Although newer and 'better' varieties are available nowadays, IR 64 is still planted because it is, according to farmers, suitable for local conditions. Some farmers experimented with other varieties, but often these tests are not satisfactory. The newer varieties offered less reliable crops susceptible to crop failure and seeds are hard to get.

The old varieties planted have local names like *padi Bulu* (hairy), *padi Bali* and *padi Kapor*. These varieties are planted in sawah of lower quality with less reliable access to irrigation water, in upslope and thus colder areas and by farmers who prefer the reliability, the better taste and the specific cultural arrangements attached to this variety. Nowadays, in general, on sawah in the upslope region (above 800 m) old varieties are planted, whereas new varieties dominate on sawah in the mid- and low-slope zones. Farmers often combine both old and new varieties and prefer to plant these varieties simultaneously. It depends on the specific orientation of the farmers in terms of village norms and values, the location and quality of the sawah, family habits and specific household needs, which variety is planted.

During the Green Revolution years (1970s) planting old varieties below 1,000 metres was forbidden. Although most sawah in Krajan actually lies below this altitude, these varieties have always been planted in the lower parts of Krajan and Andungsari. Most villagers managed to circumvent the rigid government regulations related to the Green Revolution and continued planting old varieties on the isolated sawah of Krajan. Nowadays, control on planted varieties is less strong, and old varieties can be seen in the lower areas of Ardisaeng and also close to the road. Villagers who do not have local varieties and need some of this rice for rituals or special occasions can barter for them, but not buy them. I never came across any cases of selling and buying of these older varieties. Although organic farming has been pushed by the region government, in Krajan, it did not appeal. Farmers report difficulties in marketing and unreliable prices.

Wealth and Poverty in Krajan

Krajan is a differentiated rural society, in which villagers have unequal access to land, cattle, employment, and other forms of property or income. This section deals with the ways in which villagers, either directly or indirectly, have access to these resources. Direct access is constituted from command over and ownership of resources; indirect access is mediated by labour arrangements, shared tenancy relationships, social relationships, or inherently by specific modes of production. It considers a number of questions. How are resources distributed in Krajan? How, and by which means, do people gain access to these resources? And who are the most marginalized people of Krajan?

Wealth Ranking and Poverty Categorization

Socioeconomic inequalities are obvious to all villagers, and in assessing each other's wealth and status in the local hierarchy, people seemed to use a classification and ranking system on which nearly everybody agreed. In its most general form, it roughly follows a tripartite division of the population into three classes: the well off, those who can more or less manage, and the poor. In discussing individual cases, however, people make further subdivisions, and the overall local wealth-ranking system turned out to consist of six categories: 'rich' (*kaya*), 'enough' (*lebih* or sometimes called *maju*), 'just enough' (*cukup*), 'insufficient' (*kurang*), 'poor' (*miskin*), and 'destitute' (*susah* or *kasihan*) (see Figure 1).[26] Interestingly, similar categorisations are found in different areas of the world.

26 Throughout this section, I will use Indonesian terms if available. Sometimes, words are the same in Indonesian and Madurese, although they can have different connotations. Here I mention the equivalents of the words used in the text in Madurese. In Madurese *kaya* is also *kaya* (or *sogi*, more polite), *lebih* is *lebbi*, or *langkong* (polite). Another Indonesian/Madurese word often used for this category is *maju*. *Maju* has the connotation of being prosperous, but developing, not yet *kaya*. However, not everybody in this second class is making progress and, for that reason, I prefer to use the neutral term, *lebih*.

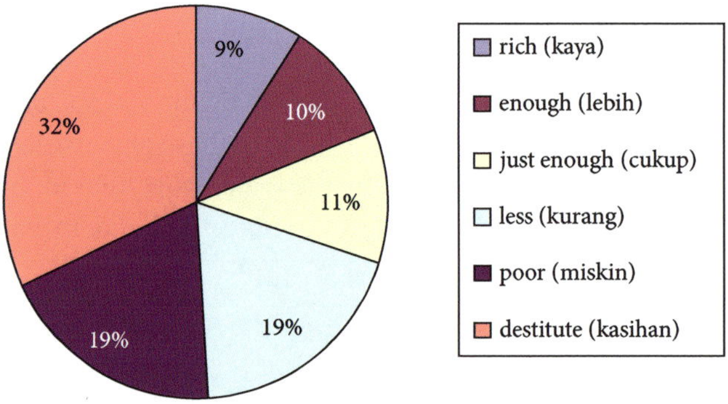

FIGURE 1 *Wealth ranking and percentage of total population*

Recent research of Ton Dietz and the PADev group shows quite similar categorizations in Ghana, Kenya, and Burkina Faso (Dietz et al. 2013, PADEV 2012).

According to local criteria, one in eleven households is called *kaya* (rich), while nearly one third are seen as *susah* or *kasihan* (destitute). The criteria, with which villagers categorize their neighbours, are rather generally agreed upon. Among the rich we find the larger landowners who produce for the market, some government officials (including the village head and his relatives), and relatives of the former village head, some large tobacco and cattle traders, and some large cattle owners. Among the *lebih* or *maju* (enough) we find well-off villagers such as large and middle-sized farmers, businessmen, teachers, and influential people such as hamlet heads and religious leaders. The *cukup* (just enough) are predominantly middle size and smaller farmers, small traders, and skilled labourers. The *kurang* (not enough) are small farmers, small cattle owners, petty traders, and wage labourers. Among the *miskin* (poor) one finds most of the landless and the people without cattle, rich relatives, and regular work. Finally, the *susah* or *kasihan* (destitute) are those who live at the margins of village society. They are often old and disabled people, or villagers who are not able to make a living and do not receive care from kin or neighbours on a regular basis. They face regular food shortages, live in small and shabby houses and face poor health.

Cukup is in Madurese *cokop, pas,* or *genna, kurang* is *korang, miskin* is *tak cokop, sakoniq, mesken. Susah* (*sara* in Madurese) means difficult and refers to people having difficulties in making ends meet. The word *kasihan* (*niser* in Madurese) is more often used in Krajan than *susah* and has different meanings in different contexts. In general *kasihan* (*niser*) refers to people who are pitiful, helpless, lonesome, having bad luck, or in grief. In a context of wealth and poverty, *kasihan* has a quite strong meaning and indicates that people are to be pitied and live a poor and destitute life. *Kasihan* in the context of poverty is somewhat stronger than the Madurese word *niser* meaning down-and-out, or poor thing.

Naturally, villagers are well aware that these categories are not static, and that people may be downwardly or upwardly mobile – as the cases of Satrawi and Patik cited show. People continually watch each other, as the relative social status of fellow villagers may change and need redefinition. Knowing the economic and social position of friends, neighbours and relatives, constitutes strategic information. It is important to know with whom social relationships should and could be established, to know expectations about consumption levels and gifts at *selamatan*, and it is important for assessing the creditability of fellow villagers. It is clear that this watching, valuing and discussion of each other's wealth and status takes place in a context of rumours, gossip and jealousy. Having a new *sarong*, radio, golden necklace, or even a new flashlight can easily lead to rumours or gossip in the neighbourhood.

> One day, Hassim, one of my poor neighbours, bought a big new flashlight. Two days earlier, his wife had borrowed some money from one of the neighbours to buy a few kilos of rice. Instantly gossip started, and the neighbour asked Hassim's wife to repay the loan instantly, as she was not inclined to finance their 'unneeded expenses'. She commented: 'Why did you not go to your husband for money. Are you married to me?' Hassim's wife had no cash money to repay the debt, and neither did her husband. The rumours made her ashamed to ask anybody in the neighbourhood for a loan, she eventually decided to sell some of her much needed maize stocks to the shopkeeper.

In the village, there is ongoing borrowing and lending[27] and information about villagers' credibility is crucial for traders, shopkeepers, village officials and moneylenders. Neighbours, friends, and relatives, are also keen to know every tiny detail of each other's household budgets: to know the amount of support that should be given or received, and the credibility of other villagers in mutual exchange and mutual help relationships.

> *Bu* Patik, for instance, is well known for her skills of gathering strategic information to regain debts. She has close contacts with women in the neighbourhood, and many guests and labourers visit Patik's house in

27 See Lont (2002) who describes these complex and multiple borrowing and lending operations for an urban *kampong* in Yogyakarta. Many villagers have simultaneously debts and loans, and fill one gap or repayment by taking new loans referred to locally as '*gali lobang, tutup lobang*'; (lit. digging a hole, filling a hole), robbing Peter to pay Paul.

search of work, gossip, a free cup of coffee, or some free tobacco. From them, *Bu* Patik obtains all she needs to know about trade, profits and prices. Being the wife of one of the richest villagers, she regularly lends money to workers, relatives, and neighbours in return for assistance and loyalty; in that way she is able to mobilize a pool of workers when she needs them urgently. Most of her loans are very small; the equivalents of a few kilos of maize or rice, but some labourers borrow larger amounts. When *Bu* Patik heard that *Pak* Sulama, one of their labourers, sold his calf she instantly went to his house to reclaim an old Rp 50,000 debt for last year's *Idhul Fitri*. When she arrived at the house, Sulama said he had not yet received any money. The next day *Bu* Patik went again, but Sulama's wife said that her husband was away for work, but others reported that he had been at home. On the third day, she went before dawn and waited in front of the house until the family woke up. She did the same the next day, and finally, after five days, she received her money. 'I will not lend to him again', she commented to other guests at her home, thus reducing Sulama's credit worthiness in the neighbourhood.

Households

Although most transactions take place between individual parties as husbands and wives tend to manage separate funds, exchanges in the village, such as *sumbangan*, gift giving and support, take place between households. In this book, I therefore take households as the units of analysis, which I define as groups of people who eat from one kitchen or fireplace, not necessary always eating together or at the same time, but as a unit that shares food and resources on a regular basis. Using households as units of analysis does not assume that all resources within the household are pooled, shared or redistributed, nor that livelihood activities, incomes and opinions are uniform or agreed upon. Naturally, households are not homogenous units with regard to resources. A household is often a place of contest, an arena of struggle, full of contradictions between the interests of men, women, children and grandparents.

Social Classes in Krajan

A clear demarcation line could be drawn in the village between the 'haves', the rich, enough, and just enough, and the 'have-nots', the not enough, poor, and the destitute. The first grouping are those who have adequate land, are financially independent, and can buy more than basic needs only, while the 'have-nots' face chronic or periodical difficulties in making a living. A general point for calibration between higher and lower classes in terms of wealth ranking is the notion of *cukup*. According to Krajan villagers, *cukup* means being able to provide basic household needs, which means that the family can eat enough (two or three meals a day); eat reasonably well (with vegetables, soy cake, or dried fish); buy clothes for the whole family at least once a year; smoke cigarettes or tobacco; chew betel; regularly buy (once a week) tea or coffee; contribute appropriate *sumbangan* and small gifts to others at weddings, funerals, and lifecycle rituals; and produce a significant number of cookies and simple meals at *selamatan* and at *Idhul-Fitri* at the end of the Ramadan. In short, *cukup* implies to have enough to fulfil household needs and to be able to live decently, being able to perform all the required *selamatan* and other social obligations in the village. At least half of the households are not able to do this on a regular basis, and another 19% faces periodical difficulties in doing this.

The Rich (*Kaya*)

In Krajan, only a dozen extended families are seen as rich. Some of them have become rich in land and cattle, others derive their wealth from business (mainly tobacco trade and cultivation), from inheritance, or from their political position. Three of the richest families of Krajan have provided all the village heads since history, and most of these richest families have members who are involved in village politics or active as village officials such as *kepala dusun*, water officer, village secretary, member of the village development board (LKMD), or head of religious affairs.

Among these rich, the two leading families compete and dominate village politics, each representing one of the two factions in the society: the secular and the religious. The secular (*abangan*) family of the village head Bagenda and his mother, Bu Ti, is currently on the rise. Bagenda owns a few hectares of sawah and tegal, a brick house, a car, a pickup truck, a new Honda motorbike, a large dish antenna and television set, and all sorts of conspicuous consumption goods such as a refrigerator, cameras, and mobile phones. He derives his wealth from privileges and levies that come with his position as village head, from government projects, from a variety of (legal and illegal) trades, and from his sawah and livestock. Moreover, his mother, *Bu* Ti, who owns another few hectares of sawah, tegal, and over 20 head of cattle, supplements his income and finances most of the trades. In addition, *Bu* Ti deals with most of the money lending and retailing from her thriving shop in the village centre.[28]

---

28 Villagers say she owns over fifty head of cattle, but I could not trace much more than a twenty. Bagenda likes to boast about his richness to impress villagers, but in many cases, his wealth was not as great as he boasted. In practice, much of his wealth is derived from profits he made from government projects, and loans from credit schemes rather than

The dominant family from the religious circle in Krajan is the Haji Feisal family living in Mengkuara. The father of Haji Feisal was village head from the end of the 1960s until 1992. In that period, the family prospered and acquired much of its current wealth. Moreover, since they came to power in Krajan, seven family members have been to Mecca to become a Haji. They own a few hectares of second-class sawah, and over fifteen hectares of tegal on which they grow predominantly cash crops such as tobacco, onions, groundnuts, and improved maize. Besides this, they have at least fifty head of cattle, which are tended by poorer families in the neighbourhood. Their compound consists of three brick houses with marble floors, a private praying house to teach Koran to the children from the neighbourhood, and a shop. Moreover, they own a truck for trade and transport, a luxury car, and several motorbikes. They maintain good trading relations in the tobacco area towards Maesan and Jember, and with the most important religious leaders (*kiai*) in that region. During peak times in the tobacco season, they employ over 100 men, women and children. Unlike the Bagenda family, they do not contribute much to *selamatan*, weddings and funerals of the people who work for them, and they rarely loan money. Since Bagenda became village head in 1992, business and political competition between these two families is fierce. From around 1998, it seems that the Bagenda family is doing better,[29] while the Feisal family is losing some of its hegemonic position in the lower Krajan zone. The Faisal family made heavy losses during the droughts of 1996 and 1997, due to low tobacco prices in 1997 and 1998, and are relatively hard hit by the need to pay higher wages to the labourers these days.

The other rich families of Krajan mostly live in Dluwang, Wringinkurung, and Pakualas, and derive their wealth mostly from local resources such as good quality sawah and tegal, and large numbers of cattle. Some of these families belong to the religious, others to the secular, camp and invest in land and cattle, fighting bulls, prestigious *selamatan*, or cattle trade. They control large numbers of poorer families in the neighbourhood who work on their lands for a share of the harvest and who look after their cattle. Although one or two of them have built brick houses, most of these families live in traditional wooden, decorated, houses, do not own motorcycles or television sets, and try to stay slightly aloof from the cash economy. One of the newly rich families has a child in Malaysia who regularly sends money. She is said to be working as a domestic

---

from earnings out of farming or business activities. Much of his business has collapsed soon after being started.

29 Success continues. After 2000, Bagenda became member and later chair of *komisi III dprd* in Bondowoso for several terms.

worker, but some others say she is a sex worker. 'How would she be able to send so much money home?'

The Enough (*Lebih or Maju*)

The enough villagers are well off. Among them are some *nouveaux riches* like such as businessmen, teachers, and some returned migrants;[30] influential people including hamlet heads, and religious leaders; and also families who once belonged to the village elite, but have now somewhat fallen back. The new rich usually own brick houses with ceramic-tiled floors, while the older and former elite often live in wooden, decorated, houses with cement floors. The enough generally own enough sawah to be self-sufficient in rice, but they own considerably less sawah and cattle than the rich. Many of the enough own large plots of tegal. Many of them are involved in tobacco cultivation, large-scale trade, and borrow or lend large amounts of money. Due to sharp fluctuations in prices and quality of tobacco over the years, their wealth is not always steady and their money comes and goes easily.

Other people ranked among the enough are skilled craftsmen, such as constructors, and educated people who have become members of the village administrative system. Teachers and health workers are generally ranked among the enough due to the combination of a steady income from their profession, and several additional income sources. Also, upwardly mobile families (*maju*) are within this category. In the past, people could accumulate wealth from local resources such as cattle and land (e.g. *Pak* Patik) but, increasingly, *maju* people have made their money outside the village from (trans)migration, their profession or business.

The Just Enough (*Cukup*)

Among the 'just enough' are those villagers who generally own some sawah, tegal and cattle, but less than the 'enough'. In general, they have access to relatively good or stable incomes or trades. Moreover, many of them are not that heavily engaged in tobacco farming, although some lease or sharecrop tegal from larger landowners, but rely on non-agricultural forms of income to finance household needs. Their houses are made from wood, or bamboo, with concrete floors, and sometimes they own a radio or a small battery-powered television. They do not own motorcycles, except for one or two families who

30 In five cases, villagers were able to gain money from migration. Among these were returning female migrants from Malaysia and a few families who followed transmigration programmes, succeeded, and sold their lands to return to the village. Not a single spontaneous migrant returned prosperous.

gave way to demanding children and sold assets to buy their children one. Most of them do not produce enough food on their own fields to fulfil household needs and combine farming with a variety of other activities. Among the 'just enough' are many of the shopkeepers, owners of coffee stalls, and peddlers and small traders selling livestock, chicken, fish, or baskets. An example of a 'just enough' is *Pak* Has whose lands produce enough to feed his family for about six months. In addition, he is a tailor, hairdresser, shopkeeper and part-time religious teacher in the *surau* of his father. He and his wife have put their hope in their son who they send to a nearby *pesantren* (religious school) hoping he will become an important religious leader like his grandfather. An uncle of *Pak* Has, living near the *pesantren*, pays most of the expenses of the boy.

Among the 'just enough' are also skilled labourers, such as carpenters and bricklayers, and musicians. A number of Krajanese participate in the dry season in folk theatre groups (*ludruk*) and music (*gamelan*) performances all over the region. Some of these earn relatively large amounts of money from these activities, but the earnings are seasonal.

The Not Enough (*Kurang*)

Those who are considered 'not enough' do not have enough to make ends meet the whole year round, and have never been able to establish a stable income or trade. In normal periods, these families earn enough to make a living, but periodically, they face shortages for which they could not prepare themselves. In these situations, they have to borrow, sell things or cut down on expenses. Remarkably, the not enough have, on average, somewhat larger landholdings and cattle stocks than the enough, but these lands tend to be of lower quality. A relatively large number do not have land, but live from a good job or trade. Among the not enough are many villagers who work the land of large landowners for a share of the harvest, and who look after the cattle of others. Also, most of the wage-labourers can be found among the *kurang* and here also the people who migrate for certain periods of the year can be found. Due to periodic shortages and migration, they cannot always meet the demands of the gift and labour exchange economies in the village, and this makes their networks smaller and more vulnerable. Therefore, they do their utmost to keep up exchanging gifts and perform the main *selamatan*.

The not enough (*kurang*) differ from the just enough (*cukup*) primarily in that they lack property and a stable income. The not enough have smaller networks and fewer relations that might offer labour opportunities, information, or assistance. Moreover, the not enough generally lack the skills to engage in the somewhat better paid types of work. In monetary terms, they live just at the Indonesian poverty line.

An example of a not enough family is the Hasan family from Mengkuara. They live with their two children in a bamboo house with an earthen floor close to the road to Pakem. In the house, a bamboo bed, some kitchen utensils, an old cupboard, a table and a few chairs, and a flashlight make up their belongings. On their tegal, they grow maize, which they mix with rice, and which provides them with food for about six months. After the maize crop, they borrow money from an uncle at 50% interest to grow tobacco. In good years, the tobacco brings in an equivalent of six months of rice, in bad years they are hardly able to repay the loans with interest. At the back of the house, a bull is share-raised for the same uncle. Every morning and every afternoon, *pak* Hasan goes out to cut fodder along roads and trails, on the land of his uncle, and along the river. In the dry season, he walks hours to the forest to collect fodder, or cuts edible leaves from trees in the neighbourhood. He also works in the fields of others, or in the fields of his uncle. Sometimes, his uncle gives him bamboo to plait and weave for sheets for walls (*dinding*) to make some money. On other days, he goes to his fields and tries to break up the rocks in his field to sell to road constructors or house builders. His wife sometimes works on transplanting rice seedlings, weeding fields or cutting tobacco. She also helps regularly in cooking and cleaning at the uncle's house in return for some rice or maize, or a meal. Sometimes, she joins her husband in going to the forest to collect fodder or firewood to sell. In slack periods, they only eat two meals a day, and skip drinking coffee or tea, smoking, and chewing betel. Sometimes, they borrow money from neighbours, the shopkeeper, or ask for a cash advance on the bull, to enable purchases. On several occasions, they have pawned or sold gold to obtain cash. A couple of times, Hasan has followed bands of men from the neighbourhood in search of work, but he was never very successful. Once he was, and he returned with some money with which he bought a radio that he then had to sell a few months later for a much lower price. In 1999, the oldest daughter of the Hasan family was married out to someone in Madura when she was 14. Madurese are among those who marry youngest in Indonesia (Jones 2001).

The Poor (*Miskin*)

The poor, own hardly any land, cattle, and consumer goods. They have no regular cash incomes, and cannot make ends meet. Their houses look shabby, and if their children go to school they do not have a school uniform. They live below the generally acceptable standards of living. They have small networks and, at best, a small piece of land which does not bring them sufficient rice or maize to last even a few months. Moreover, they do not have a stable income, capital or cattle, and are not sufficiently well connected to get access to the resources of others. Moreover, they lack the strength, the health, the skills and the information to engage in stable labour relationships. Last, but not least, they are generally regarded as not creditworthy, and can only borrow very small amounts, or only with collateral which they often do not have.

Each year they experience periods of food shortages in which they need to cut down on expenses and consume only two meals a day. They structurally lack funds for additional costs such as clothes, house repairs, and medical costs. They live below the village poverty line (below *cukup*) and below the Indonesian poverty line, but are able to work, and in that way do gain some income from working other people's lands. They work as wage labourers, becoming migrant workers or produce handicrafts at home. Sometimes, they perform a *selamatan* and try, at great pains, to stay a part of the 'decent' village families. However, they are never able to save or plan for these occasions in advance. Many of the poor turn to potential patrons hoping that they will provide them with some stable work or support. An example in this category is the Satrawi family as described in the introduction. They face regular shortages, have hardly any land and maintain social relationships with great difficulties. Regularly, there is no food or money in the house, and the children roam around the neighbourhood in hope of a free meal. Often, they end up in the kitchen of people like *Bu* Patik who offers them leftover meals and snacks.

The Destitute (*Kasihan*)

The 'destitute'[31] are all those who permanently live far below the village poverty line. They include widows, the chronically ill and the unemployed who are virtually without land, cattle and caring relatives. The destitute have lost their pride and can no longer contribute gifts, assistance or anything else to others. Within strict boundaries of decency, they need and ask for support or assistance on a regular basis. Old and disabled people without relatives; and handicapped people not able to work, walk, see, or having leprosy; are called pitiful, or needy (*kasihan*), and can expect little from social relationships in terms of access to resources. However, due to their obvious vulnerability, they are entitled to some help and might receive some social assistance and privileges from the community at a daily basis. This help however remains somewhat limited and does not exceed an incidental free meal, exemption from village taxation, small sums of money or food donations, basic medical care and, sometimes, labour assistance in collecting firewood or repairing a house. In general, this category of people cannot borrow any money at shops, from neighbours or friends, and live constantly at the absolute minimum level.

31 Dietz (2012) in the PADEV research speaks of ultra-poor PADEV 2012.

Material Indicators of Wealth

So far, in distinguishing these social classes, I have adopted an emic approach to wealth and poverty by making use of local concepts and classifications. Adopting such an approach has a number of implications.[32] First, it is idiosyncratic, and will not always coincide with (but in practice it does have) an 'outsiders' categorisation'. This wealth ranking is relative and locally-based, and therefore comparison with other regions or populations is difficult. Such classification runs the risk of being particularistic and highly context specific. It might produce an adequate case study, but it can make it rather difficult to communicate with other researchers, to related fields of study, and to social policy and development practitioners. On the other hand, such a relative approach has a number of advantages since it overcomes some of the difficulties inherent to some mainstream definitions of poverty that are static and overlook the value of social relations and the social embeddedness of poverty.

In the following sections, I try to overcome the limitations of using a relative approach by relating the local wealth-ranking scale of Krajan households with more quantifiable and material indicators of class such as property and ownership of land, cattle and labour.[33]

Sawah

The differences and inequalities between rich and very poor are most striking if one looks at direct sawah ownership (see Table 1).[34] While the rich have, on average, one hectare of sawah (while some own up to four or five hectares), the other social classes have much smaller plots: 1/5 or 1/6 hectares for the enough

32 See: Breman 1980, 1994, 2000; Dixon and Macarov 1998; Townsend 1993.

33 The definitions of ownership in the survey are: (1) *tanah milik dan bisa pakai* (land ownership where there are usufruct rights), and (2) *tanah tidak milik, bisa pakai* (*ambil gadai, sewa, etc.*) (land not owned, but with a usufruct right at the time of interview such as rented land, land under share tenancy, and land taken as pawn or collateral. Excluded is the arrangement of *babunan* (taking a 1/5 share of the harvest in return for labour), which in fact is not a share tenancy relationship, but a payment for labour by giving a fixed share of the harvest.

34 By direct *sawah* ownership I mean ownership rights (*hak milik*) and use rights (*hak pakai*) thus including land that is *de facto* controlled. This includes rented land (very rare in Krajan) and land that is taken as pawn (which is quite common). These pawns sometimes stretch over several decades. In the case of sharecropping (rare), I take the use right as the proportion (usually fifty-fifty) of the arrangement as both parties are entitled to use half of the returns of the land. See also discussions on the differences in ownership rights in Nooteboom (2001).

TABLE 1 *Ownership of* sawah *and* tegal *per social class*

	Percentage of total households	Average *sawah* ownership (ha)	Percentage of total village *sawah*	Average *tegal* ownership (ha)	Percentage of total village *tegal*
Rich (*kaya*)	9	0.97	53	2.47	37
Enough (*lebih*)	10	0.21	13	1.37	23
Enough (*cukup*)	11	0.16	11	0.49	9
Less (*kurang*)	19	0.11	13	0.47	16
Poor (*miskin*)	19	0.05	6	0.28	9
Destitute (*kasihan*)	32	0.02	4	0.11	6

and just enough, and 1/10 to 1/40 for the poor and the destitute. Taken together, the rich households (9%) control more than half of all village sawah, and, in most cases, they have the better quality fields, which produce substantially higher yields than the small plots of poorer villagers. Of the destitute, two-thirds do not own any sawah at all, and often they do not even own their home lot.[35]

The rich own 53% of the total sawah.[36] The poorest 32% of the population own only 4% of all sawah owned by Krajan villagers.[37] Fig. 2 illustrates this inequality of sawah ownership by wealth category.[38] Similar, but slightly less significant inequalities can be seen for dry lands.

Tegal

Although inequality in sawah ownership in Krajan is high, such irrigated rice fields make up a tiny proportion (around 4%) of the village lands, and are not

35 One should note that most Krajan widows are ranked in the lowest category. Some of these widows had once owned land but have given it already to their children. Only widows heading an independent household were included in the survey.

36 This does include the ownership of *sawah* outside the village of Krajan (mostly in Ardisaeng and some in Andung and Tamankursi (rice fields close to the Dluwang River)).

37 40% of the population of Krajan have no *sawah* at all, and half of these can be found in the lowest wealth category. Of the poor, 53% have no *sawah* at all. And of the category of the not enough, 37% have no *sawah* at all. In the category of just enough everyone has at least some *sawah*, while of the richest villagers interviewed, 11% do not own any *sawah*. This is because they no longer need it due to other sources of income.

38 If quartiles are calculated, the richest 25% of the survey population owns 74% of all village *sawah*. The poorest 25%, virtually own no *sawah* (0.7%). Of the 25 poorest households, only two had a tiny piece of *sawah*.

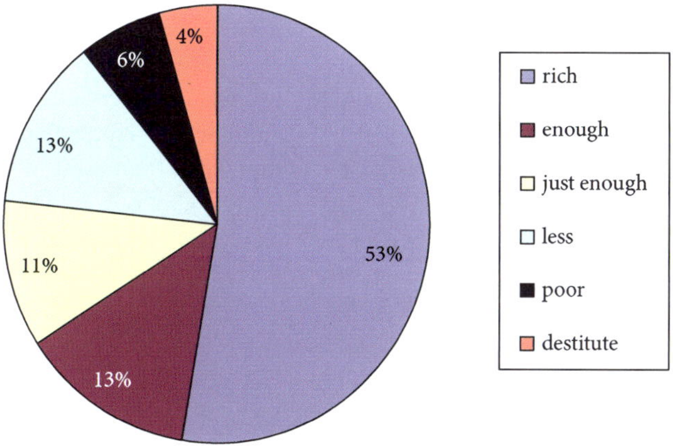

FIGURE 2 *Share of sawah ownership by wealth category*

the only important resource for village households. Most of the arable land (over 75%) is tegal – generally valued at one-third of the price of sawah– and it is suitable for maize, bananas, cassava and tobacco. As most villagers mix rice with maize for their staple food, maize production on tegal is an important source of livelihood and food security.

There is a more-or-less similar unequal pattern of average tegal ownership as with the ownership of sawah (see Table 2): the rich own, on average, about 2.5 hectares and the *lebih* 1.4 hectares. They control about one-third and one-quarter of all village tegal respectively. Also here, the poorer section of the village population owns only small plots ranging from one-tenth to one-third of a hectare.[39] If there are differences between sawah and tegal ownership, then it is that the *lebih* have a greater relative proportion of all the dry fields in the village, and the *kaya* somewhat less.[40] The *lebih* concentrate more on dry land

39 Despite these inequalities in direct ownership of land, it does not follow that the owners use all their land. Direct access to land differs slightly due to sharecropping and harvest-sharing arrangements. In Krajan, sharecropping is not very important. Less than 5% of all *sawah* in Krajan is sharecropped, and only 11% of all tegal in the survey was shared in 1997 and 1998 for the production of the cash crop tobacco, and not for maize. These differences due to sharecropping are included in the calculations where one-half is added to the property of the landowner and the other half to that of the sharecropper. Applied to tegal, with a sharecropping arrangement for one harvest of tobacco, I counted one quarter for the sharecropper and three quarters for the landowner.

40 The enough (*cukup*) own only 9% of all village tegal. This can be explained by the fact that most higher educated, skilled labourers, small traders, and construction workers can be found in this category. These are less inclined to own tegal or *sawah*, as many in this category receive wages and can buy rice on a regular basis. These people are often more oriented

TABLE 2 *Ownership and control of cattle per household*

	Percentage of total households	Average number of owned cattle per household	Percentage owned cattle of total stock of cattle	Average number of controlled cattle	Percentage controlled of total stock of cattle
Rich	9	5.2	42	3.1	25
Enough	10	1.7	15	1.6	14
Just enough	11	1.4	13	1.4	14
Less	19	0.7	13	1	18
Poor	19	0.5	9	1	17
Destitute	32	0.3	8	0.4	12

agriculture because it is difficult to purchase sawah, and because they are more often engaged in tobacco production.

Tegal can be pawned for one or more head of cattle which can then be sold to cover expenses. Also migrants tend to pawn their land to pay the trip to Kalimantan. They hope once to return wealthy and to get the land back. In Krajan, dozens of local terms exist that indicate different types of cattle according to the age and height of the animal. Nowadays, transfers are usually made in cash, although the pawn price is still set as the price of a cow or bull of a certain colour and age to safeguard against the risk of inflation; and, still, pawned land is often paid back in animals.

There is barely a free land market in Krajan. Villagers can only increase their acreage by taking in pawned land from families in urgent need of cash. In general, it is the rich who have cattle or ready cash available to exchange for land in pawn. However, middle class farmers (*lebih*) – and sometimes the better-off lower classes (*cukup*) – also take land (*ambil gadai*) for one or two heads of cattle. In this way, social mobility is possible. Notwithstanding the possibilities for social mobility are available through migration, accumulating cattle and education, there is a tendency towards a concentration of land in the hands of richer families, like elsewhere in rural Java.[41] Rich families can also lose land. Among the most common reason why descendants of richer families have lost

towards the outside economy and less inclined to eat rice mixed with maize, less oriented towards investing money in land, but rather in houses, on motorbikes, and sometimes cattle.

41 See: Edmunson 1994; Hart, Turton and White 1989; Hüsken 1988, 1989.

access to land is the inheritance system. In customary Madurese inheritance law, male and female siblings receive equal shares, whereas if Islamic law is applied, daughters inherit one-third. Children with small pieces of land were more likely to run up debts, move away, or become marginalized which force them to sell the land. In the reverse sense, only a few villagers – such as *Pak* Patik – were able to move from smallholder to prosperous landowner. Such families managed to save and invest in cattle and slowly build up a big herd, which then could be used to acquire pawned land or to buy land.

Cattle

Despite the concentration of land in the hands of richer villagers, not only large landowners are counted among the rich of Krajan. Traditionally, cows and bulls have been an important basis of wealth because they can be converted into other forms of capital, and because of their symbolic value. Nowadays, consumer goods such as motorbikes, cars, radios, television sets and stone houses are competing with, and replacing, the symbolic functions of cows and especially bulls.

Owning cattle is an important source of income. First, a cow or bull contributes to the livelihood of its owner and serves as a saving device. However, often it is not the owner who takes care of feeding and cutting grass, but someone else who, for this work, receives a share (usually half) of the proceeds. In the case of a cow, the tender will be given half of the cattle's offspring (*mengobu*-arrangement), and in case of a bull, the tender receives half of the profit when the bull is sold (*oanan*-arrangement[42]). In the past, *oanan* relationships were important for status and prestige. Owners of good bulls gave them to professional caretakers who trained and prepared the bulls for *aduan sapi*, the Madurese bullfight.[43] Today, the two arenas for bullfights are closed for religious reasons and bullfights are forbidden. Prices of bulls have fallen relative to normal market prices where traders buy bulls to be butchered.

Share-raising arrangements for cattle are very firm, and in Krajan always on a fifty – fifty basis. Because of this, caretakers cannot easily be changed; and

42 Hefner (1990: 107) notes for this 'halving' system *paron*. 'Under the terms of this contract, the animal tender gets to keep all the manure produced by the animal. At sale, the original purchase price for the animal is deducted from the sale price, and the remaining cash is then divided equally between the tender and owner'. In the context of upland commercial vegetable-farming in Tengger, he records a market for manure. In Krajan, I came across only one case of people selling manure; to one of the farmers experimenting with high yielding maize varieties.

43 See: De Jonge 1990; De Jonge 1994.

caretakers of cows can use the cows to plough or for carrying goods, and usually have a say in buying or selling the animal. In practice, this means that the caretaker does indeed have around 50% of the control of the animal minus the initial value.[44]

The importance of cattle becomes evident from the survey that showed that 81% of all villagers[45] are involved in cattle-raising; either as owners, or as tenders. Only elderly widows and some of the destitute, as well as households from the 'higher middle-class', do not raise cattle for physical, organizational, or social reasons.[46] Thus, nearly every Krajan villager who is willing and able either owns or cares for cattle, but in no sense do they all have a more or less equal share. As with land tenure, property rights over cattle are very unevenly distributed, as Table 2 shows. While the rich owned on average five cows or bulls, the rest no more than one or two. As in land tenure, the rich owned nearly half (42%) of all cattle, while the *lebih* and *cukupan* owned one-quarter, leaving the poorest classes (*miskin* and *kasihan*, 51% of the population) with control over 17% of the village livestock.

Considering only the actual ownership of cattle is misleading as figures will then be distorted by the fact that most of the richer villagers do not look after any cattle themselves, and no-one can tend more than two adult animals by himself. Poor relatives, neighbours or friends of cattle owners, look after the other animals, in return for half of the profit or offspring (*oanan* or *mengobu*), giving them thus significant control. If we include the cattle that are cared for by share tenants, the distribution is less skewed. Then it turns out that most households have at least some control over the proceeds of cattle – if they

44 Control of cattle is calculated as actual control: the sum of the number of owned cattle, owned cattle but share-raised by others (0.5) and not owned, but share-raised for others (0.5). The number of controlled cattle indicates the number of cattle whose proceeds (profit, offspring, manure) are available to a household. The manure is used by the tender.

45 This is a high figure, but not unusual in upland farming systems in the Eastern Salient. Compare with Hefner (1990: 106) who shows for the Tengger that in the midslope area two-thirds of the population own or share-raise cattle. One-third of the landless, and about 40% of the landless and small peasants, are tending cattle. According to Hefner, cattle raising is less profitable than the production of commercial vegetables. In Krajan, where these opportunities are scarce, cattle is one of the few cash generating activities.

46 12% of these 19% not caring for cattle are old widows who cannot for physical reasons, widows supported by children, and destitute villagers could not get access to a cow. The other 7% are mostly upper middle class villagers (*cukup* and *lebih*) with other, more profitable, work opportunities, or seasonal migrants making it impossible or not so necessary to care for cattle.

want it. The three poorer classes – who amount to two-thirds of the population – on average, control the proceeds of about 0.7 animals per household, amounting to nearly half of all cattle in Krajan. Presented in this way, the distribution of control over cattle turns out to be more equal than for other resources and a means of levelling inequalities somewhat.[47]

Finally, it should be noted that the ability to tend cattle relates to the ability to gain access to grass. Here I cannot elaborate at length on the specific difficulties in obtaining fodder in the dry season, especially for poor families, but, in general, grass can be cut along roads, trails, rivers, and in the forest. Night-time thefts of grass do occur, and sometimes competition over grass is so fierce that fights occur. Those who own sawah or tegal often plant elephant grass along the dykes and ditches of their fields, others are dependent on the goodwill of landowners. In many cases, tenders have some rights to the grass along the ditches of the owner of the animal. In addition, taking harvest shares give rights to the grass along the edge of fields and the crop leftovers. In general, the less resources a household owns, the more difficult it is for them to obtain grass of good quality (except for those living near the forest).

Consequences of Inequalities: Food Production, Self-Sufficiency, and Access

What does this inequality in landownership mean for the food production of households? During the survey, I asked each head of the household – and often the wife – how many months the household would be able to eat from the production of their own, rented, and sharecropped fields. The results in Table 3 show that differences in self-sufficiency between the social classes of

TABLE 3 *Number of months of self-sufficiency in food*

	Number of months self-sufficient
Rich	9.8
Enough	8.4
Just enough	7.5
Less	5.1
Poor	2.7
Destitute	1.6

47 If quartiles are calculated, the inequality is still striking. The upper 25% control 48% of all cattle proceeds, while the lower 25% controls only 10%.

villagers are almost as sharp as in land ownership. Through share cropping arrangements (*babunan*), even the poor are able to gain some income in kind, but inequalities remain.

An important fact hidden here is that richer families do not mix much maize with their white rice, and so finish stocks more quickly, while poorer families generally mix in more maize with their rice to reduce costs and prolong stocks. Additionally, feeding agricultural labourers puts a strain on the food stocks of especially large landowners. Poorer villagers, especially those in the '*cukup* and *miskin*' categories work regularly as wage labourers in the fields of others, and save their own food stocks by eating frequently at other people's houses, while they rarely employ and feed labourers themselves.[48]

The poor and destitute are worst-off as their own supplies last for no more than 1–3 months – a supply which hardly stems from their own land (of which they have virtually none) but from sharecropping participating in harvests or gleaning the leftovers after harvest, from roots and tubers which they collect on wastelands, and from food given to them by children or neighbours.

The data from Krajan show that ownership rights are vary unevenly distributed, with the richest class owning about one half of the village's main resources: rice fields, dry fields, and cattle; while the poor own only tiny plots at best. To some degree, share-tenancy on village land, and share-raising of the village cattle, provides the poorer classes with at least some access to resources. Sharing arrangements thus mitigate somewhat local inequalities, but the overall picture of a small number of households in firm control of the village economy remains. The poorer households – who together make up two thirds of the village – have to rely on other sources of income to survive. An obvious source for the property-less is income earned from working for other people. The next section will discuss the different labour arrangements in more detail.

Labour and Work

Some households earn incomes from a variety of sources, other are dependent on only a few crops or sources of income for their livelihood. Essentially, for those poor who are healthy and able-bodied, the main resource they have is selling their own labour. By working they secure income, and they also maintain their social networks which are, as I will explain, crucial for their survival in the

48 The classes described are not tenure classes, but social classes and that *lebih* and *kaya* also include rich people who are not dependent on farming, such as traders, returned migrants and teachers.

village. Access to employment, however, is not easy and can never be taken for granted. People try hard to obtain work, and they do this in many different ways.

Although the land and cattle are very unequally distributed in the village this does not mean that the landless and small farmers completely lack access to land. Villagers with little or no land can get access to a part of the harvest by sharecropping or taking harvest shares. Sharecropping (*paronan*[49] or *paron* Mad.), a 50–50 sharecropping deal of sawah in Krajan seldomly occurs. Only about five Krajan villagers give their sawah out in sharecropping. Some 75% of the poor families in Krajan are involved in *babun*[50] (Mad.), a system of payment in kind through harvest-shares of friends, neighbours, patrons and relatives. There are basically two types, *babun* (Mad.) and *beton* (Mad.). In *babun* arrangements, people receive a one-fifth share (maize or rice) in return for their labour; and this arrangement lasts in principle for one cropping season. *Beton* arrangements are long, often life-long, arrangements with the same share. Both arrangements, *babun* and *beton*, are only used with food crop cultivation. In addition to the harvest share; two meals, coffee and cigarettes are provided during workdays. The *babun* share of one-fifth has to be divided among the workers. Sometimes, the owner of the land is included if he has worked alongside the labourers. In the case of larger landowners, this is seen as greedy and indecent, as it means a lower share for the workers.

As sharecropping through *babun* contracts is common practice on the fields of the large landowners, these contracts imply some kind of redistribution – albeit that, in the end, the landowner benefits most as this payment-in-kind covers all his labour expenses.[51] Given the fact that the richer classes (*kaya* and *lebih*) together own 66% of all sawah and 60% of all tegal, and that the standard

49 *Paronan* refers to the practice where *paron* is the root word (comparable with *maro* in Javanese). In the following, I will give the root words only (and leave out *ke-…– an* constructions which are used to refer to the practice of and the deal itself).

50 *Babun* (*beton* in case of long-lasting arrangements) is a Madurese term for wages in kind (in rice or maize) as a 1:5 share of the crop in return for labour. In the case of old rice varieties and maize, the workers chose one bundle out of every five. Compare with the Javanese word *bawon*, which means literally: '(1) a share of the rice harvest received for one's services during the harvesting […] (2) a certain size bundle of newly harvested rice plants' Horne 1974. It is the best part, or the biggest bundle. *Babun* should not be confused with the Javanese *bawon*, the latter of which is generally referred to as a harvesting arrangement. *Babun* is comparable with the Javanese *kedokan* arrangement Van der Kolff (1937); Wiradi (1984) but differs because the share in Krajan is always fixed (1:5). *Babun* applies to old and modern rice varieties in the same ratio (and also often to maize).

51 Except for costs on meals (one or two per working day), coffee (one glass), and something to smoke (tobacco or one or two *kretek* cigarettes).

workers-share is 20%, this implies that poorer villagers, through their *babun* work, acquire access to 13% of the sawah produce, and 12% of the tegal – insofar as food crops are concerned (tobacco is not cultivated in *babun* contracts).

As keeping cattle and food crop production are closely related in Krajan, gaining access to fields by taking on *babun* also means access to fodder. *Babun* workers need to have cows at their disposal to plough the fields. On some rare occasions, people can get a *babun* contract without having a cow; when the worker is young, recently married, or when a cow is still in training, or when one's cow has recently died. While, in the case of *beton*, the worker has to turn up when summoned, in the case of *babun*, workdays can be negotiated. If one of the workers is not able to come, he can send someone – usually a child or relative – to replace him. If he does not, he will lose his right to a share of the harvest, or his share will be reduced. Moreover, the arrangement is part of a patronage relationship in which the landowners often also give small loans, pay part of funerals, give gifts, and the like.

Many villagers favour being paid in *babun* over receiving a day's wage because of these reasons. Moreover, the average returns from *babun* are significantly higher than those from wage labour. On average, *babun* workers earned about 3 kilos of rice for a day work. Further, it is not only the cash value that counts, villagers prefer wages in kind over those in cash because they can store the rice and maize and thus secure sufficient food for the coming months. 'Money cannot be saved', villagers often commented.

Villagers make strategic choices when opting for wages in kind instead of cash. They also say that they like to get several *babun* contracts because this enables them to spread risks over several fields (different locations and altitudes) or over several rice varieties and over several bosses. However, the unstated main reason is also that often wage labour jobs are very difficult to get. In years when many harvests failed because of diseases and irregular rains, people say many villagers even more strongly preferred *babun*, a way of saving 'in others'. In fact, they are building up social capital, and labour arrangements such as *babun* are a crucial investment for creating and maintaining solid ties between workers and landowners.

Babun arrangements contribute an important element to the food security of poorer Krajan households because they contain a firm right to a fixed share of the harvest. Some small farmers spread risks by sharing their own land through *babun* while, at the same time, taking up *babun* in the fields of others. To an outsider's it might have seemed more profitable to work their own land alone, to minimize labour costs and reap all the harvest. However, people consider working together on land in small groups to be more efficient, and to spread risks as it provides access to other plots of a different quality than their own. Moreover, it offers access to knowledge and information, and helps to finish the work more quickly. Again, the main reason is that it extends social networks and thus the chances of getting help when it is needed.

Not everyone can get a *babun* contract as one needs to have a good relationship with the owner. If one gets *babun* then social relationships with the employer can become stronger over time and the employer can become a kind of friend. Satrawi described this dual advantage of *babun* by using a well-known Madurese saying: 'A friend can become a relative, while a relative can turn into an enemy'.[52] By working one makes friends, and therefore labour contracts with large farmers are highly desirable. For him, this is the major reason that he prefers good relationships with many people and wages in kind, over a cash wage.

Beton, and to a lesser extent *babun* contracts are often a part of patron-client bonds. *Beton* workers are supposed to do other jobs for the landowners, and also their wives and children might help around the house or in the kitchen of the landowner, and help at the preparations for a *selamatan*. Patron-client relationships offer many benefits in getting and guaranteeing access to resources. As Hefner described for the Tengger mountain area: 'Many poor villagers seem to prefer the loss of personal freedom above the insecure way of living of those who have no access to this kind of tied land-labour relations' (Hefner 1990:80). It is not just a 'fear of freedom', but mainly because patronage relationships and friendship are the most obvious ways to gain access to land, cattle or work, and to be eligible for help in times of need: in short, to survive in Krajan.

Payments in kind, like harvest shares, meals, drinks, and cigarettes have been common all over Java, but locally there can be differences in the way these payments are made. In Krajan and surroundings, the one-fifth harvest share for *babun* is fixed, and according to villagers it has always been so. For new varieties of maize introduced in 1998 however (which are regarded as a cash crop, rather than a subsistence crop), a share of one-sixth or even one-seventh was sometimes used because landowners say that their expenses have gone up, and that harvests are bigger anyway so that, in the end, the workers will still receive the same amount of rice or maize.[53] Though common across

52 Madurese saying: *'Kancah bisa detdih taretan, taretan bisa detdih mosoh',* (*teman bisa jadi saudara, saudara bisa jadi lawan*).

53 *Babun* is found across the whole district of Pakem, Wringin, and Besuki, and probably in the whole of Madurese East Java. In Javanese Java the very similar arrangement of *kedokan* is generally found Van der Kolff (1937); White and Wiradi (1989).

East Java, *babunan* contracts come in several shapes and there are minor variations between villages and hamlets, and also between crops. Apparently, *babun* is interpreted, negotiated, modified and adapted according to local circumstances and conditions. Over the years, there seems to exist a clear connection with population pressure and researchers in the past has explained the size of the share by population pressure, as a levelling and redistribution arrangement, as an exponent of the moral economy, and by the ability of the poor to claim a share of the rich. Many of these writers expect the disappearance of these arrangements after commercialisation and a breakdown when too many people migrated. Both did not happen in Krajan. The arrangements turn out much more flexible and subject of negotiation than often assumed.

Local Variations in Labour Arrangements

The hamlets of Dluwang and Pakualas are the most remote, and for a long time the most isolated and, probably, the most closed communities. They belong to the most recently settled parts of Krajan and the fields were cleared only one or two generations ago. The two hamlets are therefore relatively homogeneous; including from a religious perspective since most inhabitants belong to a single orthodox group belonging to one *kiai* represented by organizations such as NU (*Nahdatul Ulama*) and PKB (*Partai Kebangkitan Bangsa*).[54] Land is relatively fertile and abundant, and people use few chemical inputs as cash is scarce in these two hamlets. However, given the remote location, labour is also relatively scarce as not many workers from elsewhere go to these hamlets looking for work. Mutual labour arrangements are therefore more important than in the other hamlets and the share of *babun* is larger, up to 25 %.

Harvest arrangements vary depending on crop, place, type of community, culture and form of ownership. Moreover, in upland areas, many of the traditional arrangements have survived the agricultural reforms of the New Order regime. This also questions the linear, political economic expectations that farmers will increasingly be dispossessed and only a few large farmers will remain. Reality is much more complex. In the higher areas of Krajan, old long-stalk varieties are often grown for economic, social and cultural reasons. These varieties require time-consuming manual ear-by-ear harvesting. Due to this increased workload, the harvesters receive an extra bundle of rice (1.5–2.5 kg) on top of their *babun* (*kedokan*) share. Usually, those who planted the rice have the right to harvest. Harvest shares also vary accordingly to social closeness: it is often only the wives or female relatives of *kedokan*-takers who are accepted

54 In these hamlets, over 90% voted for the PKB during the last elections. In Krajan proper, Mengkuara, Sayuran, Wriningkurung and Morsungai, the majority voted PDI-P.

as harvesters. The free access, as described by Geertz (1963) and others,[55] in lowland Java before the Green Revolution, where villagers could harvest without personal invitation, has never existed in Krajan. Who is invited depends on the labour arrangements and the preferences of the farming family; if they want to tie certain labourers to them, they will only invite those labourers.[56] Free access to harvests applies only to 'new' IR varieties of rice that can be cut with the *arit*, the Madurese sickle, and threshed in the field. Here, harvesters help in cutting and threshing the rice and get a share of the straw for cow fodder. Sometimes these uninvited harvesters receive some food, or something to smoke. In the dry season, when fodder is scarce, such harvests are overwhelmed with people trying to get a bundle of straw. *Babun* workers, also in need of animal fodder, often try to keep the day and time of the harvest secret, or start harvesting in the middle of the night or very early morning to be ready before dawn and be able to take all the straw home. Thus, the poor exclude the poor.

Unlike in rice cultivation, in tobacco farming tegal is share cropped, albeit on a seasonal basis only. Almost one in seven households that are engaged in tobacco farming share their crop. Sharing contracts for tobacco last one growing season and, generally, the costs of land and inputs are shared, or landowners provide the money and others the labour. Essentially, it is a way to control labour as the worker is not free to choose when and where to work. Further, it is the middle-level farmers who have their tobacco sharecropped by others. This means that the tobacco sharecroppers engaged in sharecropping are generally the 'just enough' (*cukup*) and the 'not enough' (*kurang*) villagers. The poorest villagers (*miskin* and *kasihan*) are excluded from these sharecropping

55 Abdullah and White 2006; Hart, Turton and White 1989; White and Wiradi 1989; Wiradi 1984.

56 As noted previously, the Madurese word *babun* might seem similar to the Javanese word *bawon* but the arrangements are different. *Bawon* refers to the open harvest of old, long grain, varieties of rice which have to be harvested by the labour intensive *ani ani* method. *Babun* refers to a one-fifth share of the harvest plus meals in return for all the work involved. It can be applied to the harvesting of rice and maize. It can probably best be compared with the Javanese *babon*, which refers to the choice of the biggest bundle after the harvest Hüsken. It is a kind of a mix of the Javanese *sambatan* (mutual help) and *pakehan* (*bawon* share of harvest in return for planting and harvesting) Van der Kolff (1937). According to Van der Kolff: (1937:15), these forms developed into *kedokan* in response to increasing population pressure. In the original form, workers received larger shares and had to do less work. Van der Kolff notes one-quarter shares of the harvest, without soil preparation before planting, in 1936. Due to population pressure, shares have decreased. This shows that the arrangements are fairly universal and can survive over many generations, but that the contents of the arrangements are more flexible.

arrangements as they cannot afford the costly inputs and are reluctant or unable to take on the huge risks involved in tobacco farming. The richer villagers, who have enough land, cash or credit facilities to grow tobacco themselves, prefer to manage their own crop and reap all the profit.

Arrangements for Cattle

In securing a livelihood, cattle have similar functions as land but the ownership of cattle is much more widespread than that of land. According to many of the poor, share raising cattle is productive, secure and provides status. Although the actual ownership of cattle is nearly as unequal as that of land, there are two arrangements for share-raising (*ngobu*[57] Mad. and *oanan* Mad.) that offer many poor villagers access to some relatively stable income. In the first arrangement, the caretaker gives the first calf born to the owner and is allowed to keep the second. In the second arrangement, only the profit is shared. The caretaker has total control and responsibility for the cattle. They can be used for ploughing and preparing rice fields. These share-raisers are thus able to engage in *babun* contracts and gain access to land as well as an opportunity to save (in the form of cattle) and build up property. Many villagers share an ideal of owning their own herd, but very few are able to succeed and build up a stock of cattle. For the destitute, who do not own any assets, this is particularly problematic as any calves they receive as payment for their work often have to be sold soon after they are born to repay debts or cover household needs. Sometimes they even sell their calves before they are born at a much lower price. About two dozen Krajan families from the fourth and fifth categories have managed over the last fifteen years to rise from partakers in *ngobu* to independent cattle owners.

While sharing arrangements for cows and bulls are crucial to the income of poor villagers, cattle serve as a saving mechanism for nearly all the households in Krajan. The question is if this arrangement protects or exploits the poor. It has a dual nature, and can be seen as doing both. Those without access to

57 Leunissen (1982:152/204) mentions the Madurese word *ngobu* for an arrangement where seed (such as peanut or soybeans) is borrowed under the condition that half of the produce will be returned to the owner of the seed. I did not come across such an arrangement in Krajan for seeds, only for cattle and chicken (the caretaker takes half the offspring). Koning Koning 2001 describes a cattle-sharing arrangement in her paper on Central Java and mentions *gaduh*: 'for goats and cows the *gaduh* system (taking care of the animals owned by someone else) is practiced. In case a goat has two young, one of the young is for the caretaker who can chose which animal he wants. Usually the male animals are preferred as these grow faster and have a higher value. For cows in Krajan a similar system is used but with more strict rules as the price of cows is much higher' Nooteboom (2001).

cattle can face serious difficulties when they need money. This applies in the first place to widows, the elderly and the sick who cannot collect fodder, and thus are unable to gain a shareholding contract. It also holds for the destitute (*kasihan*) of Krajan of whom 36% do not own or share-raise cattle, they are simply not trusted and not considered sufficiently reliable to care for cattle.[58]

Getting Rich in Krajan: (Social) Mobility

Where the Patik family was able to rise from rags to riches by slowly accumulating property through acquiring village resources, they reflect no more than ten per cent of the villagers who have been able to significantly improve their living conditions. There are essentially four upward trajectories in Krajan to escape poverty: through the accumulation of cattle to then buy land, through education, through trade and through migration. The production of cash crops such as tobacco, chillies or, increasingly, timber is only available to those who have sufficient land.

During the last four decades, another 10% have slowly slid from a relatively prosperous rural livelihood into poverty. They include the Satrawi family living beyond their means, and also families who lost fortunes in tobacco trade and speculation, through gambling, divorce or through sheer misfortune and loss of productive family members. It is often a combination of the above that lead to families falling into poverty.

The majority of the relatively affluent families with land and cattle have been able to remain prosperous and almost all of the old landed village elites have been able to add to their land and their number of cattle. Moreover, they occupy important positions in village politics or religious affairs, and they thrive on the new opportunities Indonesia has to offer. They trade in tobacco, give loans on credit, transport goods to nearby towns, trade in the city and allow their children to study. They maintain good connections with the outside world through religious networks, politics or trade. These families are the drivers behind the slow but steady process of land ownership becoming concentrated in ever fewer people.

A large majority of the Krajan population, almost 80%, have become slightly poorer or slightly richer or stayed in their wealth class. The basic agrarian

58 Thirty-six per cent of the *kasihan* of Krajan (including widows) do not own any cattle whereas 64% do, or share-raise cattle, and in that way have access to some income and stability. Of the *miskin*, 21% do not own any cattle, while all *kurang* have or at least share-raise cattle.

structure of unequal land ownership and low paid labour has not changed. Over the last four decades, the proportion of poor villagers has neither increased nor fallen, while the group having just enough has also not grown. Over the years, tobacco prices have slightly improved, but not soared, rice and maize production in this dry land area has not increased and almost no new cash crops have been introduced. The only exceptions being the newly established state-owned coffee plantation and the growth in planting fast growing trees such as *sengon* (*Paraserianthes falcataria*), and mahogany (*Swietenia macrophylla*). Wages in the coffee plantation are low and the growing of trees will benefit only those who have firm access to land.

The only other way to escape the constraining village structure has been migration. It is very hard to reconstruct migration figures over the last four decades as no records are kept and village statistics are unreliable. Through life histories and through systematic surveying and explicitly asking about the migration histories of the surveyed families, their neighbours and relatives, a basic picture emerges. Migration from Krajan has slowly increased since the 1960s. In the beginning, it was only the lower middle-class families who had enough capital to send one or more sons away to find work. They found seasonal work in the region in tobacco, coffee and sugar cane, and some settled in the area between Bondowoso, Jember and Banyuwangi. A few found work in the towns of Bondowoso and Jember as craftsmen. After the mid-1980s, some Krajan families were able to join transmigration projects to Sumatra and Kalimantan (Madurese from Madura were never part of transmigration programmes), some of them returned, but the majority of these families simply 'disappeared' and connections with the village ceased. At the end of the 1980s, labour recruiters increasingly found the village and recruited labourers from the poorest families to work in Kalimantan. From this time onwards, out-migration increased rapidly with 100 people a year migrating, or 3 to 5% of total village population between 1987 and 1997 (estimates of village officials and survey). During this period, young women first started to work as domestic helpers in town, but numbers remain low until today as women tend to marry very young and Madurese values are not in favour of letting women travel, work or migrate alone. In 1997, around five per cent of Krajan villagers had a family member working outside the village. Today this has risen to more than 10%.

Many young men try to find their luck beyond the vicinity of the village. Young men migrate to work for a few years in the oil palm plantations of Kalimantan, in construction or in brick kilns or stone quarries, while women stay in the village, care for cattle, work as agricultural labourers in the tobacco industry or find a job in town. Today, increasingly, also women move out of the village to find work. In Krajan, this did not happen before the end of the 1990s.

This chapter has highlighted the poor agricultural resource base of Krajan, one of the many Madurese villages in Bondowoso district. It has dealt with existing inequalities, poverty and ways of accessing resources in Krajan. With a focus on inequality and access, rather than on a precise poverty line delineating incomes, I have shown the structural inequalities among large groups of the Krajan population both in direct and indirect access to resources. Inevitably, this chapter therefore dealt with the old, but still relevant, theme of widespread inequality and poverty in rural Java.[59] Starting from an insider's viewpoint, it shows the continuing structural gap between rich and poor by taking local definitions of rich and poor.

The crux of the matter in understanding poverty is not the lack of income as expressed by a poverty line, but the lack of and exclusion from access to resources, and the realisation that poverty can be temporary and dynamic. Rather than measuring income, the analysis of direct and indirect ways of gaining access offers a better picture of inequality in Krajan. We saw that the large inequalities in direct ownership of sawah, tegal and cattle are reduced by up to 20% by four factors. Firstly, the property of richer villagers is shared through sharecropping, share harvesting and the share-raising of cattle. Secondly, most labour arrangements for working on the lands of richer villagers include the provision of meals, thus reducing the pressure on the household food stocks of labouring families. Finally, sharecropping arrangements are primarily about social relations. Workers are often entitled to social assistance in times of need. Nevertheless, even after these adjustments to the apparent inequality in access to resources, the gap between rich and poor is still astonishing. A small minority, of about 9% of all households, controls over half of the village's resources of land and cattle, while over 60% of the villagers face hardships in securing basic needs on a regular basis. This final figure has hardly fallen in recent decades: the only way out is to move out. Further, the figures show a tremendous divide between the haves and the have-nots. These inequalities are widely reproduced in the power relationships between rich and poor villagers, so maintaining and perhaps even enhancing the inequalities. It is from this unequal situation that many of the poorer people, and often not only the poorest, have decided to try their luck in Kalimantan.

59 See for debates on poverty in Java among others: Alexander and Alexander 1982; Breman 1980, 2000; Edmunson 1994; Hüsken; Hüsken and White 1989; Jellinek 1991; Levinsohn, Berry and Friendman 1999; Singarimbun and Penny 1973.

CHAPTER 3

Bonds of Protection; Structures of Exclusion

Social Security in East Java

The examples of the Satrawi and Patik families at the beginning of the book show the importance of establishing and maintaining good relationships with others. At the same time, it shows the paradoxical nature of support networks, as other people can also be a major source of insecurity. This chapter analyses the everyday risks and insecurities involved in making a living as well as the scope and limitations of the available arrangements and institutions. It also discusses the crucial issue of inclusion and exclusion in communal support systems in a Madurese village on East Java. In Chapter 4, we then move to the ways in which Madurese-speaking villagers handle insecurities themselves, both alone and together.

In the mentioned cases of Satrawi and Patik, the state did not play a major role as a provider of support to the needy and poorer members of society. This is not surprising since, for poorer sections of the population in rural Indonesia, state programmes for poverty eradication and social security often fall short. Moreover, the Madurese, as relatively poor, poorly educated and often living in remote areas, are among those groups that largely fall outside the system of state patronage. In general, they have few opportunities to benefit from the state and need to rely even more than the urban poor on communal forms of social security. This becomes increasingly problematic as village institutions and social security arrangements are changing and do not stretch to migration areas, while new forms of social security tend to be rather specific. As Hüsken and Koning conclude: 'these institutions lost their "naturalness," and new ones are increasingly exclusionary [...] As such the changing social security situation underlines the general profound transformation that Indonesian communities have experienced in the past decades where old, more or less open-access forms of communality and solidarity are rapidly dwindling or becoming increasingly exclusivist' (Hüsken and Koning 2006:25–26).

Local Forms of Social Security

The scope and meaning of such local social security arrangements in rural areas or village societies have been regularly debated over the years. The literature concerning Indonesia falls into two categories. There are those who take poverty as a starting point and, from that position, look at social protection – or more often the lack of it; and there are those who look at institutions and arrangements which might offer social protection, but which often fail to do so and leave people exposed to risks and the negative consequences of poverty. The first group contains the many poverty studies on rural Java that discuss inequality, poverty and social class, while the second group takes poverty sharing, support and cooperation as its starting point.[1] Many of these studies only partly or indirectly touch upon the lives of people in coping with insecurity and social security, and tend to offer a limited, sometimes static, romanticized or distorted picture of rural societies in Java.

The inequality and limited protection reported in these studies contrasts sharply with the rosy image of the communal Javanese village as presented by Clifford Geertz and others (Alexander and Alexander 1982, Geertz 1963, Jay 1969, Koentjaraningrat 1967b, Robinson 2000). The Javanese village has been often mythologized as harmonious due to the presence of various arrangements for mutual help (Hüsken and Koning 2006:17–18, Koning 1997:33, White 1983, 2000). The widely held belief that, in rural Java, levelling mechanisms of shared poverty were widespread and still exist, and that rural populations in Java will react to population pressure and decreasing resources by sharing their poverty, has proved wrong.[2] White (1983) gives a clear analysis of this view on shared poverty:

> ...No observer would dispute the existence of a pervasive public ideology of sharing and reciprocity in Javanese society - nor the widespread, actual 'sharing of poverty' within the marginal and landless classes, the crucial error of agricultural involution lies in assigning to this ethic a determinant role in regulating the actual relations of distribution between classes.
>
> WHITE 1983:27

---

1 For studies on poverty and inequality see, among others: Alexander and Alexander 1979; Breman 1980; Edmunson 1994; Marcus and Asmorowati 2006; Mishra, Kristiaji and Perkasa 2009; Singarimbun 1996; Singarimbun and Penny 1973; Strout 1974; Suryadarma, Widyanti, Suryahadi and Sumarto 2006; Suryahadi and Sumarto 2003. For studies on sharing, village institutions, redistribution and cooperation see, among others: Abdullah and White 2006; Alexander and Alexander 1979; Alexander and Alexander 1982; Bouman 1995; Geertz 1962; Geertz 1963; Ingleson 1996; Jay 1969; Jellinek 1991; Jellinek and Rustanto 1999; Kanó 1980; Kawagoe, Ohkama and Bagyo 1992; Koentjaraningrat 1967a; Koentjaraningrat 1967b; Koning and Hüsken 2006; Vel 2008.

2 See for extensive debates on Geertz's shared poverty ideas and agrarian involution thesis as discussed extensively in: Hart, Turton and White 1989; White 1983; White 1983, 2000.

The discussion on inequality and poverty versus sharing and support in rural Java has lingered for a long period, and few new studies on this topic have appeared in the last decade.[3] No indisputable conclusion has been reached, and the debate remains highly relevant for understanding poverty and social protection in Indonesia. Some authors conclude that although moralities of sharing can be found in many villages, these societies tend to remain highly non-egalitarian with regard to the distribution of resources (Hüsken and White 1989:260, Mishra et al. 2009, Suryadarma et al. 2006) or that shared poverty institutions have become more exclusivist (Hüsken and Koning 2006). 'Access to such communal institutions is increasingly exclusionary and limited [...] and has therefore acquired a more transactional or calculating character [...] institutions in themselves are under pressure. Being unable to participate in balanced exchanges, they [the poor] are forced to withdraw from those networks that are still viable in present day Indonesia' (Hüsken and Koning 2006:25). Associated with this debate is another one: whether New Order changes in agriculture led to greater wealth for all, or to a new schism in society, and if these processes have been reversed following the demise of the New Order regime. Edmundson (1994) argued that, on average, inequalities in the distribution of wealth in the rural areas did not increase. Others have shown that the incomes of the larger landowners have increased and that labour wages have also increased, 'but slower (while still being among the lowest of Asia)' (White and Wiradi 1989:81) and that the gap between rich and poor continues to grow (Mishra et al. 2009, Suryadarma et al. 2006). At the same time, other important changes in the rural wage structure took place through diminishing harvest shares (wages-in-kind) (Hüsken and White 1989: 249).

This all stands in stark contrast to the shared poverty and communal image maintained in many policy circles (Li 2007:232–233, Tsing 1999:175, 179). Why is this image of harmonious villages so persistent such that, even in the late 1990s when the economic crisis had started, shared poverty ideas regularly cropped up in the thinking of Indonesian governmental and academic elites?[4] Even

3 A notable exception being the book 'Ropewalking and safetynets: Local ways of managing insecurities in Indonesia' by Koning and Hüsken (2006).

4 The anthropologist Jellinek stated in Kompas (10 February 1999) that the crisis that had hit Indonesia a year earlier did not affect rural people very much. On behalf of the World Bank, she had carried out a rapid appraisal of the effects of the crisis in Indonesia in certain urban and rural areas. According to her, the effects of the crisis were much worse in the cities because of the lack of social support networks there (and assuming these were still present in the villages).

At the beginning of the 1997 crisis, Harmoko (parliamentary spokesman and prominent member of Suharto's Golkar party) visited some rural areas in Central Java to observe the

today, these images still lead to inertia in dealing with the problems of the rural poor. It could well be that it is beneficial for policymakers and urban elites in Indonesia to maintain the discourse on the existence of a viable communal social security system in rural Indonesia and so retain a certain level of ambiguity. 'Ambiguity is often used by those in the best position to take advantage of the fluidity of possible interpretations of their own decisions' (McGoey 2012:11). Best adds that 'because ambiguities allow for flexibility in interpretation, they can be used strategically by those in the best position to take advantage of that interpretative power' (Best 2012:93). During the 1997–1999 crisis, for instance, politicians readily believed that the effects of the crisis were not as bad in the villages as in urban areas. Recognition of the problematic impact of the crisis on poverty in rural areas would have required taking action. Instead, they clearly opted to focus on the huge urban problems, and leave the village communities to make ends meet through supposed systems of mutual help (*gotong royong*) and solidarity. They could adopt this position relatively easily because urban elites rarely went and stayed in villages, and simply did not want to know about disharmony, inequalities between groups and classes, and between local regions within those villages as we have indicated elsewhere (Kutanegara and Nooteboom 2000, Nooteboom and Kutanegara 2003).

If we want to connect present-day social realities in Indonesia through a Madurese lens, we need to set aside such stereotypes and classical views of the East-Javanese countryside, and move beyond the agricultural involution, social class and poverty debates, to understand the delicate balance between livelihood and security today. A close look at the existence and performance of local social security at the local level, with its power differences, offers the first step forward.

Property, Power and Prestige

Observing hierarchies: the Bagenda family

Bagenda is the unrivalled village leader. He is the big man of Krajan, both feared and respected, believed to possess great – almost supernatural – powers, with a weak spot for women, known to be a daredevil, keen

situation in the villages (*safari Ramadan*). He spoke to village officials and had dinner (*buka puasa*) in one of the villages visited. The dinner was well prepared and, after his visit, Harmoko stated in interviews on television and for newspapers that the situation in the rural areas was not so bad because he had had a good meal, and 'solidarity is still strong in the villages', implying that plenty of food was available for everybody (See also: Jawa Pos, December 1997).

on business, and an incurable gambler. He is judge, mediator, patron, moneylender, tax collector and caretaker for the village all at the same time; and one of the richest and most generous villagers, helping many others in times of need. He owns things most villagers can only dream of: a big brick house, a luxury car, a pickup truck, the newest mobile phones, good connections with military and police officers, he has liaisons with women, a huge television set, and a laptop. It is this television set which is the catalyst to enlightening the pecking order of the village.

In front of the television and around this table, village politics are transacted and the most important businesses and political problems are settled or discussed. Financial transactions, however, are rarely completed here. Money nearly always passes hands in the office, a side room, separated by thick curtains and only to be seen by a few insiders. During the fieldwork period, my position shifted slowly from being with the guests on the second row, to the first bench, and then to the floor in front of the television. I also witnessed many of the transactions and discussions in the office. I never got to hold the remote control, though.

Just as the seating arrangements for guests at rituals, weddings, and funerals reveal people's social status and relationship with the family involved, so the positions of villagers in front of Bagenda's television set reveal much about village hierarchy and social distance. In general, these seating arrangements not only point to social and political inequalities in the village, but also suggest the likelihood of extra income, a windfall, or support in times of difficulties. The greater the distance from the television, the smaller the chances of making a profit or receiving support from Bagenda during difficult times, and consequently, the less courage villagers have in asking him for a job, a loan, or mediation. This only increased now he has become member of the commission on infrastructure and development in the district parliament (*komisi III* DPRD Bondowoso).

In the surrounding villages, Bagenda is well known for his success. In his eight years in power, he has been able to improve the economic conditions of his family and the village, and to establish a firm rule. Having good contacts with government officials in town, with loyal villagers, and a keen sense for business, he has been able to implement a considerable number of governmental projects that have been beneficial both for him personally and for the village as a whole. During his rule, he has also been able to reduce the number of thefts, violent conflicts and cases of sexual abuse. Not because of good governmental rule, but only due to personal capacities and relationships with police officers, criminals, bureaucrats, and military. Sometimes the lines between these people get blurred.

People like Bagenda are flexible political actors. Converted from petty criminal (*preman*) to village leader. In the mid-1990s, he succeeded in being elected both as a village head and a royal ruler of his people and a loyal bureaucrat in the Suharto franchise through strong rule and a well-kept balance between self-interest and redistribution of jobs and resources is the key to this success. In return for redistributing most of the money from governmental development projects, he demanded, and received, loyalty from the village people by which he is able to get better access to local resources and government money. After the fall of Suharto, he easily shifted to the Megawati's party of struggle and supported democracy. Later he followed Megawati's PDI-P and now he is part of Gerinda, the president's party. From a village perspective, Bagenda is a great patron possessing powerful connections with the military, police and the regional government. He is not seen, in the first place, as a continuation of the nation government in the village. In practice however, both functions development agent and local strongman amalgamate.

Resources and Power

Social inequality in Krajan involves more than unequal access to resources alone, it has an inherent power dimension. The wealth ranking system itself already reveals some of the existing power differences in the village. In economic and political matters, the relationship between rich and poor, influential and marginal people has long been marked by tension. Poorer villagers have asked, over the years, sometimes loud, sometimes mute, for support and redistribution of the resources of their fellow villagers. Moreover, the poor are part of the system of power differences themselves. The labourers and share raisers of cattle for a large part contributed to the riches of the village elite and at the same time, they might form a treat for these rich. By calling themselves poor or marginal, the poor accept at least some of the authority that makes wealth and poverty a proper, even foundational, frame of reference in the local society. According Van der Ploeg (1999: 453): 'Power is a relational concept. It is constituted where different projects in society are combined, and in such way, that they mutually enforce each other. There will also be situations where there is powerlessness, mutual exclusive projects. No connections are being made. The needed cohesion, without which a society cannot function for long, is lacking [my translation]'. Power is firstly not an individual quality, or the ability to carry out your own will in the pursuit of goals of action, regardless of resistance, but often also part of a structure of domination. In Krajan, both the active, conscious, and intentional exercise of power, and the structural, hidden understandings embedded into society and polity, play a role (Antlöv and Cederroth 1994, De Jong 2006, Li 2007).

In terms of access to resources, I understand the exercise and consequence of power as the capability to get a larger share of land, cattle, and money than the average villagers (Hall et al. 2011:2). This can be both intentionally, by using and enforcing a privileged position, and unconsciously as a consequence of structures of authority and domination such as local and cultural forms of hierarchy – as for instance reflected in patron client relationships, village leadership, and state policies. Here, I will not discuss power relations at length, but these two faces of the exercise of power are reflected in two of the case studies; those of *Pak* Patik who has become an important patron, and of Bagenda, the village head. In the following, I will briefly elaborate on issues of power in these two cases.

> *Pak* Patik regularly employs about ten villagers from the neighbourhood who are largely dependent on him for work, income and support. Most of these villagers simultaneously till his land, take *babun* contracts in his fields, raise his cattle, and are financially indebted to him. Their wives assist in some of the agricultural tasks, and often work for the wife of Patik at harvest times, hulling maize, cleaning paddy, searching for firewood and assisting in the kitchen, without payment. In the return, they can borrow rice or maize in cases of severe shortage and receive free meals (including for their children) while carrying out those activities.
>
> Patik's main activity – besides his cattle trade - was tobacco cultivation: during the first year of the research, he planted 12,000 seedlings in his own fields, and bought another 10,000 standing plants in the fields of others. The total costs amounted to Rp 2 million: Rp 500,000 on food, coffee, etc. for the workers; Rp 500,000 on wages for cleaners, planters, harvesters, and for transporting the harvest to his house. Further, he spent Rp 600,000 on the purchase of the standing crops, and on fertiliser, tools and seedlings. Finally, he paid Rp 400,000 to the two families who worked for two months of a stretch, day and night, cleaning, storing, cutting and drying the tobacco harvest. That year, Patik sold his tobacco for Rp 7 million, making a profit of Rp 5 million, the price of two adult bulls.[5]

5 These figures were calculated carefully by noting and adding up all expenses and profits each day. This information could only be gathered through daily visits to the house of *Pak* Patik (often twice or thrice a day), lengthy participant observation, and a good relationship with the family. *Pak* Patik hid information about the expenses, and especially the profits, he made in town by selling tobacco for his wife, daughter, neighbours, friends, and labourers, but told them to me. On the other hand, his wife and daughter secretly hid small amounts of the tobacco each working day, stored it under their beds, and sold it in small quantities whenever they needed money.

> When asked, the workers spoke of their activities as help or mutual help, not as labour. In addition to the pleasant atmosphere during the long nights cutting tobacco leaves, they said they enjoyed the opportunity to be able to help the Patik family. On later occasions, and in other places, I heard them calling *pak* Patik a scrooge because of his low payments. Even if they resented him, they had to show up and help at every occasion when they were called. 'We are only small people. We need to stay close to them', one of the workers said. 'We are totally dependent on him and his wife for work, credit and small gifts of food in the dry season, so what should we say?'

In the case of the Patik family, their ability to mobilize labour is quite strong and Mrs. Patik turned out to be a key player. In other cases of patronage in Krajan the hold on labourers can be less strong. Nevertheless, in most cases of large tobacco farmers, similar patterns of patronage could be seen; a use of large quantities of unpaid labour of whole families of dependents, free meals, and low, or absent, payments. The more unpaid labour that could be used, the more successful the landlord.

At tobacco harvest time, the family of Satrawi, one of Patik's most dependent and most loyal client families, worked day and night, including their children, for a total wage of Rp 200,000 cash and a pair of new slippers for each family member. They all ate good meals for free during that period and *pak* Satrawi was allowed to take tobacco from Patik's pouch whenever he wanted.[6] Nevertheless, the worth of all this was far from a 'decent' wage and definitely lower that daily wage labour standards.

Labour is tied to patrons through relationships of debt, share tenancy and gifts. Patik would never have been able to mobilize this amount of cheap labour if he had been an ordinary employer. However, through his personal charisma – and especially that of his wife – his wealth and through loans, they controlled many poor families. In this way, he was able to make a considerable profit from on his tobacco crop, while most other tobacco farmers had to sell their harvest at or below cost price that year. It is especially his authority as a successful farmer, and his personalized unequal relationships with individual farming families who hoped for help, which made the difference with these farmers. (This is in contrast to Bagenda, the village head, who has an open

6 As a loyal client and a frequent visitor to the house of Patik, he was allowed to take small plugs of tobacco from Patiks tobacco pouch (*pak lopak* Mad.) the whole year round. Rolling paper, however, he did not receive and frequently, when he had no money, he had to use corn leaves instead.

ambition for personal, symbolic and governing power). The second example of using power to gain better access to resources is Bagenda, the village head.

> Bagenda ordered villagers in 1997, as part of village *gotong royong*,[7] to plant hundreds of fast growing trees along the road, footpaths, the river and on other wasteland. According to local law, the person who plants a tree – or ordered the tree to be planted - even if the land is not his or hers, is the owner of that tree and is allowed to cut and sell the wood years later.[8] By using *gotong royong*, the village head created a huge stock of trees on the waste land of the village for future profit.
>
> He has also been able to force many villagers to plant other crops as ordained by the government. From 1994 to 1996, he used government regulations to convince villagers that they had to plant tobacco. In the meantime, Bagenda obtained a monopoly on the tobacco trade from the tobacco factories and was able to make huge profits. The factories supplied credit facilities to the tobacco farmers through the mediation of the village head who added additional interest on the loans or lent the funds illegally to other parties. After 1998, this was no longer possible. In 1999, after the economic crisis hit Indonesia, the village head could use this favourite ploy again, by using credit facilities meant for rural development. He borrowed more than 60% of all the KUT (*kredit usaha tani*) funds available for the village by making fake groups.[9] In this way, he gained access to at least Rp 180 million of credit meant for small farmers and rural development. This money he used to start businesses, trades, and construction activities in the village: offering work to dozens of villagers and financing his forthcoming re-election campaign as village

7 Official village programme for mutual help that functions as free corvee labour for public work. See also Bowen (1986).

8 For that reason, trees planted by others at disputed places as borders of rice fields or home gardens seldom survive. Neighbours do not want others to have them planted and damage them, or let them die of damage caused by either animals, fire or playing children. Trees planted on land that is rented out to others and especially on pawned lands stay property of the one who planted the tree. Generally, permission should be asked though. This is especially relevant for house lots, where the house is built on someone else's land and might be transferred to another place, while trees planted in the yard remain property of planter.

9 He has been able to do that by stimulating friends and followers to establish borrowing groups. He himself established some fake groups also. From the 13 established groups in the village he borrowed 10–50%. From the ones he established himself, he borrowed all. Total amount of money he borrowed exceeds Rp 200 million (of which Rp 180 million I have seen proven in hidden bookkeeping records of the groups).

leader. Further, he lent it to military and police personnel in Bondowoso who were in need of cash, to other village heads in the area, to villagers, and to the election campaign of the PDI-P in the area. Slowly, he gained in his relationships outside the world of the village. This certainly helped his election into the district a few years later.

Although this example of the village head is the most extreme example found, it further illustrates that those with power are able to eat a greater slice of the resource cake. It also illustrates how local forms of domination can be derived from power structures at the national level. Powerful villagers are able to mobilize their networks more effectively and in this way, they get better access to resources. Moreover, they have better access to credit and information, and are thus able to trade successfully, or to influence decisions concerning who is able to work on the land or in projects, and who is not. At the same time, they can more easily withdraw themselves from social obligations.

When Life becomes Difficult: Limits and Potentials of Local Forms of Support

Although people in general are able to eke out a living in Krajan, as I described in the previous chapters, this is not always a stable or secure affair. Setbacks and adversities such as harvest failure, death, illness, unemployment, and sudden drops in income are recurring risks and threats to villagers' livelihoods. All people run these risks in one way or another, but not all livelihoods are threatened, and not all people perceive the risks, in the same way and as insecurities. Poor villagers are, generally speaking, more vulnerable than others (Blaikie et al. 1994, Chambers 1989:2, WorldBank 2012b) as vulnerability largely depends on their sources of income, ways of access to resources, and the specific constitution of the livelihood (Ellis 2000:58–62). In this chapter, I turn to the experiences and interpretations of risks, threats and insecurities, and to local institutions, arrangements and mechanisms which can provide support to different categories of villagers. In the next chapter, I deal with the different ways, the styles, in which people and households combine livelihood options and social security to cope with these insecurities in everyday life.

Mimona: when the bad days come

Neighbours describe the Mimona family as poor but able to make ends meet. In the village survey and wealth ranking exercise, they came out as belonging to the category of small farmers occasionally facing shortages (*kurang*). A year later, in the second village survey, they had dropped to the category of destitute (*kasihan*). They live somewhat unnoticed in Wringinkurung, but near to the road and the mosque. Not many villagers from outside the hamlet know them and, if they do, they cannot tell much about them. In the close neighbourhood, they are known as reliable and hardworking people.

Their house is of the common Madurese type with the typical tapering tiled roof, bamboo walls and an earthen floor. Inside, a simple cupboard, a few chairs, a table and a bamboo bed make up all their material possessions. At the back of the house is a small fireplace made from clay. The Mimonas are around 30 years old and had been married for more than ten years when their first child was born. They care for the widowed mother of the wife who lives in a small shack leaning onto the house. She eats with the family and helps occasionally with basket weaving. Her production, however, is low due to her bad eyes and poor health. Her daughter occasionally buys some betel nut and tobacco for her to chew. Next to the house of the Mimonas lives a brother of the husband. The only sister of Bu Mimona has migrated to Kalimantan some years ago, but to date she has never sent a word, let alone, any remittances.

When we interviewed the Mimonas for the first time, they were able to make ends meet. They cultivated a small plot of some 0.1 hectare of low quality sawah, which they inherited from the parents of the husband, and about a quarter of a hectare of tegal inherited from the wife's parents. Together, the land provided them with three to four months of food per year and they made an additional income for a few more months of the year from a second tobacco crop.

For the rest of the year they increase household incomes by a few days of wage labour, by weaving baskets, and by engaging in mutual labour exchanges that brought them free meals in addition. The husband and wife often combined tasks and shared their incomes. In the year 1997 the household income from their tobacco crop yielded them Rp 270,000, which they used to repay small debts, buy clothes, rice, and maize. Besides this, *Pak* Mimona worked that year ten days on fields of large landowners harvesting and carrying tobacco leaves which brought him Rp 20,000 per day plus a meal per day, coffee and something to smoke. With a further seven days hoeing and weeding tobacco, he received Rp 10,500 per day, again with a meal, coffee and some cigarettes. In both 1996 and 1997, Pak Mimona went for three months - with an experienced friend - to work in Madura as an agricultural labourer and brought home

Rp 75,000 in 1996 and Rp 150,000 in 1997. In 1997, Pak Minoma bought with this money a radio cassette player for Rp 55,000 and ingredients for snacks and cookies needed for *Idhul Fitri*. Harvesting and cutting tobacco at the houses of large landowners yielded husband and wife together Rp 60,000 plus snacks, coffee, and cigarettes. This money was all used to buy rice and maize to cover consumption needs in the slack (dry) season.

In this year, *Bu* Mimona earned on average about Rp 5,500 per week making *besek*.[10] This money she used for buying rice, maize, and small kitchen needs such as salt and cooking oil. The rice price in this period was about Rp 1,000 per kilo (for low quality rice) and the maize price ranged from Rp 400 to Rp 600.[11] By combining all these jobs, they were able to meet their basic household needs and build up a relatively stable livelihood.

After that year, their only child died and things changed rapidly for the worse. On the funeral, about fifteen neighbours and relatives came to donate rice, money or sugar. In total, they received 25 kilos of rice (10 kilos from the brother of Mimona), two kilos of sugar, and Rp 15,000 in cash. Some poor neighbours came with firewood or with nothing and helped with cooking, serving the guests or digging the grave. To cover the expenses of the funeral and seven days of *selamatan* and praying, the family borrowed Rp 250,000 from two neighbours in short term loans with interest of two and five percent per month. To repay these loans, the Mimonas pawned their tegal to Maryani, a local tobacco trader. Later that year, when memorial rituals for the deceased had to be performed, they could use their own rice stocks (partly saved from the funeral) and four of their own chickens for the *selamatan*. When later that year, *Pak* Mimona fell ill for some time, they had to sell the radio for Rp 35,000 to cover the costs of medical treatment.

When we visited the family again a year later, the situation had clearly deteriorated. According to them, since the start of the crisis, they had had to work harder while earning less. Food prices had gone up while the low tobacco prices caused a drop in labour demands. To make matters worse, the extended rains and cold weather had almost completely destroyed their rice crop on their small sawah, their only piece of land that time. The family was trapped by the downward spiral of falling incomes, rising

10 These baskets (*besek*) are woven for tape, a sweet fermented cassava snack. I do not know how many weeks she stopped working due to delivering the baby. After the baby was born, she told she continued making *besek*.

11 In 1997, on average, for one week of *besek* weaving, she could purchase five kilos of cheap rice.

prices, and large debts. The family started thinking of migrating to Kalimantan. One of the travelling labour recruiters had offered them a job as labourer in an oil palm plantation.

In that year, *Pak* Mimona earned only Rp 17,500 with wage labour. In search of money, he went regularly to the forest to cut bamboo which he partly sold to *besek* makers (twice a week earning Rp 5,000 each time), the rest he used to make baskets with his wife, the sale of which brought them in one week only Rp 8,000[12] (for 100 pieces) as prices were going down. To complement their income, they cared for livestock of others. Their first cow came from the husband's brother and still had not produced any offspring. The second animal, a bull under cash sharing, came from the landlord who usually employed *Pak* Mimona in tobacco cultivation and this landlord would probably be willing to give cash advances on this bull when asked. As they now had to care for two animals, and as economic conditions were unstable, *Pak* Mimona did not have the courage to search for work in Madura again. They also postponed the plan to go to Kalimantan.

Overall, they managed to earn more cash as they did the year before. However, with soaring prices for basic needs this meant a drop of over one-third in real income. Moreover, as they now earn their income mostly from the sale of *besek* and bamboo, the number of free meals has declined, and as they still have to repay their debts, they are in a much more vulnerable position than the year before. To make ends meet they cut on consumption costs (by eating less dried fish and *tahu*, no longer coffee or tea, and by mixing cassava and maize with their rice). This did not make Pak Mimona to give up smoking: he started to smoke even more and now bought a packet of cigarettes a week. The government's cheap rice programme (offering, each month, 10 kgs of rice for Rp 10,000) has helped in keeping expenditure low.

When the mother of *Bu* Mimona died, again this household was confronted with huge costs. They covered the lion's share of the costs. They received from neighbours and relatives 50 kilos of rice (including 25 kilos from his Mimona's brother), a pound of coffee, four kilos of sugar,

12 On an average, with one week of working *besek*, now – due to inflation – three to four kilos of rice could be purchased. Although the rice price stabilised somewhat at the end of 1998 and in 1999, it was nearly Rp 3,000 at the beginning of 1999. At the time of the interview, under the influence of the cheap rice programme, it had gone down to Rp 2,300 per kilo. Compared to the returns from *besek*, this is still a decrease in real income out of *besek*, and thus purchase capacity, of 30%.

two packets of cigarettes, and Rp 45,000 in cash. (In total, these gifts were worth about Rp 200,000). They spent Rp 550,000 on the first seven days of *selamatan*. To cover the difference, they borrowed from the owner of the cow they were share-raising and from the village head. For the 40th-day memorial *selamatan*, they still had some rice in stock and sold only three chickens which was enough to buy the most important ingredients for the *selamatan*. At the end of the year, they had some debts at the local shop (Rp 30,000) and with one of the neighbours (Rp 15,000), while the other debts were repaid by pawning all their sawah. *Pak* Mimona hopes to be able to repay the remaining debts at the shop and his neighbour from his daily earnings. By next year, they also hope to redeem their pawned land with another calf of the cow they care for, so that they can grow maize and tobacco again. The cow is now being trained to plough. If trained well, Pak Mimona can try to earn some money by working other people's land or even manage to get a *babun* contract. But since the crisis started, chances have dwindled and he did not succeed. The share tenancy contracts went to another villager. Two years later, they left for Kalimantan.

The combination of crisis, misfortune and death has caused a drop in their incomes and the loss of land and capital. The family received some help, but nowhere near to cover all their costs. They first survived under these circumstances by working hard and by carefully spending their money but, when new misfortune occurred, they fell through the poverty line and eventually were forced to sell their fields.

This example of the Mimona family shows that a combination of several shocks and stresses can seriously threaten a family's livelihood. It also shows the potential strength and limitations of village social security systems. Their life seemed secure enough, but turned out to be vulnerable when confronted with high funeral costs and declining earning opportunities as a result of the economic crisis in Indonesia. Not only did prices go up drastically, the crisis also forced many farmers to change from cash crops to subsistence crops, leading to a major drop in wage labour opportunities. Although the case of this family is special in the sense that they lost both their child and a mother within the course of two years, their situation resembles many of the village poor, whose security can be blown away by a single mishap.

This example also shows that under such conditions, people basically have to fall back on their own. True, neighbours and relatives may come with *sumbangan* while others may be willing to provide loans and help – materially and emotionally – through the first difficult days, but this was not enough to cope with their misfortune. Village social security institutions and arrangements helped them in covering their first costs, but did not help them much in regaining strength, resources, work or a sustainable livelihood. Nevertheless, without the help from others, the Mimona family would have gone down the drain.

The good reputation and social relationships that they had established with neighbours and large farmers enabled them to borrow money and to tend extra livestock. Because of this network, they also remained candidates for share-raising cattle, and, probably, for *babun* contracts. It is hard to calculate the importance of these social relationships and their good reputation in economic terms, but it is obvious that their efforts to remain respectable and decent villagers was not in vain and made them eligible clients and labourers in the eyes of more affluent villagers even though this would not protect them against a further fall into poverty.

Pak Mimona told me with a tired and sad voice: 'Hopefully, our crisis will not last long, and hopefully, my living will improve, not always facing these shortages'. Thus expressing his wish for a better future but also not expecting much at the same time. The year before, he had been more confident about the future and told me he was going to spend less, cooperate more and work harder to overcome his poverty. But when he had to face their further downfall, he expressed deception and thought of retreating from mutual help relationships. 'What can I give to others if I don't have anything myself?'

The Mimona family is a good example of some of the possible insecurities of landless and near-landless households who earn a living from small-scale farming, wage labour and handicraft production. Their story reveals some of the adversities people are confronted with, the ways in which they perceive and cope with them, as well as the scope, strength, and limitations of social security arrangements and institutions in Krajan. From the Mimona family, we can move on to the wider field of social security in Krajan: what are the specific threats, risks and insecurities for different categories of villagers? Are there any social security arrangements and institutions to protect and maintain access to resources in times of adversity like misfortune, contingencies and ill fate and, if so, how do they work, and under what conditions?

Insecurity in Krajan

To understand village social security we have to depart from local perceptions of risks and insecurities and their cultural interpretations of the probability and possible effects of a hazard, calamity or crisis. These risks, the livelihood literature speaks often of shocks and stresses (De Haan and Zoomers 2005,

Kaag et al. 2004), severely threaten the livelihoods of villagers. Villagers in Krajan never speak about *risk* in a broad and general sense as is common in English. The Indonesian word risk itself (*risiko*) is a loanword (from Dutch) and only used in the context of gambling, speculative (tobacco) trade, and sometimes in contexts of opting for migration where there is a risk of not making any profit. It is used in a narrow sense and confined to a context of wagering where there is a clear and calculable possibility of gain and loss. There is no Madurese and no original Malay equivalent for risk and, in the village, other words are used to refer to the possible occurrence of misfortune and contingencies.

People in Krajan use words like danger or threat (*bahaya*), fear (*takut*), and uncertainty or doubt (*bingung*). Conversely, the word safety (*keamanan* or *jamin*) is often used to indicate the state of absence of these threats, fears and uncertainties. *Rezeki* (luck), means profit or blessing, and is used as the opposite of misfortune, although *rezeki* is never stable and can be taken away. If you have or find *rezeki*, you do not have to fear a lack of food, income or safety, and thus can be called secure. *Rezeki* has a materialistic connotation and is often not a result of making the right choices, but rather something that occurs, a blessing that can come, or be withdrawn. In practice, this means that villagers are much more concerned with the question how to gain safety or *rezeki* than how to prevent insecurities. For that reason, rather than discussing risks, I prefer here to use the word insecurity – referring to dangers, threats, and fears; and the specific ways of perceiving them.[13] These insecurities form a problem for an individual and often the household and to overcome setback they need the support from others. People's main insecurities concern their basic needs: food, shelter, healthcare and social status. When these are threatened, they need support in the form of food, labour, knowledge, cash or some combination of these.

In the following, I will focus on these insecurities at the household level while acknowledging that households are made up of different members who face different insecurities and sometimes have conflicting interests. The security of the husband, for instance, can be at the expense of his wife or children. First, I deal with threats and dangers regarding household members' food security, then the threats to the incomes needed for the household's livelihood. After this, I will turn to the threats related to profit and trade and, finally, to threats related to shelter, healthcare and social relationships in the village. Here, I will not relate these threats to different categories of people, although

13 See Chapter 5 for deliberate risk-taking behaviour in a context of gambling, sexual relationships and speculation.

it is clear that poor people are more affected than the rich, but describe insecurities and ways of support. In Chapters 4 and 5, I will deal with the relationship between insecurities and different categories of people, and their different ways of responding to them.

Food and Income Insecurities

Frequently, poor and landless villagers in Krajan have good reasons to worry about insufficient income or food. Securing a stable food supply heavily depends on seasonal variations and economic cycles, as well as on the weather and the health and skills of household members. Over the years, especially villagers in the poorer categories have experienced recurrent crises in their food supply.

Among farming households, seasonal fluctuations in agricultural output are the most common threat to food security. Ellis (2000: 58–59) mentions that seasonality is an inherent feature of rural livelihoods and that these seasonal factors apply just as much to landless rural families as they do to farming families.

For landless labourers and smallholders, the possibilities of earnings are heavily dependent on the season and on climatic irregularities such as the intensity of rainfall. If there is no rain, there is no work. Both for landless, smallholders, and larger landowners alike, incomes may be threatened if rains start later than usual, or if there is less rain or if crops are damaged by strong winds, diseases or pests. Villagers who work for a share of the harvest in the fields of others, share-raise cattle, or make baskets, feel more secure and have little chance of losing their work except in the case of chronic illness, inability, or bad work. Other types of work such as wage labour and contract labour are more volatile and casual and, hence, its incomes are less stable.

The insecurities in trade and markets are manifold, but villagers perceive them foremost as the presence or absence of luck (*rezeki*). The price of tobacco has fluctuated considerably over the years, and so have – to a lesser extent – the prices of rice, fertiliser, cigarettes, coffee and food. People often feel uncertain about expected returns and whether they will earn enough to buy the increasingly expensive foods. For traders, moneylenders, and shopkeepers, financial worries are even more a part of daily life as they face insecurities through fluctuating prices, unreliable partners, stock decay, inflation, losses and non-payment. For this reason, interest rates on loans are high.[14] The main

14 Interest of 50% for a loan of one tobacco season are no exception. The risk of default on loans, and the absence of collateral to put up against loans, are amongst the most frequently identified.

ILLUSTRATION 1 *Rice harvest in Krajan*

concern for shopkeepers is that people will not pay their debts.[15] At some points in their lives, most middle and lower middle class women in Krajan have started small business or trading in coffee, dried fish, vegetables, maize or rice. Many of them have failed, however, as friends, neighbours, and relatives bought on credit and never paid for the goods. The number of collapses was greatest in 1998 when, as a consequence of the monetary crisis, food aid, and the concomitant inflation, about half of the small shops collapsed. Not everybody has a knack for business and only 20% seem to have good entrepreneurial skills.

Ceremonial Expenses, Health Care and Education

Some threats are more endangering than others. Franz and Keebet von Benda-Beckmann (1994: 7), observed that the most devastating uncertainties are those concerning people's most basic needs: food, shelter, health and care; and in connection with them the experience or expectation of destitution, of a sudden loss or severe reduction in the means of existence, and of access to other people or social institutions which might provide help. A serious assault

15 Many conflicts between villagers are related to such old debts that have never been settled, and shops often collapse due to the large number of people who do not repay debts on time.

on household reserves in Krajan is the untimely death of a family member, as it does not only imply a severe emotional loss, but also involves huge unanticipated direct and indirect costs. The loss of a family member involves an expensive funeral (the same day as passing away) and a series of *selamatan*, and if it concerns a productive household member, it severely affects the household's income-earning capacity. Both poor and rich villagers are confronted with such costs, but the poor have to spend relatively more on burial costs, as they have smaller networks of support and receive fewer contributions. A series of *selamatan* for an adult household member can easily cost the equivalent to one bull (or two or three if the household is more prosperous).[16] In the case of poorer families, funeral costs often amount to more than half of the saleable or pawnable household assets (bulls, land) and it can take years to recover.

Then there are expenses related to health and pregnancy. Expenses on health care can be a source of urgent needs for cash leading to indebtedness as these may involve high costs for hospitalisation, medicines or local healers (*dukun*). The costs of hospitalisation can easily go beyond the capacity of a family and may force them to sell or pawn land or cattle to pay the bills. As in the case of funerals, money has to be provided quickly and often the same day (doctors and hospitals often ask for money before treatment is given to a patient). Even now, when most of the poor of Krajan have a health card of the national health insurance programme (Jamkesnas), significant amounts of money are asked for. As fast cash is expensive and hard to get, and interest is high, health expenses come dear. In the case of a need for hospitalisation, the poor often wait long and even decide not go to the hospital at all in fear of these high costs. Moreover, transportation adds to the costs. In some cases, especially when it concerns younger people, or pregnant women, they will ask neighbours or the village head for help. Occasionally, he is prepared to drive the patient to the hospital and pay the costs of hospitalisation. He knows that these families will try their utmost to repay these debts, either by selling land or cattle later, or by providing labour or lumber. Nevertheless, not all succeed in doing so.

For wedding and engagement ceremonies similar, or even higher, amounts are spent (depending on the wealth of the family). However, here the situation is different in that wedding dates can be planned in advance and people can prepare themselves. Although most costs should be covered by the parents, in middle and poorer households the couple themselves are expected to contribute. In these families, boys start raising a calf or care for someone else's cow in order to save for the wedding. Only if enough money, wedding gifts and a house

16 The price of an adult bull in mid-1998 was about Rp 3 million.

are available, can the marriage take place and will be approved of by both sets of parents. Sometimes, parents, already at an early stage, start to collect the wedding goods or wood to build a house (in the case of a daughter). If all the building materials (wood, sheets of woven bamboo, roof tiles, and foundation stones) are available, then the house can be built by making use of a collective housebuilding party, *tolong menolong*, where neighbours, relatives, and friends join in constructing (or repairing) the house.

People often referred to the first years after marriage as the most difficult years in their household's life. The majority did not, or not yet, inherit enough land to be self-supporting and had not yet established a strong network and therefore had little chance to get work or a sharecropping contract. After setting up a separate household, these couples faced, in the first years, periodical food and income shortages.

After children are born, costs increase, and, usually, another difficult period starts due to higher consumption, an increased need for support, and lower labouring capacity. When children get older, costs of education increase. At primary school age, these costs concern some school fees, uniforms and learning material. When parents want their children to continue at secondary school or even further, they are confronted with high, and often steep, costs. After children have grown up, engagements and weddings concern huge costs for parents. If the children stay in the village, they are supposed to take care of their parents when they get old. Last, but not least, if people grow old, and income earning capacities decrease, the need for support increases. This can be difficult if elderly or widows do not have any children, or if they do not have any children living in the village, who can care or support.

Insecurities Related to Other People

There are other, idiosyncratic, causes that can lead to indebtedness, forcing farmers to sell their land and lose their main source of food security, or affect income. There are good reasons to fear other people as they may cause insecurity from theft, deceit and destructive rivalry. Items which are regularly stolen in the village are radios, cigarette lighters, and even chicken, small stocks of rice and maize (both from houses and from the fields), and in the dry seasons, sometimes irrigation water and grass. In Krajan, cattle and motorbikes are rarely the target of thieves although cattle thefts in the region are regularly reported in the local newspapers. Generally, people point to outsiders as the perpetrators, but more often than not, thefts come from local conflicts, jealousy, and unsettled scores. The majority of the thieves of maize and rice who have been captured, turned out to be former workers of large landowners who had been fired by their employers, or had had a conflict with them and were after revenge.

ILLUSTRATION 2 *Widow with children and land*

Within the family, children or close relatives can be a threat to the livelihood of the household. Children can be very demanding for expensive consumer goods and push their parents to spend the household's resources on such items. Other, usually male, members of the family can also endanger its livelihood by taking high risks in gambling, womanising and conspicuous consumption.

Outside the family, relationships with neighbours can be tense because of an unsettled case of deceit, or due to envy and jealousy, or jealous rivalry (*cemburuan*). In Krajan, quite often, imagined extramarital affairs lie at the basis of such conflicts. These conflicts occasionally even result in murder (*carok*).[17]

17 See for similar cases of *carok* in the area and on Madura: Latief Wiyata 2002.

In the four neighbourhoods I moved around on a daily basis, under a surface of courteous friendliness, quite a number of families lived in a kind of silent conflict with one another, while, with half of the villagers, relationships in the neighbourhood seemed to be somewhat distrustful, envious, jealous, or suspicious. Such neighbours rarely visited each other, or talked much with each other on the road or in the fields, nor shared tobacco. They also were often outside the local exchange networks of goods, gifts, or labour at weddings, *selamatan*, house repair parties or agricultural activities with these people, and concentrated themselves on relationships with other neighbours.

Other dangers and fears stem from local politics (contested leaderships) and relationships with richer farmers. In private conversations, villagers often expressed their fear of influential leaders, the village head or the religious leader and of political violence in general. Bagenda was especially feared for his power to put people down. Good relationships with him were highly valued, although this could become a threat to work and livelihood if he were to lose the next election.

In conclusion, these insecurities boil down to six major interrelated sets of problems to which people need to find solutions. The need for support might occur in the field of: (1) food provision; (2) when organizing communal activities (*selamatan*, *arisan*, housebuilding, and labour parties); (3) around life cycle crises (death, illness, or childbirth); (4) around old age care; (5) in the event of natural or economic disasters; and (6) when desiring education.[18] People try to overcome these adversities either at the household or nuclear family level, or with help from others. The next paragraph goes further into the available options and specifically into the sources available for dealing with these difficulties, ranging from the nuclear family to main village and government institutions of social security.

Arrangements and Institutions for Social Security

In principle, there is a wide range of sources that can provide support in times of need.[19] In Krajan, the most important ones are parents or children, close

18 The case of education is somewhat exceptional since not everybody is willing (or able) to aim for a good education. To many families, the need for, and importance of, education is not clear as good jobs are scarce and Krajan youths are unable to win the competition with urban applicants.

19 From the literature a long list of institutions and arrangements which may provide social security in Southeast Asia (and especially Indonesia) can be derived. On kinship: Jay 1969;

relatives, neighbours and friends, wider kin, patrons and village leaders, village and religious institutions (such as reciprocal labour relationships, rituals, *selamatan*, forms of gift and alms giving, and saving and credit associations), and government programmes or institutions (both permanent and temporary ones such as development and poverty eradication programmes, social safety net programmes, free health services and cheap rice programmes). Their respective roles are discussed in the following sections.

Institutions and Arrangements of Mutual Help and Labour Exchange

In Krajan, the basic principle for support arrangements is that those who need help have to ask for it, and ask for it delicately, humbly and with the right tone, without losing one's pride. In the agricultural domain, this can be rather straightforward as mutual help is task-based and calculated carefully because it has to be balanced and reciprocated. In other domains, approaching other people for support needs more finesse in order to be not turned down briskly, and to build trust and reciprocity. Unlike a general view of reciprocity and mutual help as investment in social relationships that insure against certain risks and, as a collective action to support members of that community in times of need, village life shows that reciprocity is often contested. Interests of people are not equal and not all exchanges and reciprocal relationships serve a pure insurance purpose. Most of the clearest risks are covariate and can hit everybody at once (drought, rain, pests, crop failure, economic crisis) while, as

---

Koning 1997; Von Benda-Beckmann 1990, Von Benda-Beckmann, Casino, Hirtz, Woodman and Zacher 1988; on fosterage: Schröder-Butterfill and Kreager 2001; neighbourly assistance, institutions of mutual help: (*gotong royong*) Abdullah and White 2006; Bowen 1986; solidarity and shared poverty: Alexander and Alexander 1982; Geertz 1963; Koentjaraningrat 1967b, peer networks of friends and fellow workers: Koning and Hüsken 2006; Nooteboom 2006; share tenancy: White 1989, 2000; sharing arrangements and patronage: Breman 1980; Cederroth 1993; Hefner 1990; saving and credit associations (*arisan*); Bouman 1983, 1995; Geertz 1962; Lont 2000; Lont 2002, 2005; the state, and religious charity institutions (such as alms giving (*zakat*)): Von Benda-Beckmann 1990. Others, not dealing specifically with Indonesia: shared poverty Feeny 1983; Streefland 1996; share tenancy Abdullah and White 2006; Cashdan 1985; Cederroth 1993; Ellis 1989; Ellis 2000; Wiessner 1982; patronage Breman 1980; Jackson 1974; Platteau 1995; Scott 1972; Scott 1976; Wolf 1966. The edited book of Koning and Hüsken 2006 is so far one of the latest contributions. This list is not complete, but it shows the widespread recognition of the existence of institutions and arrangements in Indonesia with a social security function. At the same time, such an overview of the literature makes clear that coherent studies of care, support and social security, taking all institutions and aspects into account, are generally lacking.

indicated in the introductory paragraphs of this chapter, other forms of insecurities are not so clear and are not perceived of as risks.

From a utilitarian perspective, reciprocity is the equivalent of insurance, because people involve themselves in reciprocal relationships out of a conscious strategy of risk spreading. Although people sometimes act very strategically, they are not only driven by calculated motives but also by other factors, such as custom, culture, habit, expectations, peer pressure, and worldview. Those factors, at least partly, shape their participation in local networks. I will come back to this issue in the next chapter on styles of social security. Here I concentrate on the most important forms of village support available to villagers.

A special, and clearly defined, form of reciprocity is labour exchange in agriculture such as: *giliran* (also the Javanese word *sambatan* is used) (Van der Kolff 1937), and *keajegan* Mad. These rotating and mutual labour arrangements are often part of patron-client relationships although, in theory, they are labour exchanges on an equal basis (Abdullah and White 2006). *Giliran* is a form of rotating labour where groups of farmers work on each other's land in turn. *Keajegan* is an arrangement in which neighbours can be asked 'to help out'.[20] Tasks which can be done using *keajegan* include the peeling of maize, planting tobacco, cutting trees or firewood, preparing, drying and cutting tobacco, housework in emergencies, and assistance during parties. *Keajegan* is not used in a context of funerals and *selamatan*, where it is just called *bantuan* – helping out. These labour exchanges usually take place between households, and are personalized and negotiatable, as the following example makes clear.

One afternoon, *Pak* Patik called for (*ajeg*) his labourers to help with planting tobacco seedlings, but they were not very willing as they know him as a greedy person. The workers from the neighbourhood of Satrawi complained to Patik's neighbour, *Pak* Asus, and said they were fed up with planting tobacco without seeing any benefits for them. *Pak* Asus approached the wife of Patik and she went with her daughter to the workers to talk with them. In a cheerful way, she

20 *Keajegan* (*ajeg* Mad. lit. take along) is mostly used for the planting of tobacco. Tobacco is often planted in the late afternoon to protect the seedlings from too much sun. Neighbours are called for help because the planting has to be done very quickly. Other examples are repairs to rice fields destroyed by landslides or river floods. In these cases, friends and neighbours can be asked for help. *Keajegan* is not strictly reciprocal in nature. Balanced reciprocal forms are *tolong menolong* (mutual help) for house building, replacement, and repair is not referred to as *keajegan*. Scott comments: 'There is a particular rule of reciprocity – a set of moral expectations – which applies to their exchanges with other villagers. Whether or not the wealthy actually live up to these minimal moral requirements or reciprocity is another question, but there can be little doubt that they exist' Scott (1976:42).

told some stories about her greedy husband and then asked the men to work as if she knew nothing. With a nod to her daughter, she promised to cook a nice meal for everybody who joined in. When she came home, she asked her son to ask Patik for money to quickly buy some cigarettes for the workers. He was surprised, and thought it unnecessary, but gave the money. Later, in the field, the workers commented: 'I work for her, not because of him', some of the workers told me, and 'she's a good woman, always willing to help if needed'. This illustrates that mutual help arrangements are never static and uniform, nor organized according to fixed rules and principles, but, depending on the people involved, that they can be negotiated and adapted to specific situations.[21]

Selamatan

The most important institution for redistribution of food and resources among co-villagers is the *selamatan* with its communal meals, praying ritual, and food packages to bring home, organized around birth and death and at other certain stages in the family life cycle. It is here where social relations are reproduced. The family organizing the *selamatan* offers free meals and entertainment to neighbours and guests in exchange for prayer, and in so doing, renews networks and social relationships. The richer the family, the larger the *selamatan* and the wider the network of guests. Guests bring gifts or donations (*sumbangan*), usually consisting of rice or money, and receive a good meal and a basket with rice, meat or soy cake, and biscuits to take home. That *selamatan* are not purely altruistic sharing occasions becomes clear because the gifts and donations are meticulously recorded in notebooks which are used in future occasions to decide what gifts are to be returned.[22]

---

21 Mutual help exists in many forms and for many reasons in Indonesia. Koentjaraningrat (1967b) gives an overview of mutual help arrangements (*gotong royong, tolong-menolong*) in rural Indonesia. He makes a distinction between different domains where mutual help takes place. His four domains are mutual help in agricultural activities, mutual help in domestic activities, mutual help for activities in organising parties and ceremonies and, finally, mutual help in the case of contingencies, disaster and death Koentjaraningrat (1967b:166–167). Some forms of mutual help go across these domains and apply to different domains, and others link agricultural activities with parties and ceremonies. There is no doubt these arrangements still exist in rural Java and Madura, but seldom their effectiveness has been assessed and changes over time have been recorded. An exception is Hüsken and Koning (2006:25–26) who attempt to map changes in these arrangements over time.

22 These are balanced, generalised forms of reciprocity. See Sahlins (1965). Gifts are also exchanged at funerals (rice, money), at engagement and weddings (presents, biscuits, or money), at house-building parties (rice), and at *Idhul Fitri* after Ramadan (biscuits,

At *selamatan*, many things come together. Such occasions reveal networks of social relationships and support, are indicator of status and prestige, and show the wealth and power of the organizing family. Visitors are seated by order of importance and status, but generally also poor guests, and uninvited visitors can come and receive a share of the food. Villagers who are invited try at all costs to contribute a decent gift. Poor neighbours, friends or relatives who are unable to contribute are too shy to join in. If they have a close relationship, or live nearby, they will try to help with cooking, carrying firewood or water, serving the guests, or with organizing the activities. In this way, they make themselves acceptable and become entitled to a free meal. *Selamatan* are expensive to organize, and although guests offer contributions in the organizational costs, in Krajan most families incur a net loss. Only at a handful of occasions were families able to make a profit (received more *sumbangan* than they paid out on organizing the *selamatan*). All such families belonged to the upper classes of society and received relatively large contributions from participants, while the number of non-contributing guests was low. For the poorest villagers, reciprocity worked the opposite.

Sumbangan are not only a source of support that helps in organizing communal activities, it can also cause insecurity among the contributors. The high costs of gifts and many invitations may constitute an assault on household reserves. Contributions to *selamatan*, especially when there are many of them in the same period (such as during the house repair, wedding, and circumcision season), can cause financial headaches to those who are invited for many selamatan. In particular, poor villagers may find themselves in a position that they have to borrow money or rice from friends, neighbours or patrons to fulfil their social obligations. The poorest among them are even unable to get a loan and therefore never contribute, or contribute only to the most important ones, and hardly ever organize *selamatan* themselves (except for those related to burials and weddings). Consequently, they do not receive significant contributions when they themselves have a lifecycle crisis.

Often over-estimated as a source of social security, the figures are showing the limitations of *sumbangan*. From participant observation at dozens of *selamatan* and from the survey, I aggregated that about two-third of the Krajan households contributes a minimum *sumbangan* (1.5 kg. of rice or the equivalent in money) more than two times a year as part of an engagement, wedding,

snacks, or sweets). At all these occasions, guests receive a meal, coffee or tea, and something to smoke (men) or chew (women).

or funeral.[23] One-third of the people who came to these events did not contribute anything. Another category of people never contribute because they are too poor. This means that more than one-third of the village population is only marginally included in these exchange networks or not included at all, these largely correspond with the group of extreme poor as described in Chapter 2.[24] If there are events such as a birth, circumcision or wedding, they will invite only one or two of the closest neighbours and a patron, or simply not organize a *selamatan* at all. They will apologize by saying that the *selamatan* is postponed until there is money or a suitable date, which will often never come.[25] Instead, they will have a small family meal with someone who is performing the praying ritual, often a neighbour or acquaintance who knows the ritual. The *selamatan* itself is nothing more than a slightly better evening meal than usual (rice mixed with maize, vegetables, and some dried fish, egg, noodles or soy cake as a luxury). I witnessed several of these 'unobtrusive' ceremonies in the neighbourhood I lived, where less than a handful of people were present and no *sumbangan* was exchanged.

Funerals are a different case. At funerals, always more people come but, as with *selamatan*, not all bring *sumbangan*. Those who do not bring anything,

---

23 In a village survey, the number of *sumbangan* contributions of both wife and husband in the last year were covered as well as the number of *sumbangan* contributions they had given in the last five years. *Sumbangan* gifts are often recorded and remembered very well. Most people were able to list all their 'outstanding debts' as they called them, the name of family, the amount, and the occasion. For a limited number of families I cross-checked this with the other party and figures were accurate. Moreover, I collected, copied and discussed *sumbangan* lists from funerals and weddings from a handful of families. Rich families had sometimes very long lists, while those from poorer families fitted on the wrapping of a cigarette pack.

24 Most of the poorest households (*kasihan*) had not given any *sumbangan* in the last year, or only once or twice. Of the poor families (*miskin*) about half of the families did not give more than three times a year. Of the rich (*kaya*) and the better off (*lebih* and *cukup*), many families were found who gave more than 30 or 40 times a year (including both men and women) although they were not always able to remember exactly all the amounts and these instances included *sumbangan* outside the village. When giving *sumbangan*, these families did not check their lists all the time, but just gave some standard donation (1.5–2 kg. of rice, or an equivalent in money; Rp 2,500 in 1997 and Rp 5,000 in 1999) depending on the status of the family and the relationship they have with the family. After 1999, amounts rapidly increased and followed inflation suit.

25 It has to be realised that the number of widows in the poorest category is high. Widows do go to the *selamatan* of other people and can do some work in the kitchen to avoid the obligation to bring a gift, but widows usually do not organise many *selamatan* themselves except for those around burials of family members.

help in the kitchen, comfort the family, care for small children, mourn over the body (women), or help in digging and constructing the grave, cutting firewood, or praying (men). More affluent neighbours are expected to bring some rice or money, but never in large quantities, and the funerals of poor people are very sober and simple. Meals are often nothing more than a simple dish of rice with vegetables and soy cake or dried fish with a cup of tea.

It is however, not just a matter of financial means which determines participation in these *selamatan* exchanges; of the poor families, at least half gave *sumbangan* more than three times a year and some even up to ten or fifteen times, while among the richer villagers, there are large variations depending on their willingness to engage in these exchanges. The survey showed a considerable variation in the donations between families of similar social economic classes. Some donated less than five times, while others donated for over forty times a year. More on this variation, and the motivations and reasons behind them, are given in the next chapter. There I will go into the background of these differences, people's motives, orientations and reasons for sharing or not. For *sumbangan* counts: those who need them most, receive least.

Credit, Saving and Arisan

Krajan men and women borrow often and a lot from each other, from credit schemes, and from the *toko*, from neighbours, from patrons, and from moneylenders. From the household survey, I learned that the higher the class the more loans and lending took place with higher amounts depending on the economic activity. On average, large tobacco farmers had many more outstanding loans and debts than large cattle farmers, although some of the cattle farmers had given considerable cash amounts to share-raisers of their cattle. The richest had average loans of over two million Rupiah, while the 'not enoughs' had, on average, a few loans and debts at the same time worth about Rp 105,000, while the poorest (*orang kasihan*) had virtually no debts and loans at all. Poor widows cannot even borrow Rp 5,000, or buy on credit in shops. They can only get a cash advance on the baskets they make. In terms of saving and credit in Krajan, the poor generally most urgently need loans, but are least able to get them.

In many societies, alongside the old arrangements, new private arrangements and microcredit schemes have emerged (Van Ginneken 1999:34) such as co-operatives or mutual benefit societies, benefit burial societies, and rotating credit societies. Rankin (2001) speaks in this respect of micro-finance entering the most remote corners of society as a result of global neoliberalism. This does not hold in Krajan. Most of the villagers do not have access to any formal form of credit, except for landowners with proper ownership certificates, which is almost nobody. The best-known Indonesian example of such an emerging arrangement is the *arisan*, a rotating saving and credit association[26] in which members deposit small amounts at regular times, and in turn, through a lottery system receive the full deposit fund. These tend to be privately organized associations of a few dozen participants at most, but sometimes these *arisan* are linked to banks, government programmes, and religious and community institutions. As a means of saving and credit, *arisan* can have social security functions, although recent studies question this analysis (Lont 2002). They tend to increase the burden of the poor.

Unlike in urban areas in Indonesia, where *arisan* are common and many people are a member of several *arisan*, in Krajan, only a few *arisan* were found. This might be due to the high rate of illiteracy, mismanagement, distrust and seasonality in agricultural production, leading to periodic shortages of cash in Krajan. In the terminology of Hospes (1995), in Krajan, there is no 'fertile financial landscape' enabling the development of *arisan*. Many households do not have daily access to cash since they receive most income in kind.

Over the years, several people have tried to establish *arisan*, but most have collapsed after one or two rounds. The *arisan* that have survived require only very small deposits and are related to village or religious institutions and one part of government promoted programmes in which the arisan is thought to be a development instrument, well-adapted to local culture and assumed to be effective to facilitate saving. Leo Schmit (1994) describes the history of microcredit in the Dutch Indies between 1895 and 1935. In this period, two understandings of microcredit dominated the debate: microcredit as a means of social protection for the poor and as a development instrument promoting economic growth. In 1962, Clifford Geertz wrote about the Javanese *arisan* as a 'middle rung' in development. According to him, the group based petty saving institution marked an intermediate stage in the transition from traditional societies to modernity with its rational economic markets. It turned out not to be so. Until today, where monetary borrowing and saving has deeply entrenched Indonesian society, as well as massive borrowing for motorbikes, *arisan* still exists. The *arisan* was not an intermediate form and evolutionary convictions do not hold (Lont 2002:278–279, 2006). The recent attention for microcredit and group-based lending in Indonesia ignores discussions on these earlier programmes and fails to learn from previous lessons on using it as part of poverty reduction and social protection. Between the late 1990s and 2010, the enhancement of microcredit has been

26 See for a description and discussions: Bouman 1983; Geertz 1962; Hospes 1995; Lont 2002, 2005.

pushed all over Indonesia. Most state sponsored microcredit schemes have not become a success.

The largest *arisan* in the village is run by the wife of the village head and has more than 150 members. Each week, they each deposit a very small amount of money and a winner is drawn. Members do not feel particularly committed since one only receives the kitty once every three years, and as the wife of the village head is dominant and decides – secretly – whose turn it is to receive the kitty. The other *arisan* in the village are concentrated in the hamlet of Wringinkurung and are organized within religious praying groups, and aim at saving money to buy flour (women) and meat (men) for *Idhul Fitri*. The direct impact on social security of these *arisan* is limited except for its saving purposes and its network function through which potential support might be channelled if needed.[27]

To Whom or Where to Turn?

Fostering Children and Care in Old Age

Children are nurtured, fed and raised with great love and care. Having no children is a great regret for couples, a reason for loneliness, feelings of incompleteness and often a source of shame. In talking about the future, and who will care for them in their old age, villagers often first mention children as the most important means of support. When parents get older, and are no longer able to work, they expect their children to care for them, to provide food, basic healthcare and company, and to organize *selamatan* if asked. However, in many cases, children are not prepared to live up to these expectations.

In the village survey of 100 households, 17 families claimed to be caring for an elderly father or mother (in two cases both), aunt or elderly neighbour who had no children of their own. However, most of these elderly were still living on their own, often with their own income and cooking independently. In general, to the informants, care meant giving whatever was needed and possible, such as food, clothes, firewood, attention and help at *selamatan*. Sometimes this did amount to full daily support but, in many cases, care entailed no more than irregular visits, an incidental meal or financial or material support on special occasions such as house repairs, *selamatan* and at *Idhul Fitri*.

About half of the elderly in Krajan are not being cared for in a substantial way or on a regular basis. Many of them are childless, while the rest have children who do not, or only partially, care for them. Children who do not provide

27 See Lont Lont 2002, 2005 on explaining the social security functions of *arisan*.

care for their parents include those who are away from the village and not sending remittances, those who are a drain on the parents rather than supporting them (referred to as *anak nakal*), those who neglect their parents or leave small grandchildren in their care (in cases of migration and remarriage) and children who are too poor to support their parents.

Of the 25 elderly widows in the survey, 12 did not receive any significant help from their children. Eleven of these 12 were considered to belong to the lowest social class. These widows (ages ranging from 45 to about 70) had to make their own living, and survived by weaving baskets, taking care of cattle, gathering firewood, by doing small agricultural jobs (harvesting and transplanting rice) and by gleaning at rice and maize harvests. Of the other 13 widows, eight were also active in trying to earn some income and only received help from children in the event of shortages. Only five widows were fully taken care of by their children (in two cases by their grandchildren).[28]

For those who do not have children, fostering could be an option.[29] Roughly one out of five Krajan children are fostered. Of the elderly in my survey, eight widows or couples (aged over 40) had neither their own or fostered children. In the surveyed families, 24 children had been fostered (in 20% of the households with children at least one was fostered). By fostering a child, new or closer kinship relationships are formed and existing kinship ties between families are articulated. Often richer families (with or without children) invite the children of poorer relatives to live with them. If no close kin are available, they might

---

28 Some of them were widowed by the death of a husband (*janda mati*), others were divorced (*janda cerai*).

29 Hull and Tukiran (1976), show that East Java ranks among the highest areas in Indonesia in terms of childless ever-married women aged over 30. In 1976, nearly 17% of rural and 23% of urban women fell within this category Hull and Tukiran 1976. These women will now be over 50 years old, indicating that there is a large group of childless older people in East Java. Research in rural Malang found that 21% of the elderly (men and women) claim never to have had children Schröder-Butterfill 2004. The author also noted that this figure is likely to slightly overestimate primary sterility as 'some people without children may never admit that they have had a child who died'. Others will lose children later in life and become childless. As such, one can expect there to remain a significant number of childless elderly. Moreover, a similar number of people in Krajan are childless in the sense that their children are unable or unwilling to care for their parents, with children's old age care function maybe only applying in about half of the cases. This is at odds with the views of demographers and politicians who assume that children are, and should be, the primary source of elderly care, and that local practices of fostering can be interpreted as a child substitution mechanism. I found that widows foster for other reasons, such as company, and that caring for a child is often only a temporary arrangement.

foster a child from another family. Under fostering arrangements, the foster parents pay the schooling expenses of that child and sometimes also wedding expenses. Depending on the situation, a foster child might be given inheritance rights on land and cattle while they may also inherit from their biological parents if they care for them in their old age.

In Krajan, the fostering party usually takes the formal initiative to invite a child to join them, although sometimes the child-giving family implicitly raises the idea. There are essentially two types of fostering: live-in and full adoption. Both families benefit from the relationship, and often the poorer family the most. For a poor family, the advantage of giving a child to foster parents is that one of their children receives better care, food, education and future prospects. They save the costs of rearing a child (education, paying for the necessary lifecycle rituals (*selamatan*) and the costs of a wedding including bridal gifts). Further, their ties with the richer family members will be strengthened and thus also their support network. A foster child living with a richer family is still expected to help its biological parents in times of need.

For the richer families with children of their own, moral considerations often seem more important than economic ones. From their perspective, they care for their relatives by giving fostered children a better future that contributes to their social status. On the other hand, they are also able to use the adopted child for household chores and other jobs. In the case of boys, the fostering family can raise additional cattle and frequently an adopted child can be used to do domestic and productive tasks that their own children cannot, or are unwilling to, do such as hauling water, fetching firewood, preparing meals, cutting cow fodder, cleaning stables and watching over cattle, goats and chickens. It is here that boundaries are blurred. In the case of live-in fosterage, care and misuse are hard to distinguish, and fostered children are sometimes little more than house slaves. A couple I interviewed in Kalimantan, who had left their daughter with a richer family in the neighbourhood, complained: 'our daughter is not treated equally and she does not get the same benefits as the other children'. Another father noted: 'She can go to school, but cannot do much of her homework as she always has to fetch water, cook and help with heavy household chores'.

If a married couple remain childless, they tend to adopt at a very young age and raise the child as their own, and by performing and paying for all the necessary lifecycle rituals show publicly that the child is fully theirs. Such a child automatically receives the right to inherit, but also the obligation to care for the parents. In general, it will lose the right to inherit from the biological parents, but never the moral obligation to care.

I came across a few cases where fostering 'as insurance' for old age care had failed. In one case, a couple had adopted a young boy but, after his marriage, he turned to gambling. He asked his foster parents for help to repay his debts and they gave him a bull which he sold to cover his debts. After a while, he started to play again. When he came for money a second time, the foster parents refused and declared him to no longer be their child. The man left the village and went away. They have completely lost track and do not know where he is and what he is doing. Since then, the couple again refer to themselves as childless. In another instance, concerning a childless widow, the biological parents took an adopted child back as they did not believe she was taking good care. Clearly, in both cases, the arrangement had failed.

A special case of fostering concerns childless widows. Widows living alone and without caring children are often given a daughter by a relative, firstly to care for, and then to provide care when the widow gets older and is unable to work. The child is considered as offering good company to the widow who would otherwise be living alone. When older, the girl can care for the old woman and will then inherit her belongings. Of the 24 fostered children I came across in my village survey, seven were living with six widows, meaning that around a quarter of all widows in Krajan have a child living with them.[30] Two-thirds of these were a grandchild.

I found, in the survey, eight cases of childless people (not having any surviving children) of whom five were widows and three were couples without their own or fostered children.[31] If we include widows who lack *caring* children, either because they are not living in the village or because the children are unable or unwilling to care, the figures are much higher. Five other widows have been given a grandchild to care for, and are not considered locally as childless. In Krajan, this practice of 'giving' children to live with older women is not explicitly seen as a fostering arrangement, but is in response to the often-mentioned view that it is so pitiful (*kasihan*) to see a grandmother living alone. In reality, however, these widows do not receive much care, but at least they receive attention and have daily company. Moreover, if married children move to Kalimantan, one of their daughters is expected to stay to 'keep grandma

30 The number of childless widows and fostered children is too low to provide a statistically reliable interpretation. However, observations in the village and other studies in East Java produce similar figures. See: Marianti 2002; Schröder-Butterfill 2001, 2004.

31 I did find two childless men who had remarried childless widows. In both cases, the men had become childless through divorce. In one of these cases, the children stayed with the man's former wife in another town. In the other case, the man married a woman without children after his only child died.

company'. In return, these widows have to care for these grandchildren, in order to lessen the burden on their own children who are not able or unwilling to care well for their own children. In some cases, this becomes a real burden for them.

Kinship

In discussions on vulnerability and social security, kinship is often mentioned as an important or even crucial mechanism offering social security and a safety net for people in times of need or adversity (Von Benda-Beckmann et al. 1988:12). Van Leliveld, for instance, discusses at length the rights to economic resources and assistance from relatives in Swaziland: 'Kinship has its function in distributing wealth in Swazi society. The kinship system not only regulates

ILLUSTRATION 3 *Widow without children*

social life and relationships of people, but also attaches, at the same time, a variety of economic obligations and rights to kinship members' (Leliveld 1994:178). In most societies worldwide, strong normative conventions exist pointing to the moral responsibility to help relatives in times of need. In reality, however, practice may differ from this morality, and the importance of kinship differs between societies. How relevant is kinship as a form of social security in a context where many people are poor?

In Krajan, it is important to know your kin and to maintain good relationships with them for a variety of reasons. These relationships are expressed and reproduced at weddings, funerals and *selamatan*, and at *Idhul Fitri*: people go and visit kin and family to share meals, presents, sweets or snacks, and to pay tributes to their relatives, thus maintaining and rebuilding relationships. Women make biscuits and distribute them among both far and close kin. Even very poor families try to produce at least enough biscuits to stress their relationship with their richer kinfolk. In Krajan, rich villagers know more kin, and are able to trace more-distant wealthy relatives and more often express the importance of kinship as a way to keep contact, exchange information or ask for help.[32]

A closer look at the actual support received from relatives in Krajan provides a different picture. In the event of temporary food shortages, or the need for small loans of food or money, people rarely go to relatives such as brothers, sisters, uncles, nephews, nieces or cousins. They first try the shop, parents (or children) or neighbours. In finding work, kin are important and keeping in regular contact does help in finding a job or business opportunities. In addition, share tenancies or the share-raising of cattle is often granted to kinsfolk. At *selamatan*, weddings and labour parties, kin are important providers of *sumbangan*, and the donations of relatives are usually the most substantial, albeit never enough to cover the costs of rice, animals and meat.

Kin support for covering the costs of funerals, severe illness and hospitalization varies considerably between households and amounts to an ambiguous practice. With funerals, the mourning family itself pays most of the expenses and the huge costs involved in a burial, the associated meals and the *selamatan*. Usually, they have to sell cattle, sell or pawn land, gold or goods. If these resources are insufficient, they seek loans from neighbours, patrons or relatives. In some cases, neighbours and patrons contribute most to covering the costs, or provide loans while, in other cases, relatives covered the lion's share.

32 Hüsken (1988:226) observed, in rural Central Java, that kinship relationships are often more important and more extended in richer families than in poorer ones. In general, poor villagers know their rich kin better than vice versa.

Relatives covered the majority of the costs in less than one-third of all cases. The types of support that were mentioned by relatives in the survey covered financial support, emotional support and support in kind (with goods or rice). In most instances, aid from relatives is not sufficient to cover the required financial help. On these occasions, it seems that, contrary to my expectations, the neighbourhood is the primary supporting agency, and only if individual savings and the neighbourhood fall short will kin provide the necessary aid and loans. Detailed observations over long periods of time showed that, except regarding parents to children and vice versa – and to a lesser extent between siblings, the contributions of kin generally failed to exceed the contributions made by good friends and close neighbours. In a number of the cases surveyed, siblings even asked for interest on loans provided for funerals and hospitalisation costs. Relatives were the main providers of support in less than 15% of funerals, and the same was true when it came to hospitalisation. In a number of cases where a family was confronted with a death of a household member, they could not pay for a decent funeral because relatives did not give any financial support even though they had the economic resources. Sometimes, there were conflicts or long-lasting feuds involved, but it was also reported that relatives were said to be unwilling or unable 'to waste money on a party for other people's friends'. Others reasoned along similar lines: 'we would never receive any *sumbangan* from these visitors in return'.

Although the assistance from relatives in the event of a bereavement turned out to be limited in a financial or material sense, support is always important in the emotional and practical sense. It is close relatives who help prepare the food, give advice, comfort, distribute invitations, find buyers for cattle or land, broker loans, negotiate prices, do the shopping for meat in town and lead the praying groups. In old age, the elderly without children can fall back on close relatives for food support, minor financial aid and care. Where children are absent and the husband or wife has died, and an old man or woman is ill or can no longer earn an income, close kin are seen as responsible for taking them into their home and caring for them until they die. In reality, it is remarkable how often this does not occur. At the turn of the millennium, the village contained 64 widows, called *kasihan*, who were not cared for, or not fully cared for by close relatives. In one-third of these cases, relatives were absent. In roughly another third of the cases, close relatives provided some care and support on a regular basis, but not enough to cover all needs. In the other one-third, the widows were largely left alone and perceived as able to and responsible for earning their own money by doing agricultural work such as rice and tobacco planting, weeding, collecting and selling firewood, making *beset* or herding goats.

When it came to weddings, in a quarter of the cases studied, close relatives[33] paid most of the wedding costs (often as a loan), or lent cattle to be sold and repaid later. If relatives paid for these events, they rarely asked for interest and, sometimes, they provided 'loans' without really expecting to ever be repaid. This both contributes to the good name of these uncles and aunts and it underscores the family hierarchy. Uncles and aunts feel a strong moral responsibility to care for the children of their brothers and sisters at the time of their marriage. A good wedding is part of family pride.

The support of kin becomes most visible when brothers, sisters, uncles, aunts and cousins become brokers of property and money, ceremonial leaders or organize funeral practicalities. Moreover, when it comes to engagements and weddings, relatives play an even more important role in negotiating bridal gifts, extending loans and sending out invitations. I came across several instances where uncles or other close kin paid for higher education, or towards the tuition fees of nephews, nieces or cousins.

In my judgement, it is in the economic sphere that these relatives, as brokers of knowledge and information, are the most important source of support. They will help when one needs work or trade contacts, and can be a valuable source of information, can mediate political support and can broker loans. The socioeconomic value of relatives thus lies more in their intermediary role in gaining both direct and indirect access to resources and various forms of investment, rather than as a source of direct financial support in the event of adversities.

Friends and the Neighbourhood

Provided relationships are sound, neighbours and the neighbourhood are a major source of small-scale daily support and assistance. Maintaining good relationships with neighbours is crucial to insure against small everyday insecurities. At funerals, for instance, neighbours are often the first to help with all the work and organizing activities and, if the neighbours are wealthy, they may provide significant contributions in the form of animals, money, rice and loans. The neighbourhood is important, not because it covers all expenses and offers full protection, but because it is the first and prime source of help such as small contributions in cash, labour, or

33 Primarily uncles and aunts, but also nephews and nieces (*keponakan*), are of special importance and more often take responsibility to help financially in times of need. They are viewed as almost as close as siblings and sometimes even closer. In the survey, villagers indicated that they want to help, and are more inclined to lend money to nephews and nieces than to other kin.

commodities.[34] In this respect, the neighbourhood is much more important for social security than relatives, patrons or village schemes (although these often overlap as neighbours may also be relatives, friends and patrons). It is in the neighbourhood that most redistributive lifecycle rituals, *selamatan*, take place. Further, it is at this level that small loans, free meals and snacks (for children), small gifts of food, practical assistance during illness, funerals, house building, harvesting and care for small children are provided. While baby-sitting and elderly care is primarily the responsibility of parents and children, neighbours provide important additional support and often contribute to keeping an eye on small children and taking care of the elderly in a familiar and spontaneous way.

As such, the neighbourhood is the basic *locale* and unit of organization for most village institutions offering support, assistance and mutual help,[35] although it does not always function as such. Relationships are not always good between all members, and not all neighbours join all voluntary activities. Krajan neighbourhoods are dense, relationships and exchanges can be intense, but neighbourhoods are certainly not the romantic islands of harmony assumed in many government circles.

An example of the support and minor care provided in a typical neighbourhood is the neighbourhood of *Pak* Marjam in lower Dluwang. *Pak* Marjam has leprosy and, over the last few years, his condition has deteriorated as he somehow lost contact with the leprosy health programme that used to regularly supply medication. Due to his illness, he is not able to work and sits most of the time in front of his home watching passers-by. His wife weaves baskets, works occasionally in neighbours' rice fields and grows some maize and cassava on their tiny plot. The money she earns is nowhere near enough to support her husband and their three children. *Pak* Marjam's parents and some aunts live nearby, but they are too poor to support him. The eldest son of the Marjam

34 Although severe tensions can exist between neighbours, relationships are never bad with all neighbours and, in the event of a burial or other severe event, conflicts and bad feelings are temporarily put to one side.

35 The importance of these small forms of social security in neighbourhoods is difficult to assess. In the village survey, most informants could mention a few significant cases of neighbourly support they had either provided or received. However, they never spontaneously mentioned these day-to-day forms of support – they were too natural to mention. These had to be observed by spending long days at key informants' houses in various neighbourhoods. In daily observations and interactions, the importance of having good relationships in the neighbourhood was stressed repeatedly: 'because we need good neighbours', or 'we ought to do it here together'. The saying, 'a good neighbour is better than a far friend', definitely resonates in Krajan.

family is fostered and cared for by distant kin in Tamankursi. The other two children are five and seven years old, do not go to school, and roam around in the neighbourhood. In the mornings, when *Bu* Marjam is away working, they go to relatives, or to other neighbours, and receive free breakfast, snacks, boiled cassava or a roasted maize cob.

If there is no food at all in the house, and borrowing has become impossible, *Bu* Marjam walks for three hours to her parents and relatives in Tamankursi, a neighbouring village across the Dluwang ravine. Sometimes, these trips are successful and she is given some money, but often she only receives a meal and some food to take home for the children. On such days, *Pak* Marjam also goes out to visit friends from the past, distant kin and maybe even the village head. On these trips, he generally receives at least some coffee, an occasional free meal and something to smoke. If his children join him, these trips are more successful as they are more to be pitied (*kasihan*). It is apparent that he uses his obvious handicap as a means to more effectively ask for help but without begging openly. The village counsellors regularly give him some money and his house was once repaired as a gift from the village head.

Nowadays, *Pak* Marjam has lost most of the control over his fingers and is no longer able to roll his own cigarettes. A couple of times a day he goes to his neighbours and asks them to roll one for him. Coming so often, he is not invited to share a meal, and people still consider him able to find a meal for himself. As one of the neighbours commented: 'I know he has leprosy, but why does he not try to work at least a little? I work hard every day, and I still have nothing; he doesn't work at all and receives a new house for free'. Paradoxically, help often leads to jealousy and less help from others.

Living close together makes the needs of others highly visible and, between neighbours, their close ties make assistance in times of need seem a logical thing. However, this closeness and visibility can also easily lead to tensions. Although limited in scope and importance, social relationships in the neighbourhood are still the most fertile setting in which to organize *selamatan*, mutual labour arrangements, small loans, *arisan* and prayer groups, as other sources of help tend to be more restricted.

Patronage

There are two types of small-scale patronage in Krajan, one based on control over resources such as land and cattle, as in the case of *Pak* Patik, and another based on political and sometimes religious power, as in the case of Bagenda. In the first type, patrons allow their clients to have a share in cultivating their lands or raising their cattle. In the second type, usufruct rights over local resources can also be granted, but also jobs or gifts. In the event of an emergency, patrons are expected to 'care' and provide assistance. This can be financial, or by 'helping out' such in finding a good doctor or negotiating to get someone out of prison.

Crucial to the first type of patronage is the share raising of cattle described in the previous chapter. Caring for cattle and dividing the profit is one of the most common and stable ways of making an income, of saving, and securing assets for times of need. As shown earlier, the shared tenancy and harvest shares (*paron* and *babun*) labour arrangements do offer landless villagers some, albeit limited, access to resources.

When it comes to *babun*, cattle-raising and cooperative mutual labour arrangements, the fringe benefits of the relationship with the employer often outweigh the direct material revenues. Establishing and maintaining good and close relationships with such landowners, the *orang kaya* of Krajan, for instance increases the likelihood of loans, cash advances, aid in times of emergency, work, new cattle sharing contracts and small gifts at *Idhul Fitri*. In the event of adversities or sudden deaths, a patron or his wife will, if no other support is available, often provide emergency loans, provide a white burial cloth, some rice or other small necessities needed for the burial, praying ceremonies or *selamatan*. Without such a relationship, it is hard to claim support in times of need. If these relationships are maintained over time, they take the form of more permanent patron-client bonds in which both parties have rights and obligations. As Hefner (1990) writes:

> In private conversation, full time laborers underscore themes of trust and personalized attention, insisting that they work not just for their wages but because of special kindness the employer shows. In part, of course, these comments are intended to put a good face on a demeaning situation. However, the social implications for the labor relationship are real. The employer-become-patron assumes responsibilities beyond those of the wages he pays. He provides a new set of clothes each year, gives bonuses when his worker has a ritual festival, and allows time off with pay if the worker has family problems. Most important, the patron provides a significant measure of social insurance by advancing interest-free loans during difficult times. In the long run, these loans may not be repaid even if the employee severs ties with the employer.
>
> HEFNER, 1990: 151

Such observations reflect reality in Krajan since labourers will always try to call upon the moral obligation of their patrons. However, not all patrons respond. It is rare for patrons to take responsibility for all the expenses or structural help required for a *selamatan*, or during the period after a funeral. Some large landowners turn down many demands for help, as in the case of Patik and Satrawi. However, even Patik will provide some minor forms of help such as clothes, tobacco and share tenancy contracts for land and cattle. His wife is probably more important in this respect by providing small gifts of food, small loans of money, rice and maize, free meals for Satrawi's children, and used clothes and free biscuits at *Idhul Fitri*. If a real disaster were to hit the Satrawi family, one suspects that even such a greedy patron as Patik would accept his responsibilities and help the family through the early days by providing food, loans and small cash gifts.

In exchange for these gifts and incidental meals, and employment and small loans, the patrons benefit from the acquired labour force and the loyalty of their clients. On balance, patrons probably benefit the most from the relationship in terms of economic and political aspects.[36] As Scott (1976: 39) comments on patronage in general, clients in Krajan seem to give up individual freedom, maximum returns on labour and also justice in return for the security provided by a patron. An easy access to a landlord's credit is often the motive for remaining part of a patronage relationship with security being preferred to short-term income gains.

The second type, political patronage, is provided by local political and religious leaders, such as the village head, village officials, forest officials and religious leaders (*kiai*). These patrons provide their clients with work, and access to credit and business opportunities, in return for loyal political support and friendship. Establishing a group of loyal political followers is important, especially for the village head and his village officials such as the secretary and hamlet heads, as they can assure votes for re-election, hide and legitimize the embezzlement of government money, and help push unpopular deals or unpopular regulations.

Political patrons are also important as providers of support in the event of an emergency. About 40% of all emergency cash loans, in the event of death, illness or bankruptcy, where a family could not pay and did not receive any support from others, were provided by the village head, his mother, the village secretary, or the head of the hamlet. Even if these political patrons did not provide the cash themselves, they were able to negotiate credit, assistance or help for their clients through other contacts. Many significant loans and material assistance have to be paid back with labour, in kind (tobacco, lumber, or wood), in services but primarily in long-lasting political loyalty or dependency.

36 See the cases of the tobacco harvest of *Pak* Patik, and the loans of the Satrawi family.

Religious leaders seldom give direct support or credit, but use their influence to mediate in obtaining credit from landowners and businessmen in their network. As brokers between the needy and the affluent, they have moral, religious and political authority to call on rich followers to help. As in other forms of patronage and brokerage, they receive in return long-term loyal commitment and piety from their clients. These networks will be mobilized at key moments, such as at elections.

State Support and Village Politics

From the early 1970s until the beginning of the 1990s, rural Indonesia was the main focus of government development initiatives but, in the mid-1980s, government interest started to shift towards urban areas, the industrial sector and agro-business development beyond Java. Nevertheless, government-funding remains relevant to the village, and a gradual shift can be seen from investment to social assistance. As with most villages in Java, Krajan benefited, albeit rather late, from investments in agriculture, education, healthcare and infrastructure. As they were the ones handling the funds, the village head and officials benefited from all such projects. By appropriating a sizeable amount of these funds and distributing the rest mainly among relatives, friends and loyal clients, they were both able to improve their own livelihoods and to enhance their positions.

In Krajan, since the early 1980s, not only roads, but also irrigation works, have been improved, schools have been constructed, a health post with a nurse established, as well infrastructure for piped water, electricity and some basic sanitation. Although some of these services are badly maintained, facilities have without doubt improved in the past two decades. With the improved road, public transport to Bondowoso has increased and access to the market has become easier.

Since the late 1990s, in addition to the above projects, programmes such as the founding of village cooperatives KUD (*Koperasi Unit Desa*) and the establishment of rural credit programmes KUT (*Kredit Usaha Tani*) have come to the village, although the KUD has since declined in importance. Krajan was classified as a remote and underdeveloped IDT (*Inpress Desa Tertinggal*) village in 1990 and, since then, special development projects to alleviate rural poverty have been carried out. An important element in the village modernization programmes of Suharto's New Order regime was schooling, which focussed especially on educational development in rural communities. All children were obliged to attend primary school, and the bright ones were pushed further towards the vocational school.[37] Over the last decade, transportation to

37 See for a description of this development in central Java: White 2012.

and from town has increased due to regular transport and the 'motor bike revolution'.

The benefits of all these programmes in the development of the Krajan economy are difficult to assess. Today, most irrigation canals, dams and sluices operate, not least because important village members watch over them, and cash crop production has clearly intensified since the opening up of the area although it is not clear if this is the result of government policies. Seasonal migration has also increased. The village cooperative has, however, collapsed due to mismanagement, attempts by the regional government to influence and control the village economy, distrust among the village farmers and corruption. The village credit programmes have had variable effects. In some periods, loans were successfully obtained and repaid (mostly by richer villagers) but, in other years, the schemes were a disaster, as in 1999 when two-thirds of KUT loans were appropriated by the village head and invested in his private enterprises.

In retrospect, one can say that these New Order investments did not directly improve the living conditions of the landless and the landed poor. They were more effective in helping the middle classes (*cucup*) and the 'poor with potential' (*kurang*). Richer farmers with a surplus of land and capital benefited far more than the village poor and, in particular, village heads and village officials reaped the profits from projects and the new cash flows. Well-connected poor villagers could temporarily gain employment in constructing roads, schools, irrigation canals and village buildings, but wages remained low. A significant proportion of the funds leaked away into the hands of the village head, district government employees and junior village officials to finance luxury items such as motorbikes, television sets, radios and cars (all purchased outside the village).

Prior to 2000, only a few programmes had any significance for the poor. A free healthcare scheme could have helped them, but it collapsed soon after its start, and the new programme following the *Reformasi* only partly works as doctors and hospitals still ask additional fees. However, the government policy of boosting agriculture certainly did increase employment. Some poor families also received intermittent help such as boxes of tools to enhance village craftsmanship, coffee seedlings, ducks, goats, chickens and calves. In general, however, most programmes were a crushing failure: the gifts were sold as soon as possible, the goats ate the coffee bushes, ducks were stolen and chickens died due to chicken pest. Only in a few instances were villagers able to really make a difference and start something new: by raising goats, a few people were able to purchase a cow or improve their house; and those who had planted coffee and guarded the bushes against the goats reaped a windfall when, at the start of the economic crisis, coffee prices rose dramatically. Three villagers earned substantial amounts by using the tools provided by the government to make wooden cabinets and furniture for the local market.

Good relations with the village head, the village secretary, representatives of the village developmental board (LKMD), and its successors, and the heads of hamlets are essential if one is to obtain help and support from the government or take part in projects. If you are not well known to these people, there is little likelihood of working for them. As money-earning jobs are scarce and therefore valuable political instruments, Bagenda always tries to ensure that people from different fractions and hamlets gain some benefit from them. The more he spreads the benefits, the more loyal followers he can generate.

Before the crisis in 1997, a World Bank sponsored road improvement project was launched in most of the remote *desa* of rural Java. This project targeted infrastructural improvement and, further, all villagers were supposed to be able to join the project and so earn some money. In 1997, Krajan received over 50 million Rupiah to upgrade the dirt roads towards Pakuarah, Dluwang, Pakuarah and Andungsari, and those who joined the work were paid Rp 5,000 a day, enough to buy more than 4 kg of rice, and more than they could earn in other jobs. Loyal families, close to the village administration, got most of these jobs. Moreover, relatives and close friends of these people got the better jobs, as foremen, instructors and coordinators, and could earn much higher daily wages. The project administration was supposed to be open, and long lists and documents were displayed on the walls of the *balai desa* (village office). However, behind this official facade, costs could be reduced and incomes improved by using second-rate building materials, and by purchasing stone, sand and wood directly from the village head and village officials.[38] A double bookkeeping system was used to suggest to officials that these items were being purchased at market prices. By the time the project was completed, most village officials had bought television sets, motor cycles, fancy phones or improved their houses.

After the reforms following the turn of the millennium, similar patterns continued although more programmes became available for the poor. These included subsidized rice (Raskin), free health cards (Jamkesmas), cash transfers for poor students (BSM), conditional cash transfers (PKH) and temporary unconditional cash transfers (BLT) (WorldBank 2012b:12). The first of these

38 For instance, the village head determined that the iron bars supposedly in concrete constructions would be replaced with bamboo for small bridges, ducts and walls. Two years after construction, the bridge at Wringinkurung collapsed under the weight of a truck loaded with sacks of rice.

certainly helped the poorest families in the village. Although less poor villagers also received a share, the cheap rice rations especially help the poorest of the poor. The later programme for free healthcare is now running and offers a major improvement in health insurance, but hospitalisation remains a major risk for poor families as not all costs are covered. The conditional and unconditional cash transfer programmes do not yet run in Krajan, and the cash transfers for students have not had a significant effect as few children proceed to higher education.

How successful the infrastructural development has been depends on the importance of these roads for the poor. Java now has excellent road access far into the most remote areas which, while symbolically important, has no practical meaning for those who are not productive and in much greater need of 'make-live policies' (Li 2009).

Religious Charity

The Madurese consider themselves good Muslims, carrying on the tradition of the great Madurese *ulama* who spread Islam to Madura and East Java from the 17th century onwards. Other Indonesians regard the Madurese as pious, orthodox or even as 'fanatical' Muslims. Being Muslim, and a member of NU (*Nahdatul Ulama*), has become part of the Madurese cultural identity. Two of the three main *kiai* in Krajan belong to a relatively moderate strand of Islam, whereas the third is of a stricter vein. Besides the three religious leaders, other Islamic scholars, who have been educated in one of the numerous religious boarding schools (*pesantren*) in East Java or Madura, teach praying and Koran reading in small schools (*surau*).[39] Also among these leaders, we find a range of strict to liberal adherents.

In Krajan, *kiai* play an important role in that they are seen as learned men, often able to contact the supernatural world. They teach the ordinary believers how to pray, and the norms and values of Islam. They are often also healers,

39 As religious leaders, the *kiai* have much political prestige. Their political importance became explicit during village elections where followers of the most orthodox *kiai* voted for the PPP, and of the others for the government party Golkar. In the reformative 1999 elections, the PPP followers switched to PKB, and the others to PDI-P, supported and strongly influenced by the village head. Since the beginning of the twentieth century, less strict syncretic Muslims (*abangan*) and religious families have been rivals in controlling village resources and village leadership. Frome the mid-1960s onwards, strong religious families ruled the village. Since 1991, Bagenda has been the village head of Krajan, and he is a descendent of the first postcolonial village head who had strong ties with the military and was not very religious. Since the start of his rule, Bagenda has never been on very friendly terms with the more orthodox *kiai* of Krajan.

believed to control white magic, they advise on marriages, and lead and pray at weddings, funerals and *selamatan*. Besides all this, they are often consulted over conflicts and marriage problems, and for economic advice. In return for such services, they receive small gifts, in rice or cash, which constitute a significant part of their income.[40]

Officially, the *zakat* is one of the most important Islamic institutions, and relevant to providing social security. This is one of the five pillars of Islam, and includes giving alms to the poor and needy. The Koran indicates, in Soera 9: 60, how alms should be used: for the advancement of Allah's cause, for freeing prisoners and debtors, for distribution among the poor and needy, for travellers, for converts and for those engaged in collecting alms. The amount of money or goods is not fixed (Van Dijk 1994). Two forms of alms are given to the local *kiai*; the *zakat-mal* and the *zakat-al-fitra*. *Zakat-mal* entails giving a percentage of the harvest or livestock and is applicable for richer people, but is not very often practised by NU Muslims. *Zakat-al-fitra* is paid by everyone after the fasting month of Ramadan, and entails a small gift of two kilos of rice to one's religious leader.[41]

Institutionalized religious practices such as almsgiving at the festival following Ramadan have hardly any social security function as donations are small and used by the religious leaders themselves.[42] For most of the *kiai* of Krajan, these contributions are a welcome addition to their food stocks as they themselves struggle to make ends meet. None of the alms were redistributed among the village poor; on the contrary, the village poor felt obliged to contribute to the *kiai* as a form of universal taxation.

The slaughtering of cattle or goats by rich villagers at ceremonies during the Islamic festival of *hari korban* (*Idhul-adha*), when the birth of Mohamed is remembered, has more of a redistributive character. Neighbours, friends and relatives can come to such a meal or receive free meat from the

40 These contributions are explicitly referred to as gifts, not as payments. At *selamatan*, some money is put in the basket with food for the *kiai*. If *kiai* are visited to ask a favour, for advice, or to pray, they receive money on the first greeting hidden in the palm of the hand.

41 Usually, this is the *kiai* who has been their religious teacher for praying and reading the Koran.

42 I observed that all villagers paid the necessary minimum, around two kilograms per person. Each villager paid this to the religious leader from whom they had received education. Villagers perceive the gift as a means to honour their *guru* and as a kind of religious tax. Even the poorest people pay *zakat*, and I did not hear of anyone ever not paying, although it was said that widows did not have to pay. For the poorest families, finding this two kilograms of white rice is yet another burden, especially because the rice redistribution does not happen in Krajan.

organizing family. In practice however, few animals are slaughtered in Krajan, and meat portions are very small since they are distributed among many families. Further, most of the poor are not invited, or do not dare to come.

A similar kind of institution with a redistributive function is *kaul* (vow), a sort of thanksgiving *selamatan* with free food and meat. These are organized when someone is especially grateful, maybe for a large profit, the birth of a child or has made a promise to Allah. Both rich and poor villagers can organize *kaul* but the extent of giving differs. So, although religion-based charity could, in theory, be important, its impact remains limited and, in practice, the major redistributive Islamic institutions such as *zakat* contribute little to poverty alleviation in Krajan.

Who Cares? Evaluating Locally Organized Support Systems

From the discussion above, it has become clear that if people and families are confronted with an emergency or adversity, such as death, illness, fire, misfortune or a loss of shelter or assets, most of them can initially fall back on their social networks for basic help. Support from these networks is, however, rarely sufficient to cover all needs and does not protect against slipping back into poverty, or a deterioration in one's livelihood base and the long-term consequences of shocks and stresses. To avoid these outcomes, people have to take action themselves, by selling or pawning land, adjusting needs to income, by accepting poverty or by leaving the village in search of a better future. The State offers little in this respect apart from keeping rice prices artificially low, assuring basic education, by providing work through village projects, providing health services, paying subsidies and recently by improvements in health insurance. So far, these interventions have not proven fully effective and they clearly do not represent a solution to widespread poverty and inequality in Indonesia.

To sum up, the most significant forms of support in times of an emergency in Krajan are *sumbangan*, loans, labour assistance and a helping hand from the neighbourhood, from kinsfolk and from patrons (see Table 4). The neighbourhood is a very important place where social security is organized, and support from neighbours is often the prime and most import source of support. Some caution should be noted here: neighbourhoods are neither harmonious entities, nor locales of uncontested, unconditional or charitable forms of support. Neighbourhood assistance is often enforced, calculated and strictly reciprocal in nature.

Among these forms, political patronage, provided one's patron remains in power, is a benefit for those who have secured a position as a loyal client and, in some cases, political patrons will take care of the poor. After careful calculation, I conclude that clients invest more time, money and labour in the relationship with patrons or richer villagers then most of them will ever receive in return. They are effectively paying an 'emergency premium' to claim the moral right to assistance when they most need it and when they need it urgently.

Occasionally, government assistance plays a role when money is provided for village development projects or poverty alleviation and is distributed to the village creating labour opportunities. However, considerable amounts of such funds are used privately by village officials, either for their own consumption, or for supporting relatives, friends and clientele. Table 4 summarizes the insecurities and different sources of support as discussed in this chapter.

A complicating factor in assessing the role of village social security is that local institutions and arrangements are often of a dual nature and paradoxical in that they not only offer security but are often also a source of insecurity. The practice of gift giving at weddings, *selamatan* and funerals, for instance, provides the receiving family with support in coping with the expenses and food provision in the expensive period around such an event. However, at the same time, the contributions are a burden for those invited. Despite these difficulties, most people and households do try to remain part of, and invest in, reciprocal relationships of all sorts. Others try to escape the pressures and expectations of neighbours, kin and village institutions, and retain resources for their own use (see the next chapter). Many villagers experience this balancing of resources, claims and obligations as a dilemma, torn between taking part in the ritual exchange economy, and so being eligible for return support, or opting for individual solutions which are neither sufficient nor secure.

Here we return to the key question of this chapter: how viable and how important are these forms of village-organized social security? Different views exist as to the quality of these forms of social security. Some researchers state that these arrangements and institutions have been successful in guaranteeing social security for village members in the past, but have broken down due to external influences such as colonialism, capitalism and globalization.[43] Others assume that some of the 'old indigenous social security' arrangements have survived throughout different periods in history and functions and, to a certain extent, survive until the current day.[44]

43 Dixon 1985; Geertz 1963; Koentjaraningrat 1967a; Midgley 1994; Scott 1976.

44 Hefner 1990; Midgley 1994; Platteau 1991; Van Ginneken 1999.

TABLE 4 *Insecurities and sources of support*

Insecurities Sources of support	Temporary food Shortages	Communal obligations (*selamatan*, house building, labour parties)	Lifecycle crises (death, illness, childbirth and hospitalization)	Old age care	Ecological and economic disasters (covariate risks)	Education needs
Nuclear family (own resources)	–	++	++	++	++	+
Parents or children	++	+	++	++	+/–	++
Brothers or sisters	+	–	+	+/–	–	+/–
Neighbours and friends	++	++	++	+/–	–	–
Other relatives (uncles, aunts, nephews)	–	+/–	+	+	–	+
Patrons and village leaders	(+) (patrons)	+	+	–	(+) (village leaders)	(+) (in some cases)
Village and religious institutions	–	++	+	–	–	–
State and government institutions	(+) (very occasionally)	–	+/–	–	+	+

Many Indonesian elites also share these views of an extant village social security system. The mythology of mutual help and exchange in the countryside makes up an important part of national political and academic discourses. This belief in the existence of the harmonious Javanese village, where people still care for each other, is a powerful and archetypical one. For instance, the *bupati* (district officer) of Bondowoso told me that I was very lucky to be able to live in the *desa* and to study 'real' Indonesian society. He believed in the existence of widespread forms of mutual help as strong bonds between the rich and the poor in the villages. When I told him some stories of people not receiving any support, he became irritated and quickly shifted to another subject as this was clearly not what he wanted to hear and especially not from an outsider.

The myth of a 'real' and 'good' Java, that is most closely to be witnessed in the villages, remains a functional ambiguity. The maintenance of ignorance of the exploitative and often disharmonious nature of village societies is important in the 'construction' of a Javanese-Indonesian identity and helps to deal with changes such as modernization, monetization and globalization in the cities. That is, at least in the villages, something of the 'good' harmonious past has remained despite the massive changes in Indonesia. Reality in Krajan, however, is different. Competition over resources is fierce, solidarity between the poor is hard to find and jealousy, rivalry and hate are more common than cooperation. These subjects will be further addressed in the next chapter.

The best known early academic representative of this romantic view is Clifford Geertz who states: 'In East and Central Java [we find] villages of "just-enoughs" and "not-quite-enoughs" in which a Byzantine maze of land, sharecropping, and labour rights have tended, until recently, to provide villagers a minimal niche, albeit at declining levels of welfare for all' (Geertz 1963:Chapter 5). In reaction to these 'shared poverty' ideas, Hefner writes, 'the analyses that emphasize "poverty-sharing" have inevitably misperceived the nature of agrarian hierarchy and overlooked the profoundly differential effect of inequality on welfare and politics' (Hefner 1990:114). He continues, on mountainous Java, 'first, and most important, the primary guarantor of household welfare here has never been sharecropping, privileged access to work, or any of the other patronage arrangements so widely reported from wet-rice areas of Southeast Asia (Scott 1976; Hart 1986; Hüsken 1979). Household welfare has instead depended on the ability of a man and woman to reap the fruits of their own piece of land'. In other words, village-based social security has always been down to people's access to resources, income and poverty. The large inequalities in access to resources serve as a continuous basis for inequality (Hall et al. 2011).

If we look at Krajan, we see that this does not mean that these institutions and arrangements are meaningless. On the one hand, their function and performance should not be romanticized or taken for granted but, on the other hand, the majority of villagers are in principle entitled to several forms of emotional and material support in the event of misfortune. When they are down and out, they do receive considerable support and contributions (although never enough to cover all costs) from similar and sometimes from richer villagers. The real problem is that a significant number of the population are effectively *excluded* from most exchanges and forms of support, and that these are the people who need support the most. It is the 'little-less-poor' who exclude the 'poor'. In reality, one-third of the Krajan people receive practically no support to cover the many insecurities experienced in daily life.

In Krajan, the iron law of social security postulated by Macarov (cited in Von Benda-Beckmann and Von Benda-Beckmann 1996) that 'those who need most, receive least' holds: the poorest villagers are unable to secure their welfare and receive insufficient support. These poor, who make up one-third of the Krajan population, need the support of village institutions but cannot contribute to these institutions, arrangements and forms of reciprocity, and have poor networks, meaning that they face social exclusion from most of the potential benefits. Moreover, even if they still manage to meet some of the expectations of the ritual exchange economy, they pay relatively more than their richer neighbours, and more than they will ever receive back. The mid-level and richer categories get more out of village social welfare than they put in to it.

These paradoxes of local social security can be summarized as follows. Firstly, poorer villagers are more vulnerable to insecurities than richer villagers, and they have fewer means of protection. Poorer villagers pay relatively more (as a proportion of their total income) for their funerals, *selamatan* and weddings, while receiving less support and *sumbangan* on these occasions because their networks are smaller and their friends and relatives are generally poorer. Those poorer villagers who are engaged in mutual help and mutual labour groups generally give more labour to their richer neighbours, due to their larger plots, than is reciprocated. Corvée labour and services given to richer village members, politicians, relatives and patrons are seen as investments and premiums but these generally cost more than the social security ever provided by these politicians, patrons and relatives. Moreover, their labour contributes to the prosperity of such patrons and thus sustains or increases the gap between rich and poor in rural Java. Those who most need credit can borrow least, and pay the highest interest. Finally in the sphere of consumption, those who have little money pay more for goods as they buy only when absolutely necessary, in smaller quantities and from the smaller, more expensive, shops in the neighbourhood.

Clearly, the institutions, arrangements and social relations in the village are inadequate to overcome the 'insecurity trap' and will likely remain so. If this situation is to be changed, well-targeted interventions through poverty alleviation and social security programmes will be needed. To date, the Indonesian government has promoted education, health and development in rural areas, and has helped protect the poor by keeping rice prices low. While this has contributed to the survival of large populations, the performance and significance of these programmes was limited and they should clearly be extended, continued and enhanced if livelihood security is to be available to all poor citizens.

Generally in Krajan, people and households have to primarily rely upon their own resources. In financial terms, local institutions and arrangements for social security are only supplementary and never free of charge. Thus, village institutions only partially work and in general are more important for richer than for poorer categories of villagers. Selfless sharing and simple solidarity among the poor, or between social classes, is rare or non-existent, and the few saving groups serve social rather than social security purposes.[45] Institutions and arrangements such as kinship, fostering, neighbourly assistance, patronage, reciprocal gift-giving and mutual help do exist and can be important but their scope depends on the individual networks of villagers and they can never guarantee significant welfare or social security in the long run. Given this reality, villagers are left, at least to some extent, to their own specific combinations of income sources, savings and ways of accessing resources and social relationships. In the next chapter, I focus on how they achieve this by combining different resources and relationships in following their own individualized social security style.

45 See: Lont (2002) who also argues that the social security functions of *arisan* are limited in an urban context. In Krajan, where few villagers engage in *arisan*, and the contributions are small, the importance of *arisan* for providing social security is negligible.

CHAPTER 4

Styles Matter

Coherent Diversity in Livelihood and Social Security

Closely-knit webs of social relationships, village institutions and arrangements for support are important for the Madurese in East Kalimantan. They can be of help in the event of misfortune or an emergency, but they do not offer sufficient, stable, steady and long-term social security for all. On the contrary, access to support varies between households, social classes and regions. In most cases, when Madurese villagers are confronted with an emergency or adversity, they first have to rely on their own resources; either directly by using any savings, cattle or land they might have or indirectly by turning to others for help or loans which can be later repaid through labour. To maintain these options, villagers have to balance short- and long- term household needs, and individual and household consumption, with investments in mutual help and social relationships.

In this chapter, I take a closer look at the ways people deal with the tensions which arise out of choosing between these options: between individual consumption and saving, and investments in social relationship and village social security in general; and between wages in kind and village resources, and cash-generating opportunities and outside opportunities. I look at the different ways in which people organize their livelihoods and social security, and the inherent logic in anticipating and reacting to various forms of setbacks and adversities. For the poorest Madurese, options are naturally limited and they have little room for manoeuvre. Nevertheless, even among lower social classes, different mixes of social security exist, and these mixes show similarities with those of other classes. As described in the introduction, I use the concept of styles to analyse patterns in these different mixes.

The guiding questions for this chapter are: how do people cope with contingencies and emergencies, and how do they balance investments in livelihood and in social security? What patterns or trajectories can be found in the diverse ways of coping and preparing against emergencies? What rationales are behind the specific mixes of social security? In answering these questions, I first explore the concept of style. Secondly, I present a number of cases that illustrate these styles within the complexities of everyday life and illustrate the different orientations, choices and limitations of people. Thirdly, I present an overview of the major social security styles found in Krajan and how these are spread among the population. Finally, I will discuss the concept of style in a broader perspective.

 | DOI 10.1163/9789004282988_005

From an analytical perspective, social security can be viewed as a recurring tension between individual spending and collective investment. With regard to individual and household security, villagers have to choose potentially conflicting options such as investing their labour, time or capital in communal activities and mutual help, or in livelihood activities for direct consumption and personal accumulation. Investing in social relationships, arrangements and village institutions requires trust as there will only be a return on the investment if the majority of the network's members are willing to return the favour. Further, short-term interests and immediate needs contrast with long-term concerns and less certain future needs. This rises to the surface when, for instance, choosing between waged labour with direct cash returns but with only weak ties with the employer, or taking a *babun* share of a later harvest, which is less certain but involves a much closer tie with the landowner and, as such, enhances the opportunities for future support.

Investments against insecurity can be made in social relationships and networks (by gift giving, marriage and making friends) and by engaging in reciprocal mutual help relationships; or by individual and household accumulation and savings in the form of cash, cattle or gold. Accumulation and investment options are confined by practical financial and social limitations and are not simply a matter of free choice. Nevertheless, this wide range of options results in diverse, complex and, to a certain extent, unique combinations of social security arrangements. Notwithstanding this diversity, we see patterns in this complexity of options, here referred to as 'styles'.

Styles: Balancing Livelihood and Insecurity

Based on local definitions and categorizations, I distinguish four major patterns in ways of dealing with insecurities that I call 'styles of social security'. A style is a coherent and distinctive manner of acting and doing things. It can be argued that social security styles reflect solutions for making a living, about a 'good' and secure living, and about the best ways for people and households to prepare for the future. We can see a style of social security as a general mode of ordering life: a somewhat systematic and ongoing attempt to create congruence in all domains of everyday life. A social security style can thus be defined as an observable pattern in the actions and perceptions of people and households in making a living while dealing with the insecurities, threats and risks that endanger their livelihood. Analytically, it helps to explain structured heterogeneity.

In the process of trying to obtain and maintain a secure and stable livelihood, people have a specific style of doing things. These styles are the outcome of dealing with tensions, and reflect for instance contrasting orientations and practical behavioural alternatives. The first tension we see is between support, mutual help and cooperation versus self-insurance and individual accumulation. The second is the tension in economic activities between livelihood activities based on subsistence and local resources against those oriented towards the cash economy and economic opportunities beyond the village.

The styles referred to here are based on the specific knowledge and the folk concepts used by local people. Folk concepts reflect categorizations and stereotypes that exist in local society. Nevertheless, at the same time, this local knowledge and its categorizations and stereotypes are abstractions that do not fully reflect the actual hustle of activities people employ. In ordering the diversity of threats and options, the actors themselves make qualifications to indicate differences between themselves and others concerning individual orientations on livelihood, survival and willingness to support. I will now present a few cases to illustrate what this means in daily life.

Styles in Daily Life

The Norwana business family: 'making money by people'

Fifteen years ago, when the Norwana couple married, they did not have many belongings and were ranked as a poor household (*miskin*). The father of Norwana was a peddler, who had died young, and the family of Norwana's wife were former members of the village administration, but they had become impoverished after 1965. The couple did not inherit any land except for a small piece of tegal. Nowadays, they are ranked as having enough (*cukup*), able to make ends meet, organize *selamatan* when needed and contribute to those of others. Recently, they bought a small television set. 'Now, it is time to take a second wife', *Pak* Norwana joked.

Over the years, *Bu* Norwana made *besek* and secured a small income to cover basic household needs. In the early 1990s, *Pak* Norwana was involved in all kinds of agricultural work and took *babun* work on fields of large landowners. However, he did not like agricultural work that much and was always looking for other opportunities to make money. In search of work and profit, he travelled a couple of times to Bali and Madura. In Krajan, he tried to earn money by trading in *besek*, he cut forest wood illegally and worked as a carpenter. When the new road was opened, he abandoned the *besek* trade due to the increased competition from traders from town. In 1995, he was caught by the forest police while hauling lumber. The police demanded a large sum of money for his release.

He was only freed after two days and intensive mediation by the village head Bagenda. Bagenda paid the police, but did not say how much. Nowadays, *Pak* Norwana has abandoned his illegal activities and earns a living as a carpenter, cabinetmaker, speculator, trade-advisor and go-between for large traders and for Bagenda. He seeks out farmers who are willing to sell cattle, tobacco, land, trees, antiques etc. and brings them into contact with Bagenda. If a deal goes through, he receives a share of the profit; if not, he does not lose anything.

Norwana and his wife go to many *selamatan*, assist at all mutual help activities and go to many funerals (often beyond their own neighbourhood). At these occasions, his wife always donates small gifts of rice. She has got a good name for not being greedy and always willing to help. He is seen as a clever and bold man in trade, and as having many valuable connections and good relationships. In the house of the village head, he sits in the second row, is familiar with family members and is sometimes consulted by Bagenda for advice on village matters. For this reason, villagers often seek Norwana's advice and ask him to accompany them to the village head to mediate help, a loan or assistance. Also in the event of conflicts between families, heirs or in marriages, he is often asked to mediate or settle a conflict. Moreover, he has negotiated many weddings and bride prices for young people in the neighbourhood. Over recent years, his livelihood has slowly improved and he and his wife are now able to give small loans to fellow villagers who are in need of some cash. In return, those people pay interest or provide the family with firewood, timber or information on promising deals.

When a governmental aid or construction programme involves the village, Norwana is one of the first to be selected as a beneficiary. Over the years, he has received a goat, some ducks, a calf, a toolbox with implements and several jobs in infrastructure projects. He has been a foreman on an irrigation canal improvement project, the village piped-water project and on the latest road construction project. He has made good profits with the goats: when offspring came, he sold 'the whole bunch' in Bondowoso and, with the profit, bought a young heifer to be taken care of by a neighbour. The ducks have multiplied and roam around the village producing eggs that his wife sells to neighbours and local medicine traders. The offspring of the heifer have formed the beginnings of a small herd of three animals. Two were lent to families in need of money in return for small pieces of tegal and sawah. On these lands, the Norwanas now grow rice, high-yielding maize varieties for the market and tobacco. The other animal, a bull, is share-raised by a neighbour and the cash

> profits will be split evenly. Of the fifteen toolboxes donated to Krajan, only two are still owned by the original recipients, the others have been sold, stolen or lost. Norwana was one of the ones not sell his tools. With these tools, *Pak* Norwana started to make furniture and cabinets. Nowadays, he is one of the best furniture makers in Krajan and every spare day he spends making cupboards, which are popular as wedding gifts. Most of the wood he uses is illegally cut by poorer friends and neighbours and stored at the back of Bagenda's house. In this way, he uses patronage and political protection to maintain access to good and cheap wood while avoiding the risks and dangers of illegal logging.
>
> When asked about his success and his way of living, he mentions his good relationships, risk-spreading activities and the wish to make money without working as a manual labourer. 'I cannot do heavy labour and for that reason I had to do something else. My father taught me that it is better to be clever than to sweat.' By taking part in all the mutual help activities in the neighbourhood, and through his good relationships, he receives information about business opportunities. With these relationships and his rising status, he is never short of work. 'If something happens to me or my house, other villagers will help with labour, food and loans' he commented. 'Moreover, even when I get old, or become less healthy, I can continue trading.'

The Norwana family is strongly oriented towards social relationships, participation in village institutions and forms of mutual help. Nevertheless, they are primarily oriented towards cash earnings, and achieve these through social relationships and have gained access to more land by taking tegal and sawah as collateral for loans. Social relationships are important according to the Norwana family: they bring earning opportunities and goodwill.

> The Niwati money family: working alone
>
> *Pak* Niwati was born in Tamankursi as the third child of a local artist family specializing in popular Madurese theatre plays (*ludruk*) at weddings and festivals.[1] He learned the skills, songs and jokes from his childhood and accompanied some travelling players for a few months each year. After ten years of marriage, he wanted to marry a second wife in Krajan and – according to him – his first wife agreed. However, soon problems arose.

1 See for a comprehensive study on Madurese theatre and art Bouvier: Bouvier 2002.

'Don't say to me that there is no money [because all the money goes to the younger one] I don't want to be pushed aside', his first wife said. Quarrels increased and Niwati started to live with his second and younger wife, her nine-year-old son, and *Bu* Sunami, her mother. This was unacceptable to his first wife who sent the village officials to force him to return. Niwati refused and, eventually, the case was settled through a divorce leaving the house, wedding gifts and kitchen utensils to the first wife.

At the time of my first encounter with Niwati, he had just divorced was still head over heels in love with his second wife and quite optimistic about his future. He and his new wife had no sawah (ten years earlier her sawah had been washed away by a flood) and the income from his work as a *ludruk* player had dwindled because he did not want to travel around all the time. He hoped to find a trade, or other work to care for his new family and planned to rent sawah, to grow tobacco and to work together with his wife as wage labourers. However, finding work was not easy, as the divorce had added to his bad reputation. 'We will do it alone', he said angrily. 'We don't need other people to make a living. The best thing is to eat less for a while.'

In the decade after, they were not successful. Shifting to another profession turned out to be difficult. Tobacco yields were low and of poor quality and with a dubious reputation as a *ludruk* player - not many people offered him work. When I searched for the couple again, they had left for South Kalimantan to work in the oil palm plantations to repay the debts Niwati had made in his attempts to grow tobacco and establish a trade. The child of Niwati's wife stayed at home with her mother and I interviewed her mother instead. Since their departure, Bu Sunami had not received any messages or money. Unfortunately, she fell ill for more than 40 days and was no longer able to earn anything. Her grandchild, being too young to work, could only earn a little by cutting and selling grass and cattle fodder to others. *Bu* Sunami said: 'I can live on rice with salt, but even for that we have no money.' Eventually, she sold her four chickens one by one to buy food, and some of her neighbours took her for treatment to the local health post and she received some injections. She then felt slightly better and could occasionally help neighbours with light work such as pounding and sifting coffee beans, cleaning rice, or peeling maize, in return for a meal or some money, rice, or salt. Alternative work opportunities are not available, and she is seldom asked to help with transplanting rice by the large landowners in the neighbourhood. 'I am too old now for that work, nobody wants me', she sighs. 'If I need rice, I borrow from the shop or from neighbours, but the debt already

> exceeds seven kilos and, if they know that I cannot repay, they will not allow me to borrow again.'

The complicated history of his marriage in Krajan gave Niwati a bad start in his new neighbourhood (Dluwang). Moreover, he first adopted a haughty position of not being interested in his neighbours, exchanges and mutual help. 'I will take care of my new family, not of my new neighbours', he said at the beginning. Conversely, his neighbours were not very willing to support him when he was in need of help later.

I have never been able to trace this family in Kalimantan and it must be doubted whether they were successful there given that many Madurese migrants have difficulties in making ends meet (see Chapter 6). They never send money back. So far, most Krajan migrants searching for work in Kalimantan have not done very well. Those who roam around seeking temporary work in slack periods in the region do sometimes have more luck. However by no means all of them, as the next case illustrates.

> Ernawa: opting out
>
> Pak Ernawa lives in the hamlet of Mengkuara and belongs to the category of the poor (*miskin*). He has no land but cares for two cows of an uncle. In Mengkuara, opportunities to work in return for a share of the harvest are few, so he went to work in Jember with a group of workers to cut sugar cane. While away, his wife and children cared for the cows. Wages in sugar cane fields are very low although food is provided for the labourer. If careful, Ernawa can save a little each day, but sometimes there is no work and savings are used to eat, smoke and roam around in search of other work. The first time when he returned home, he was successful and bought 15 kg of rice and a radio from his wages. After a month, he went away again because the food stocks in the house were already finished. This time he was not so lucky. His clothes, which he had put at the side of the field, caught fire during a cane fire. It was not only a set of clothes he lost, but also money. He had put his savings (after 13 days amounting to Rp 100,000) and his identity card in his sleeves. A friend from Krajan lent him a shirt and some money for the trip home.

The families of Norwana, Niwati and Ernawa are poor and primarily oriented towards cash incomes and wage labour. They prefer to work for a wage, but they also see very few opportunities to make a living in another way. Niwati and Ernawa do not invest much in mutual relationships in the village world of

Krajan and, for several reasons, they as far as possible make their own living. Ernawa is an exception in that he is a member of a group of young villagers who roam the region in search of work. When at home, they spent their days gathering cattle fodder, with occasional jobs and by playing cards together. When money and credit opportunities are finished, they depart for job-hunting again. The leaders of such bands of 'wage hunters and gatherers' (Breman 1994) have useful contacts and know the places to find work. Some work in sugar cane or rice harvesting in the lowlands of Besuki, Bondowoso, or Situbondo. Others go to Madura, work as loggers or in the coffee plantations and vegetable farms at Ijen plateau, southeast of Bondowoso. Since the crisis at the turn of the millennium, such working groups increasingly go to Kalimantan to work on oil palm plantations, in illegal coalmines, in brickmaking kilns and in stone quarries (see Chapter 6). Membership of such a labour-searching gang offers close contacts and the security of a peer group. However, it makes establishing and engaging in mutual exchange relationships in the village difficult.

> The Horati family: high ambitions, low contributions
>
> *Pak* Horati has no land and works as a jack-of-all-trades, a craftsman and occasionally as a *gamelan* musician. Both his, and his wife's, parents were labourers with little or no land. They are ranked as not having enough (*kurang*). In the Suharto years, he was well known for his lobbying activities on behalf of the governmental party Golkar, and Bagenda's faction during village head elections. Before the elections of 1999, he first continued to work for Golkar and was paid for these activities but, later, when he saw that most villagers were favouring Megawati's PDI-P, he switched to that party. He often goes to *selamatan* and weddings of other people to make music. As a musician, he seldomly pays *sumbangan* and gets to know many people. He is quite ambitious, and perceives himself as clever and progressive, able to rise from rags to riches. In the eyes of others, he has not yet made it because he has not saved any money and working as a musician does not bring much status. Further, he is known as a notorious gambler.
>
> The wedding of his first son in 1998 was planned as a big event, where he could show the world that he was able to achieve and organize something. He borrowed money from the village head and other political friends, and distributed many invitations around the whole sub-district. Each invitation contained a pack of cigarettes with a written announcement of the wedding, the place, the date and the kind of entertainments. He bought about a hundred packs of expensive Gudang Garam *kretek*

cigarettes and more than five hundred cheaper Grendel packs. Through the invitations, the expensive packs were given to wealthy and important people and the cheaper ones to poorer families. If people accepted the pack, and people usually do, they were expected to come to the wedding and to contribute.

He openly said that he had invited many rich people on purpose. By inviting many important and rich people, he hoped to receive large donations. To further stimulate more money to be given, all wedding gifts were to be announced by a speaker (which is not common in Krajan but is usual practice in neighbouring Tamankursi). Simultaneously, he and his wife tried to keep costs low by asking neighbours, relatives and friends to cook and to assist in all the other kinds of work at the wedding. *Ludruk* friends and fellow musicians played for free 'to help him out',

The wedding was a disappointment as many of the important invitees did not come. Even many fellow villagers did not show up. He had clearly boasted too much, and the villagers gossiped for days about his impious intention to make a profit out of the feast. Some decided simply not to come for this reason, others felt free to donate only small amounts. Unfortunately for Horati, many people came with presents in kind and villagers faced problems in obtaining cash. After the wedding, Horati sold most of these gifts to repay his debts. After long calculations it turned out that he had made some financial profit, but much less than he had expected.[2] His aim to make a big smash and gain some prestige had clearly failed.

Villagers reacted resentful. *Pak* Horati had tried to use arrangements and the institutions of *sumbangan*, neighbourly assistance and mutual help to give a huge wedding, much grander than his status would require or even allow. The returns however were disappointing and he failed to accumulate wealth or status by free-riding local social security. Misuse is clearly punished and reciprocity a guiding principle. Horati had never given much to others and had not accumulated credit.

Horati is widely known as frugal, not donating much at *selamatan* and weddings, nor quick to join in mutual help arrangements with others. His wedding

2 We laboriously noted down all the expenses, visitors and gifts during the three days of the wedding. Weeks before the wedding, we started to write down all Horati's expenses and during the three days of partying, we calculated all. Many of the *sumbangan* in kind, such as cookies and snacks, were put on the tables and served right away to the visitors, other things were left for the married couple, so, only a part of the gifts could be sold. Overall, his net cash profit was slightly more than Rp 1 million where he had hoped to earn at least Rp 5 million.

strategy was too clever and too cheap in the eyes of many wealthy Krajan villagers and therefore they donated relatively little. The large wedding impressed poorer villagers and neighbours, but these could not afford to donate much. Moreover, he was not regarded as a dependable investment, as he does not own cattle or land and prefers to roam around, searching for contracts to play music, for radios to repair, a good bet, or for work in woodcarving or house construction. Such activities do not make him a reliable investment and it is not likely that he will become more reliable in the future. Another example of a frugal and stingy villagers, albeit much richer, is the Patik family know from the introduction of this book.

'Scrooge' Patik: rich and stingy

Patik was born into a relatively poor family with many children, but has managed to become one of the ten richest villagers in Krajan. He has worked hard and managed to save and to invest in local resources such as land, cattle, trees and bamboo. Generally, he is called the '*kreket*' (Scrooge) of Krajan. A son of Satrawi once commented: 'If we need help or loans, *Pak* Patik never has money, but if we have a cow, or land to sell, he is always willing to buy; 'to solve our problems' he hypocritically says.'

In the perceptions of both *Pak* and *Bu* Patik and their two adult children, they acquired their wealth by working hard and spending little. 'Especially in the first years of marriage, we tried to eat very carefully, live very simply and spend as little as possible' Bu Patik said. They never contributed much to *selamatan*, funerals or weddings – often *Pak* Patik did not go at all. He could sustain basic relationships by sending his wife who was clever in making cookies and gifts, thus saving costs. If he was explicitly invited and had to go, he contributed as little as possible. 'On the other hand, these occasions were moments when our children and ourselves could have decent meals, and we always took our children along to *selamatan* and weddings. In this way, we earned our contribution back right away.' Only in the case of close relatives, he would had to contribute significant amounts. The daughter of the Patiks (married and living away) recalls these *selamatan* as big parties. 'There was never something special at our home. For me, these *selamatan* were great moments and I was nervous the whole day. Finally, when it was time to go to at these parties, I could not eat much and never tried all the delicious food, as I was too afraid, nervous and shy.' She explains her Spartan upbringing: 'My father was very hard and strict not allowing anything to be wasted. We never ate white rice, never got money for sweets or

> snacks and were never allowed to buy something nice for ourselves even when there was money.' Her mother always supported her husband in his thriftiness and became well known for saying: 'Don't spend; let's buy a calf first.' However, even when they had acquired many cattle, their simple lifestyle continued. Once, when the daughter was 5 years old, she was so undernourished that she lost all her hair and people thought she was going to die. 'Neighbours told me I was a very ugly child at that time and that my mother told others to take me for free, as she wanted to get rid of me.' Because of such statements, her grandfather got angry with Bu Patik and took her to live with him and his wife. There, she slowly recovered and felt much better. 'Although I returned home when I recovered, I often went to my grandparents when I felt miserable, I helped them with small tasks and there I received care, attention and proper meals.'
>
> *Pak* Patik thinks positively about the future, and sees himself in clover now: 'I own a number of bamboo bushes in various fields. I bought them cheap and harvest a few stalks to keep the bushes strong and healthy. If I become old and have given away my sawah to my children, I will still be able to sell bamboo canes every now and then to drink coffee in the coffeestall. I will not be dependent on anyone.' His orientation on helping others is very clear, he says: 'My poor friends and neighbours are often helped by my wife who offers them small loans of rice. Those who raise bullocks for me, I sometimes give a cash advance or a loan if needed, as it will be returned. Other people have to work for themselves; they can never borrow any money from me.'

The Patik family is one of the clearest examples of *orang pelit* in Krajan. They are extremely cautious in generating their own livelihood, and share and cooperate as little as possible with fellow villagers. This has helped them to accumulate. They save money by staying away from expensive social obligations and do not contribute much to arrangements for mutual help. Today, they are self-prepared for hard times.

> Supandi: hoping to save his cattle[3]
>
> The Supandi family is much poorer than the Patik family and ranked as *kurang*, but they are also referred to as stingy or '*kreket*'. They own some land and care for a few heads of cattle of larger landowners. In the previous two years, they have been able to get two calves of their own. The

3 *'semoga tidak sampai jual sapi'.*

> husband and wife describe them as their 'hope for the future'. Moreover, they claim to be trying to be self-sufficient and acquire more cattle and improve their cash income in the coming years.
>
> When I visited them again later, their strategy showed as having been quite successful. He was able to raise the two cows and train them for ploughing; she had established a small shop and saved some ten grams of gold. 'If friends or neighbours come to borrow money, or buy on credit, I always refuse and answer that I have no spare money and have a debt myself at the shop in Bondowoso. Now they know, they seldom ask.' However, when they life came under severe stress due to a tobacco harvest failure, the death and costly burial of the wife's mother, and the 1998 economic crisis, they were forced to increase their debts. 'God willing, I will not have to sell my cows', Pak Supandi said. 'Without cattle I cannot borrow, I cannot work and I cannot make a successful living. I am a real Madurese you know, without cattle I am nothing because I am not used to getting friends to help me.' They decided to sell the wife's gold to cover the costs of the tobacco harvest failure.

For years, he and his wife had tried to save and accumulate wealth by remaining as independent as possible. He avoided going to *selamatan*, weddings and mutual help activities whenever he could, and his wife paid over only the essential tributes at these occasions. In his view, he had never invested much in friends and social relationships, and his wife had maintained only a few contacts so as to be able to accumulate some money. However, due to the relatively poor subsistence basis of the household, they have not been able to save enough to be totally insured against misfortune. Now that they are in trouble, they cannot expect much help from neighbours and friends as they have never invested much in them. *Pak* Supandi fears the sale of his cattle that are not only his savings, but also most of his working capital.

Also those who do invest in social relationships do not always get the desired returns. The Satrawi family offers an example of people who value close social relationships, subsistence production and village solidarity. Here we return to the story of the Satrawi family first described in the introduction to this book.

> The Satrawi family: poor but respectable
>
> The Satrawi family is widely known in Krajan as good people who have encountered many misfortunes in their lives. They were born to relatively wealthy families and their futures looked bright enough. Their fields produced more rice than they needed, and they employed many labourers in

> return for a meal and a share of the harvest. They had status and prestige and lived according to the expectations of their class. However, their wealth and status became a burden. Meals, *selamatan*, and the weddings of their children were abundant, expensive and well attended. They never failed to contribute *sumbangan* to others even if those families were poor and would never be able to return the favour. Although their wealth did not increase, their reputation of being good and generous spread across Krajan. The Satrawis once said: 'If we are good to others when they need it, others will be good to us when we need it.' On another occasion, *Pak* Satrawi explained further: 'My parents always did it this way, and my father taught me to be a good and responsible villager, always ready to share and to help. That's why I try to follow his example. My parents were good and respected people.'
>
> In the first years after their marriage, the parents of the Satrawi's were active and organized large *selamatan*. Years later, when their parents had died, things started to decline in the house of Satrawi. Due to a chain of misfortunes and tragedies, their wealth decreased and their incomes declined. As a result, at their *selamatan*, guests were fewer and *sumbangan* contributions dropped considerably. Moreover, many of their previous friends had died, migrated or become impoverished, and not able to return the help that the Satrawis had provided earlier.
>
> In short, their investments were not returned, and reciprocal arrangements of support did not help them through these difficult periods. They needed to sell land and, gradually, they lost all their property and became one of the poorest families in the neighbourhood. For a couple of years, they have been ranked as *miskin*. For the wedding of their third child, their last plot of land had to be pawned to pay for wedding gifts, and they cut down their coconut trees in their garden in order to obtain some money for new clothes to wear at the wedding. After the wedding, they were regularly short of food, and Pak Satrawi was sometimes not even able to buy paper to wrap his cigarettes.

The Satrawi family offers a good example of villagers who invested in social relationships and mutual help, but who did not get back as much as they ever invested in it (see Chapter 3). Organizing large weddings and rituals proved not to be a solid strategy to insure against severe setbacks in livelihood because. The problem is that in their present poverty, people do not think it to be worthwhile to provide large contributions as even their children will never be able to repay them as investments in local forms of social security tend to be 'upward looking', not 'downwardly protective'. Fewer people turn up at their *selamatan* and their social network has shrunk.

Are social relationships meaningless? Not at all. Although their living standards have fallen drastically and the returns on former investments have been disappointing, they still enjoy some status in the village and their extensive network is of use. *Pak* Satrawi is often invited to pray at *selamatan*, freeing his wife and himself from the obligation of providing a contribution. Further, he is known as a good man because he always joins in *selamatan*, *gotong royong*, house building and funerals and helps with the work. His good reputation and sociability helps him to find work in the fields of others and in getting share tenancy contracts. Regularly, when their food stocks are used up, they go to some of their wealthier neighbours and their patron Patik's family to do some odd jobs or occasional work and receive a meal or some rice. Even the Patik family never refuses them a meal on such occasions, even though they complain to others afterwards about the Satrawis chronic lack of money. 'Even if they have money, they cannot keep it and spend it right away'.

Perhaps the Satrawis have not 'chosen' the best style if viewed from an economic angle since they have lost all their land, but at least they still eat due to their former relationships. To be able to compare and evaluate the different styles, we first need to know more about their characteristics. Below an overview and outline of styles in Krajan is provided.

Styles in Krajan

These cases show that people can benefit and receive some assistance from existing networks such as kin, neighbours and village institutions; and that they do make choices within boundaries and opportunities. Often, this help from others is inspired by moral considerations or mutual interest, and reciprocity is important, although not always reliable and never enough. At the same time, the examples show that villagers actively make choices and have some coherence in their ways of living in order to enhance their livelihood and to obtain protection in times of need. Significantly, families of equal class clearly make different choices reflecting their different orientations on the future.

The cases also show that the arrangements that structure and enable human action as well as the strategies that villagers employ cannot be separated. The two dimensions of local social security action are intertwined and presuppose each other. The cases also show that the distinction between livelihood and social security is difficult to establish. A strategy that seems to be oriented towards earning money can turn out to be one that generates help in times of need.

Nicknames and Folk Concepts

In Krajan, villagers often use nicknames and categorise fellow villagers based on their values, orientations and practices towards livelihood and social security. Examples of these locally used categories are 'enterprising people' (*orang bisnis*), 'money people' (*orang duit*), 'stingy people' (*orang pelit*), and the 'traditional or naive people' (*orang asli* or *lugu*).[4] 'Money people' for instance are those who prefer to earn cash and depend on the opportunities of the cash economy for securing their livelihood. 'Stingy people' are those who try to benefit from the support given through the old mutual exchange economy, minimise investments, and ignore as far as possible the claims of others in reciprocal relationships.

Behind these nicknames lie distinguishable patterns that I label styles. These styles are based on empirical distinctions in the everyday activities which people employ. Styles are the outcome of tensions between different interests, needs and priorities that calibrate the tensions between mutual help and self-insurance and between economic activities based on share tenancy and local village resources as against the opportunities of the cash economy and the outside world. The categorisation of styles is a sliding scale. Some families are much more 'typical' than others. The majority of villagers can be classified as being attached to a predominant style by their orientation and choice from the available repertoire, but they sometimes intermingle the various options from other styles. Moreover, having a certain style is not always that conscious a decision, and can be habitual, customary, traditional and safe. If it has proved, by chance, to be a successful one, then actions reveal the style and reproduce it.

I distinguish four major styles in Krajan based on qualifications made concerning the surveyed families. While carrying out my survey and during the interviews, I asked, both directly and indirectly, about orientations in life, means of livelihood, the rationale behind choices and about hopes and fears concerning the future. During these interviews, I also tried to get informants to

---

4 In the village, sometimes Indonesian and sometimes Madurese words were used. Examples of Madurese words are: *oreng bisnis, oreng pesse, oreng cerre* or *kreket,* and *oreng esak.* Not all of these qualifications are used equally frequently. *Oreng kreket, pesse,* and *bisnis* are the most commonly used, for *orang esak* also Indonesian words such as *lugu* and *asli,* are used. In the text, I will use the most appropriate Indonesian words: *bisnis, duit, pelit,* and *lugu.* (The *orang esak* are often called *orang asli, orang lugu,* or simply *orang baik,* I use the word *lugu* as a style indicator as *lugu* expresses both the connotation of original or traditional people and of good, rustic, natural, or country people and it has a connotation of *naivité*). *Orang lugu* are, in this understanding, the good, but sometimes naive people from the past who represent and reproduce the good village life and its inherent communal values Barlocco (2010:405).

reflect retrospectively on the choices they had made and on the differences between them and others regarding livelihood, resource use and mutual help. Outside the survey, I collected nicknames, qualifications and categorizations in the village about these families.

The nicknames, which can be regarded as folk concepts, are interesting in that they indicate an awareness of differences in livelihood orientations and sharing attitudes. Being *lugu* has both a morally superior and a somewhat backward and naive connotation. Morally, they are seen as good people, who are believed to be the true followers of traditional values of support, exchange and reciprocity. However, economically, *orang lugu* are seen as somewhat naive and backward. Those who are oriented towards wage labour, trade and beneficial economic opportunities are seen as much more successful. This successfulness, however, can change over time, depending on climatic conditions, market prices and political-economic developments. After analysing the survey, I found that these patterns made sense empirically.

Folk concepts are indicative of patterns in the diversity and reflect a more or less coherent way in which people try to make a living and organize their social security mix. These 'modes of ordering' reflect their attitudes and expectations of protection, effectiveness and stability in their livelihood. They are to a great degree ideal types and metaphors for different patterns of social security, based on distinctions made by the actors themselves. At the village level, these styles are based upon different responses of actors to insecurities that arise from the agro-ecological, economic, political and social contexts.

Dilemma's of Sharing and Accumulation

Villagers' styles also reflect different value orientations toward the dilemma of sharing and accumulation. We can put these value orientations on two axes, the first axis formed by incomes from subsistence production and local resources on the one hand versus cash incomes and outside opportunities on the other. The second axis shows the orientation towards individual accumulation versus reciprocity and cooperation. We thus arrive at four types of villagers who follow different styles in achieving a secure and viable livelihood (see Table 5).

In analysing this information and other data about savings, the number of contributions (gifts, help, support and labour) both to and from others, debts and savings, etc. I put each household on two axes and positioned them according to: (1) their orientation towards support and mutual help as against being self-insured; and (2) in the production sphere to their orientation towards cash incomes and the outside economy as against subsistence and the local economy. Nearly all the families could be ranked according to these orientations:

TABLE 5 *Value orientations and styles*

Orientation on	Subsistence	Cash
Reciprocity	*Orang Lugu*	*Orang Bisnis*
Accumulation	*Orang Pelit*	*Orang Duit*

some very clearly belonged to an identified style; others were less clear as they combined several different aspects in their lives, or because the orientations of the husband and wife were not aligned. The statements made by the people themselves were important to link people to a certain style. As a second step, I checked their statements with their actual practices as reflected in types of income and property, number of occasions they gave help or contributed to labour activities and contributions to *selamatan* and *sumbangan* (see Table 6).

There were a few cases in where I could not classify people at all. Some of the destitute and pitiful people of Krajan were effectively excluded from any style, as they were so poor that they had little choice other than to eat carefully and adjust to their poverty.[5] Despite this, even among the destitute, differences in orientations and alternative patterns could be observed. Another odd category is the so-called wayward people (*orang nakal*). These are mostly young men who deliberately take huge risks by heavy gambling, womanizing and stealing, and whose behaviour can be perceived as a style in itself, or rather a contrary style with people rejecting the established ways of earning a livelihood and investing in the social security of mainstream society. The *orang nakal* are described in the next chapter.

The most important feature of styles is that they do not always coincide with the socio-economic categories of wealthy or poor and provide an addition to social class analysis such as described in Chapter 2 and static

5 *Orang kasihan* live in a state of constant social insecurity and have few options left. Some of these people do not really follow a style as they are socially excluded from all the styles. They cannot invest in social relationships, are not acceptable as wage labourers, and do not own anything to be coveted upon (see also Singarimbun and Penny 1973). Although they are entitled to help, since they are to be pitied (*kasihan*), they are often not helped, do not have caring relatives or neighbours and are often neglected by aid programme. Among these people are commonly widows, the old and very poor, chronically ill and other vulnerable people without caring relatives or productive assets. *Orang kasihan* are relatively invisible in village life and even neighbours sometimes do not know them very well. In Krajan, at least fifty widows – sometimes with grandchildren – lived in very difficult circumstances.

TABLE 6 *Styles and orientations*

			Styles			
			'Enterprising people' (*orang bisnis*)	'Money people' (*orang duit*)	'Stingy people' (*orang pelit*)	'Village people' (*orang lugu*)
Orientation	Livelihood	Money, wage, cash, outside	+	+	–	–
		Subsistence incomes	–	–	+	+
	Social Security	Support and mutual help	+	–	–	+
		Self-insurance	–	+	+	–

understandings of poverty. Both poor and rich villagers can share similar orientations towards livelihood and thus adopt security and follow the same style. In all the styles identified both poor and richer villagers are present, although not always in similar numbers. In general, upper class villagers are more to be found among the *orang pelit*.[6] Obviously, one needs at least some assets, to be oriented towards on self-support and greed. Most of the village poor are found among the *duit* and the *lugu* categories. Some of the poor live from waged labour (and hope for stability based on and direct incomes from regular employment) and rely on incomes in cash. Others live mainly on subsistence incomes from local resources; putting their hopes on village institutions and social relationships for protection and social assistance. In Table 7, the spread of the styles across the Krajan population is given as well as the relative number of wealthy and poor as a percentage of the total in each style. The most common style in Krajan is that of the village people (*lugu*), followed by 'money people' (*duit*) and 'enterprising people' (*bisnis*). 'Stingy people' (*pelit*) are least.

It is also interesting to look at the age distinctions among styles. The average age of *bisnis* people is 42, of *duit* people 39, of the *pelit* 38, and of *lugu* 45. The average age of all the interviewed people is 42. The differences are relatively small, but the traditional, or good, village people (*orang lugu*) are

6 When I speak of rich (wealthy) and poor here I mean, by rich, the categories of rich, enough, and just enough. The poor are the not enough, the less, and the destitute categories.

TABLE 7 *Styles and social classes in Krajan (in percentages)*

Style Social class	'Enterprising people' (*orang bisnis*)	'Money people' (*orang duit*)	'Stingy people' (*orang pelit*)	'Village people' (*orang lugu*)
Upper and middle classes	73	41	36	23
Lower classes	25	59	64	77
Total population	13	25	36	26

more often found among the elderly. As one gets older, less can be expected from wage labour, or from being stingy. However, this does not mean that their style is going to become extinguish or is doomed to vanish. A large percentage of the younger villagers are interested in waged labour or in being enterprising, although the enterprising style includes many older villagers who use their capital now that they are older and less inclined to do heavy labour on a daily basis. Also a number of unmarried young people can be found in this style who – often with capital from their parents – wish to make a living by trade, but remain embedded in closely knit networks of support and mutual help. Often, these attempts are not successful and lead to a change of style later. The characteristics of the orientations underlying the various styles are described in more detail below.

Styles in Krajan

'Entrepreneurial People' (*Orang Bisnis*)

'Entrepreneurs' (*orang bisnis*) are oriented towards the cash economy and look for opportunities outside the village to make money. They focus on social relationships to maintain trading opportunities and long-term protection. For their livelihood, they depend primarily on incomes from trade, peddling, cash crop production (for instance tobacco) or running a small shop or coffee stall. For richer and poorer *orang bisnis* alike, incomes are not only generated by using local resources but also by using outside opportunities, such as government or bank-related credit facilities, contacts with traders operating on a regional or national scale, and goods from markets and shops in Bondowoso, Besuki and Pakem. Also in consumption patterns, they are oriented towards new goods and status products from outside the village, such as radios, televisions, mobile phones, motorbikes and jeans.

As trade and business opportunities in Krajan go together with social ties, social relationships are crucial for the *orang bisnis*. In order to be successful in business, they need to invest in and maintain reliable relationships with customers, traders, suppliers and politicians. This network of social relationships provides them with goods, credit and information about good deals, prices, and the credit worthiness of suppliers and customers. These networks usually extend beyond the small world of the village. Access to information is very important as the threats and risks in trading are manifold. Profits and prices can fluctuate, stocks can decay, crops can fail and the risk of default by customers is substantial. For these reasons, *orang bisnis* need these networks not only to generate profit, but also for their protection, support and assistance in times of difficulty. They realize that these networks need to be maintained for the future. Difficulties in life and urgent cash shortages are often solved by taking loans (often from outside the village), by selling or pawning assets, or by asking for the support of friends, trading partners, or political patrons. Moreover, most of them say they are keen on maintaining a reputation as a good village member. They are frequent visitors to weddings, parties and funerals; ready to share and contribute in an attempt to bind people and maintain reputations. As most *orang bisnis* keep ties with the village, they often operate in groups, share profits and are cooperative. Some small cattle traders, without sufficient training capital, work together to buy and sell cattle. In this way, they are able to pool risks and accumulate cash. Others engage in alliances with retail traders from outside the village and obtain credit. It is especially the *orang bisnis* who tend to be the most active in mutual saving and credit groups (*arisan*).

Poorer *orang bisnis* include small traders and peddlers selling chickens, eggs, dried fish, sugar, wood, local medication (*jamu*) and those who run small shops or coffee or food stalls from their homes. Among these people, daily incomes are just enough to make ends meet, and are spent immediately on basic needs. When things go wrong, they rely heavily on the social relationships that they had built up.

'Money People' (*Orang Duit*)

The *orang duit* ('money people') in Krajan are also oriented towards cash incomes, but differ from *orang bisnis* in their orientation towards social relationships, sharing, support and cooperation in that they exhibit a general reluctance to contribute to social village arrangements and institutions. As a consequence, they do not expect much help and support in times of need. They rely primarily on cash for survival and livelihood, and hope to be able to earn money until their children are old enough to support them. They try to be, and remain, independent and self-prepared.

Although, naturally, everybody in Krajan would like to have and earn cash, this group is specifically oriented towards fixed and direct incomes such as incomes from wage labour – sometimes outside the village – and they try to ensure a stable livelihood by investing and combining different sources of cash incomes such as waged labour, political activities and a profession. Their cash incomes, their untied labour relationships and opportunities beyond the village economy make them flexible and relatively independent of village institutions.

The *orang duit* include many poor wage labourers who work in Krajan or who are constantly in search of work in the East Java region, in agriculture on Madura, or as street peddlers in Bali. Their cash incomes are their main basis for coping with difficulties in life, and as long as cash incomes are relatively stable, regular and reliable, they are doing well, meeting these wishes. The difference with the 'entrepreneurial people' is that this group tries to earn money wherever possible, and are not very inclined to invest in relationships of mutual help and exchange and do not engage in patron-client bonds in the village. They were doing relatively well during the second half of the New Order period and acquired higher esteem and status than the *orang lugu,* who depended basically on wages in kind.

Care and support for the *orang duit* is mainly organized within the household, the nuclear family, or within peer groups of fellow workers. Elderly, handicapped and ill people are generally cared for by family members. Difficulties in life and urgent cash shortages are often solved by taking out loans, either from inside or outside the village, by selling or pawning assets, or by asking for support from fellow workers or within peer groups. Also as part of this style, villagers having surplus money on a regular basis, may engage in saving and credit arrangements, such as *simpan-pinjam* and *arisan.* Examples of richer *orang duit* in the village are relatively scarce. Examples include teachers living from their salaries, certain village officials, and *rentenir,* people living from their pensions, or interests on property or loans. It should be mentioned, however, that the crisis did change the economic situation of this group quite substantially.

'Stingy People' (*Orang Pelit*)

'Stingy people' (*orang pelit*), conversely, are oriented towards the village economy and its resources of land, cattle and labour. They try to accumulate wealth based on local resources and make use of village institutions and arrangements, while they try to avoid the social pressures of sharing, redistribution, care and mutual help, and so keep costs as low as possible. According to other villagers, 'stingy people' are those who want to profit as much as possible from the social security benefits of the older cultural arrangements, but who do not want to invest much in them. In general, *orang pelit* share the opinion that not much can be expected from village institutions, such as mutual help, and that it is better to insure and prepare oneself. In their view, *sumbangan* is often seen as a must, a money-consuming necessity, rather than as a way of improving future support, investment or social capital. They are wary of redistributing their wealth, even if they have plenty of money, rice or assets available. Family labour, and sometimes bonded labour, plays an important role in their way of making a living. They prefer to invest in their own assets such as cattle and land rather than in other people.

Although there have always been stingy villagers, this group includes many younger as well as richer families, and families on the way to becoming richer. Moreover, it seems this style has gained popularity in recent decades. It offers the opportunity to ignore the claims of others while still obtaining some benefits of the ritual exchange economy and related institutions and arrangements of mutual help and exchange. Later, in old age, some of these people may shift their orientation towards a more reciprocal attitude although they do try to prepare themselves for old age.

The poorer stingy people combine wages in kind from *babun* and cattle raising, with waged labour, making *besek* and other handicrafts. They visit as many parties, funerals, and *selamatan* as possible, as these occasions include free meals for low costs since poor villagers are not expected to contribute much to these parties. In times of need, they beg from richer villagers and cling to, and emphasize, traditional village values of sharing and redistribution in order to get some support. This support is often not that substantial, since they never contributed much to others, but they might receive a free meal, some rice or a small gift of money. In this respect 'stingy people' are the free riders of the village social security system with their attitude of benefiting from, rather than investing in, reciprocity, sharing, cooperation and the village community at large.

'Village People' (*Orang Lugu*)

The 'village people', or 'traditional' or 'good people' (*orang lugu*), are oriented towards traditional village values of exchange, and are active in *sumbangan*, *selamatan*, rotating labour arrangements and mutual help. They clearly put their hopes on obtaining help and support from village institutions and in the form of mutual help if they are in need. Often, they have a strong orientation towards the local non-cash economy. If involved in cash-earning activities, they see this as subsidiary to their other activities. Work and care-taking activities are not only a way to earn an income or to obtain food, these are also ways to engage in and maintain a relationship.

These villagers frequently have conservative ideas concerning out-marriage of children, the village hierarchy, and norms and values of sharing, gift-giving, labour relationships and exchange. Giving large *selamatan* and owning land, traditional rice varieties and cattle offers status and security (both spiritual and practical); and organizing these activities demands extended relationships.

Using social relationships and mobilizing networks of exchange in the first instance, constitute the livelihood of *orang lugu*. Poorer people who adopt this style try to gain access to work, status and protection by engaging in social (patron-client) relationships. Richer people use their networks, land and cattle to bind workers to them. The poor *orang lugu* anticipate mutual help, emotional support and ritual gifts (*sumbangan*) from fellow 'traditional' people and from the large landowner for whom they work. Increasingly, during recent decades, this style has declined, and lost much of its previous status during the New Order regime, as new forms of status and upward mobility than *selamatan*, cows and land became available. Nowadays, a relatively large proportion of the people adopting this style are the poorer and older people of the village.

'Religious' and 'Wayward People'

Alongside these four major social security styles, some sub-styles can be distinguished. One of these subgroups is the 'religious people': *orang muslim* or *orang santri*. Being – or pretending to be – a pious Muslim can be beneficial in achieving a reasonable position in society as well as entitlements. A few religious teachers and local leaders (*kiai*) in Krajan earn a solid income out of religious functions and combine it with farming and trade, while they are ensured of support in difficult times. In the way they earn a living, they show similarities with *orang bisnis* and they have been ranked as such.

Not all styles are oriented towards a sustainable livelihood, or long-term social security. In Krajan, there is a category of villagers who deliberately take and combine risks. Locally, the term '*orang nakal*' is used for these people. It means something along the lines of wayward, madcap or naughty people. The *orang nakal* are people who do not follow the mainstream norms and values of society, are ignorant of livelihood security, and deliberately take huge risks. Wayward people are not specifically outcasts, but excessive risk-takers who live dangerously such as gamblers, womanizers and vagabonds. Although many other villagers take risks in business, agriculture, or in other spheres of life, usually these risks are taken within a context of security. These are seen as acceptable risks, which can be taken after a certain level of subsistence has been reached. The orientations of the *orang nakal* are different. They seem not to care about the risks of losing their livelihood and the things that they have, and are more interested in the chances of winning something and for the thrill of the day. In the next chapter, a more comprehensive description of the *orang nakal* will be given.

Deliberate risk taking is not an exception in peasant societies, but an attractive style for some villagers who search for an alternative to complying with the village norms and the social pressure urging large investments in social security and reciprocal relationships. Probably, this lifestyle is less risky than it appears since partners in the household and social relations in society can sometimes still offer a minimal safety net. Some of those who lost rice fields, cattle, and their family through heavy gambling, switched to another style and found a place in society by becoming a client, or a labourer, on their former land. Others continue to live dangerously and roam the region in search of work and fun, often joining Madurese theatre groups (*ludruk*) and only return to their house, parents or relatives when in need of a meal or a loan. Many of the *orang nakal* play an important role in demonstrations and political campaigns during election times.

Concluding Remarks

Many studies on local arrangements, institutions and mechanisms of support and assistance to other community members in times of need share a common perspective in that they are oriented towards the supply-side and tend to focus on *institutions of support*. There is another group of studies oriented towards the demand-side of support and on individual strategies. It is these individual efforts to make a living and safeguard security that have been at the heart of a range of studies focussing on people's *strategies* to achieve support and security.

The two views are usually presented as mutually exclusive: it is either communal institutions and village structures, based on long-term bonds of reciprocity, which provide support in times of need, or it is individuals designing strategies to cover their own risks through maximizing profit and sharing among only a small groups of social equals. In practice, the structural and the strategic views can be highly complementary because they address two sides of the same coin, albeit from different perspectives. Social structures do not determine individual behaviour, but they do shape it and set limits: individuals cannot act in a social void and have to take contexts, structures and institutions into account. Moreover, depending on the specific conditions, there may be more, or less, room for individual efforts and strategies to further one's own interests. In my fieldwork, I tried to ascertain both the role of communal institutions in providing social security, and the room that individuals have, and use, to achieve such security.

The conclusion is that it pays to look at common patterns of protection, coping and security strategies. People do not randomly invest in reciprocal relationships, or opportunities for social security, but make specific and meaningful combinations that reflect their orientations, perceptions and assessments, as well as their capabilities and resources. Further, not every combination is open to everyone. Wealthy people can largely rely on their own resources and networks, while their less fortunate neighbours must invest heavily in mutual support and care in order to be eligible for social security when they are in need.

These combinations can also be gender-specific since men and women can have different orientations and resources. Often, women are much more concerned than their husbands with household food security and livelihood protection. These differences may be smoothed out at the household level as most activities require the involvement of both husband and wife. At the village level, there is therefore a large heterogeneity in strategies and arrangements for social security. These stem from the differential responses of actors to the ecological, economic, political and social insecurities that they face and the varying resources to which they have or can mobilize access. In this heterogeneity, one can distinguish patterns or pathways, or as I prefer to call them styles of social security.

As explained earlier, styles of social security are analytical constructions based on local knowledge and emic categories. This does not mean that villagers are necessarily aware of their own style, or those of others, but that they indicate and refer to some of the apparent features of styles. Contrary to what these folk concepts might suggest, it does not refer to people, but rather it refers to patterns and ways of ordering, and to households. In addition, villagers themselves indicated their orientation towards the future and the relative stability of their livelihood. It is an analytical tool that helps to understand pathways out of poverty.

People have a certain style because they were raised in a particular fashion, share a cultural repertoire or because neighbours expect them to conform to their style. When conditions change, people could turn to new, and probably more profitable, ways of organizing their social security. However, for social and economic reasons, a shift of style is not always that easy since styles carry a history and a legacy: if one has been strongly involved in profit maximizing and individual arrangements for social security, it is well-nigh impossible to suddenly switch to a style based on strong ties with neighbours, relatives or patrons. There is, nevertheless, room for gradual shifts if one moves out of tight networks, or if one's economic position changes dramatically.

Of equally importance is that some styles are more vulnerable to certain risks and threats than others. For instance, people following a style oriented towards the money economy – such as wage labourers and migrants – are often quite successful these days. They are able to generate a good income and buy new high-status goods. For adversities in life such as severe illness, they have strong networks of fellow workers who offer some basic security and assistance, or they can depend on savings and other sources of income in the extended family. For migrants who return without money, and self-focussed villagers, who are confronted with multiple difficulties, it can sometimes become painfully clear that migration, or a sole orientation on the cash economy, has meant that they have neglected many aspects of their social relationships and networks of mutual help, and that this has made them extremely vulnerable. They can no longer fall back on the old societal insurance mechanisms and face major setbacks in their livelihood, security and status in times of individual or collective crisis.

In comparison, people oriented towards the old village economy of wages in kind, share tenancies and patron-client relationships (*orang lugu*) do relatively well under these conditions. They remain part of basic networks of balanced reciprocity. The thrifty people, those freeriding on the old institutions of insurance and village social security, while reaping the benefits of the new economy, are probably doing the best. Nevertheless, it cannot be foreseen how they will do in future. If increasing numbers of people follow the thrifty route, the social fabric of society will continue to change and the social security system of the village will weaken or completely disintegrate. It also cannot be said which style will dominate in the future. If the agricultural production system in Krajan becomes increasingly commercialized and commoditized, less space will be available for non-cash labour relationships and non-cash forms of cooperation and exchange. The *orang lugu* will become less important and, with them, the position of many women in these households who now dominate food production and systems of gift exchange, redistribution and food exchange. The implications of these changes need to be studied.

A style is to an extent 'inherited', villagers may be caught in a social security style by being born into a family and acculturated with an orientation towards strong ties with neighbours, relatives, mutual help and reciprocal relationships. If one has a certain style, having learnt and internalized its related values, orientations and skills, it is difficult and disadvantageous to abandon established ties and switch to another social security style such as being oriented towards self-support (as an individual or a family), saving and withdrawing from mutual exchanges. If one is engaged in commercial agriculture and waged labour, it is impossible to shift quickly to subsistence farming or share tenancy relations as these require a completely different set of relationships. However, this does not mean that it is completely impossible to break with a style and escape to another. Styles are constantly reproduced and 'restyled' by the changing needs and orientations of villagers. An example of such a disruption of style is the youngsters who travel (*merantau*) to Kalimantan, Bali or Madura in search of work and fun, and aim at a future different from that of their parents. Education also often serves to change styles and being oriented towards education can become a style in itself.

In this chapter, I have only been able to give a rough outline of styles as patterns of behaviour that echo the value orientations towards the vicissitudes of life. To what extent these styles apply in other areas remains to be determined. The implications of using a style concept are manifold. At the policy level, if oriented on poverty eradication or social welfare enhancement, it implies a more differentiated approach. As long as general goals and general solutions are presented as solutions to people's specific problems without taking diversity into account, then social security and anti-poverty programmes will never be fully effective. Moreover, the approach shows that vulnerability is not only a matter of poverty or inequality, but also a question of style. In understanding why some people and households cope better than others, social security indeed turns out to be a matter of style.

CHAPTER 5

Risk Taking

Sex, Gambling and Power

In the introduction of this book, I discussed what I see as a major bias in social security studies. Many of these studies deal with a range of institutions and mechanisms for support and assistance that exist to protect people against the consequences of adversities. However, rather than looking at agency and the reasons why people take risks or seek to protect themselves, they focus on institutions and community arrangements that potentially offer support in times of need (Hüsken and Koning 2006:11, Lont 2006). Similarly, disaster studies tend to focus on protection and external risk reduction instead of considering the individual and collective risk-reduction practices of people (Bankoff 2009, Hilhorst and Bankhoff 2004, Van Voorst 2014, Van Voorst and Handgraaf 2012). Implicitly, most of these studies appear to depart from the assumption that people prefer security to risk, and that social relationships and village institutions are oriented towards enhancing some form of social security rather than disrupting it. In this chapter, I intend to draw a more nuanced picture by taking a closer look at Madurese people in East Java, both rich and poor, who are involved in risk-taking practices that potentially endanger their livelihood base. Why do people 'at risk' (Blaikie et al. 1994, Wisner et al. 2012) take on large risks?

Poor people are generally assumed to be risk-averse and security optimizing. This emphasis on the presumed human need for security rather than insecurity is also clear in human needs approaches and studies on social welfare. Macarov quoting Goodin (1988) writes:

> All societies hold as dogma that social welfare deals with needs, rather than wants. […] Although there is no good, clear-cut reason to give meeting needs systematic priority over satisfying desires, almost all social welfare programs define themselves as meeting needs – and indeed attempt to defend themselves from the charge that they are answering 'mere' desires.
>
> MACAROV 1995:17

This observation is still widely accepted. However, during fieldwork in East Java and East Kalimantan, I became increasingly dissatisfied with explanations of poor people and peasants being risk-aversive and primary focussed on physical needs and security. Although this assumption no doubt holds for a proportion of the population, and might help to explain some of their actions, I noticed that nearly all villagers sometimes take risks and some deliberately increase risks even when their livelihood base is neither stable nor secure. Moreover, there is a specific category of people, both in East Java and East Kalimantan, who actively take risks rather than search for livelihood security. These people are at the centre of the analysis in this chapter. They take not only profit-enhancing risks, but also ones that endanger the security and the continuity of their households' livelihoods. How can we understand this 'excessive' risk-taking given the above-mentioned assumptions?

This chapter provides examples of Madurese villagers in Krajan, in upland East Java, who deliberately take and combine risks. Locally, the term '*orang nakal*' is used for these people, which can be translated as something like wayward, wicked or naughty people.[1] I prefer the word wayward, as *orang nakal* are people who do not follow mainstream norms and values of society, are ignorant about livelihood security and deliberately take huge risks. These risks are not the customary risks related to farming and entrepreneurship, but excessive risks that, at least at first sight, are not oriented towards establishing a sustainable livelihood or long-term social security but seen rather as potentially devastating, putting livelihood security at risk. The focus of this chapter is the practice of excessive risk-taking rather than outcasts in society. It will, however, be shown that risk-taking and deviancy do often, but not necessarily, go together.

In this chapter, I want to show that deliberate risk-taking is not an exceptional event for poor people, but an attractive livelihood style for some villagers who search for an alternative to complying with the village norms and social pressures that urge huge investments in social security and reciprocal relationships. I describe gambling and risk-taking in the village of Krajan, elaborated with some examples taken from case studies. Taking into account the examples of wayward people, I will discuss whether the assumption of inherent risk-aversion in poorer households is justified. I will focus on the local and everyday practices and notions of people in terms of experiencing, avoiding and deliberately engaging in risks.

Whereas the risk-taking in the examples provided in the introduction, such as in vegetable farming (Hefner 1990, Lewis 1992) are accepted and embedded culturally, Vel's (1994) description of Manu Wolu, a bird-nest collector on

---

1 *Nakal* is diffiicult to translate into English. A common translation is naughty (often used for children, but also for men who flirt with women, who gamble, or who do not behave according to morals, who are petty gang leaders and the like). Throughout this book, I use the term *nakal* to refer to people who are daredevils or somewhat wayward.

Sumba, Indonesia, is an example of unacceptable risk-taking and deviancy. In Sumba, gathering birds' nests from caves is highly disapproved of as it is believed that entering caves brings people into contact with evil spirits. Vel sketches the dilemma of the village poor such as Manu Wolu: 'Either they submit themselves to the rules of the local community and live a life of hard work and may be sure of a basic level of existence. Or they engage in cash earning activities that are beyond the limits of what is approved of by the local community, and subsequently may be rich at times, but excluded by the community' (Vel 2000:35). Despite disapproval and danger, a group of mainly youngsters, sometimes described as *kuat jalan* or vagabonds, take risks and engage in such, often physically dangerous, activities. Although they make good money, they lose, to a large extent, access to village networks of support and social security and most of them are still poor in the end. As Vel (Vel 2000:45) argues 'Deviant behaviour such as "gathering birds" nests is the option for people who are on the outer edge of the local economy, for whom there hardly is a viable alternative to make a living. Coping with insecurity is the permanent theme of their life. In their own assessment, a deviant way to earn cash can be preferable over access to local social security arrangements, if that would imply permanent drudgery merely for the benefit of patrons'.

Normative and Contextual Landscapes

As described in Chapters 3 and 4, the social-security system in Krajan is largely based on two normative principles: reciprocity and self-insurance. Self-insurance reflects those individuals and households that protect themselves against adversities through their own savings, independent of social arrangements and institutions. Alternatively, such village institutions and arrangements, often built upon reciprocal relationships, can offer some security and assistance to their members in times of need. This mutual support encourages villagers to contribute to assisting others.

However, these institutions and arrangements do not cover all expenses in times of need. The importance of village social-security institutions is often more non-material than material. When encountering hardship, villagers are first expected to cover their expenses out of their own savings, capital and resources. Only if they do not have resources can they call on social relations for support and then, more often than not, this support is insufficient and coping becomes extremely problematic. For instance, in the case of a burial, the family of the deceased will have to sell its cows or land even if these are its only sources of livelihood. If they do not have any savings, the deceased will be buried without much ceremony. Risky behaviour and squandering attitudes that endanger the capacity of a household to fulfil the expected obligations and rituals in times of need are highly disapproved. Nevertheless, some poor, and often young, villagers do not want to face the prospects of life-long compliance to these established norms of the ordinary and try to find alternatives. They pin their hope on earning quick cash and opt to violate norms rather than avoid risks.

I frequently visited such people, most often men, when at home, while labouring in the fields and at places where risk-taking practices come to the fore such as cattle markets, coffee shops and gambling dens. Through these frequent meetings and by taking part in activities such as gambling, friendship led to mutual trust. Based on careful observation and participant observation, made possible by these good social relations, I could gain in-depth insights into risk-taking behaviour. Besides this, these activities enabled me to collect detailed life histories and to touch upon sensitive questions concerning loss, debts, conflicts, sexuality and shame. Men, women, husbands and wives were often separately observed and interviewed. Further, my wife and child played an important role in establishing good relationships with women, in gaining access to women's stories in 'backstage' places, and by cross-checking male stories within female domains.

Risk-Taking in Krajan

In Krajan, three kinds of risk-taking practices are predominant. First I deal with gambling, then with the practice of engaging in extra-marital relationships, and finally with speculation. For the purpose of this chapter, I limit myself to the risk-taking practices of those villagers who take major risks, ones that threaten their own and their household's future livelihood: the '*orang nakal*'. I translate this as wayward to reflect that *orang nakal* do not follow the norms and values of society, ignore livelihood security and deliberately take huge risks without being physically excluded from society.

Gambling

In Krajan, about one-third of the male population gambles every now and then. Except for members of some orthodox religious families, nearly all men have gambled at least once. However, less than 5% of these men are referred to as *orang nakal*, wayward and wicked people who violate established village norms of behaviour in a deviant way. For the other gamblers, gambling does not directly threaten livelihoods, it has more the character of pastime.

During the first two months of fieldwork, I was not aware of the importance and prevalence of gambling in village life. I was still busy paying visits to all the important families in the village (including religious leaders), making good impressions and learning the basic rules of village life. Sometimes, I came across a group of people playing cards or gambling at big festivities like village festivals, weddings and bullfights. Initially, I thought that gambling was a rather isolated activity of a small group of diehards. Each time, I tried to get to know more about gambling, I received vague answers, or negative stories about these *orang nakal*. Friends and close neighbours, who obviously wanted to maintain a good impression, answered vaguely or assured me they were not like those gamblers. As long as you are an outsider, it is extremely difficult to study deviancy in Indonesia, because negative behaviour will be euphemized to the outsider.

One day, I heard rumours about regular gambling going on in a coffee shop (*warung*) nearby. I asked if someone knew where it was and when the gambling usually takes place. My neighbours remained silent and only after repeated questions they told me they were not able to take me there, as they did not know the time and exact location either. I was not satisfied with this answer and decided to ask some of the youngsters with whom I already had established good relationships. One of them agreed to take me to the gambling place, which turned out to be only two minutes from my house.

The gambling den was at the back of the *warung*, where I used to chat and drink coffee in the morning. It was run by an old widow who lived in a small house, a dozen metres away from the back. Then, I noticed sounds of rolling dice, and when I entered the room, they all rose, looked surprised or scared, and gazed at me. The small place was lit with a shimmering light and occupied by more than a dozen people, all from the same vicinity including the village head. I smiled and said: 'I heard there is gaming around and I wanted to join'. Immediately, I drew out some small money and threw it on the playing board. They all laughed relieved, allowed me to join, and the game continued.

That night I played carefully and long. Eventually I won a significant amount of money (ten days' wages). The next day, I was the talk of the neighbourhood. All neighbours, also those who had assured me they were not gambling, congratulated me, and asked me to recall the story of the game. Some now admitted they were playing every night and others warned me for playing too recklessly, because they had lost huge amounts in the past.

Some of the women in the neighbourhood came to my wife, trying to find out if she knew that I had been playing that night. When she told them, she did not mind, as long as I would play for fun with small amounts, they smiled understandingly. All people in the neighbourhood seemed very relieved to find out I liked playing and was not too conceited. This event meant a breakthrough in my fieldwork and cleared the way to discuss more-sensitive subjects.[2] From this time onwards, I felt more accepted and people started to open up.

The Rules of the Game

Most kinds of gambling are illegal, but every time there is a large ceremony, wedding, music (*dangdut*) or theatre (*ludruk*) performance, there is gambling on the outskirts of the festival terrain. Sometimes empty houses or the houses of players are used. If there is no house available, a garden, behind some trees or the back of a shed provides a convenient gambling place. Such places are needed to prevent outsiders from spotting it, as gambling is illegal. To make these events possible, police, military and sometimes village administrators are usually paid off. It also happens that the military directly sponsor gambling activities and then neither the police and village officials nor religious leaders dare to take action.

Most of the gambling is organized by a group of people. They work together with a creditor (*bandar*). The *bandar* does not need play, others play for him. He adds or collects money every now and then and maintains good relationships with village officials and policemen to safeguard the play. An example of such a *bandar* is Patik. Being a trader and moneylender, he always has ready cash available and is willing to lend it to organizers of the game. Since he is not playing himself, and seldom watches the game, he always stayed out of trouble when gamblers were seized. He never took responsibility when players were seized. 'I have the risk of losing money, you the risk of being caught, I do not want to be in trouble', he said.

Most of the gambling in Krajan is petty gambling where bets are small and villagers play occasionally and irregularly, often only at special occasions like festivals. For many villagers, this type of playing has the character of a pastime and amounts lost do not exceed much of a day's wage.[3]

2 Something similar happened later at the start of the Ramadan (after two months of fieldwork). I decided to fast with the others. Every night, those neighbours still fasting prayed in the prayer house attached to my house. After six days of fasting, I had difficulties with working and I became very thirsty, so I decided to stop fasting in private and took some drinks and food. When I told this to my neighbours the other day, they smiled relieved. From that time on, I spotted many of them smoking or sipping coffee at daytime in their house. That night, nearly nobody showed up in the praying house anymore.

3 Before the 1997 economic crisis started, a 100 Rupiah coin was the normal bet for these common games (like playing cards, dice and a kind of lottery). After the start of the crisis, due to high inflation, 500 Rupiah notes had become the minimum bet. After the year 2000, in

There are three basic categories of gamblers in Krajan: those gambling for pastime only at special occasions such as *selamatan* and weddings, those who gamble regularly, but carefully and strategically, and the addicted gamblers who can hardly resist playing at any occasion. The most common games are cards (*judi ceki*), balls (*judi bola*), and dice (*judi klodok*).[4] In cockfights (*aduan ayam*) and the typical and popular Madurese bullfights (*aduan sapi*), larger amounts of money are at stake than when playing cards, balls or dice. Before the 1997 crisis, at *aduan sapi* and *aduan ayam* bets of one million Rupiah (€416) or more were no exception.

Most of the cases I was involved in, the bets are contained within realistic financial limits of the gambler. Most occasional gamblers do not put more money at stake than brought to the game. However, there are people who have ruined themselves by gambling away cash, land, goods and even the house in which they live, or are on the way to ruining themselves. In the last five years before the fieldwork, at least twelve families in Krajan lost nearly all their belongings due to a gambling husband or gambling son. Most of these families could not be interviewed as they had left the village, many to Kalimantan, on the run from creditors and/or in the hope of returning some of the lost possessions. Many of the Madurese migrants looking for work in East Kalimantan, who I interviewed there, gave gambling debts as a reason for migration.

Gambling in Krajan is a purely male activity. Women in Krajan do not gamble, apart from the occasional ticket for legal lotteries in town. Many women know that their husbands are playing, and they are highly opposed to gambling (even petty gambling). They believe that gambling is a major threat to the livelihood security of the household, an irresponsible waste of money and an illness that needs to be cured.

The women are convinced that, even if their husbands win, they will not get hold of the money as the money will not last long. Money earned from gambling is hot (*uang panas*), earned too quickly, and cannot enter the household domestic unit as such money is spent 'as fast as it is earned'. Apart from this, the belief that gamblers in the end always lose is strongly rooted in society. This is true to a large extent. Most of the notorious gamblers are not successful in the end due to money leaking out of the circuit. Organizers (*bandar*), patrons (often military), moneylenders and shopkeepers take their profits and they are usually the only ones who are making a profit in the long run. On the

---

Krajan, notes of Rp 5,000 and later 10,000 became the norm. In cockfights in East Kalimantan, Rp 20,000 and Rp 50,000 notes were the standard.

4 Indonesian words I came across: Card *judi: main gaple, main ceki, main remi, cap beki,* ball *judi: bola adil,* dice *judi: main dadu, judi klithik.*

other hand, these stories also function a great deal to scare and to prevent people from engaging into gambling.

Among women, stories of women who lost all possessions due to an 'irresponsible' husband are told and retold. A well-known example is the story of *bu* Sulama. Her husband's gambling behaviour caused them not only to sell his own land, but also his wife's property she inherited from her parents. Now, the couple has to work as labourers on the fields of others to make a living. According to the female audience, *bu* Sulama should have divorced him before all the land was gone. 'She must have noticed that he (her husband) had the fever', one of the women commented.

Although women cannot divorce easily in Krajan, a gambling husband is generally accepted as a legitimate reason to divorce. Women usually try to keep away their husbands from gambling in many ways. A common strategy is to ask money for household needs as soon as the husband earns something in order to prevent the money from being wasted. From this earned money, most husbands keep a minor proportion for their own benefit, used for expenses like coffee, cigarettes, sweets for children and the like. Usually, husbands try to hide the exact amount of earnings, but networks of women constantly exchange information about payments and earnings of their husbands and thus strengthen their bargaining position.

During extended case studies of a few families who we were able to visit regularly, we spoke to husbands and wives separately and observed that spouses already knew the earnings of the man before they met. Frequently, I found women (secretly) saving some of this money for bad times, or for expected expenses such as a *selamatan*, school fees or uniform. This was particularly the case if husbands were notorious gamblers. Nearly half of the wives of the gamblers we interviewed admitted (privately) that they had small savings (*celengan*). In most cases, husbands admitted they knew or at least suspected their women to be saving, but they were never sure about the exact amounts. The gamblers in the area around Krajan included both rich and poor villagers and older and younger villagers. Although most of the gamblers are young, the gamblers for bigger kitties are often older and successful villagers. A special category appeared to be the village heads. Out of seven neighbouring villages, at least four village heads were known to be excessive gamblers. Among whom Bagenda, the village head of Krajan is the most notorious, but due to his power, slyness, and influence, he is called a *jago* (a fighting cock), rather than a wayward.

Who are these Gamblers?

In four hamlets of Krajan, with about 400 families, I came across twenty to thirty notorious gamblers. About half of them were poor. Among these heavy gamblers of Krajan, villagers distinguish two classes: the rich, or children from rich families, and the poor or newly poor. Especially children of richer families are explicitly referred to as *orang nakal*. These children have never had to work hard and are spoiled in the eyes of fellow villagers. 'They never learned to take responsibility'. In Krajan, there are at least ten cases where children gambled away family property sometimes with disastrous consequences. Their parents have not been able to stop these children. They often operate in gangs and very often the gambling goes together with other illegal, or semi legal activities as having sexual affairs (outside the village), theft, conspicuous consumption (demanding motorbikes), and drinking.

An example of such *anak nakal* is Abdul, the brother of *Bu* Sumyati (30). Her family used to be one of the richest families of Krajan. Twenty years ago, they had more than fifteen hectares of sawah and tegal. The decline in the family's wealth started with an attempt by Sumyati's grandfather to run for village head. He failed and lost some of the family capital. The family stayed relatively prosperous and Abdul and Sumyati were sent to secondary school in Bondowoso. Abdul started a notorious lifestyle there and wanted to live like his classmates from town. He demanded from his parents a trendy motor bike, good clothes, pocket money etc. They willingly paid as they thought it right to give their son a good education. Gradually, an increasing proportion of the cattle and some of the family's rice fields had to be sold or pawned.

Abdul finished his education but was not able or willing to find a paid job. He continued to live a high style at the expense of his parents, and started several small trades and businesses. When these went bankrupt, he took the initiatives to sell most of the already pawned rice fields secretly. Sumyati and her grandfather were very angry when they found out. The last two plots were put in Sumyati's name preventing Abdul from spending more of the family capital. When all the parents' property was gone, Abdul returned to live in Krajan where he received disapproval but food and lodging in his parents' house. Soon, he left for Kalimantan in search of luck or money. Not much later, his parents, without work and income due to the loss of the land followed a transmigration program to Sulawesi in the hope of recovering some of the previous prosperity.[5] Since then, Sumyati has tried little by little to repay debts and to return at least some of the pawned fields.

From the rich gamblers in Krajan, gambling traders form a prominent group, who rarely risk their own livelihood completely and who are generally able to

5 In 1999, they returned to Krajan. Although not prosperous, they at least had been able to secure a plot of land in Sulawesi and sold it. With the money, they bought a couple of cows in Krajan and returned the pawned land of their daughter.

compensate huge losses from gambling with profits in trade. Moreover, networks of gamblers serve for them as networks of information and often these networks lead to new business opportunities. Apart from this, as money circulation is high in these networks, borrowing opportunities are manifold and credits and profits are also used for trade. Some of these businessmen occasionally operate as the organizer (*bandar*), moneylender or pawn-taker, and are able to make a living out of gambling.

Village officials and village heads from the neighbourhood who often play in Krajan form a special category of rich gamblers. The village head of Sumber Dompyong, *Pak* Zeinol (age 45) bets mainly at bullfights. He owns a number of bulls himself and he would go to the Bondowoso bullfights every week. Sometimes he lost millions of Rupiah in one week, in other weeks he won similar amounts. In addition to betting at the bullfighting arena, he is a notorious cock gambler and dice (*klithik*) player and pays weekly visits to Krajan gambling dens. During big weddings and similar large events, I would always see him gambling. There were rumours that he compensated for his losses by using village development funds.

The village head of Gadingsari lost a few cows, a car and a motorbike in the course of four years through gambling. After the fall of Suharto in 1998, large demonstrations by villagers and complaints to the heads of the district (*camat* and *bupati*) led to him being deposed. The former village head of Andungsari lost a number of cows, at least one hectare of sawah and another two or three pieces he had pawned because of reckless gambling. He also took huge amounts of cash from village funds. He was not re-elected at the 1998 elections. His illegal use of village funds was investigated and he lost access to funds. To cover his debts, and to repay village funds, he had to sell his parents' land. The village head of Poler lost huge amounts of money to Bagenda, the village head of Krajan. Bagenda offered huge credit and lent him a car indebting him for tens of millions Rupiah. At the same time, Bagenda had a secret affair with the man's wife. After the situation got out of control and the affair became public knowledge, her husband was unable to take action against Bagenda, because of his financial ties. This sexual affair lingered on until the end of 1999.[6]

6 I spoke to a few villagers who had seen Bagenda taking this woman to town. When I asked Bagenda in a confident moment about going with that woman, he himself admitted he made the husband on purpose dependent on him, '*dia diikat kepada saya karena punya hutang besar. Sekarang saya bebas di sana* [the house of the village head]'. Besides this, I received much information from one of the confidants of Bagenda who had to provide alibis to the wife of Bagenda. Finally, the affair was confirmed by Prima, a local journalist and friend of Bagenda who had witnessed the couple entering a hotel in town.

Of all the seven village heads, only the new village head of Andungsari is not known as a notorious gambler. He is the oldest son of an orthodox religious family that has provided several village heads in the past. The values of his religion and strong social control in the family prevent him of being wayward or a gambler. In business, however, he took considerable risks by speculating with rice and tobacco prices.

Among common villagers, two categories of gamblers can be distinguished. Children from rich families and children from poor or newly poor families. Often, children of rich families are explicitly referred to as *orang nakal*, because they never had to work hard and are spoiled according to fellow villagers. One informant said: 'They never learned to take responsibility'. In Krajan alone, there are at least ten children who have gambled away family property, sometimes with disastrous consequences. Parents clearly have not been able to stop these children from asking for money, motorbikes or other expensive goods. They often operate in gangs and very often the gambling goes together with other illegal, or semi-legal, activities such as having several sexual affairs (often outside the village), fighting, thieving and drinking.

The largest group of gamblers can be found among the poor of Krajan. They come from families who have always been relatively poor, but had some property and income like one or two plots of land and some cattle. The poorest people of Krajan do not gamble regularly, because they do not have cash and cannot get any credit. Moreover, they need all the money they earn for instant consumption. The *orang nakal* among the poor started gambling wishing to improve their situation quickly in some way or another. They were not inclined to wait long, or save, and invest in social relationships. Some expressed this by saying that they preferred to live high for a short moment, or to have at least a chance of a better life than to live all days in poverty without ever changing anything.[7] Often, gambling becomes its own trap and turns into an addiction as players hope to win back their stake leading to even higher debts.

Bagenda, the village head and other upper *bandar* of Krajan have good relations with police and military active in the area. Some of these police and military are directly involved in Krajan gambling as well. Bagenda's good relations with the police are important to protect the gamblers. If villagers are caught by the police, they go to Bagenda and seek his support.[8] In return for his

7 *'Kalau saya kerja keras, atau malas, tidak ada bedaan. Tetap miskin. Lebih baik saya hidup betul satu hari dan coba menang daripada miskin terus'.*

8 Village heads being involved in gambling is common in Java. Among others, Cederroth (1995:194) notices the same for a village in the west of East Java: not only the village administration, but also the police and military are heavily involved.

protection and mediation, Bagenda receives regular grants. In the years before my fieldwork took place, he sometimes played a double role in this. Although he is a passionate gambler himself, he is often the *bandar* and seldom loses exorbitant amounts of money. Besides this, he supplies credit, buys goods or land from those who lost large amounts and tries to tie people to him by creating long-term debt relationhips. According to himself and to some informants who confirmed this, there have been instances where he informed the police so that they would raid gambling places in Krajan. Often, these were games of competing *bandar*. In this way, he showed the regional government he was willing to seriously tackle gambling in his village. At the same time, he received bribes from villagers to free the captured villagers.

I also received reports from different sources that on a few occasions in town, when Bagenda had lost huge amounts of money to Chinese *bandar*, he informed the police about illegal gambling going on. The police captured the players and the money and decided to divide it equally. His excellent relations with police and military make him a feared rival and most villagers choose to cooperate with him. His involvement and success in gambling adds to his status as *jago*, his reputation as a daredevil and strong man.

Gambling as a Way of Life

There are good reasons to assume that risk-taking behaviour is not an exception, but that it can be found in most towns and villages in Java. Some of these excessive risk takers show deviant behaviour, but this does not need to be the case. In many societies, there seems to be a small proportion of people of gamblers and non-conformists who take these kinds of risks. Cederroth (1995), who conducted research in Central, East Java, mentions: 'However, there is a group of dedicated gamblers, many of whom have completely ruined their personal finances by gambling' (Cederroth 1995:195). In most societies, there is a vast group of gambling deviants violating the norms of mainstream society.

Poverty is often mentioned as a major reason why people gamble according to Cederroth: 'For many people, their income is not even sufficient to cover their daily economic needs. Such people frequently turn to gambling in the hope of gaining instant wealth. Gambling then has an important role in the household economy of many families' (Cederroth 1995:6). Later, Cederroth contrasts saving to gambling: 'Those who cannot, or are simply too impatient to adhere to the boring strategy of long saving periods before getting their reward, frequently try to find shortcuts and instant fortunes by various kinds of gambling' (Cederroth 1995:170).

I belief that these interpretations are too simple. Many villagers said, they started to gamble in hope for a quick fortune, but after some time, these motivations changed and the game became a reason in itself. At the gambling place, their eyes start to flicker, they meet with friends, and experience moments of total ecstasy or despair. Often, gambling is an addiction and gamblers refer to it as the real thing, the game that makes a boring life interesting. At the gambling places, friends are made and alliances develop which compensate for social disapproval from society at large.

Further, from the examples in this chapter it can be seen that gambling, sexual promiscuity and speculative trading often go together. This is not a coincidence, as these practices are often related and once being *nakal*, it becomes difficult to go into society again. It slowly develops into a style of living with attributed expectations, social relations and an inherent repertoire of choices. The *orang nakal* represent a way of life that is probably not that economically attractive as most of them do not accumulate much, but it is appealing for many youngsters and older men in search for some thrill to enliven dull village life.

Moreover, being *nakal* offers poorer villagers the change to acquire some status (and not only among their own folks) as daredevil and true men. Risk taking represents machismo, the he-man, and probably the only chance to obtain a better life which otherwise could never be achieved. Being wayward and *jago* enables one to win at least some kudos in the cultural, sexual and political domain of Krajan. Sometimes, being *nakal* develops into a creative counter strategy, a life filled with gambling and dangerous living offering an opportunity to distinguish oneself from the bourgeois, the common folk, the people who never become anything special.

An example of an *orang nakal* who has become successful is Bagenda, the village head. Since his teenage years, he was known and feared in the area as an uncontrollable daredevil, involved in all kinds of semi-legal enterprises, able to resist and cooperate with local leaders, the police and the military. Often, villagers used nicknames for him referring to famous fighting cocks or bulls. He was elected village head at the age of 26. Until now, much of his power and prestige is based on his past and his rigid, creative and sometimes violent style of leadership.

The similarity between him and the fighting cock (*jago*) is clear and this term is also used by villagers for other reasons. Within and outside Krajan, he is well known for his brutality, his success as village leader and for his sexual escapades. *Jago* is a word commonly and historically used for gang leaders and their machismo in Indonesia (Schulte Nordholt 1991). The relationship between gambling and crossing sexual borders is often mentioned by (religious) opponents, by women, by spectators and by players themselves. *Jago* not only receive status from daring bets, but also from having many extramarital affairs as well. Engaging in illegal sexual relationships can be more risky than gambling.

Extra-Marital Relationships in Krajan

Another form of risk-taking in Krajan is the engagement in extra-marital relationships. Although the risk of revenge (*carok*) is high, the number of men and women engaging into extra-marital relationships is considerable. Of the sixty adults in the neighbourhood, a large majority of the men and about half of the women have had sexual experiences or relationships outside marriage.[9] Often these affairs remain hidden but sometimes, when a couple is discovered, the case is brought to public trial.

The general norm is that no extra marital relationships should take place but, within certain limits of decency, extramarital relationships can be acceptable. It depends on the people involved, who knows about it, and how the relationship develops. Love relationships outside forced weddings, or relationships of widows with married men, and relationships of first wives in polygamous households are sometimes acceptable, but only if they remain hidden and invisible, which is difficult as houses stand close to each other and are always open. Often, sisters, brothers or mothers of the girl who know or are suspect about an affair, protect the couple if needed. Often, neighbours also know or suspect an affair, but do not bring it into the open as long as maintaining good relationships with the families involved is considered more important than moral considerations. In addition, the fear of the revenge by the man involved, or his friends, refrains people from bringing it to the fore.

If an affair is not socially acceptable, continues too long, becomes too visible, or is disapproved by most relatives and neighbours, and leads to gossip, a discovery is likely and in the most extreme cases it will be reported to the village counsel. Most of the discoveries I studied during the research period, concerned men from outside the village such as peddlers, tobacco traders, schoolmasters and the like who had a relationship with a woman or girl

---

9 In the area I lived, quite some cases have been discovered over the years. Other stories I received from men and sometimes women and healers (*dukun*) who told me about their sexual escapades and of those of close friends for whom they had ever provided an alibi. Many of these stories could later be crosschecked by my wife, or by friends. Sometimes we accidentally came across signs of such relations as for instance when our domestic helper, put a bag with water in our fridge. When we asked for what purpose she did this, she told that a close friend and neighbour had asked her secretly for a large bag with ice. She had not menstruated this month and she was afraid she was pregnant. Her husband had gone to Kalimantan four months ago. Other stories provided indirect clues such as illegal abortions and women inquiring privately for abortion pills.

from Krajan. In some other cases, the relationships came to the fore when the man or his family was not liked by the relatives and neighbours of the girl. If brought to the open, cases have to be settled according to local law, the couple is publicly scorned, huge penalties have to be paid and the couple are often forced to marry.

Men and women having or having had extra-marital relationships are not automatically called *nakal*. It depends on the frequency and the kind of relationship. If the relation and the flirting is too public, playful, macho, short term, or multiple, and lead to gossip, women run the risk of being called *nakal* or cheap (*murah*). *Nakal* is used where women flirt actively, take initiatives, or visit places where men can be found (for instance at certain *warung* and gambling dens). Women who easily give in to pressure from men or to temptations are called *murah* (cheap, or easy; without having any backbone). Being called *nakal* has a very negative connotation for women. Nakal behaviour of women is disproportionably sanctioned.

Despite the tremendous risks of discovery, a love relationship can go on for years despite the fact that other people know about it. Pak Oke told me: 'The best way and the safest is to search a girl far away in Bondowoso or in another village. Every now and then, you meet in a place where nobody knows you. To love a girl in the neighbourhood is very dangerous because you have to establish very good relationships with the parents, husband and with neighbours of the girl in order to establish a regular visiting pattern to make your presence in the house unobtrusive. You have to make yourself trusted by those most closely related to the girl'.

Another way of diminishing risks is meeting in the house of a friend or relative. This is the safest if you have a friend who does not talk. Some of the *warung* in Krajan and along the road to Bondowoso have this function too. Most *warung* comprise an area to drink and sit and a kitchen with one or more bedrooms, and these beds can be 'borrowed' for some time. It is not difficult for women to slip in to a *warung* from the back or to enter the kitchen as most *warung* sell vegetables, *tahu* or dried fish. Men often sit in the front, chatting and drinking coffee. The lover can easily slip into the back of the *warung*, leaving a friend in the front as an alibi. Two or three *warung* in Krajan make quite a good living out of this business.

Clifford Geertz in his famous 'Notes on the Balinese Cockfight' explicitly links cockfights with sexuality. He argues that Balinese men identify themselves strongly with their cocks, a symbol for male masculinity, where the fight between cocks is a fight between men (Geertz 1973:417). In accordance with Geertz' observations, De Jonge analysed the Madurese bullfight on East Java as a symbol of Madurese masculinity and sexuality offering a valuable picture of aspects of society which in other spheres of life tend to stay invisible (De Jonge 1990, 1994).

De Jonge draws a parallel between Madurese bullfights, *aduan sapi*, in the arena of Bondowoso and Madurese society at large:

> The *aduan sapi* is replete with sexual symbolism. The arena and its immediate surroundings are a stage for the expression of 'male sociability', and the fights as well as the surrounding phenomena serve 'male identity functions'. Bulls are symbols *par excellence* of sexual vigour, courage, power, and aggressiveness [...] To watch and take part in the contests, even through betting or by hanging around the arena, enhances the masculine identity of those concerned. This way their machismo is strengthened and they are encouraged to display the connected behaviour and continue in this. The sexual symbolism [of the bull] is confirmed down to the last detail, as is apparent from the rubbing of the area around the bull's genitals and the painting, polishing and decorating of its horns, which are phallic symbols (Blok 1981: 427). The high point of the event [bullfight] is perhaps the dance [...] of the winning bull. At that moment, the bull's power is metaphorically taken over by the men and displayed to the woman. (*cf.* Douglass 1984:243) The events inside and outside the arena unambiguously emphasize and reinforce Madurese ideas about relations between the sexes.

Indeed, the sexual connotations in the Madurese bullfight and jokes surrounding the animals and owners are manifold. In analogy to the bullfight, Madurese men fight for money and women. In showing force and masculinity, they get more attention from women and receive more status. This fighting often takes the shape of gambling and wagering family life, status and safety as the consequences of discovery can be high and sexual affairs – or even rumours about it – easily lead to fights, hatred, or even revenge murder (*carok*). The play for women and status does involve non-material chances and losses, although money is often involved and the financial risks can be high.

Since colonial times, Madurese men have been known for their touchiness, suspicion, temperament, hot temper, fierceness, vengefulness, combativeness and violence (De Jonge 1995:13). Since 1994, no murders have occurred In Krajan due to repression by the village head, but some villagers have been wounded in fights during the research period. In the same period, at least four men have been killed by *carok* near the village.

Given the dangers and risks involved, one might wonder why women take these risks and get involved in extra-marital relationships. For women, there are a number of reasons to engage in risky extra-marital relationships. Among the reasons are love and desire, financial reasons, status and the 'thrill' – the wish to live more dangerously. Although not allowed by the government, Krajan girls often marry at the age of thirteen or fourteen.[10] Madurese women in East Java are among the youngest to marry in Indonesia (Jones 2001). Often this first marriage is seen by girls as a way to fulfil the wish of the parents, or just as a logical consequence of having finished primary school. Often, these marriages break up after two or three years and then the girl is free to marry a more desired partner. Around 30–40% of first marriages break up after a few years.

A marriage is really counted as a marriage if there has been sexual intercourse. An inability to perform sexual duties can be a legitimate reason for divorce (Niehof 1985). Often the potential husband, or his relatives, try to force or persuade a girl to sleep with him. However, girls who do not want to marry the choice of their parents can fiercely refuse. If they resist their parents, they might be beaten, refused food or locked up until they do agree. Sometimes, relatives even take watch in the house of the new married couple to ensure they stay in the same bed for the whole night.

Although sexuality in Krajan is connected to marriage, pleasure and reproduction, marriage usually has nothing to do with notions of romantic love. A popular Indonesian saying is: 'Marriage teaches you to love your husband' and some female informants added: 'or to hate him'. Nevertheless, many marriages stay unbroken. Common reasons to marry and to stay married are that an independent household forms an economic and autonomous unit and offers social security, care and access to an income. Only by marriage can a couple gain access to crucial resources such as land, cows and collective labour arrangements.

Hidden sexual relationships outside the marriage might be a better option for both men and women frustrated in their marriage. For instance, Mega, a young woman, who was forced to get married eight years ago, managed to continue a loving relationship with her former boyfriend. In her case, maintaining her marriage and keeping a secret love affair is satisfying. She keeps on good

10 For marriage, a health and age certificate is needed. All girls have to be checked by the local health post if they are already physically ready for marriage. At this occasion they receive also information about anti-conception. As girls usually do not know their age, the local nurse gives a statement that the girl is sixteen years old. Another possibility is that the girls marries and only gets permission from local religious leaders. As soon as the girl is sixteen, the marriage is officially registered. Often marriages are not registered at all due to expenses involved.

terms with the relatives of her husband, she respects her parents, and keeps a good image in the society. With the help of her mother, she is able to meet her lover every now and then. The marriage stays together, while needs and desires can be satisfied elsewhere. Some of these women (and often their mothers) actively use and enjoy the room of manoeuvre created by attention and financial gifts from lovers.

The foregoing description of engagement in sexual relationships might be too positive. Especially for women, the risks of extra-marital relationships are high. Not all young women are able to deal with their loving relationship in a positive way. Some urge their lovers to marry them and threat with suicide if he does not want to. In more than one case during the fieldwork, young women committed suicide when their love affair came out and their lover refused to marry her, or meeting became impossible. Often, thwarted love, or being deserted, leads to sorrow, frustration, and pain among young women.

In addition, the behaviour of *jago* is often threatening to women. Some are lured or forced into a relationship with some of the *jago* men and cannot resist the demands of these men. In other cases, women were raped. In societies like this, often women become victims of subordination and power of macho men and for them, machismo and other attractions of male behaviour are more often a heavy burden than a pleasure.

Speculation

Among the wayward people in society are also those who, according to villagers, take reckless risks in farming and trade. Insecurities in crop output are normal in that farming in Krajan is insecure due to fluctuations in rainfall, market prices, etc. According to villagers, reckless risks are those risks that endanger livelihood security in the long run. Often, risk takers in agriculture are also daredevils in other sectors of society. A good example is the family of Limatus. They invested a lot of money (the price of a small cow) into tobacco farming while resources of the family were already limited due to excessive gambling. By borrowing a lot of money, they wagered the subsistence of the family and when they lost, few options were available. No more money could be borrowed and relatives and neighbours no longer wanted to invest in social relations or mutual gift giving with this family.

Not all speculation in farming is reckless speculation. Traders, large farmers and local businessmen constantly speculate on possible future profits. However, if they lose, they usually still have a buffer of protection avoiding a total fall in livelihood. Here we are concerned with most reckless speculators. Generally, these villagers believe that every couple of years there is a big smash and huge amounts of money will be made with tobacco farming. While most farmers watch market prices of the previous years and contribute to an economic cycle of rising prices when little tobacco is planted followed by declining prices in the years after because of an increase in supply, the wayward people counter the expectations of the majority and take huge risks. Limatus indeed had made some good profits in previous years but, in those years, he was better equipped to counter the negative effects if losing.

Many of those who lost their bets on tobacco and could not repay their debts went to Kalimantan in 1997 hoping for a better future or to recover debts and then start farming in Krajan again. After the 1997 tobacco season, about 40 indebted families left for Kalimantan. Besides those indebted, many others went to Kalimantan in search of a quick profit. Only a very few of these migrants were successful and returned with savings. Most of them were not able to save as gambling in Kalimantan is common, prices are high and returns were disappointing. Given the recent outbreaks of violence against Madurese in Kalimantan, migration turns out to be a very risky choice.[11]

Migrants, Ramblers and Vagabonds

A last related type of risk-taking can be found among migrants, ramblers and vagabonds travelling around with local theatres. Some of these migrants have upped and left without much preparation, 'just to try their luck elsewhere', others departed well prepared. Most of the Krajan people migrated to Kalimantan to work in the oil palm plantations for a couple of months up to several years. Some never returned. Those who returned have not been very successful. Only few Krajan villagers got the opportunity to follow a transmigration program. Another share of the migration has a more temporary and cyclical character. If there is news of good working opportunities, some depart for Bali, Madura, lowland Java or the area of Banyuwangi to work as peddler, waged labourer, sugarcane cutter or in logging. Often, villagers travel in bands in search for work.

It is remarkable in this migration process that some of the poorest villagers seem so desperate that they depart with hardly any money, just to try their luck somewhere else. Among them are notorious *nakal*, who feel the fiery breath of debtors or angry villagers, or whom simply want a change of scene and to try their luck elsewhere. Some villagers take the bus to Denpasar, Bali, and leave with just a borrowed Rp 10,000 (1999 prices). The only thing they know is that there is a businessman probably in search of people to sell brushes and sunshields. After paying for the bus, they only have money for two meals.

11 In spring 2001, when the most violent outbreaks took place, at least 55 Krajan villagers returned. No casualties of Krajan people have been reported.

Sometimes, these people return to the village with some money or goods and are able to buy a bag of rice. Mostly, they return with nothing, because of bad luck, theft, prostitutes or heavy gambling and need to borrow again from neighbours and relatives who would rather see them leaving than arriving. In their absence, they cannot contribute much to the welfare system in the village and are often excluded from village social security.

They exchange village networks for the viable and fluid relationships along the road with fellow ramblers that can be strong for a short time, but often turn out to be unreliable. Participating in migration, criminality and commercial activities is not a sign of innovation or development (Vel 2000:45). It is an option for people who are on the outer edge of the local economy, for whom there is hardly a viable alternative to make a living. Coping with insecurity is the permanent theme of their life. From their own viewpoints: a deviant way to earn cash can be preferable over access to local social security arrangements that do not have much to offer for its poorest members.

Analysing Risk-Taking in Krajan

Deliberate risk-taking by the very poor seems to be a reaction to poor prospects and dull and tied village life. Some people no longer want to work each day for a small wage without any prospect of improvement and a better livelihood with fewer difficulties. They might opt for the thrill and the change of success, even if that means they risk their minimum subsistence. However, even for them, this style is less risky than it seems because gender structures in the household and social relations in the society sometime offer a minimal safety net. Some of those who lost rice fields, cows and family by heavy gambling, switched to another style and found a place in society by becoming a client, or a labourer on their former land. Others continue to live dangerously and roam the region in search for work and fun, not seldom joining theatre groups (*ludruk*) and only return to their house, parents or relatives in need of a meal or loan. If they run out of possibilities at home, they still can flee to Bali or Kalimantan to start a new life there.[12]

The aforementioned does not imply that other villagers are not taking risks at all. Most of them do take risks in farming, trade, and social relationships, but

12 Migration to Kalimantan has increasingly become risky as ethnic violence against Madurese has shifted to the Central and Western provinces of the Island in the 1990s and early 2000s. As a result of the violent clashes between 1999 and 2001, migration is increasingly oriented at cities and towards safe sectors such as plantations and mines.

they do it within a reassuring context of subsistence base and resource reserves. Huijsman, who concludes that one farmer can be both risk aversive and risk preferable at the same time applies to the situation in Krajan. His other conclusion that some farmers, confined by structural differences in society, cannot take risks in farming simply because they are not able to due to poverty (Huijsman 1986) does not hold in the context of Krajan. Further, poor villagers take huge risks if they play with their last penny. Especially for those living on the edge of existence without any chance of improving their livelihood, breaking out of the accepted ways of living might be an attractive option. Based on my fieldwork I conclude that risk-takers are to be found among both rich and poor and old and young farmers. An exclusive focus on the financial aspects of risk-taking does not give enough attention to cultural and normative decisions of farmers, which are not directly related to farming, but affect farming strategies as well.

Risk-takers, who break out of the (social security) system of the village, form a potential threat to the functioning of the society according to many villagers. If too many villagers, or youngsters, follow their example, the whole social fabric of reciprocity and mutual support (village social security) is at risk.

Orang nakal are expected to experience a lot of resistance from those who live a 'decent' life, and, more importantly, who are interested in maintaining the local social security system. Besides this, the orthodox Muslims in society are very much opposed to *orang nakal* and the village head was pressured to forbid gambling and sanction promiscuity. Unlike the past, in case of violation of village norms and traditions, now Islam offers the strongest arguments by those feeling threatened by these deviants. Usually, the most orthodox villagers are not directly engaged in social relations with the deviants. They often react with hostility as they have internalized the moral norms now being violated and experience this violation as a personal attack. Their lifeworld and their group feels most threatened by this behaviour. Radicalisation of Islam in Indonesia is a severe threat for the *orang nakal*.

This partly explains some of the furious and violent actions of common villagers and orthodox religious groups against gambling and 'immorality'. During the research period, on several occasions, orthodox Muslims tried to ban gambling and increase penalties on adultery in the village. In the Ramadan of 1998, the bullfight arena in Bondowoso was burnt down as well as places of prostitution. At the same time, they succeeded in banning cockfights in Krajan. Around the 1999 elections, public gambling was also prohibited and gambling places were raided by local followers (*pagarnusa*) of religious leaders (*kiai*). Despite these threats, gambling continued, but even more unobtrusively than before.

Concluding Remarks

This chapter has addressed excessive forms of risk-taking by villagers, with customary risk-taking being outside the scope of this chapter. In describing peasants' excessive risk-taking, I wanted to question the assumption that peasants are inherently risk-averse. The practices of the *orang nakal* (wayward villagers), who take and combine risks and in this way put a severe strain on their financial and non-financial resources, are described. Moreover, a focus on such 'deviancy' reveals the norms and structures in village society. I concluded that deliberate risk-taking can be an attractive option for peasants. It seems that the *orang nakal* see compliance with the village norms, and the inherent social pressures to make huge investments in social security and reciprocal relationships, a price too high.

Over the past two decades, an increasing number of people in Indonesia have seized the opportunities available: cash in the villages has greatly increased, as have risk-taking, gambling and travelling. A number of people have deliberately taken risks and bet on a better life, others just gave up living 'a decent life', went nuts or became addicted to gambling or a thrilling lifestyle. In Krajan, around 5 per cent of the population – mostly male – follow such a style of risk-taking, and one that seriously endangers their families' livelihoods.

Wayward people are deviants in the sense that they 'differ in moral or social standards from what is considered normal' (Hornby 1990). By studying deviancy in a society, something about that society can be learnt.[13] Behaviour cannot be described in the abstract, but has to be related to the norms that are socially defined as appropriate and morally binding for people in the society. For the wayward members of society, these norms, coupled with the disapproval of their behaviour, make cooperation and interaction with common villagers difficult. The failure of *orang nakal* to live up to socially defined expectations often makes life for them both miserable and difficult. Merton (1957) in writing about deviants observed: common people cannot count on them, although in fact they must. Deviants are difficult to predict (also by the scholar analysing societies) and to penalize.

Depicting wayward peasants as deviants does not explain why they live as they do and why, in so many societies there are a number of gamblers and risk-takers. Are they all stubborn and bad people, unsuited to doing good or

---

13 Deviancy is an inappropriate term as it has a negative connotation and suggests society is somehow uniform or has a consensus about norms and values. Therefore, I opted to speak of a wayward livelihood and social security style in this book. This style is but one of several possible styles in a society.

following mainstream society? Is risk-taking a viable livelihood style in itself, or just a strange way to make a living, an alternative to a dull life that will never yield a big reward? To answer these questions, I believe, a more differentiated approach is needed, one that offers insight into the reasons and the creativity of the people involved.

The studies by Hefner (1990) and Lewis (1992) discussed in the introduction show that risk-taking is often facilitated by the specific economic and agro-ecological context. In their studies, vegetable farming by its nature invited farmers to take risks in the hope of higher returns. Tobacco has much the same characteristics as vegetables: a cash crop needing expensive inputs with highly unpredictable returns due to fluctuating market prices and climatic risks. Although conditions for speculating are not similar in each society, can they explain everything?

Maybe excessive risk taking is a reaction to, and an unintended consequence of, pressures from policy, culture, religion and social control by the family or village society. Whatever, for some reason some people decide to take an alternative road. Some villagers expressed it as that they simply could not breathe within existing patterns. One said: 'I just cannot work only for my daily rice. Especially, when I was young, I could not live quietly here in the village, I had to escape every now and then'. Once depicted as *nakal*, such wayward behaviour can develop into a style that becomes perpetuated by stereotyping, stigmatization, government policies and exclusion from credit or certain forms of income. Thus, societal reactions and non-conforming responses create a 'spiral of deviancy' through which relatively minor deviations may be amplified. This is particularly the case for machismo, sexual and gambling behaviours, and for drifting, but much less so for speculation and risk-taking in other spheres of life. Wayward villagers gradually develop a deviant identity, a lifestyle that is difficult to leave behind in village life.

This lifestyle can best be described as reflecting those living dangerously as gamblers, risk-takers, speculators and so-called 'wayward' people, the *orang nakal*. It is a kind of counter-style, contrary to the other styles in society which are oriented towards sharing, accumulating wealth or mutual help. The *orang nakal* are people oriented towards chance, thrills and risk-taking rather than security. They are the minority of a population who do not want to live according to the rules and regulations of the society, who take deliberate huge risks and are 'unreasonable and irresponsible' in the eyes of others. Among these wayward people are some youngsters, criminals, gamblers, prostitutes, some migrants and *jago* (macho gang leaders).

Engaging in sexual relationships can, for instance, be very risky for the Madurese. Both male and females gamble with their lives, livelihoods and social positions. Heavy gamblers can endanger their work, land, the family's capital and thus the household's social security. Migrants may give up everything at home for an unsure and dangerous future. *Nakal* youngsters can consume the family capital by demanding parents sell land to give them money for clothes, a motor bike or other things without contributing to the village economy or to the care for their parents in return.

Risk-takers are to be found among both rich and poor and among old and young farmers. A focus on only the financial aspects of risk-taking overlooks the cultural and normative decisions of farmers that are not directly related to farming but also affect farming strategies. In the eyes of many villagers, these risk-takers, by breaking out of the village system, form a potential threat to the functioning of the society. If too many villagers follow their example, the whole social fabric of reciprocity and mutual support (village social security) is at risk. This partly explains the sometimes furious and violent reactions of common villagers and orthodox religious groups against gambling and 'immorality'. During the research period, orthodox Muslims tried several times to ban gambling and increase penalties for adultery in the village. During Ramadan 1998, the bullfighting arena in Bondowoso was burnt down along with places where prostitution was carried out. During the same period, cockfighting was banned in Krajan and, around the 1999 elections, public gambling was also prohibited and gambling places were raided by local followers of religious leaders (*kiai*). Despite these threats, gambling continued but more hidden than before.

The village head of Krajan is a good illustration that daring risk-taking can become a successful lifestyle. He used to be one of the most notorious *jago*, or delinquents, in the region, but is now highly successful in politics and business. Moreover, his experience and status as a former gang leader, womanizer and daredevil is an important basis of his power and influence in the village, and shows to others that a risky lifestyle does not always end in failure. The reverse might also be true, that those who comply with the village norms and values, and invest in social relations and social security, might also have backed the wrong horse as village social security is not that strong and does not always yield the expected outcome.

Many villagers take risks in business, agriculture or in sexual relations, but these risks are usually taken within a context of security. These are 'normal' risks that are reasonable to take once a certain level of subsistence has been achieved. The orientation of *orang nakal* is different: they do not seem to care about risking the things they have, and are more interested in the chance of winning something and the thrill of the day.

Deliberate risk-taking by the very poor seems to be a reaction to their limited prospects and dull and tied village lives. Some people no longer accept working every day for a small wage with no prospect of improvement and a better livelihood with fewer difficulties. They might instead opt for the thrill and the chance of success, even if that means risking their minimum subsistence. Maybe also for them, this lifestyle is less risky than it first appears because gender structures in the household and social relations in society will sometimes offer a minimal safety net. Some of those who have lost rice fields, cows and family by heavy gambling have switched to another style and found a place in society by becoming a client or a labourer on their former land. Others continue to live dangerously and to roam the region in search of work and fun, often joining theatre groups (*ludruk*) and only returning to their house, parents or relatives when in need of a meal or loan. Another possibility might be to run to Bali or Kalimantan to start a new life there. Now our attention shifts to East Kalimantan and to these migrants. In the next section, we turn to how they fare on arrival.

PART 2

East Kalimantan

Between 1997 and 2007, hundreds of men and women departed from the village of Krajan alone. To today, there is no end to the exodus. On October 5, 2009, a small article appeared in the Surabaya Morning (*Surabaya Pagi*) entitled: *Seribu warga eksodus ke Kalimantan* (Thousand residents in exodus to Kalimantan). It describes the migration wave after Ramadan 2009 from Krajan and three adjacent villages (Andungsari, Sumber Dumpyong and Ardisaeng) through Surabaya: 'A wave of more than 1000 inhabitants of [the villages] leave for Kalimantan. They leave the island with the hope of gaining a better life [literally: a life with more dignity]. In a single day, around 100 people from these villages charter a truck to board one of the ships in Surabaya's harbour Tanjung Perak with destination Kalimantan. The travellers consist of people who have visited their home village and now leave and take along new family members and neighbours'.

'In the villages where they come from they are farmers or landless labourers who leave for various places in Kalimantan. Some go as far as Sulawesi and even to the Moluccas', the article continues. 'The final decision to go was taken after they felt they could no longer survive in their village because of the lack of economic opportunities. After *Lebaran*, [the festive period following Ramadan] every visiting person, who had migrated earlier, took at least five relatives and neighbours along. [...] According to the village head of Krajan and the former village head Bagenda, now member of the DPRD in Bondowoso, the government should do something about the poverty in the villages'.[1]

This article summarizes the nature of Madurese migration from East Java: the migrants come from poor rural areas, they go to islands where large land development and crop booms are taking place, they use the cheapest possible transportation and they use networks of relatives and neighbours to find a job. In the following chapters, I provide an overview of how these Madurese migrants live and settle, and how they constitute a secure livelihood. The key questions are: how do they make a living, what role do social relationships play, and how and in what ways do they cope with insecurities in the migration areas.

The story of the people from Krajan is not unique. The migrants from Krajan are but a tiny part of the enormous diaspora of Madurese who have moved to Kalimantan, to other islands in Indonesia, to cities, to populate frontier areas, who flock to construction sites and occupy sidewalks and market places in search of income and a better life. They have left communities in which they

1 Surabaya Pagi. *Seribu Warga Eksodus ke Kalimantan Dihimpit Ekonomi*, Monday, October 5, 2009. http://www.surabayapagi.com/index.php?3b1ca0a43b79bdfd9f9305b8129829628 5c6e8d592665bd610ccc737db3ab13d.

ILLUSTRATION 4 *Brickmaking family from Bondowoso, East Java*

are embedded in unequal relationships of clientage, closely-knit webs of social obligations, religious affiliations and wider networks of leadership and government control. Migration offers new opportunities but also insecurities. It offers a life in which they are partially freed from the social obligations of village social-security networks, but also creates a need to engage in new relationships of support and subsistence. As a result, the old networks of community-based support are becoming increasingly weak and exclusionist, while the new networks of support are no longer community- but rather kinship- based and built on personal relationships with bosses, land owners, credit suppliers and even policemen (see Chapter 7).

This brings us back to the observations on the changing nature of local forms of social security in Indonesia as described by Hüsken and Koning (2006). They conclude:

> ...indeed the role and scope of networks and institutions that were considered to supply social security at the local level have changed during Indonesia's 'Great Transformation'. Access to such communal institutions is increasingly exclusionary and limited because, on the one hand, there are simply less people eligible or entitled and they cover less specific social needs. The primary foundation for any social security is based on direct balanced reciprocity and has therefore acquired a more transactional or calculating character. Ties between members of the networks have weakened because people's lives no longer take place in mainly one social setting, whether the hamlet, the village or the urban neighbourhood, since the huge growth of urban migration, of education, transport facilities and communication lines (2006:25).

People are often creative in finding new ways to cope with risks and adversity, and the Madurese are no exception. They deploy a wide variety of strategies and build new networks or find new forms of protection. Now, in this second part of the book, the whereabouts and livelihoods of Madurese migrants in Kalimantan are analysed in more detail. Some of the villagers from Java could be traced to East Kalimantan's brickmaking and plantation industries, but the story deals mostly with other Madurese from similar backgrounds who struggle to make a living in a hostile and insecure environment.

In East Kalimantan, I have been able to study the livelihoods of East Javanese villagers who came in the earlier waves prior to 2009. A few of them actually came from Krajan, others from nearby villages and from Besuki, Probolinggo, Bondowoso, Jember, Lumayang or Malang. I also interviewed many migrants who came from rural and poor areas on the island of Madura itself and I took part in their daily activities whenever possible. They told me about their backgrounds and reasons for migration, the importance of social relationships, relationships with other ethnic groups and about the maintenance or disruption of ties with their area of origin.

In the last decade, the large majority of these migrants have ended up in Kalimantan's oil palm plantations, in the mining and construction sector or in the informal economy. Few have been able to buy land. Some have gone back to their home villages as successful migrants, and presented another rosy example for yet another wave of migrants to follow. The majority however simply vanish and never send back any remittances or news. Although the widespread availability of modern means of communication is changing this situation, still many areas in Kalimantan lack a phone signal and phone coverage in Krajan is low. Many Madurese migrants eventually hope for a prosperous return, but very few actually achieve this, and most slowly settle down in East Kalimantan (see Chapter 6).

The reasons for migration also vary. Some were forced to migrate as a result of debts, or as a result of gambling or risky behaviour. Some of them were spurred on by death threats. Others were simply lured into what turned out to be disadvantageous labour arrangements by middlemen and recruiters who promised work and a good income. Many of these had almost completely lost their ties with their area of origin, or had cut these ties on purpose. Other migrants I spoke to just hoped for a better life, just to be free from regular food shortages and debts, and to be able to make a decent living and give their children a better future.

For practical reasons, the following chapters focus on three sectors of economic activity, the construction sector, the brickmaking sector and the agricultural sector. All the studies take place in one area, the city of Samarinda and its vicinity in East Kalimantan. Within these sectors, the livelihood activities of Madurese, embedded as they are in larger contexts of political change and economic insecurity, are described and analysed. Risk-taking practices such as speculation, gambling and engaging in criminal activities, as well as threats and interpretations of violence, will be discussed in detail.

In Chapter 6, the livelihoods of Madurese migrants in and around Samardina are described with a focus on the three sectors. The chapter is situated in a period of turmoil, the aftermath of the economic crisis and reforms at the turn of the millennium. Chapter 7 deals with ethnic violence and its threat to migrants in relation to livelihood strategies, and the final chapter, Chapter 8, returns to the issue of risk-taking, this time focussing on one aspect, the engagement in criminal activities and relationships with police officers in Samarinda. Although sketchy at times, these three chapters offer an image of how Madurese from East Java eventually fare in migration areas and how they deal with the vicissitudes of their new lives in an often alien environment.

CHAPTER 6

Badlands

Madurese Livelihoods in East Kalimantan

A Short History of Madurese Migration to Kalimantan

It is difficult to find exact figures for Madurese migration to Kalimantan since details of ethnic descent have not been provided by Indonesian statistics during most of the twentieth century. It is clear however that considerable numbers of migrants from Madura first started to migrate shortly before World War II when work opportunities Kalimantan's oil industry, plantation sector and logging industry started to grow in importance (Harjono 1988). Earlier, between 1867 and 1920, the population density of Madura had more than tripled, a faster growth rate than in other areas of Java (Cribb 2000:69). Madurese were the most popular cheap and reliable labourers and they were also part of the first Dutch transmigration projects (at that time known as colonization) in 1921 in Kalimantan. In 1938, the settlers in the Madurejo dry land transmigration area of South Kalimantan were all Madurese (Harjono 1977).

Contrary to what has generally been said,[1] Madurese were seldom part of the large-scale transmigration programmes of the post-war era. The majority of Madurese migrants came spontaneously to Kalimantan. The first major wave of Madurese migrants, including migrants from the Besuki – Bondowoso area, came after the oil boom in the mid-1970s. They chased the new labour opportunities and their migration was only indirectly stimulated by the transmigration programmes. Madurese from East Java and Madura migrated in the slipstream of the opening up of the area and they settled in the niches of opportunity created by the large programmes. According to informants at the bureau of transmigration in East Kalimantan, it was official policy not to include Madurese in transmigration projects because they were perceived as risky and problematic groups that might cause turmoil or ethnic tensions. Madurese from mainland East Java were included if they happened to live in source areas for transmigrants, such as Malang, Pasuruan and Lumajang. In several of the blocks, established since the 1970s, of East Javanese migrants in East Kalimantan, we came across Madurese speakers.[2] During fieldwork,

1 The wikipedia page 'Madurese people' also repeats the common misunderstanding that transmigration programmes brought the Madurese to Kalimantan (accessed 14 Feb 2012).

2 Survey in Samarinda and East Kutai district, East Kalimantan, 2003.

whenever I was able to trace the first generation of settlers, they were always born in Madurese-speaking areas of Java (such as Malang, Pasuruan, Besuki, Bondowoso and Jember) – we did not encounter a single Madurese-speaking person born on Madura itself.

The transmigration programmes have been indirectly important for Madurese. The transmigration programmes opened new areas, provided infrastructure and opened the way for spontaneous migration, not only for Javanese and Madurese, but also for Bugis, Banjar and Toraja. In these early years, most migrants did not experience much resistance from other ethnic groups and often peacefully lived and worked together with other ethnicities.

From the early 1970s, when the numbers of immigrants in Kalimantan increased dramatically, friction has regularly occurred with the local population and with other migrant groups. Due to the strong military repression under Suharto's New Order, these frictions could never develop into large conflicts and, further, migrants, especially from Java and Madura, were generally well protected in contrast to the ethnic Chinese in West Kalimantan (Hendro 2001). In the early 1990s, the New Order developmental model started to show cracks. Local groups in the outer islands started to contest the Jakarta and Javanese based domination, and more openly expressed their resentments. The often corrupt and internally divided police and military forces were no longer able to stop ethnic and religious inspired clashes against migrants and ethnic Chinese. Widespread and repeated looting and ethnic violence in Java (against Chinese), the Moluccas, Central Sulawesi (Poso) and in the outer islands (against Madurese and Chinese) was an early indication of the shortcomings and weaknesses of the Indonesian New Order political system which suppressed tensions rather than resolving them (Antlöv 1999, Breman 2000, Hill 1999, Lont and White 2003).

In 1999 and 2001, when government legitimacy had severely declined due to the crisis, large ethnic conflicts occurred in Sambas and Sampit (West and Central Kalimantan).[3] Most of the Madurese in these provinces originate from Sampang and Pamekasan at Madura Island and from the eastern districts of East Java. After the conflict had peaked, over 300,000 Madurese were expelled from Kalimantan and sent 'back' to Madura or East Java (Brusset et al. 2004). In Krajan, at least 300 people were resettled in a refugee camp in the lower area of the village (*dusun Sayuran*). It was not clear to me if all these people were originally from Krajan, or if some came from the three adjacent villages.[4]

---

3 For an overview of the conflicts in West and Central Kalimantan see: Davidson and Kammen 2002; Peluso and Harwell 2001; Schiller and Garang 2002.

4 Information based on interviews with Krajan residents on a Pelni ship (regular interisland shipping line) from Surabaya to Samarinda in 2003 and with Krajan people working in Samarinda's brick industry (interviewed in 2004 and 2005).

For East Kalimantan, the situation is slightly different. Most Madurese from Madura who migrated to East Kalimantan originate from Bangkalan, with some from Sampang and mainland East Java. Generally, they do not own land and work as unskilled labourers for logging companies, in road construction, for contractors and in the plantation sector. Nowadays, some have been able to start small- or medium- sized businesses, but the majority remain poor. The migration patterns of Madurese in East Kalimantan differ from those in West and Central Kalimantan as, in the latter, large proportions of the Madurese settled in rural areas and obtained land (Peluso and Harwell 2001:95).

Madurese Migration to Samarinda

It is difficult to say exactly when the first Madurese came to Samarinda. Of the Madurese currently living in Samarinda, those living there the longest came to the town in the early 1960s. They worked as unskilled labourers and, at least since the mid-1960s, a few Madurese have been active as brickmakers. Before that period, all the houses were made of wood and occasionally Madurese were reported to be working as carpenters or traders. Until the late 1960s, living conditions in Samarinda were difficult due to poor roads and facilities. When, at the end of the 1960s, large transmigration schemes were established in Samarinda, Madurese found work in road and house construction, in logging and in the construction of irrigation dikes, canals and ditches.

After 1970, things started to change. Employment opportunities grew, large transmigration areas around the city brought larger populations and Samarinda started to develop as a provincial city. In this period, logging activities in the vicinities of Samarinda also increased, a large number of sawmills were opened along the Mahakam river, government buildings were established and the demand for unskilled labourers for road construction and building activities increased sharply. Moreover, the demand for gravel, stone, bricks and building materials rocketed and many newcomers seized the opportunities to start a trade or business. Nowadays, Madurese make up an estimated 5% of the population of Samarinda and 3.6% of East Kalimantan.[5] This makes them the sixth largest ethnic group in East Kalimantan – after Javanese with nearly 30%,

5 This is a rough estimation. The secretary of the KKMM (Madurese cultural association) estimated the number of Madurese household heads in the areas of Balikpapan and Samarinda in East Kalimantan in 2002 as at least 35,000 (compared with 30,181 individuals listed in the 2000 census for East Kalimantan as a whole). Given that most Madurese live in or near these two cities, and that about half of these Madurese immigrants bring their families (with an average of two children) with them, suggests at least 87,500 Madurese would be living in East Kalimantan. This makes up 3.6% of the population (three times the official 2000 census figures).

Bugis with 18%, Banjar with 14%, Kutai with 9% and Dayak with an estimated 5% (BPS 2001, Suryadinata et al. 2003).

The ethnic division in terms of economic activities is as follows: Javanese dominate farming in the transmigration areas as well as the middle and higher ranks of the services sector, in government bureaucracy and in education. Buginese immigrants from Sulawesi dominate petty trade and transport, as well as large trade in wood, vegetables and fruit, they own restaurants and some large production enterprises. Banjarese are farmers, factory workers and owners of many small shops and restaurants. Kutai, the original population, can be found in agriculture and business and in the higher ranks of government personnel. Chinese dominate the retail and supply sectors, own most of the larger shops in town, many sawmills and they dominate the capital-intensive branches of the economy. Most of the Dayak people in East Kalimantan are to found in the faraway forests of the upper Mahakam and in the Berau and Nunukan districts.

Some of the Madurese settlers who came in the early 1970s are now well-off and own houses, cars, transport businesses, recycling firms, construction companies, gambling dens and brothels. A quick count in 2005 showed that about 25 Madurese families own medium or large companies with over 25 workers and more than 10 vehicles. These successful Madurese in Samarinda can all be traced back to 7 families from either Bangkalan district (4) or mainland East Java (3), but none of them came from Krajan or its vicinity. Some of them have developed into real tycoons dominating road construction, recycling and contracting. They made their fortunes during the late 1980s and 1990s when the economy of Samarinda was booming as a result of the increased logging and mining activities. All the migrants I spoke to started without virtually any capital and a number of them told me that had migrated to escape troubles in Madura such as poverty, but several also mentioned accusations of crime, theft, murder, gambling debts and adultery.

The majority of the Madurese in Samarinda have, however, not been very successful and remain poor. They have limited education (with illiteracy rates of over 40% to 50% for men and over 70% for women) but are known for being hard workers. This makes them desirable in sectors where hard labour is required such as in transport and construction work. Many porters in the harbour and on the markets are Madurese, as well as road workers, construction workers, garbage collectors, stonecutters and brickmakers. Some have become security guards, policemen, carpenters, owners of repair shops and hairdressers. The banana trade and the *sate* sector are dominated by Madurese as well as the majority of the canteens on the university campus. Nevertheless, in general, Madurese migrants remain in the lower strata of society.

ILLUSTRATION 5 *Brickmaking family from Bangkalan, Madura*

This chapter and those that follow are based on material gathered during a larger study on livelihood and social security styles of Madurese migrants in East Kalimantan in the context of crisis and decentralization in Indonesia. In Kalimantan, I studied Madurese settlers in three clearly demarcated clusters of economic activity: brickmaking, stonecutting and vegetable production. The first two sectors are dominated by Madurese from Bangkalan (West Madura) and Sampang (Central Madura) respectively, whereas, in the vegetable production area of Lempake (northeast of Samarinda), Madurese-speaking migrants from Malang (East Java) dominate economic activities.

Most brickmakers work on the outskirts of Samarinda and stonecutters can be found in the hills of *Batu Putih* and *Batu Besaung* west and north of the city (see Map 4). Within these relatively homogeneous clusters of economic activity (in terms of place, descent, social class and ethnic identity), I observed a wide range of different ways in which people try to make a living, interpret crisis, maintain contacts with other ethnic groups and strive for 'success'.

The research consisted of both quantitative and qualitative methodologies and comprised three phases with increasingly narrowing scopes. In the first phase, the different economic activities, locations and backgrounds of Madurese migrants were mapped. After this phase, three sectors that were dominated by Madurese were identified. In the second phase, a large-scale survey was conducted on livelihood constitution, livelihood patterns, incomes, remittances, social security, perceptions of crisis and interethnic relationships. In the final phase, a dozen families from the first and second phases were again approached for lengthy interviews and life histories. These families were visited on a weekly basis and studied more intensively as case studies.

Some members of these families were traced back to the island of Madura and family members were visited in Bangkalan, Madura. In practice, the second and third phases overlapped as the case studies started while the survey was still running. In total, 79 brickmaking families and individual workers were surveyed, as well as 45 stonecutters, 20 farmers and 10 contractors. In addition, Dayak, Bugis and Javanese key informants were interviewed, as well as members of the police and the administration.

In summarizing, one can say that the majority of Madurese migrants came spontaneously to Kalimantan, with major waves after the oil boom of the mid-1970s. They followed the new labour opportunities, and their migration was only indirectly stimulated by the transmigration programmes. They took the opportunities provided by infrastructural development and newly opened areas, and were attracted by economic growth in other parts of the archipelago.

Since the early 1970s, when the numbers of immigrants in Kalimantan started to increase dramatically, friction with the local population and with other migrant groups regularly occurred. Due to the strong military repression under Suharto's New Order, these tensions could not develop into larger conflicts. Migrants, especially from Java and Madura, were generally well protected. However, in 1999 and 2001, when government legitimacy as well as police and military forces had severely declined due to the crisis and regime changes, large ethnic conflicts occurred in Sambas and Sampit (West and Central Kalimantan).[6] Most of the Madurese in these districts originate from the remote Sampang and Pamekasan districts of Madura Island and from the eastern districts of East Java. A significant proportion of the migrants from the island of Madura managed to obtain land and had lived for two or three generations in the area. Among them were people from Krajan, but the majority from Krajan remained rural labourers or had established a small trade in town.

In East Kalimantan, one of the richest provinces in Indonesia due to its large reserves of oil, gas, minerals and timber, the situation is slightly different. Most Madurese who migrated to East Kalimantan originate from Bangkalan, with smaller numbers from Sampang and the eastern districts of Java including Krajan. Generally, in East Kalimantan, the Madurese migrants live in and around the main cities of Balikpapan, Samarinda and Tarakan, and work as

6 For a good overview of the conflicts in West and Central Kalimantan see: Davidson and Kammen 2002; Peluso and Harwell 2001; Schiller and Garang 2002.

ILLUSTRATION 6 *Brickmaking settlement in Balikpapan*

unskilled labourers for logging companies, in road construction, for contractors and in the plantation sector. Some have been able to start small or medium-sized businesses, but the majority remain poor. The migration patterns of Madurese in East Kalimantan differ in this respect from those in West and Central Kalimantan as, in the latter, a large proportion of the Madurese settled in rural areas and a significant number managed to obtain land.

Madurese Livelihoods in Samarinda

Of the migrants studied, the stonecutters (quarrymen) are the most marginalized. They work in the hills around Samarinda (10–20 kilometres from the city) and live in small barracks or sheds. Labourers earn on an average Rp 15,000–20,000 (€2) per day. Male workers carve rocks and stones from rocky mountain ridges, while women cut larger stones into smaller chippings. Most of the employers have Bugis, Chinese, Banjar or Javanese origins. Wages for labourers in the brickmaking industry are only slightly higher (an average of Rp 17,500 per day, ranging from Rp 15,000–25,000) but living conditions are better, labour conditions are more stable and in some cases transport and some basic social security is provided by the employer.[7] The wages in both these sectors are somewhat lower than the Rp 25,000 paid to unskilled labourers from Java

7 Sometimes, social security benefits are provided to the labourers such as payments for visits to a doctor or hospital, for medication, by giving loans (without interest and to be paid back in bricks) or free transport to return to the area of origin. These benefits are mostly given to labourers who are from the same area as their employer.

working on large construction projects in Samarinda. Nevertheless, they are well above the Rp 6,000–7,500 which could be earned on Madura or in rural East Java if work was available.

During the last decade, the brickmaking industry in Samarinda has been booming. In the survey, we found 350 brickyards (usually only a simple barn where stones could be parched and burned) which had been operational for an average of five years. One-third of these brickyards were family enterprises without labourers, the others employed an average of six labourers, mostly couples working together. Ninety-two per cent of the brickmaking entrepreneurs as well as 58% of their workers come from Madura. In fact, 80% of the entrepreneurs and 39% of the workers came from one village, Geger, in Bangkalan district, West Madura. Another 19% of the workers came from other areas in Madura, and the other 40% of the workers come from Madurese-speaking areas in East Java with the largest proportion from Bondowoso (32%) including some from Krajan. Most labourers return home before the festivities the follow the Islamic month of fasting (*Idhul Fitri*), but those tied through debt and those who had established a trade, bought land, married locally or established a business never or only seldom went back. On average, savings after ten months of working amounted Rp 1.2 million (€120).

Average incomes for the owners of brickmaking enterprises range between Rp 1 million and 4 million a month (€100–400). The brickyards are usually situated just outside the city and are rented or leased for the purpose of producing bricks. Only 15% own the land they are working on. With the growth in negative sentiments against Madurese in the last couple of years, landowners are increasingly reluctant to rent or lease land and demand higher prices.[8] A local Banjar leader commented: 'We, as the original inhabitants here, have decided and say to all: "Don't give any land to Madurese to make bricks. Why should we help them to make money out of our land? Let them buy it honestly". To gain a clearer image of how Madurese make a living, and how they perceive the situation in East Kalimantan, we now zoom in on the practice of brickmaking and its key event, the firing of the bricks.

Brick firing

One Friday night in November 2004, *Pak* Dapi, originally from Geger, Bangkalan, Madura, put a bench in front of his brickyard and held a small ritual (*selamatan*). He said a prayer with his two sons and attached a tiny piece of wood with some flowers, a leaf, a red pepper and an onion at the

8 Lease prices doubled between 2001 and 2003.

ILLUSTRATION 7 *Worker from East Java preparing clay for bricks*

corners of the carefully constructed stack of unbaked hand-formed bricks. Following this, they took a simple meal and went to bed. Early next morning, Dapi lit the fire and, a few hours later, his sons and some of their friends came to help. Dapi organized the firing and the younger workers followed his orders. It takes knowledge and experience to get a good firing, and a fire that is too hot would crack the bricks, while slow baking would be inefficient. During the day, they sit on the bench, watch the fire and play cards. Every now and then, the game is interrupted and new wood is added to the fire. At regular intervals, Dapi's wife serves a meal.

After two days, the fire is really hot and then needs to be fuelled almost continuously. Dapi's two sons, two relatives and a neighbour help with the work. Large flames pour through holes in the stack of bricks and illuminate the sweat-covered bodies. Dark silhouettes fuel the hungry oven. One hand throws in the firewood, the other protects the face. A young daredevil even climbs on top of the pile to show his vigour and rearrange some of the bricks. In front of the barracks, a man pours water over his face and in his mouth. Even at night, the work is deadly hot.

During the five days it takes to fire the bricks, relatives, friends and maybe neighbours – all Madurese - come by for a short visit every now and then. Some of these visitors had provided credit, firewood or rice to Dapi; others just sat down, chatted and smoked. Some of these visitors offered Dapi a pack of cigarettes. They discussed Madura affairs, or the difficulties they had in obtaining land, firewood, loans and reliable deals. 'Since the violence in Sampit [2001], people don't want us here anymore. They are making our lives hard and insecure. We Madurese have to look after ourselves.'

The firing of bricks is the most important event for a Madurese brickmaker in East Kalimantan. Through studying this event, all the major ingredients of successful migrant entrepreneurship become visible. Important elements to be achieved include the successful mobilization of labour and capital through ethnic and kinship networks, the maintenance of close links with Madura, sending remittances regularly, helping each other out, keeping on good terms with police officers and local power holders and avoiding problems with other ethnic groups.

Brickmaking involves a number of tasks that cannot be organized alone. Land needs to be 'borrowed', leased or purchased, and the clay must be mixed well and manually moulded into bricks. These bricks are then dried in long rows outside the brickyard after which, a few weeks before the firing, they must be carefully piled up into the shape of a kiln. The construction of the barn, barracks, drying lanes and moulding tables, as well as the payments for leasing land and wages involves a lot of money. At the same time, truckloads of firewood need to be purchased, as well as sawdust, food for the workers, coffee, sugar and cigarettes.[9] Most entrepreneurs do not have sufficient money to finance all this so they borrow from relatives, friends or fellow brickmakers.[10] Besides this need

9 Required investments prior to production range between Rp 15–25 million (€1500–2500), and each cycle of firing the bricks involves another Rp 7–20 million (€700–2000) depending on the size of the enterprise.

10 Borrowing and lending is a complex matter. Nearly all entrepreneurs need cash before the firing of the bricks and not everybody burns at the same time (they take turns in firing).

of cash, many helping hands are required to build a barn, to construct an access road, to get the land ready for clearing and to periodically fire the bricks. Moreover, relationships with landowners, usually non-Madurese, need to be maintained and fees or rents need to be paid to them after each firing. Further, as land titles are far from clear in East Kalimantan and many brickmakers occupy land previously idle, good relationships with policemen and government officers need to be maintained to obtain licences and protect against land claims (see Chapter 8).

All those who have a stake in the enterprise will show up during the firing of the bricks; either to provide a helping hand or just to show their presence (and to ensure that premiums are paid and loans will be repaid after the bricks are sold). Entrepreneurs who are, for whatever reason, unable to manage all these relationships will not be able to stay in business.

Regular access to cash and credit is necessary to recruit a sufficient number of labourers since entrepreneurs who are not able to provide loans and cash advances to their workers will not be able to mobilise sufficient labour. Young single male workers especially need regular money for smoking, entertainment and drinking parties at the roadside or market at night. Regularly, these parties end up in fighting with other youths. When such fights break out, the entrepreneur needs to go and settle the conflict. Besides these internal managerial tasks, outside influences are also important for the success of these enterprises. Brickmaking enterprises are sensitive to external changes (such as a crisis) that influence market prices, interpersonal trust or inter-ethnic relationships.

Four Types of Migrants

In East Kalimantan, four categories of Madurese migrants can be distinguished: seasonal migrants, semi-permanent migrants, semi-permanent settlers and settlers.

(1) Seasonal migrants seasonally travel to and from Madura or eastern Java. They are most often males travelling alone but sometimes couples who leave dependent children with relatives in Madura where life is cheaper

Virtually everybody is indebted to each other at some stage, and many are indebted to each other almost continuously. The credit landscape resembles a carrousel of revolving money in which entrepreneurs are alternately debtors and creditors to each other. In almost all cases, the money is borrowed from fellow Madurese from the same village of origin, or from close relatives (siblings, uncles, parents or nephews and nieces).

ILLUSTRATION 8 *Carrying clay to the brick moulding place*

and perceived safer. As soon as some money is earned they send it to family members or return home (savings of Rp 1–2 million (€100–200) are considered adequate to return). Most of these seasonal migrants work as waged labourers in construction, agriculture, brickmaking or stonecutting and are organized by Madurese middlemen. They come from East Java or from Sampang and Pamekasan (including refugees from West and Central Kalimantan) and usually travel to Kalimantan by boat although, nowadays, the plane option is becoming popular. Lengths of stay range between three months and two years. These workers have the lowest incomes (gross individual and family wages average between Rp 15,000–20,000 (€1.5–2) per day) in the region, but these are still double what can

ILLUSTRATION 9 *Firing bricks in Samarinda Sebrang*

be earned on Madura or on mainland East Java. It should be noted, however, that prices for basic goods in East Kalimantan are also about 50% higher than elsewhere.

(2) Semi-permanent migrants. Among the brickmakers and stonecutters in Samarinda, people can regularly be found who have worked for over 20 years in Kalimantan but who still return home nearly every year at *Idhul Fitri*. These peoples can hardly be called seasonal migrants since they have lived most of their lives in Kalimantan and only travel to Madura for short periods each year. Every year, as soon as their savings are used up on Madura, they return to Kalimantan. Nevertheless, they still regard themselves as living on Madura and as only temporary dwellers in Kalimantan. Some of these people own houses and sometimes cattle 'at home' in Madura, but the majority have never been able to accumulate any substantial property in either Madura or Kalimantan.

The average incomes of semi-permanent migrants are higher and more stable than those of the seasonal migrants. They work as waged labourers, traders and sometimes as subcontractors (*barongan*). They tend to invest their savings mainly in Madura by buying land, cattle, a motorbike or to improve their houses. Every year, they try to go home for *Idhul Fitri* and visit relatives and children who have stayed on Madura (girls usually stay on Madura to care for parents and, if sufficient money is available, boys are sent to an Islamic boarding school (*pesantren*)). If possible, they send regular remittances to family members, parents and relatives in need of support or a loan. The difference between them and the (semi-permanent) settlers lies in their self-definition as being a migrant (*perantau*) and their orientation towards their place of descent. This is for instance expressed in their wish to invest in their home villages on Madura or in eastern Java rather than in Kalimantan.

(3) Semi-permanent settlers. This group can be rather successful, some own good businesses or trades, and among them are many entrepreneurs, owners of brickmaking sites and transport companies. Among the semi-permanent settlers are also people who are unable to return to their place of origin for a variety of reasons such as indebtedness, low wages or 'trouble'. The successful semi-permanent settlers send regular money home to support parents or relatives and to accumulate assets, but they tend also to invest in Kalimantan (in enterprises, trucks and land). As the years go by, ties with Madura get weaker and children, if they decide to live in East Kalimantan, tend never to return. Nevertheless, they all claim to yearn to go back to Madura and tend to maintain a home there. These houses are often used by relatives but some fall down due to neglect. Semi-permanent settlers aim to make money in Kalimantan, where 'money is cheap', but often dream of retirement 'at home'. After the 2001 violence, this dream acquired another dimension. Most Madurese migrants expressed it as that their attitude towards Kalimantan had changed. They no longer feel safe and doubt if they will ever live safely there.

(4) Settlers. The final group have simply chosen to stay in Kalimantan and do not wish to return 'home'. Many try to assimilate themselves, or hide their Madurese descent, as a result of the violence against Madurese in neighbouring provinces. Among the permanent settlers are many second and third generation Madurese. They feel little affection for their homeland. They are living with their family, and children go to schools in Kalimantan. Sometimes they are even unable to speak Madurese. They have no wish to return and generally no longer own anything on Madura. If they do send any remittances back, these are for family emergencies or bear a more ritualistic function such as contributing to the building of a mosque or religious school.

These migrant categories do not necessarily reflect social class, and especially in the last two categories both rich and poor people are to be found. Over 90% of the Madurese from the island of Madura in East Kalimantan keep close ties with their area of origin, whereas this percentage is much lower, less than 50%, for the poor migrants from mainland East Java. For those who maintain contacts, news about family members and events on Madura are constantly exchanged. This connectedness to Madura is one of the reasons why Madurese from Madura tend to maintain their distinct ethnic identity. The cultural notion of travelling (*merantau*) in search of money, rather than 'settling', is an important driver for Madurese to move from Madura. Initially they all hoped to return and this idea of *merantau* does not motivate them to invest in Kalimantan or to buy land there. This mechanism strengthened after the violence in West and Central Kalimantan, which spread fear of further ethnic violence, and more Madurese tried to accumulate assets on Madura.

Those who still aim to settle in East Kalimantan, initially tend to only invest in productive property. Only if children are born in the diaspora grow up and wish to stay, does permanent settlement become an option. Now, as lease contracts for land and business opportunities have become difficult for Madurese due to the growing prejudices, many regret not having bought land earlier.

The Madurese-speaking migrants from the island of Java originate from the Situbondo, Bondowoso, Jember, Lumajang, Banyuwangi and Malang areas. In the eyes of other ethnic groups, these people are Madurese and treated as such but, according to Madurese originating from Madura itself, they are neither Madurese nor Javanese. Generally, they are classified as of lower status by both Madurese from Madura and other ethnic groups. They occupy the lowest echelons of Madurese migrant society and often work as labourers.

Stereotypes of Madurese in Samarinda

'Madurese are always causing problems, you know. If you lend them land, they will stick to it and never give it back. They simply pushed us too far...' (Dayak commentator, Samarinda 2005).

Since colonial times, Madurese have been described as touchy, temperamental, hot-tempered, fierce, vengeful and violent (De Jonge 1995:13).[11] Further, outsiders often mention them in relation to crime and theft. Such stereotypes are still regularly mentioned and maintained up to the present day. The best-known feature of Madurese violence is *carok* – a murder committed when a man's honour is insulted. Among the main reasons for *carok* are (rumours of) someone having had a sexual affair with a wife, daughter or relative. Until recently, *carok* has been regularly committed in Sampang and Bangkalan

11 Although most remarks in this chapter about stereotypes refer to Madurese men, women are usually included in these images as the male attitudes are perceived as clear symbols representing the whole group.

districts on Madura, and cases have also been regularly reported in the Bondowoso, Situbondo and Jember areas in East Java (Latief Wiyata 2002).

During interviews and casual talks in Samarinda with non-Madurese residents, such as with Javanese, Bugis, Banjar and Chinese, the above-mentioned negative stereotypes about Madurese were often raised. Informants used them to explain 'the Madurese problem'. In general, people of Banjar and Bugis descent were the most negative about Madurese and almost always produced negative stereotypes when talking about Madurese. Other people also mentioned these negative stereotypes, but would sometimes add more positive images of Madurese such as being hardworking, clever, trustworthy and loyal (once engaged closely). Some of the Chinese strongmen and businessmen preferred Madurese workers because of these qualities:

> If you get to know them and entrust them with a position, they will be reliable and loyal. Once loyal, they would rather die for you then walk away. I like them, they are good workers and able to save and accumulate, even under harsh conditions. They are a bit like us.
>
> CHINESE BUSINESSMAN

In most other situations, anything positive about Madurese was hardly ever mentioned. Stereotypes about Madurese remain extremely negative and widespread in Kalimantan.

One of my neighbours (a Bugis) told me seriously: 'I know many of those brickmaking Madurese by name, 90% are thieves. At night, they sneak around the houses in richer neighbourhoods and if they don't find money, they steal your daughters'. Someone else commented: 'Don't ever make them angry. They stab you right away'. About taxi drivers in Samarinda: 'Beware of those Madurese. They always rip you off' and about minibus drivers and porters in Samarinda: 'Beware of those Madurese at the docks, afterwards they will charge you a higher price than agreed upon and if you protest, they call upon their friends to beat you up'. 'Those Madurese always back each other', another commented. 'If the police arrest a criminal, one of their leaders will pay the police to free him. When we search for the criminal for revenge, he has escaped to Madura where we cannot hunt him down'.

These negative images do not only prevail among lower social classes, they are also reproduced among the upper classes. At one of the university campuses for instance, staff of the demographic department told me in a group discussion that:

> They only come here [to East Kalimantan] to work and earn money. They do not really settle here. You can observe a pattern in their settlement:

> first they lived in the quarters on the edges of the town centre then, when these areas developed into residential areas, they moved to the edge of town. Then they moved again, and the pattern repeats itself. They do not settle down, accumulate, invest and rise in social status.

Another staff member opposed this speaker. 'No, I know a lot of [Madurese] who bought cars, built a house and do good business'. The other shrugs his shoulders 'maybe', and turning to me:

> They are causing problems, especially when it is close to *Hari Raya* [*Idhul Fitri* - the end of the Islamic month of fasting]. They only work temporarily here and earn little. As soon as they have money, they go back. If they don't have money for *Hari Raya,* then they try to get it in any possible ways' 'You mean they steal?' I asked. 'Yes, many of them do steal, others ask for loans but never repay them, or they take items away. Moreover, there are many small riots at this period of the year. They [here including other immigrants: *perantau*] ask for money at houses, demonstrate against rising prices, or stop cars and ask for money'.

Somewhat later:

> The Madurese cause problems with land. If you lend them a piece of land, they will stick on it and never let it go. Nowadays, we know that you should never lend land to Madurese people. Either they should buy it or not have it. Two other staff members agreed with the speaker. 'We do not want migrants like them. Our government [regional government of East Kalimantan] tries to stop them. Only skilled and desirable migrants should be allowed to come. Not those vagabonds who hamper our development'.

While ethnicity and Madurese are often mentioned in personal encounters, they are never mentioned in regional media, such as newspapers (Kaltim Pos, Tribun), television and radio. Regional newspapers report extensively on traffic accidents, crimes, fights, lynchings and police round-ups, but the ethnicity of victims or criminals is never mentioned, even if conflicts are of an explicitly ethnic nature. The collective silence on ethnicity was imposed by the regional government in an attempt to suppress the spread of the ethnic sentiments seen during the Kalimantan riots in 2001 and 2003. This stance is still maintained. However, in both lower and higher echelons of society, problems of poverty, insecurity and criminality are explicitly linked to ethnicity. In these discourses, negative images of Madurese are constantly reproduced. As few people mix with Madurese or maintain good relationships with them, and given that Madurese lack representation at the higher levels, these stereotypes seem to persist, and maintaining them would seem to benefit the ethnic elites.

Madurese Livelihoods in Crisis: Brickmakers, Stonecutters and Vegetable Farmers

In this chapter, I focus on three economic sectors: brickmaking, stonecutting and vegetable farming. I have focused on the first two as they are highly visible and known for their strong Madurese presence, the last sector has been studied for comparison purposes. Livelihoods in these sectors are not only difficult and at risk due to the stereotyping and negative impressions of other ethnic groups, they are also prone to economic risks and insecurities. In the next section, I will outline how livelihoods during the period 2000–2005 experienced various economic shocks and stresses and how people coped with them.

Labourers in the brick sector live a squatter-like existence in simple bamboo houses built on unused pieces of land and can be found clustered along most of the roads outside Samarinda. The Madurese stonecutters can be found in Batu Putih and Batu Besaung, a range of rocky hills to the west and north of Samarinda. The third group, the vegetable farmers, are not strongly identified as being Madurese, and can be found to the north and northeast of Lempake (see Map 5). They invest in land, fruit trees, cattle and brick houses.

The 'Rough' Sector: Brickmaking

In the 2003–2004 survey, my assistant and I found 350 brickyards (*serobong*) providing a livelihood for an estimated 1,400 families.[12] A *serobong* usually consists of a simple barn where stones can be parched and baked. Around the *serobong*, excavations, moulding tables, stacks of firewood and simple barracks can be found. The land to produce bricks is usually rented or leased. Only 15% of the entrepreneurs own the land they are working on.

The surveyed brickyards were on average 4.7 years old. *Serobong* are regularly transferred to other locations when the adjacent clay is used up, when conflicts occur, lease contracts are terminated or house or road construction competes for the land. Only if the land is owned by the brickyard owner will an

12 A GPS was used to locate the exact locations. The locations were then plotted on a map of Samarinda (Map 4 produced by Puslitbangwil-Unmul, the research centre for regional development, Mulawarman University, Samarinda.) Of these 350 *serobong*, 79 have been surveyed in detail and 15 have been visited more than once.

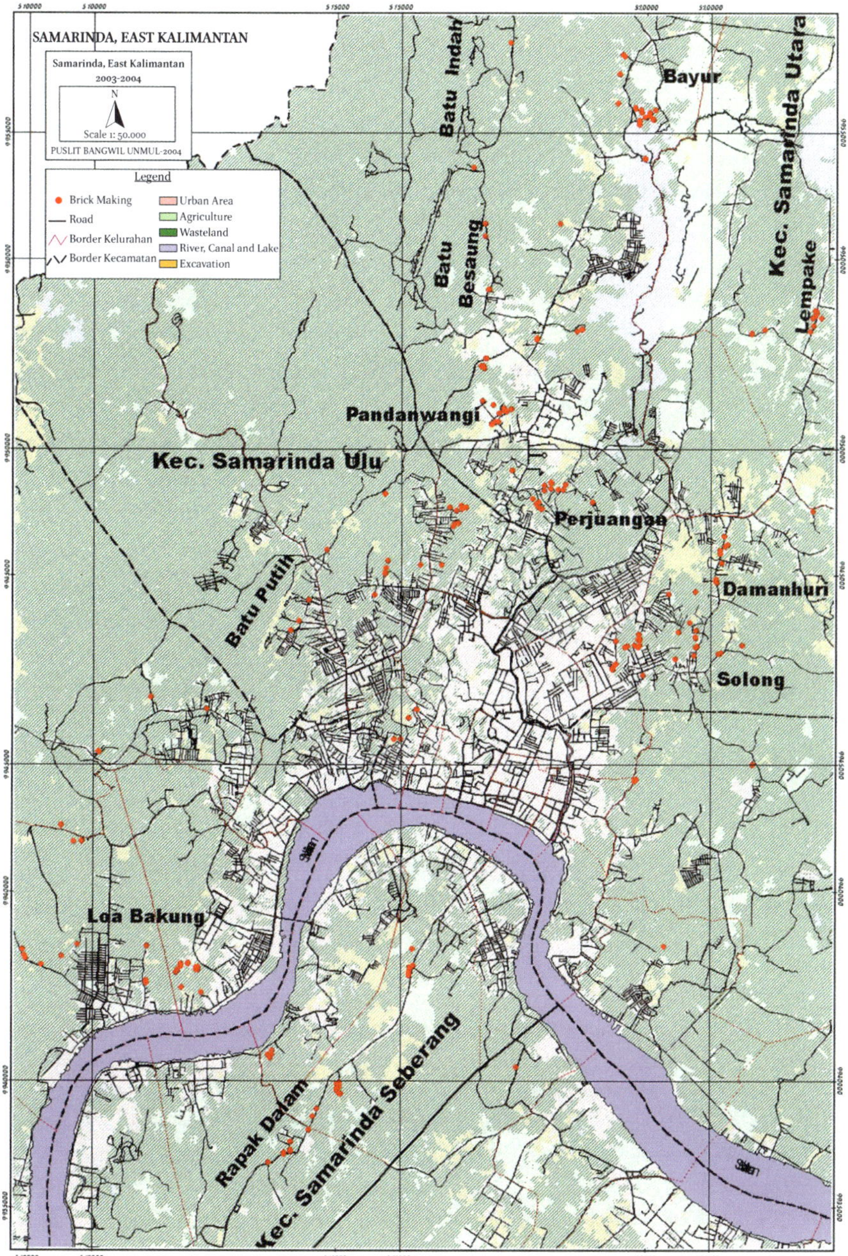

MAP 5 *Land use and brickmakers in Samarinda, East Kalimantan (February 2004)*

MAP SAMARINDA: MADE FOR THIS STUDY BY PUSLITBANGWIL UNMUL 2004, MULAWARMAN UNIVERSITY, SAMARINDA, EAST KALIMANTAN

enterprise remain in one place for much longer. Over the last two decades, brickyard locations have slowly moved from the outskirts of the older city to outer areas as a result of Samarinda's ongoing urbanisation.

About 40% of the brickyards studied were family-owned enterprises that did not employ labourers, while the other 60% employed an average of six labourers. Most of the enterprises are small and consist of one wooden shelter (*serobong*) for drying and baking bricks, a few basic barracks for the workers, and some simple production tools such as shovels and moulds. On average, each *serobong* has three teams of workers. A team, or *kongsi*, includes a husband and wife or perhaps two male workers. Many of these workers are heavily indebted to the brickyard owner and can only return to Madura once their debts are repaid. These forms of bonded, debt-incurred labour were found in about half of the brickyards. Sometimes couples bring their children along, but more often they stay on Madura (and in half of the cases wives also). Notwithstanding the simple production techniques, an estimated 50 million bricks were produced in the Samarinda district in 2003 and about 3,500 people are dependent on brickmaking as their main source of livelihood.[13]

Although there are significant differences in both speech and culture between people from Madura and from Eastern Java,[14] other ethnic groups in East Kalimantan view all brickmakers as simply Madurese. It is called the 'rough' sector, 'only suitable for strong, hardworking people who are able to endure' and for people who are not 'refined' enough to work in other sectors. Madurese are supposedly unrefined, especially according to Javanese people.

The economic activities and the ethnicity of the workers in the brick enterprises are highly visible. Brickmakers are widely known to be Madurese and their activities involve excavating, smoke and regular heavy transportation,

13 In Samarinda alone, an estimated 3,000 people from Geger are living and working, while another 2,000 can be found in Balikpapan, Bontang and Melak (the majority involved in brickmaking). More Geger people now live in East Kalimantan than in Geger, Madura. Besides working in the brickmaking sector in East Kalimantan, Geger men are also working (often illegally) in construction in Malaysia, and some are sailors or porters. A few Geger women are working in Saudi Arabia as domestic workers.

14 The Madurese language consists of two language groups: the Eastern Sumenep type, and the Western Bangkalan, Pamekasan and Sampang type, which differ in intonation and vocabulary. Madurese-speaking migrants from the eastern part of Java speak the Sumenep type. In both speech and manner, Sumenep-speaking Madurese are regarded as more refined, while Sampang are seen as almost 'rough'. Madurese from Bangkalan are regarded as not very refined. Nevertheless, they still look down on Madurese from Eastern Java who speak the refined Sumenep version of Madurese.

none of which can be hidden. Entrepreneurs in this sector face uncertainty due to fluctuating market prices and possible conflicts with landowners and local people over land and firewood. When recalling these conflicts, references are often made by both Madurese and non-Madurese people to ethnic issues. As negative sentiments against Madurese have increased in the last couple of years, landowners are increasingly unwilling to rent or to lease land to Madurese, or they demand higher prices.

It is not uncommon for Madurese entrepreneurs and workers to be accused of land grabbing, violence and criminal activities. Although some Madurese are, or have been, involved in illegal and illicit activities ranging from land occupation and gambling to illegal logging, theft and gang fighting, there are no indications that Madurese migrants are any more violent or criminal than other immigrant groups such as Buginese, Banjarese or Butonese (Acciaioli 1999:242, Nooteboom 2005:168).

Compared to other income sources in Kalimantan, the wages and profits in brickmaking are low and the wages are among the lowest in the area. They are comparable to those paid in the stone quarries. The gross earnings of teams of workers range between Rp 15,000 and 35,000 (€1.5–5) per day depending on the number of bricks produced. Net earnings range from less than zero to Rp 30,000 per team per day. Many workers, as soon as they have saved Rp 1–2 million, return to Madura or East Java. Sometimes workers chose to send their profits home and continue working. On average, workers stay in Kalimantan for 8 to 10 months, but working for periods up to two years is not exceptional. In general, their wages are saved for them by the owner of the brickyard who also provides barracks to live in and food, cigarettes and drinks on credit. For others who help with the firing (3–4 times a year) no wages are paid but food, drinks and cigarettes are provided. Net profits of *serobong* owners range from Rp 500,000 to Rp 2 million (€50–200) per month depending on the number of workers involved and the prices of wood and bricks. About 15% of *serobong* owners have additional sources of income such as trucks and trades.

Brickmaking is a dynamic sector. At the end of 2003, about 10% of the *serobong* active at the start of that year had gone bankrupt or ceased activities. Reasons given for these bankruptcies were mismanagement, heavy gambling, increased production costs, a lack of reliable labourers or credit facilities and conflicts with landowners and suppliers. The number of non-Madurese buyers who defaulted on payments had greatly increased since the 2001 violence. Notwithstanding these difficulties, the number of *serobong* rose by 5% in the same period, and the total number of workers by more than 10%. 'We have no other option', a second generation migrant sighed, 'even if I wanted to return to Madura, I couldn't. There is nothing over there'.

Brick firing is the culmination of a production process which occupies a period of some three to five months, during which brickmakers need to marshal the necessary resources of land, labour and fuelwood, and mould and dry a sufficient numbers of bricks, so that the work of stacking the bricks and wood for firing can begin. If the firing is successful and the bricks find an immediate market, debts can be repaid, remittances can be sent home to Madura, new labourers sought and relationships with neighbours, buyers and suppliers renewed. This cycle of economic activity, involving a large number of social relationships, is highly sensitive to external shocks and influences such as a crisis.

A Financial Rollercoaster

Initially, after the 1997 crisis, incomes plummeted. For a couple of months, there was hardly any demand for bricks as investors were wary of constructing houses and many labourers returned to Madura. Most brickmakers received food and cheap rice from government officials as part of the national *Sembako* programmes. 'Other ethnic groups pitied us and called us fellow countrymen'. Soon, however, higher export prices stimulated East Kalimantan's export economy, building activities skyrocketed and brick prices tripled in real terms. For the brickmakers, a period of good profits started. As few labourers were available, production could not meet demand and prices increased. 'In those days, I was able to pay all the expenses for my three remaining children and their families in Madura and even buy a motorcycle myself', Dapi, a small entrepreneur, said. 'Many of the workers who had dared to stay opened brickyards themselves'. Initially, new labourers were reluctant to come to Kalimantan seeing this as full of risk. However, after repeated phone calls from successful relatives and encouraged by a total lack of income-earning opportunities in Madura, many migrated to East Kalimantan. Due to this influx of labourers and the subsequent increase and competition in production, the price of bricks started to slowly decline in the period leading up to 2000.

This pattern repeated itself after the ethnic violence against Madurese in 2001 in Sampit, Central Kalimantan. At first, once the stories of large-scale violence against Madurese became widely known, about 15% of all Madurese labourers in Samarinda panicked and fled. Others sold their assets and sent their savings to Madura. Moreover, it became very difficult to recruit new labourers as many did not dare to take the risk of migrating to an area under threat of violence. Madurese labourers refrained from coming, while other ethnic groups refused to work for a Madurese employer. As a result, most brickmakers had to rely on family labour and individual savings to keep their production going. A brickmaker who stayed commented: 'We had neither capital, nor labourers. I tried to persuade close relatives on Madura to come, but most of them refused repeatedly. Finally, I ordered my two sons here to help me. I did not want to abandon my brickyard here, as it was the only property and means of livelihood I had'. 'We had to wait and see what happened', another reacts. 'If we had left, they would have taken over all our property'.

In fact, the violence in Sampit never spread to East Kalimantan, although a few cases of provocation were reported. However, as a result of the lack of labourers, real brick prices doubled to Rp 425 per brick (5 eurocents) offering entrepreneurs a profit of over 100%. This windfall period lasted for nearly two years, but only those brickmakers who had stayed in Kalimantan profited. They were able to buy land in Madura, a house, motorbikes or cattle. About 10% of the entrepreneurs also bought a truck in Samarinda in order to further benefit from the boom in construction activities and become less dependent on other ethnic enterprises. The majority of Madurese seasonal migrants however ceased coming and did not benefit.

In this period, an increasing number of Madurese tried to migrate illegally to Malaysia. With the declining opportunities in Kalimantan, Madurese migrants tried to enter Malaysia – many of them illegally – where real wages were much higher due to the strength of the Ringgit relative to the Rupiah. Due to the weak Rupiah, larger amounts of money could be sent from Malaysia than from Kalimantan. Except for those who were able to migrate to Malaysia, Madurese faced severe falls in income. However, by early 2003, Malaysia decided to close its borders and send all illegal workers home. It has been estimated that hundreds of thousands of East Javanese – including Madurese – had been working illegally in Malaysia (Ford and Lyons 2011, Kelly 2002, Minza 2012).

The 'Hidden' Sector: Stonecutting

There are two locations in the vicinities of Samarinda where stonecutters work: Batu Putih and Batu Besaung. In these rocky and hilly areas outside the city, large pits can be found where labourers cut and grind rocks to sell them for use in road building and construction work. Most of the work is done with simple tools such as hammers, chisels, levers and shovels. Fire is used to make cracking the rocks easier. Sometimes middlemen will hire a mechanical excavator to remove sand and rocks and to make access roads for trucks. Some people working in these stone quarries earn reasonable incomes, but most of the workers are living barely above subsistence level although workers in Batu Putih are slightly better off than those in Batu Besaung.

Both areas are part of a low, but large, mountain ridge that runs from southwest to northeast in the area north of Samarinda. In Batu Putih, the oldest pit and closest to the city, about a hundred people work. Most of these people are from Sampang, Madura and a large proportion of the population have already been living on the mountain for one to two decades. These workers brought their families with them and some, all originally from one village in Sampang, have worked there for more than twenty years. Most of these I class as semi-permanent migrants since they return to Madura once a year and all express the hope of returning permanently to buy some land or cattle or start a trade on Madura.

The working conditions are harsh and sometimes earnings, depending on one's position in the pit, are very low. The most favourable places are allocated to those who have been there the longest. They can earn up to Rp 100,000 (€10) a day provided it is not raining. Newcomers get much less favourable locations and sometimes earn less than Rp 15,000 a day (€1.5) which is not enough to meet daily expenditures however simply they live. About one-third of the temporary labourers are heavily indebted and cannot return to Madura until their debts are repaid. Usually they pay off their debt with stones while taking credit to cover their daily expenditures. Things get worse if labourers gamble away large sums of money or if they fall ill for a long period. Some of these labourers have been indebted for over four years without any real hope of ever repaying the loan. This form of debt bondage is quite common between Madurese, but is seldom found with labourers from other ethnic groups. Madurese cannot easily walk away from their debts as their village of origin and relatives are known and will be held responsible for the debt.

A few of the quarrymen have worked their way up to become transporters, middlemen or moneylenders. These usually state that they are aiming for a future in Kalimantan. Two former labourers from Batu Putih now own a small company to transport stones and a few others have become middlemen who collect fees from trucks for the pit owner, hire labourers and give loans to workers in trouble. These middlemen rarely go back to Madura.

The situation at Batu Besaung is little different to that at Batu Putih except that there are many more labourers and more ethnic groups at Batu Besaung, although Madurese still make up the majority. Batu Besaung could be called the dustbin of Samarinda's informal migrant economy. If newly arriving migrants are unsuccessful in finding a job in construction or a trade in the city, they end up in the mountains of Batu Besaung. As soon as they find a job in the city or have earned enough to return to Madura, they disappear. I did not find any permanent dwellers, although some people have worked intermittently for over five years in the area.

The mountains are divided into about twenty blocks that are owned by investors of different ethnic backgrounds such as Bugis, Banjar and Chinese. These entrust one of the workers with collecting fees from contractors' trucks and await the money coming in. Every truck pays Rp 10,000 (€1) to the owner or keeper of the pit, while labourers receive Rp 35,000 for a load. The more remote, the lower the prices are. Labourers are left in poor conditions, sometimes without proper sanitation, shelter and tools. If payments are late, or middlemen are unreliable, workers come close to starvation. Usually, all the risks are for the worker. Every year, a few people die at the pits due to accidents. If no savings or friends are available, they may be buried on the spot. In some instances where there was a Chinese boss, the owner of the land paid for the repatriation of the victim to Madura.

In 1997, just after the economic crisis hit the country, all construction activities came to a virtual standstill as did the possibility of earning money in the quarries. Most workers from the Batu Besaung area went back to Madura. In the older Batu Putih area, the local government supplied some food aid (*sembako*). This help was clearly catalysed by one of the local hamlet heads being of Madurese decent. As a consequence, the semi-permanent labourers decided to stay and wait for better times, as did many of the seasonal migrants. They just continued to work and stockpiled stones. Labourers who had savings used some of their savings to stay alive and also helped out other Madurese.

Soon after 1997, construction activities in East Kalimantan picked up as export prices rose. Contrary to the situation in the brick sector, the labourers, middlemen and transporters, most of whom where Madurese, did not compete with one another but worked together to raise the prices of stones as soon as the costs of living increased. As a consequence, stone prices have remained good and real wages have not fallen. As demand remains strong and production is relatively stable (people cannot can cut more stone than they used to do), this policy can be maintained.

The pits are a favourable hiding place for all sorts of people who have run in trouble elsewhere. In some of the most remote pits at Batu Putih, and especially at Batu Besaung, refugees from the violence in West and Central Kalimantan are working. Most of the victims of this violence were from Sampang district who were then thrown out of West and Central Kalimantan. Some fled directly to East Kalimantan while others came through IDP camps on Madura where they heard about the stonecutting work from relatives and friends. The situation in the refugee camps was difficult as not much work was available in Madura, let alone work for newcomers. An estimated 10% of the stone workers, and more in remote parts of Batu Besaung, were refugees. Since 2002, the numbers have fallen as workers have found their way into other sectors of the Kalimantan economy.

Most of the people with previous troubles work in remote Batu Besaung. Debts are often mentioned as one of the reasons given for working there. These debts may be caused by excessive gambling, but often by speculation or trade. In many cases, the tobacco trade was mentioned. During 2004 and 2005, tobacco prices had plummeted on Madura, causing many small farmers and traders who had borrowed large sums of money to go bankrupt. One worker told me that he had lost Rp 100 million (€10,000) in 2003. After selling his house and land, he still had debts of Rp 35 million (€3,500). Running to East Kalimantan was his only option. 'I will work until I can pay them back, otherwise I will never be able to return to Madura', he explained. Other reasons for finding a hiding place at the quarries are troubles due to involvement in extra marital relationships, theft and crime.

The violence in West and Central Kalimantan had shocked the stonecutting community. Many of the seasonal labourers decided to go home to Madura. Most of the semi-permanent migrants decided to stay in fear of losing their favourable spots. Contractors increasingly opted to use large excavators to get sufficient stones for their building activities, and large numbers of Madurese refugees from West and Central Kalimantan soon made it possible to satisfy market demands. Many of the refugees enjoyed the pits and the company of fellow Madurese and saw them as safe havens, protecting them from violence and far away from the urban crowds, bureaucracies and police officers in which they had lost all confidence.

The 'Safe' Sector: Vegetable Farming

Northeast of Samarinda, in Muang Dalam, a remote part of Lempake, Madurese immigrants from the South of Malang (Java) have settled over the last two decades. Originally, two brothers came as rural labourers in search of land. They had gambled away their father's property in Malang and were very eager to start a new life and to regain land. Initially, they worked as rural labourers in an area which was cleared for transmigration purposes. After a year, they returned to Malang to bring their wives to Kalimantan. They built a simple shed from leftovers from logging companies which had just cleared the area and were allowed to borrow some land to plant vegetables. The brothers planted chili peppers which they transported to the town of Samarinda by boat. These made very good prices and were able to buy a hectare of land. Slowly, they improved their property and bought more land whenever something came available. Each time they returned to Malang, they would bring back some relatives or Madurese labourers with them. After ten years, a road was opened and the brothers started to plant papaya. With the papaya, they earned a stable, steady income which enabled them to also grow more risky crops such as tomato, chilli and rambutan.

In 2009, they each own four hectares and employ four or five labourers. Relatives and fellow villagers have also established farms and now there are forty Madurese-speaking families living in the area. Not all are as successful as the first two brothers, but all of them have good stable incomes and are able to send children to school. Further, they have established good relationships with other ethnic groups in the area. Average incomes range from Rp 5 million (€500) per month for the most successful producers and traders down to Rp 1 million (€100) for those who are still dependent on waged labour on their relatives' farms. As farmers and traders, they have been very keen on maintaining good relationships in the area as these are the prime prerequisite for economic success. Moreover, they view themselves are settlers, not migrants.

During the economic crisis at the turn of the millennium, the vegetable farmers were not affected at all since they only produced for the market of Samarinda, where there was no real crisis because of the benefits accruing from East Kalimantan's export economy. Nevertheless, for the vegetable farmers, the violence in West and Central Kalimantan came as a great shock. They had burnt their bridges on Java and now saw no opportunities to return there. Further, they were very determined to hold on to their lands. As a response to the violence, and the negative perceived image of Madurese, they tried to engage in better social relationships with neighbours. Regularly they explained to me the importance of living in peace with neighbours and told me about their activities to establish good relationships.

Pak Giman, a horticulturalist and informal leader of the Madurese vegetable and fruit nurseries in rural Muang Dalam organized, as head of the Madurese neighbourhood, several peace ceremonies with Dayak neighbours from nearby forests and their regional leaders. 'We ate together, exchanged gifts, made music and agreed not to start any hostilities. I even gave them money'. They agreed to report any problem with one of their people directly so that it could be resolved. Remarkably, Bugis, with whom relationships in this area are tense due to fierce competition over land and vegetable trading, were not invited to similar events.

Although the majority of the farmers, and some of the semi-permanent migrants and settlers in the other sectors, adhere to these accommodating strategies, not all invest in friendly relationships. Especially among the farmers who live in relatively isolated communities, and this was also true of brickmakers and stonecutters, many can be found who refrain from contacts with other ethnic groups. In addition, buying land has become increasingly difficult for vegetable farmers, and they are increasingly forced to lease or rent it. As a result, they often search for cheap land further from the city that they can buy.

Concluding Remarks

This chapter has focused on those Madurese who were able to migrate during the difficult years of crisis, reformation and ethnic violence to carve a livelihood

ILLUSTRATION 10 *Newly arrived migrants from Malang, East Java*

out of the soil of East Kalimantan, one of the richest provinces of Indonesia. In this province, the reshuffling of social positions is clearly visible as new regional ethnic elites have benefitted most from the decentralization process in East Kalimantan (Casson and Obidzinski 2002, Van Klinken 2002), while other ethnic groups, including the Madurese, tend to be increasingly excluded.[15]

15 An example of such attempts to exclude immigrant groups is visible in the actions in Balikpapan against the influx of poor migrants from eastern Indonesia (East Nusa Tenggara) NTT, East Java and Madura. Local authorities try to limit this by organising raids to check residence permits (*razia KTP*).

The livelihood activities of Madurese in Samarinda, the provincial capital of East Kalimantan, have been expanding since the Asian crisis hit the country as a consequence of the growing investments and business opportunities. Notwithstanding this expansion, the entrepreneurial climate for Madurese migrants has been deteriorating ever since 1997 due to economic instability, political change and violent conflicts in West and Central Kalimantan. This violence left a deep wound and indirectly traumatized hundreds of thousands of Madurese. It was this crisis that had the largest impact on Madurese migrants.

Studying the Madurese migrants in East Kalimantan helps to uncover the dynamic processes of economic change, migration and ethnic tensions that occur between local populations and outsiders during such periods of turbulence. For migrants, such periods are largely marked by the creation of new anxieties and insecurities that cause tensions on the local level with local populations who tend to retrench into conservative ideologies and 'our people first' strategies. This process has clearly had negative impacts on Madurese livelihoods.

The Indonesian crisis, a combination of a monetary crisis, reforms, decentralization and subsequent violence, had positive short-term financial effects for Madurese brickmakers in Kalimantan but weakened their livelihood base in the longer term. After the monetary crisis, the value of remittances from Malaysia initially increased sharply and more people migrated to Malaysia. However, after the ban on illegal labourers in 2003, remittances from Malaysia declined and East Kalimantan again became important as a sole supplier of remittances. However, since 2003, the value of remittances has fallen as brick prices have declined due to overproduction. The brickmaking sector is a clear example of an economic sector that is dominated by a single ethnic group of migrants, which has then been challenged by opposing local populations. In response, the ethnic brickmakers increasingly mobilize labour, capital and resources from within their own group.

The stonecutters have been less affected in both positive and negative senses. They did not experience sizeable windfalls, but also not such deep depressions. Nowadays, when migration opportunities became scarce, that some stonecutters have to accept less favourable pits and greater impoverishment due to poor working conditions. Seasonal labourers were more mobile in this sector and, provided they are not tied by a favourable locations or debts, they can leave their tools and go back to Madura. Moreover, the system of agreed prices protected their livelihoods from the worst consequences of the crisis.

The vegetable farmers' situation turned out to be the best. They continued to make money as economic conditions in Samarinda did not worsen.

Moreover, of the three groups studied, they were the most successful in establishing peaceful relationships with other ethnic groups and in gaining prestige and a slightly better image as Madurese. As a result of these good relations, and the focus on cash crops such as vegetables and fruit, their incomes grew considerably. However, today, it is difficult to enter this sector as land access for Madurese, at least in East Kalimantan, is not easy and much of the land is unsuited to vegetable production.

The impact of the crisis and the difficulties in making a living should not only be expressed in economic terms. The violence in West and Central Kalimantan has opened up a deep wound and indirectly traumatized hundreds of thousands of Madurese living in other areas. It is this aspect of the crisis which has had the largest impact on Madurese migrants. It changed their lives, their business opportunities and their attitude towards Kalimantan. For poor immigrants, since the decentralisation policies were introduced, Kalimantan has ceased to be the promised land of virtually unlimited opportunities.

This case study of Madurese migrants in East Kalimantan illuminates the differentiated impact of a crisis, mediated through dynamic processes such as economic change, migration and ethnic tensions during such a period of turbulence. In many instances, disruption to the old patterns and practices produced new opportunities and a momentum for change but, for Madurese brickmakers and for some of the stonecutters, the turbulence has mainly been marked by the creation of new anxieties and insecurities caused by local-level tensions with local populations who tend to retreat into conservative ideologies and 'our people first' strategies. The brickmaking sector is a clear example of an economic sector dominated by a single ethnic group of migrants which has been challenged by local populations. The crisis seems to have catalysed this opposition.

Following the crisis, the composite of political, economic and social change, of elites and ethnic positions in Indonesia has been reshuffled. It seems that poor, stigmatized and poorly represented groups, such as Madurese, face a declining situation at the expense of regional elites (*putra daerah*), re-emerging elites and new religious elites. They have lost an opportunity for improvement. In Kalimantan, the 'hidden' and 'rough' sectors remain the only niches for young Madurese in search of a better livelihood.

CHAPTER 7

Experiences of Violence

The ethnic cleansing and mass killings of Madurese migrants in Sambas, West Kalimantan in 1999 and in Sampit, Central Kalimantan in 2001 shocked the world.[1] All of a sudden, or so it seemed, the original Dayak population revolted against newcomers and reclaimed their ancestral lands. Especially the display of beheaded Madurese in Western media and the stories about the eating of organs such as hearts and livers of conquered enemies stunned the international community. How did the Madurese themselves experience this violence and how did it affect their perceptions of security and their livelihood strategies?

In the early days of the 'Sambas Incident', as it was initially called, journalists and observers sought quick explanations for this 'excessive' violence and turned to exotic and simplistic observations such as that the Dayak, 'the once most feared tribe of head-hunters in South East Asia', were returning to their old practices of headhunting and cannibalism.[2] Scholars explained the violence by referring to the arrogant and aggressive 'character' of the Madurese, to the exploitation of Dayak land by foreign settlers, to the exploitation of natural resources by 'transmigrants'[3] or by religious contradictions (Schiller and Garang 2002:245).

---

1 See for instance: Bouvier, De Jonge and Smith 2006; Bouvier and Smith 2006; Chandrasekaran February 24, 2001; CNN March 19,1999; CNN March 21,1999; New York Times March 21,1999.

2 See for instance: Linder 1999 or CNN 1999.

3 During Suharto's New Order government, millions of poor farmers, mostly from Java and Bali, transmigrated to less populated islands such as Sulawesi, Sumatra and Kalimantan. Although these programmes have long been supported by the World Bank, in later years they have increasingly been criticised by scholars and developmental experts. The influx of migrants caused much frustration and resistance by the local populations of the so-called outer islands. During the New Order era (1965–1998), their protests were suppressed and not heard.

However, using the transmigration argument to explain the Dayak – Madurese violence is debatable. In fact, Madurese from the island of Madura have never been part of transmigration programmes, and Madurese-speaking people from the Eastern part of Java were only proportionally represented in the total number of transmigrants. Most Madurese in Kalimantan migrated independently and blaming transmigration programmes for the conflict is an oversimplification. The majority of transmigrants are Javanese and, if the conflict is to be explained as a resource conflict between transmigrants and the original population, then why the Javanese were not involved in the violence requires a convincing argument.

Soon, observers realized that the conflict was not that exotic and that it repeated the pattern of conflicts seen at other places in Indonesia such as in Central Sulawesi and the Moluccas (Schiller and Garang 2002). Expanding on the earlier analyses, they now explained the conflicts historically, referring to the errors of the past three decades: forced migration of hundreds of thousands people from densely populated islands such as Java, Bali and Madura to less populated islands without properly integrating the migrants with native groups in the settlement areas (Ave 2003, Dove 1997, HRW 1997, Peluso 2006, Peluso and Harwell 2001); the political heritage of suppression under Suharto's New Order (Davidson and Kammen 2002); political instability after his fall (Davidson 2003, Putra 1999); a failing justice system and probable political manipulation by Indonesian authorities (HRW 1997, ICG 2001, Schiller and Garang 2002); and deep-rooted cultural and religious controversies (Coppel 2006, Schiller and Garang 2002). Van Klinken located his analysis in a context of decentralization and blamed local ethnic elites 'who deflect democratization by stimulating ethnic conflict' (Van Klinken 2003: 70). In retrospect, these studies taken together provide a pretty convincing explanation for the violence that took place in West and Central Kalimantan, at least from the Dayak point of view. The Madurese perspective has so far been poorly represented, and their perceptions and experiences have received less attention as few scholars have worked among them and many Madurese had already fled and were hard to trace.

A History of Violence

An historical approach is needed if one is to understand the background of ethnic conflicts. Since the late 1960s, and especially since 1997, in Sambas, West Kalimantan, over a dozen conflicts have occurred between the original Dayak population (and sometimes Malay) and Madurese settlers.[4] So far, the conflicts

---

It is remarkable how often transmigrants were mentioned in reports and the media as a source of the problem and a part of the conflict. If a summary of the studies on the Sambas and Sampit conflicts were to be constructed, a steady repetition of the 'transmigration'-argument would be seen, with authors simply copying the transmigration argument. In the first months after the conflict, authors – desperately looking for an explanation – simply accepted the transmigration argument. These arguments lacked a sound basis since Madurese migrants had never been well studied and documented.

4 There are first, second and third generation Madurese in Kalimantan. In general, Madurese are Muslim, while most Dayak are Christian or adhere to animist religions.

of 1997 and 1999 in the Sambas region have been the most violent, leading to an estimated 500 fatalities and 25,000 evictions in 1997[5] and many more in 1999. In 2001, a similar but even more violent conflict erupted in Sampit, Central Kalimantan, resulting in an estimated 3,000 Madurese deaths and over 125,000 evictions.[6] All of these conflicts were triggered by relatively 'minor' incidents such as fights between youngsters at the market or a music festival, a killing, or by rumours of rape. As soon as news or rumours spread, the 'insult' was responded to by communal violence attacking members of the other ethnic group in search of 'revenge'. In these conflicts, mobs and gangs of both Dayaks and Madurese burned houses, killed at random, destroyed crops and forced people from their homes. In 1997, 1999 and 2001, things spiralled out of control and killings and evictions became widespread.[7] Since 2001, there are no remaining Madurese in the rural areas of Sambas and Sampit, and their houses and lands have been destroyed or taken over by Dayak and other ethnic groups.

In the early months following the start of the conflict in Sampit, fears arose that violence would spread across the whole of Kalimantan and to other parts of the Indonesian archipelago. This fear was understandable as the Sampit violence fuelled fresh conflicts in West Kalimantan, and Dayak from other parts of Kalimantan were reported as coming to the Western and Central provinces to fight against Madurese. Moreover, Khofifah, an Indonesian state politician, mentioned Samarinda (East Kalimantan), as the third 'S' ('Sambas, Sampit, Samarinda…') and a logical next step in the rioting.[8] Many thought that an outbreak of violence in East Kalimantan was only a matter of time. This fear was not surprising given that all the necessary ingredients claimed for West and Central Kalimantan were present including problematic ethnic relationships with Madurese, resource competition, inequalities between ethnic groups, a long history of minor violent clashes

---

5 Human Rights Watch Report 9 (published December 1997). Although they offer this figure, the exact death toll is unknown.

6 Again, exact death tolls are not known. The ICG (2001) gives a total of 500, similar to official Indonesian Government figures, whereas local sources report numbers of over 3,000.

7 Some authors refer to the powerful ritual of 'the passing of the red bowl' among Dayak communities in the region as the start of the mass violence. The red bowl is filled with blood, feathers and other ritual items, then carried from one village to the next calling on all Dayaks to wage war against a common enemy. See: Peluso & Harwell 2001; Schiller & Garang 2002.

8 'State minister for Women Empowerment/Chairperson of the National Family Planning Board Khofifah Indar Parawansa warned Saturday of the possible spread of the ethnic conflicts in Sampit and Palangkaraya to Sambas in West Kalimantan and Samarinda, the capital of East Kalimantan. "I have informed the National Police Chief Gen. Bimantoro that there are indications the ethnic conflicts will center in those areas."' The Jakarta Post, March 4, 2001.

with Madurese, widespread negative stereotyping of Madurese, hatred, political instability and ethnic, religious and economic controversies. However, contrary to such expectations, mass violence did not break out in East Kalimantan. Why did the violence not spread to East Kalimantan? Before attempting to answer this question, the history and Madurese experience of violence will be discussed.

The West and Central Kalimantan Conflicts

Between 1996 and 2002, large-scale ethnic clashes took place in the province of West Kalimantan (Van Klinken 2002, 2006). In December 1996 and January 1997, it was the Dayak and Madurese in the district of Bengkayang who were fighting each other, resulting in between 500 and 1,200, mainly Madurese, deaths and the displacement of this immigrant group from this area (Bouvier et al. 2006, De Jonge and Nooteboom 2006). In the first months of 1999, violence erupted in the district of Sambas, this time between Malays and Madurese, although the Dayak quickly joined in on the side of the Malays. Again there were hundreds of casualties, and the Madurese felt compelled to flee. About half of the almost 70,000 displaced people from these two clashes who could not, or chose not, to leave West Kalimantan were placed in government refugee camps in Pontianak. The other half moved in with relatives or acquaintances in Madurese quarters in and around the city.

In 2001, after a series of smaller incidents, serious violence broke out between these displaced Madurese and members of other ethnic groups. In the same year, violence also erupted in Sampit in Central Kalimantan with fights between Madurese and Dayak resulting in at least 500 deaths and the evacuation of almost the entire Madurese population of Central Kalimantan, about 108,000 people in all, to Madura and Java (Sukma 2005:4). In total, over 130,000 Madurese left Kalimantan and lived as Internally Displaced People IDPs in mainland East Java and on Madura (Brusset et al. 2004:13). Especially those who still had relatives or land in mainland East Java or in Madura left Kalimantan – at least temporarily (Davidson and Kammen 2002, De Jonge and Nooteboom 2006, Schiller and Garang 2002).

The atrocities which accompanied the clashes, and the scale on which these took place, shocked the whole nation and exceeded those in other conflict areas in Indonesia. In many places in Kalimantan, mutilations, beheadings and 'acts of cannibalism' accompanied the riots.[9] Although some of these were unsubstantiated reports, and facts were difficult to check, the symbolic power of these tales was massive (Peluso 2006, Schiller and Garang 2002). Soon, more

9 CNN; Jakarta Post 2001; New York Times 1999.

Dayak joined the fight against the despised migrants, and Madurese homes were set on fire, their cattle killed and other possessions destroyed. Those Madurese who did escape and hid in the forests were hunted for weeks afterwards. In rural central Kalimantan, all traces of their presence were wiped out. Also in Sambas, the Madurese were ethnically cleansed. In some places, only banana trees and disused mosques indicate where they once lived (De Jonge and Nooteboom 2006:457).

Ironically, as a result of the violence, the Madurese were in the spotlight for a short period of time as journalists, anthropologists and political scientists hurried to explain the violence. Most of the studies produced were, however, written from a Dayak perspective. The Madurese side was seldom heard, and studies among or from the perspective of the Madurese were rare (De Jonge and Nooteboom 2006:462).

According to many of the Dayak, Malay, Buginese and Banjarese informants cited in studies on Kalimantan, the migrant Madurese largely failed to adapt to their new social environment and looked down on others (Hendro 2001). Their behaviour is said to be arrogant, short-tempered, macho-like, rude, uncivilized, unfair, avaricious and revengeful: all widely-used characterizations and stereotypes that have been applied to the Madurese over long periods and which, in times of crisis, acquire additional significance (De Jonge 1995). Many of the Madurese born on Kalimantan blame this negative image on newcomers, who they claim do not know how to behave, and to *preman* (thugs) who are often members of criminal gangs involved in illegal logging, running brothels and gambling dens, and smuggling consumer goods from Sarawak into the country. According to them, these people cast a slur on the whole Madurese community. Dayak, Malays, Buginese and Banjarese tend to overlook the fact that such gangs also exist within their own groups. These various, ethnically-organized, gangs compete hard with each other, and do not eschew violence. Nevertheless, such stereotypes have without doubt contributed to a certain amount of suspicion and hatred towards the Madurese (Wilson 2011:251).

Little is known about the impact of ethnic violence in areas unaffected by the violence but with similar ethic constellations. What does violence mean for members of a threatened ethnic group who are living elsewhere, and what did it mean to the Madurese migrants? How do they interpret and experience violence? What impact does distant violence have on the livelihood strategies of Madurese migrants? To answer these questions, I carried out research in East Kalimantan from mid-2003 until early 2004 with later, follow-up, visits. Below, I describe Madurese interpretations and experiences of violence as well as the role of the government in Samarinda, East Kalimantan. I do this by again focussing on two specific categories of Madurese migrants: brickmakers and stonecutters. These two categories of migrants are highly visible and therefore vulnerable to violence.

To achieve the aims of this chapter, I will first deal with the history of Madurese violence and the violence against Madurese in East Kalimantan, inter-ethnic relationships and, again, the existence and importance of widespread stereotyping. After this, I will deal with the experiences, perceptions and interpretations of violence by the Madurese and their changing strategies regarding settlement and accommodation. Finally, I endeavour to draw some conclusions on the mechanisms and processes underlying interpersonal and collective violence, the early warning signs in East Kalimantan and possible paths that could prevent or resolve future conflicts. As such, this chapter deals with violence and how it was experienced in a neighbouring province not swept by violence. This is relevant as understanding the roots of peace and violence is not only fascinating from an academic point of view, it is also valuable for development practitioners.

Violent Backgrounds

When it comes to violence, Madurese have an especially bad name (De Jonge 2004:5). Despite this, it is difficult to say if Madurese, and as we have seen there are Madurese with different backgrounds from different areas, are really any more violent than other ethnic groups. For example, certain elements of Bugis culture have been related to the many conflicts that Bugis migrants are involved in across the Indonesian archipelago (Acciaioli 1999:242). Crime figures, insofar as they are available, do not show any significant differences in criminality levels between Madurese and other ethnic groups.[10] Nevertheless, there are certain forms of violence that are inherently part of Madurese culture (De Jonge 2002, 2004:8).

Under certain conditions, some forms of violence (for instance, *carok*, fighting and revenge) are culturally acceptable to Madurese people. However, this violence can only take place under certain clear conditions (such as injured honour or an assault), for certain purposes (to restore honour, to show courage) and by certain categories (such as married men or youngsters).[11] These

10 Information from a senior police officer who told me in 2005 that Madurese crime rates had been declining since the mid-1990s. They had been as high as Buginese crime rates, but, 'nowadays, Banjarese migrants are causing most of the problems'.

11 For studies on 'Madurese violence' see: Latief Wiyata 2002 on *carok*; De Jonge 1995, 2002 and Smith 2006. In general, Madurese migrants have a very low educational level (half of all brickmakers cannot read or write), lack political participation and representation and, therefore, violence might serve as one of the only ways to express themselves.

forms of violence bear heroic connotations and play a role in constituting the male Madurese ethnic identity. Certain stereotypes, such as being strong, hard (*keras*) or rough (*kasar*), are negatively viewed by outsiders but are seen as contributing to a positive image among Madurese themselves. Showing courage and using force give status and play a role in constituting a form of leadership (based on status, fierceness, political power and the ability to control resources and distribute them, see: Nooteboom 2002; 2003). However, not everyone follows this path and other forms of leadership are also common: leadership based on religion and spiritual power (*kiai*), or on political and economic status. In everyday life, Madurese do not use violence any more than others. Nevertheless, they are more often associated with violence than any other ethnic group.

When I interviewed Madurese migrants in Krajan who had returned from Kalimantan, they proudly told me about how strong and forceful they had been, who they had cheated and how many fights they had won.[12] An image of being courageous is important if one is to become a gang leader and gain admiration back in the village. Later, after the 1999 conflict in West Kalimantan, they told me they had also lived in constant fear and had been afraid of local populations such as Dayak and especially of their magic (*ilmu hitam*). Further, after 2001, many were hesitant to reveal their Madurese backgrounds.

History of Violence in Samarinda

In the dominant discourses on violence in Samarinda, both Madurese and Bugis are frequently mentioned in relation to brawls, killings and gang wars. This is partly due to the repetition of Madurese stereotypes, but also due to the large-scale fights between Madurese and Bugis during the late 1970 and the 1980s. In the 1980s, large feuds were witnessed between Bugis and Madurese in the major cities of East Kalimantan. These two immigrant groups were rivals for jobs and business opportunities in transport, construction and trade. At the harbour and market places of Samarinda, fights regularly occurred between bands of Madurese and Bugis. In early 1980, a Bugis gang leader (*jago*) was killed at the market after he had offended a Madurese. Seeking revenge, Bugis gang members sought out the Madurese man and tried to kill him. The perpetrator got help from friends, but was eventually killed after killing a few more Bugis. From that time on, fights between Madurese and Bugis occurred regularly, with dozens of casualties as a result. Madurese women and children were also

12 These boasting Madurese were not representative of the majority of migrants, they were part of the minority of vagabonds and drifters (*orang nakal*) who had been virtually expelled from their own society.

harassed: 'When we went to the market, we always brought knives. Our wives and children could not travel alone'. At some stages during the 1980s and early 1990s, fights between Madurese and Bugis occurred almost weekly in the market and at the harbour, with gangs competing fiercely over beneficial activities such as gambling and trade. Several Madurese boasted: 'We were better at fighting and braver than the Bugis. For each Madurese who died, at least five Bugis have been killed'. Whether this was true or not, fighting contributed to the status and machismo of Madurese men and revenge was a natural thing throughout the 1980s and early 1990s. Violence in response to an assault was, and often still is, culturally accepted and even appreciated among Madurese. In fact, violence is considered a good thing. Madurese never turned their back and a regularly heard sentiment is that it is 'Better to die with pride, than to run and be ashamed all your life. My wife and family members would disrespect me if I would have run away'.

This violence caused a climate of fear and insecurity. Innocent Bugis and Madurese were intimidated and sometimes beaten up or killed. Bugis also occasionally raped Madurese women or attacked houses or Madurese work places. In return, Madurese raided Bugis food stalls or houses, burned stocks and seized trucks. The local government was unable to stop this violence and the police appeared to tolerate such groups. Only if larger state or elite interests were endangered, such as in logging or mining, would they interfere. Moreover, some among the police and local elites maintained close ties with Madurese due to shared interests in ensuring trade monopolies and semi-illegal activities such as running gambling dens, brothels and illegal logging companies. Those who wished to fish in muddy waters undoubtedly benefited from a certain level of violence (Van Klinken 2002:103).

Until the mid-1990s, Madurese maintained these good connections with the police. There existed a form of mutual understanding built on patronage and shared interests. In return for a share of the profit, the police tolerated certain illegal activities and shielded perpetrators from punishment as long as they were more-or-less hidden and not causing too much trouble. The police regularly even recruited local Madurese strong men to suppress criminality or to control criminal activities (see Chapter 8).

After the mid-1990s, Madurese gang leaders lost most of their influential connections due to the transfer of some senior police officers and the waning of Suharto's New Order regime. When the crisis came in 1997, followed by *reformasi*, and with it several violent outbreaks against Madurese in West and Central Kalimantan (Peluso 2006), the Madurese found themselves isolated. A shift in local elites had taken place. When the old Suharto cronies disappeared, new, more regionally rooted, elites took their place. Suddenly ethnicity, carefully suppressed during the New Order, became an issue. A catalyst for this process after the decentralization process started in East Kalimantan was 'indigenous people' (*putra daerah*) claiming the right to influential positions. Moreover, the regime no longer protected immigrants from Java and Madura, and Madurese found themselves in less favourable positions than local ethnic groups. They were even regarded as a threat to the security of East Kalimantan society and many feared they could trigger another Sampit or Sambas, endangering the flow of East Kalimantan's extensive resources (Van Klinken 2002:92).

Since 2001, violent conflicts between Madurese and Bugis have ceased, and small-scale violence in Samarinda has diminished, although it remains part of everyday life. There are still fights after a traffic accident (where one party tries to get money from the other party, an activity which is often defined in ethnic terms) and fights among drunks, or between rival gangs. Thefts, burglaries and robberies occur daily, and rape and murder are also regularly reported.[13] Although gang wars between ethnic groups have declined since 2001, tensions remain. Between September 2003 and February 2004, I counted eight fights between Madurese and Bugis in which four or five people were killed and several others severely wounded. Similar levels of violence were maintained in the years that followed. In newspapers, these events, if covered at all, were referred to as conflicts between criminals or as illegal activities by unidentified actors (*oknum*). Further, these two ethnic groups continued to compete in order to establish and maintain trade monopolies. In this competition, the use of force or intimidation was not exceptional.

The examples given above not only show that images of violent Madurese have deep historical and cultural roots, but also that violence during the New Order was not as suppressed as is often assumed, and that the government allowed it under certain circumstances (Hüsken and De Jonge 2002:2–3). To a large extent, Indonesian authorities were able to hide it from the larger national and international community. Colombijn (2002) and Van Klinken (2003) go further and even depict local and national elites as the major actors and factors in constituting violence and peace: 'The *leitmotif* in state violence has been the control of disorder that elites thought threatening to their position' (Colombijn 2002:53), and Van Klinken (2002:70) blames the 'parasitic elites who deflect democratization by stimulating ethnic conflict'. According to the latter, both in West and Central Kalimantan, as well as in East Kalimantan, these local elites played a crucial role. The difference with Suharto's Indonesia was that, after 1997, the government-related elites (such as military forces) lost their monopoly on violence due to democratization and decentralization policies.

13 Reports in Samarinda Pos and Tribun (2003/2004).

However, the forms of violence found in East Kalimantan cannot be understood solely from studying the movements and interests of elites. In the first place, violence occurs between people on the street. There, ethnic identity is constructed, maintained and negotiated. Violence is not legitimate against everybody, only against those considered outsiders or enemies. That is why ethnicity is so important in understanding violence. By calling people 'Bugis' or 'Madurese', with all the negative or even inhuman images attached to these labels, outsider categories are constantly constructed, reproduced and reinvented, thus forming a fertile basis for perpetual violence. The violence against, and the ethnic cleansing of, Madurese in West and Central Kalimantan produced very strong images and anti-Madurese sentiments in East Kalimantan. Even though, after a few days, broadcasts about the violence were banned, the damage was done. Images and stories of killed and beheaded Madurese circulated within the province, and Madurese would never feel completely safe in Kalimantan again.

Madurese Interpretations and Experiences of the Violence in West and Central Kalimantan

> I cannot tell you...I simply do not know why it all happened. (A young women who fled with her baby from Central Kalimantan. She was forced to divorce her Dayak husband).

The mass violence in West and Central Kalimantan towards Madurese came as a total shock and traumatized the Madurese community in East Kalimantan. The Madurese, once bold, have been hurt in the core of their identity; some say they have lost their self-esteem:

> We are now helpless, small people without direction and no longer proud (*kami di bawah angin*). We do not dare to defend ourselves. I give you one example: a few days ago, some of my workers sat outside a food stall nearby on the main road. From the back of the canteen, a motorbike came with a screaming girl on the back. The girl was being violently taken away it seemed. One of the Madurese chased the bike and tried to save the girl. A fight evolved and the Madurese was severely beaten up by other bystanders. I think they were Banjar and Bugis. My other workers didn't do anything to help our fellow man. They did not know who was right and who was wrong, they said. In the past we would definitely have helped a fellow Madurese and beaten up all the others. Now they are

> afraid and thought that the small conflict could spread and be disadvantageous for all Madurese. Madurese no longer have any self-esteem.
>
> PAK BAKRI, SAMARINDA, January 2004

The violence in West and Central Kalimantan swept away the things they were proud of: their colonizing success as settlers, their achievements in economic terms and their courage. The stories of the hundreds of thousands who returned to Madura, as poor as when they left, defeated by 'gangs of headhunting natives' made other migrants think. They had never considered that such a massive defeat, and such a huge loss of lives, property and prestige was possible. The trauma of Sambas and Sampit had an impact far beyond the Madurese in West and Central Kalimantan: it changed the minds and hearts of many other migrants.

> A friend of mine who had ran from Sambas came to me and he cried in my house. I said: 'Don't cry, you are safe now.' But he could not stop crying after all he had seen and all he had lost. He had owned a house, land and a lot of money. Now he had nothing. Just like another man here who also ran. He always starts crying if he talks about Sampit. It makes us afraid here.
>
> Young labourer, SAMARINDA, 2003

In studying the experiences of this conflict, it is important to look at the interpretations and explanations of the people themselves, and how they deal with the trauma, as these will guide future actions. In the following, I describe four types of Madurese experiences and interpretations in order to evaluate the impact of the violence. These experiences and interpretations are reflected in specific narratives. These narratives are used among Madurese themselves to explain the violence, but they are also expressed to outsiders. Following this, some more distant implications of the violence are provided.

Four Narratives on the Interpretation of the Violence in Sambas and Sampit

In the first and most dominant narrative, the Madurese blame themselves and each other. According to this discourse, Madurese caused the turmoil. Pak Suleman, a foremen of one of the largest settlements of brickmakers expresses it as follows:

> Madurese are notorious hotheads, arrogant and violent. Those Madurese there, they thought that they could do anything. They were dishonest and broke the rules. However, this turned against them. They have gone too

> far in their arrogance and this provoked the Dayak. 'We must do things differently here'.
>
> *pak* SULEMAN, SAMARINDA, 2004

Although, in this narrative, the Madurese see themselves as part of the problem and even reproduce the negative stereotypes usually attributed by outsiders, many blame one subgroup of Madurese in particular: those originating from Sampang and Pamekasan. Madurese from Bangkalan, the area where most brickmakers come from, regarded themselves more refined and peaceful.

> I do not know who were wrong in Sambas and Sampit. What I do know is that the Madurese there are very rough (*kasar*) and hotheaded (*panas*). We [Madurese from Bangkalan] are not like the Madurese from Sampang and Pamekasan. Those Madurese from the East are very emotional. They are always fighting and do not know how to deal with their emotions.
>
> I do not know what went wrong. Madurese have been there for four or five generations. They mixed with the original populations and were doing well. I lived there for a couple of years in the early 1970s and the Dayak were always friendly and receiving. We got everything from them: vegetables, fish and meat.
>
> Some of us speak of provocation, but I am not sure. How can a few people start something so big? There must have been something more, and Madurese must have been part of this.
>
> *pak* HODI, SAMARINDA, 2004

In the second narrative, Madurese blame Malay and Dayak because they were jealous of Madurese success.

> Madurese are hard workers and they have had more success than others; they had acquired hotels, large enterprises, transport companies and sawmills. They were simply doing too well and needed to be expelled. The Dayaks cannot work like we do but people always think that wealthy Madurese have been dishonest.
>
> Eyewitness, QUARRYMAN

Indeed, some Madurese had become very rich and powerful, and this discourse suggests that they have been more successful and dominant than Madurese in any other area. It is not clear whether this image of success approaches reality or not. According to some authors, Madurese in West and Central Kalimantan were, on average, no richer than Dayak or Malay people (De Jonge and

Nooteboom 2006:461, Van Klinken 2002). In East Kalimantan, some very successful people can be found, but they are not very visible. The Madurese livelihoods I studied do not support this view at all. Among settlers, Madurese are rapid risers. They work hard and save a lot whenever conditions are sufficiently safe and stable. Their businesses tend to grow fast as we saw among Madurese vegetable producers in Lempake (Chapter 6).

In the third narrative, it is believed a larger conspiracy existed. In this vision, provocateurs ignited the conflict and were able to do so due to a failing state and a biased police. Typical statements are: 'without provocation from the outside, it would not have happened', 'the governor and the police used foul play', 'they delivered us for a higher political goal' and 'the police helped the Dayaks'. Eyewitnesses give a more nuanced picture but also mention the role of outsiders who 'poisoned' local inter-ethnic relationships and stirred the ethnic soup. The story of *mas* Bumi and Tikno reflect this.

> It all started with the killing of a Dayak gang leader (*preman*). I worked at a Malay sawmill where all the workers were Madurese. We gambled a lot. The bankers (*bandar*) were all Madurese and earned a lot of money from Malay and Dayak gamblers. The violence started after a Dayak *preman* lost once more. Repeatedly he had asked for money but, this time, he could not stand losing again and demanded more money. He got the money, but later that night, they [Madurese gamblers] killed him in the forest and disrespected his body. That man's gang members (*anak buah*) got so angry that they stirred up the other Dayak and Malay against the Madurese.
>
> At first the Madurese defended themselves, but then the police (*aparat*) came and took away the weapons of the Madurese and locked them in. Then, the Dayak came and could kill them easily. The *aparat* helped the Dayak. They pretended that they had fired on the Dayak, but the weapons only made noise and produced smoke: there were no bullets. When the army came from Jakarta, they did protect the Madurese. Unfortunately, those from my area were already dead. I was the only one who escaped.
>
> *MAS* BUMI, labourer from Bondowoso, East Java, who worked in Sambas.

> Before it happened, there were no real tensions between Dayak and Madurese. In fact, the Dayak were very friendly. They told us: 'If you are good to us, we will be better. If you are bad to us, we will be worse'. [...] There was no law there; only the right of the jungle. People were regularly killed. If there were problems with someone about money or women, he was killed some where in the forest. This often happened.
>
> *pak* TIKNO, refugee from Sambas working in the Batu Besaung stone quarry, 2008.

> The problem was that if Madurese killed someone, they always fled to Madura and the others could not take revenge.
>
> MAS BUMI, 2005.

> Even when violence flared in other areas, it remained calm in our area. Dayak friends promised to protect us. Then the outsiders came. They stirred the local Dayak up and told them how bad Madurese were and what they had all done to Dayak people in other areas. Then the Dayak people around us became very angry and within a week everybody joined in.
>
> MAS AHMAD, eyewitness, now working in road construction, SAMARINDA, 2009.

The final set of narratives are of a supernatural nature and offer explanations for the fact that 'brave and violent' Madurese could be defeated by Dayak bands of youngsters. 'The magic (*ilmu*) of the Madurese was not sufficient'. Not only Madurese, but also Dayak and people from other ethnicities often mention this kind of explanation. Belief in magic is powerful and it plays an important role in explaining success or failure. The reason for defeat, in these explanations, was the superior magic of the Dayak. Madurese explained this by the fact that Madurese magic does not work so well in Kalimantan as it is too far from Madura. Explanations such as: 'there are not enough religious leaders (*kiai*) in Kalimantan who can provide magical powers' and 'our magic does not work outside East Java' were often used. Other important stories report that, due to magic, some Dayaks are able to 'smell' who is Madurese and who is not. Madurese are supposed to smell like cows. Interestingly, it was Madurese who told me these stories. In a sense, they internalized the dominant Dayak narratives in their own experiences.

During fieldwork in Krajan in 1997, 1998 and 1999, before the large conflicts occurred, returning migrants fearfully recalled Dayak being able to fly, to kill at a distance and to make people mad. Such stories were told and retold, and new migrants were warned not to steal from Dayak people or to touch their daughters. A powerful narrative involved stories about people who engaged in a love affair with a Dayak girl but then abandoned her. They were bewitched by the parents or by relatives of the girl and became mad (*gila*). If they returned to Madura or East Java then, somewhere in the middle of the crossing of the Java Sea, the spell was usually lifted and they were healthy again. There was no *kiai* who could heal them in Kalimantan. A couple of years later, when I started fieldwork in Kalimantan I heard the same story.

Much has already been written about the importance of magic elements in the violence in West and Central Kalimantan (Peluso and Harwell 2001, Schiller and Garang 2002). A central element is the ancient war spirit that has been summoned and released by Dayak sorcerers (the most powerful sorcerers were said to come from East Kalimantan). Once released and possessed by people, this spirit fills the warrior with rage and makes him invincible. Moreover, Dayak people, and especially those from inland forested areas, were supposed to be able to make themselves disappear, to kill at a distance and to be resilient to bullets and knives. 'The spirit was in a little bottle – they showed it to me – the oil in the bottle was beating like a living heart' a Dayak from East Kalimantan told me. Also in East Kalimantan, the war against the Madurese was fought with supernatural armoury. Many Madurese have become afraid and believed that a war against the Dayak could never be won.

ILLUSTRATION 11 *Refugee from West Kalimantan working in brick kiln Samarinda*

Effects of Distant Violence

Livelihood Implications of the Distant Violence

In essence, there have been three reactions among Madurese during and after the conflicts in Sambas and Sampit in 1999 and 2001. The first reaction has been one of disbelief. There had never been large-scale violence against Madurese in East Kalimantan before. A large element did not really believe the violence would, or could, ever spread to East Kalimantan. The second category was shocked that the violence had spread from Sambas to Sampit, and realized it could spread further to Samarinda, East Kalimantan, but trusted in their fierce reputation, their good relations with neighbours, police officers and local elites, and did not want to leave their property, business or occupation behind. The last category simply had great fear and tried to escape to Madura as soon as possible. In 2001, they flocked to the harbour, some with only their clothes, gold and some money. Eventually, according to estimates by local Madurese leaders, about 15% of the Madurese (mostly labourers, petty traders and craftsmen) returned to Madura and, for a couple of months, no new migrants dared come to Kalimantan.

These relatively poor Madurese, trying to leave for Madura, had urban occupations and worked as petty traders, porters or craftsmen. They had saved some money (many Madurese women have savings in the form of gold) and could relatively simply leave taking their jewellery and a few valuable belongings. For these people, transport by water was the only option. Richer people could fly, but most of the richer Madurese tried to hold on to their property as they had acquired houses, motorbikes, cars and/or land. About five per cent tried to sell cars and land to return to Madura or mainland East Java. Most of them kept their property and left only temporarily. They all returned within a year to Samarinda.

The majority of the poor labourers decided to stay and judge the signs of what was going on around them. Many Madurese simply did not have the money to leave for Madura, or were tied to employers by debts, labour contracts or patron-client relationships. In general, employers such as brick manufacturers and subcontractors were unwilling to let their workers leave as they needed the workers and wanted to protect their property. Foremen and ethnic leaders tried all means to prevent their people going back to Madura. *Haji* Rusti, one of the larger brick makers and an influential local leader (*tokoh Madura*) said: 'If they would go, our foothold would be lost. A mass leaving of Madurese would have been a sign of weakness and a signal to take over our possessions'.

I am still not clear if the fear of a spread of ethnic violence to East Kalimantan was based on more than rumours. There are fewer Dayak in East Kalimantan than in the rest of Kalimantan and, as Van Klinken (2002:102) points out, the interests of the elites differed. Some expected to gain from political turmoil, while others clearly preferred stability. Certainly, some Madurese informants mention an increase in fights, recall provocations and describe different forms of harassment. At the university campus, people threatened to burn Madurese food stalls down, elsewhere employers refused to employ Madurese and several brickmaking compounds were threatened with violence:

> I sat here, in front of my house, when a car with three Dayak men came. One man I knew as a Dayak leader. I had seen him before in the paper. They used rough language and told me to leave with all my people to Madura within six days, otherwise they would burn down our compound. I stayed calm and told him we had never done something wrong. After six days we were prepared to fight, but nobody came.
>
> PAK SULEMAN, BAYUR, 2005.

From 2001 until early 2003, very few new migrants from Madura dared to go to East Kalimantan. Only experienced migrants and close relatives were willing to travel, and then only 'after repeated phone calls and reassuring words' of relatives in East Kalimantan. In particular, labourers from mainland East Java ceased to come. As a result of the lack of labourers, brick prices tripled in 2001 and 2002 to Rp 400–500 per brick. When, in early 2003, migrants started to come again, boosted by Sampit and Sambas refugees who were struggling in East Java, the number of migrants rose quickly and brick prices started to decline to Rp 250 as a result of over-production. In 2003, the number of Madurese in East Kalimantan continued to rise as a consequence of the lack of labour opportunities on Madura and the Malaysian ban on illegal labourers (many of whom were Madurese). By early 2004, large numbers of Madurese poured into East Kalimantan and brick prices fell to Rp 200, an absolute minimum and barely enough to cover costs of production. After this, prices recoverd somewhat. Since then, East Kalimantan has been perceived as one of the few safe places left for Madurese in search for work and money.

Impact of the Distant Violence – Ten Years Later

Now, ten years later, we can draw up the balance. What have been the implications of the violence in West and Central Kalimantan on Madurese migrants in East Kalimantan? In the following, I will describe the most important impacts that I found in East Kalimantan.

The first and foremost consequence of the ethnic violence is a continuing sense of fear. Many of the Madurese migrants fear further hostilities against them, although this fear is often hidden or tacit. This fear might be objectified, or less conscious and implicit. Some express the fear that, one day, other ethnic groups might fight against them and peaceful neighbours will betray and conspire to kick them out of the country. Others 'just don't feel comfortable in Kalimantan anymore' and say that they are concerned 'not to get rooted'. Feelings of general insecurity have become stronger and other ethnicities are no longer trusted. They are also no longer seen as a potential source of social security but rather the opposite, a source of insecurity. For most Madurese, 'Kalimantan' has acquired a new meaning. It used to be referred to as the land of unlimited opportunities, but now there is an implicit connotation with horror and hostility. The new perception is that a living in Kalimantan needs to be defended, secured and struggled for.

Secondly, the violence in West and Central Kalimantan has problematized ethnic relationships and also 'everyday forms of violence' such as fights, feuds and competition in East Kalimantan. Fights with other ethnic groups at the marketplace are now perceived as a threat to the peaceful way of life of thousands of other migrants trying to make a living. The majority of Madurese now reject these kinds of fights and interpret them as 'ethnic'; as an expression of a long history of ethnic hatred. Further, not only the Madurese perceive these petty forms of violence as a threat, but also the government: 'don't emphasize the ethnicity, view these small conflicts as problems between individual people, not between groups', is an often-heard warning from government representatives, police and ethnic leaders. The fact that these fights stand in a long tradition of fights with Bugis makes them more threatening.

Thirdly, the Madurese are once more regarded as 'troublemakers'. 'They should be tamed', according to Dayak people and high ranking politicians and police officers. 'Everywhere where there are Madurese, there is trouble', a high ranking Bugis government official said, 'we need to curtail them here'. As a result, during the period 2004–2009, Madurese in East Kalimantan needed to ask permission from the police if they wanted to organize large gatherings such as religious events, music concerts or weddings. With the Madurese, violence is perceived as a cultural problem, whereas, when other people are engaged in violent acts, they tend to be described as incidents. Bugis certainly have violent elements in their culture, but their involvement in fights is perceived differently (Acciaioli 1999).

Fourthly, the violence in West and Central Kalimantan, the belief of Madurese involvement, and the reactions of outsiders in Samarinda has brought a sense of modesty among the Madurese. There is a greater understanding that a more positive image is essential to make a successful living in

East Kalimantan. Religious and secular leaders urge their people to comply with the norms and rules set by religion, stress national values such as *Panca Sila* and show loyalty to the East Kalimantan government to try to improve the Madurese image and highlight those who make a decent living: 'they must see we are peaceful people and useful workers', 'we should respect each other and live peacefully together' and 'everybody who does not comply with these norms will be sent home'. Pak Holik commented: 'We do not want those troublemakers here'. For Madurese migrants, a strong rule of law and a strong nation state are beneficial, and many long for the Soeharto years.

A final important impact of the conflict is that ethnicity has become a political issue. Ethnicity is widely, and often implicitly, used to indicate differences between groups in society. Although formal references to ethnicity are not allowed in East Kalimantan, it continues to play an important role in political struggles over access to resources as part of the decentralization process. More importantly, however, it has acquired a meaning in categorizing people as belonging, or not, to Kalimantan. For example: 'We don't want any more Madurese here. They are poor, unskilled and unrefined. We only need to grant admission to skilled labourers'. Examples of this changing sentiment are the sweepings of illegal migrants (*razia KTP*) in Balikpapan, in late 2003 and early 2004, in an attempt to send back all migrants without an East Kalimantan identity card. The *razia KTP* were presented by the regional government as an attempt to fight criminality, begging and immorality caused by the influx to East Kalimantan of large numbers of poor and unskilled migrants.[14] There were many Madurese among those rounded up. In the perception of the government and of the leading elites in Samarinda, poor overseas migrants have become a threat to Kalimantan society, and Madurese are particularly blamed for not assimilating and mixing with 'original' populations.[15] Categorizations such as insiders and outsiders, or established and newcomers (*pendatang*), have become important in discussions on the making of an East Kalimantan society. In this society, there is no space for poor immigrants and 'troublemakers'. However, defining who the 'troublemakers' are is a matter for the regional elites and dominant ethnic groups.

---

14 Tribun, December 2003.

15 Personal communication. See also the comments of Dayak and Bugis representatives on the causes of violence in West Kalimantan and possible solutions in The Jakarta Post, a national newspaper: Madurese Refugees get Relief from WVI 1999 'It would be better if Madurese are not sent back and repatriated elsewhere'.

ILLUSTRATION 12 *Madurese road worker loading gravel at brick kiln in Samarinda*

Impact on Social Relationships

Fear and the proliferation of ethnicity leads to a number of responses from among the Madurese. Many seasonal migrants first try to hide the fact that they are Madurese. They call themselves Javanese or as 'coming from East Java' and, if they speak Indonesian or Javanese well, they can go a long way without being identified. However, as soon as they are longer in Kalimantan, neighbours come to know that they are Madurese or from a Madurese-speaking area. On the boat from Surabaya to Kalimantan, I met dozens of Madurese who only after repeated probing and series of questions finally admitted that they were Madurese. They preferred to present themselves as coming from East

Java, being East Javanese, or from the neighbourhood of Surabaya. The secretary of the KKMM, the Madurese ethnic association in Samarinda, never revealed his Madurese background to his colleagues at Pemda (Regional Government Office).

According to Madurese and non-Madurese informants alike, Madurese ended their 'arrogant' attitude and style in business, trade and interethnic relationships in order to avoid conflict. 'They are less arrogant towards other traders now', a Bugis vegetable trader commented. Several Madurese leaders admitted: 'Madurese have finally become quiet'; and *Pak* Hodi added: 'We have become careful not to make any trouble. We are here to make money, if we only make enemies, we will lose out'.

Leaders and individual Madurese alike repeatedly stressed the importance of avoiding conflicts and trouble with other ethnicities. 'If you have a problem, don't make it an ethnic issue', a religious leader told his followers. *Haji* Romli, a brickmakers' foreman in Perjuangan commented: 'If people make trouble here, I send them back to Madura. We do not want any troublemakers here'. It was not only the leaders who were trying to avoid trouble, Madurese porters at the market told me that they avoided fights and left 'hotheads' to solve their own problems:

> Just before Idhul Fitri [2003], a Madurese brickmaker was selling *ketupat* (small cubes of woven palmleaves to steam rice) at the market. A Bugis motorcyclist hit his leg and a fight ensued. He called for help, but we did not help him. It was better he helped himself or ran away, we were too afraid to mix in and strain relationships. Every Madurese is now responsible for hmself. If we unite and fight, others will unite and fight us with many more people.

As a response to the violence and their perceived negative image, many semi-permanent migrants and Madurese settlers who own land or houses have, notwithstanding their deeply rooted distrust, tried to engage in better social relationships with neighbours. This is comparable with what Susanto (2006:107) calls the 'accommodation strategies' of the Chinese during threats of violence in Central Java in 1998. Regularly, Madurese informants would explain to me the importance of living in peace with neighbours and told me about their activities to establish good relationships. Pak Gidun, a horticulturalist and informal leader of the Madurese vegetable and fruit nurseries outside Samarinda, organized, as head of the Madurese neighbourhood, several peace ceremonies with Dayak neighbours from nearby forests and their regional leaders. 'We ate together, exchanged gifts, made music and agreed not to start any hostilities. I even paid them money'. They agreed to report all problems with one of their people directly to each other to be settled. Pak Hodi visited his Dayak neighbours to stress their good relationships, and Pak Bakri made sure he paid his land rent well before the due date. Remarkably, Bugis, with whom relationships in this area are tense due to fierce competition over land and the vegetable trade, were not invited to the peace ceremonies. Nevertheless, Pak Suleman, a foreman of a group of brickmakers, gave a donation of 15,000 bricks for the building of a mosque in a neighbouring Bugis/Banjar village.

Although the majority of the semi-permanent migrants and settlers adhere to these accommodation strategies, not all invest in friendly relationships. Especially among those brickmakers who live in relatively isolated communities, and among newcomers and poor labourers, many can be found who refrain from contact with other ethnic groups. They tend to avoid any interaction with outsiders and live and work in their own communities. Food and goods are supplied by the employer, and community leaders serve as brokers with the outside world. This process is enhanced by the fact that, since 2001, Madurese seldom obtain new permission from local landowners (especially from Banjar and Bugis) to use the soil on wasteland to make bricks. Instead, they are increasingly forced to lease or buy it. As a result, they search for cheap land outside the city (see Map 5). Madurese families often combine to buy or lease this land, and this leads to the establishment of mono-ethnic enclaves of Madurese brickmakers where seasonal workers just come to work and save something before going back to Madura. Among the stonecutters, who live further from town and far from other human settlements, this isolation tendency is even stronger.

Although investment in land and lease contracts has increased (especially after the end of 2002), there is a general tendency to refrain from investments in East Kalimantan in favour of investing and accumulating assets in Madura. Many settlers spoke of no longer investing in land and large houses, but preferring to accumulate on Madura, or invest in goods which could be sold easily (such as trucks, motor cycles or gold) in Kalimantan. Many also try, and even harder than before, to get a family member to Malaysia or Saudi Arabia. However, since early 2003, migration to Malaysia has become more difficult and in reality few men and women from mainland East Java make it to Saudi Arabia.

There is a small category of very rich Madurese who seem unconcerned about all the turmoil. A number of the Madurese business people engaged in road construction, recycling (iron, plastics and tyres) and coal mining retain their aggressive business style combined with an arrogant attitude. The infamous *Haji* Noa (a member of the powerful *Haji* Su family) for instance, who

ILLUSTRATION 13 *Accommodation at one of the brick kilns of Air Hitam, Samarinda*

made a fortune in road construction and – according to former business partners – operating gambling halls, treats neighbours and minor business partners with great arrogance. In a coffee shop near his large house, a Banjar driver spoke about an accident he once had: 'His car has hit my motorbike when he came out of his porch. I asked him for one million compensation for the damage. He told me to come to his house later that day. When I came, he said: "how do you want to have it? With a straight or a bent one?" [referring to the kind of stick to beat him]. When I went to the police they laughed, they are all friends of Haji Noa'.

The Role of the Government: Conflict Resolution in Samarinda

During the 2001 violence, the provincial government of East Kalimantan adopted a proactive strategy in an attempt to stop the violence before it could even start. The governor of East Kalimantan, in close cooperation with the police, brought many ethnic leaders together with some NGOs and university lecturers and forced the ethnic fractions to make peace in public. The first meeting was held in the old stadium of Samarinda with hundreds of leaders present (*tokoh tokoh masyarakat*). Following this, monthly meetings were held in the prestigious Hotel Senyiur in Samarinda under the banner of *Forum Kommunikasi Persaudaraan Masyarakat Kalimantan Timur* (FKPMKT).[16]

In this forum, the most important ethnic groups were represented (Bugis, Banyar, Java, Kutai and Dayak) and all the expenses of the meeting were paid by the provincial government. In 2001, another forum was established: the *Forum Komunikasi Antar-Etnik* (Forkas). This forum included a Madurese religious leader (who unfortunately died soon after its start). The provincial government forced him to re-establish the *Kerukan Keluarga Masyarakat Madura* (KKMM), an ethnic association similar to the ethnic associations represented in the FKPMKT. After his death, a leadership crisis among the Madurese occurred, with Madurese community leaders from all over East Kalimantan quarrelling, and they failed to elect a new leader. There appeared to be no candidate sufficiently strong and respected to unite all Madurese.

Finally, *Haji* Su (a Madurese from Banyuwangi), pushed himself to the fore and proclaimed himself the representative and chair of the KKMM. The KKMM, however, was never successful due to diverging interests between the various ethnic sub-fractions, classes and business leaders. It ended up representing only the 'urban Madurese' such as porters, contractors and labourers in construction and road building. Brickmakers, stonecutters, farmers and small businessmen did not recognize *Haji* Su's hegemony and refused to join. They saw the KKMM as an instrument for enhancing *Haji* Su's personal power.

During FKPMKT and Forkas meetings in 2001, the government organized a number of indigenous reconciliation rituals that were supposed to be repeated at lower levels. Leaders exchanged presents and promised to settle individual conflicts between ethnic groups through communication and in harmony. The rituals however remained very artificial – especially for Madurese who are not used to this kind of ritual – and, except for Pak Gidun, this example has never been followed by any Madurese leader. Besides enforcing dialogue and reconciliation, the government banned the media reporting, and any other public

16 See also Van Klinken, 2002:50.

references to, ethnic issues and instructed local leaders to perceive conflicts not as ethnic conflicts, but as individual disagreements between people. Their slogan: 'Don't play it as ethnicity, look at the individual',[17] became known and used by almost all Madurese. To subdue negative sentiments and rumours about injustice, the government promised to establish and safeguard a fair judicial system.

Although the symbolic power of these meetings has been significant and may have been crucial in curtailing ethnic policies by local leaders, for ordinary Madurese migrants the dialogue had little meaning as they did not feel at all represented. An important factor here was the lack of an organizational structure among the Madurese and their well-educated leaders. There has never been any form of formal Madurese organization in East Kalimantan, and the influence of the KKMM remained weak. Moreover, internal divisions and personal power policies weakened *Haji* Su's bargaining position. Few inter-ethnic conflicts have ever been settled by the KKMM, and the strengthened governmental judicial policies turned out to be somewhat disadvantageous for Madurese. The government banned Madurese public meetings and established a zero-tolerance policy towards fights at hotspots such as markets, cock-fighting arenas and brothels. Security officials from the intelligence department of the police (Intel) infiltrated these places and stopped any fighting from spreading by simply firing in the air, capturing ringleaders or shooting some people in the legs.

Van Klinken (2002:70) explains the violence in West and Central Kalimantan in terms of the power politics of local elites and describes them as: 'parasitic elites who [were willing to] deflect democratization by stimulating ethnic conflict'. According to him, in East Kalimantan, the role of local elites was positive and crucial in preventing the spread of mass violence because their economic interests were better served by peace. However, I doubt if studying the interests of the elites is sufficient. The East Kalimantan case shows that ethnic elites were only able to prevent conflict with the support of the government and police. All the necessary ingredients for a violent conflict were present: problematic ethnic relationships involving Madurese, a long history of violent minor clashes involving them, widespread negative Madurese stereotyping, hatred, political instability, resource competition, and ethnic, religious and economic controversies. This chapter shows that government policies did not lead to a decrease in local-level ethnic tensions, did not eliminate the roots of violence and failed to solve the problem of the politicization of ethnicity. As a result, the Madurese remain in the black books.

---

17 *'Jangan main sampai suku, lihat individu'.*

By using reconciliation rituals, community meetings, censorship and repression, the violence seen elsewhere against Madurese did not spread to East Kalimantan. Although this provided some protection, many of the Madurese did not feel safe and remained cautious. In the concluding remarks below, the longer term impacts of the violence are summarized.

Concluding Remarks

This chapter has analysed the impact of the Sambas and Sampit violence on Madurese in the neighbouring East Kalimantan province by studying Madurese experiences and interpretations of violence and the role of the provincial government. Madurese interpretations of violence in East Kalimantan are shaped within a context of frequent, small-scale, tensions with other ethnic groups such as Bugis, Banjar and Dayak. These tensions with other ethnic groups arise out of resource conflicts, negative stereotyping of Madurese, cultural differences and competing economic and political interests. The collective memory of the ethnic cleansing of Madurese in West and Central Kalimantan in 1999–2001 has added another dimension to ethnic relationships in East Kalimantan: ethnicity has become a political problem and Madurese are no longer welcome. In general, this leads to less access to resources and fewer opportunities for Madurese to make a living. In response, poor Madurese try to keep a low profile, avoid conflicts and try to earn a more positive image.

As a general conclusion, the chapter shows that the mass violence in West and Central Kalimantan has had a large and diverse impact on Madurese in East Kalimantan. The violence in West and Central Kalimantan was a major blow to Madurese pride and self-esteem in general and contributed to the daily hardship involved in making a living. For Madurese in East Kalimantan, the ethnic violence in neighbouring provinces has been a traumatic experience and fear has spread among them. Many feel they should operate with care and modesty so as not to provoke any negative reactions. This is not an easy task, and success is not guaranteed as negative images of the Madurese are deeply rooted, and few non-Madurese are willing to acknowledge that these images do not reflect reality. There is no evidence that Madurese migrants are more violent or criminal than, for instance, Bugis, Banjar and Butonese migrants. In reality, most Madurese migrants are poor and hardworking people who make a living in sectors unattractive to other people such as stone cutting, brick making, road construction, recycling and urban waste removal. Their importance for the local economy is seldom recognised. As a result, their livelihoods continue to be under threat.

The statement of Pak Bakri, earlier in the chapter, is indicative: 'Madurese no longer have any self-esteem (*harga diri*)'. The story of Pak Bakri also illustrates that a distant conflict and a loss of pride and self-esteem have a strong impact on ethnic relationships and influence livelihood strategies. Madurese try to hide their ethnicity or tend to retreat into closed communities and the economic activities where they dominate. Although these accommodation strategies might curb conflict in the short term, in the long run, fear, distrust and frustration among Madurese could increase. This reaction does not facilitate dialogue and peaceful interaction with other ethnicities. If these local dimensions are neglected, no real reconciliation and integration can take place. It is especially here where the government could step in. Although they successfully prevented the 2001 conflict from spreading to East Kalimantan, and effectively suppressed violent outbursts of ethnic sentiments between 2001 and 2009, nothing is being done to start a real dialogue and develop sound ethnic policies oriented on intercommunity dialogue and cooperation.

It is important to not only note the far-reaching impacts of violence on individual members of an ethnic group, but also on regional ethnic relationships and policies. Madurese inhabitants perceived the violence as a collective trauma, a cultural loss of honour and a reason for increased resource competition, while others perceive them as a threat to safety and stability in the region. Although the regional government has tried to suppress ethnic sentiments and successfully prevented the spread of violence to East Kalimantan in 2001, the problems associated with the politicization of ethnicity remain unsolved. The unresolved tensions remain a potential source of future conflict. Not least because no real inter-ethnic dialogue takes place due to a lack of proper Madurese political representation. Without a change in national and regional policies that draw in the Madurese perspective, ethnic peace remains uncertain.

During the 2001 FKPMKT and Forkas (peace building) meetings in Samarinda (Van Klinken 2002), the government organized a number of indigenous reconciliation rituals which were supposed to be repeated at lower levels. Leaders exchanged presents and promised to settle individual conflicts between the various ethnic groups harmoniously through communication. However, the rituals remained very artificial – especially to the Madurese who are not used to this kind of ritual – and, except for *Pak* Gimun in Muang Dalam, this example has never been followed by any Madurese leader. Besides enforcing dialogue and reconciliation, the government banned public references to ethnic issues and instructed local leaders to perceive conflicts not as ethnic conflicts but as tensions between individuals. Their slogan, 'don't play it as ethnicity, look at the individual', became widely known and adopted by almost all

Madurese. To subdue negative sentiments and rumours of injustice, the government promised to establish and safeguard a fair judicial system. In practice, however, negative sentiments against Madurese increased. Only the relatively prosperous and socially well-embedded vegetable farmers could maintain their good position due to their ownership and control of resources. In all other sectors, it became harder for Madurese to do business and expand their activities.

Although the investments by migrants in land and lease contracts in the brick sector increased (especially after the end of 2002), there has been a general tendency towards investment and accumulation in Madura. Many settlers spoke of no longer investing in land and large houses, but preferring to accumulate assets on Madura. If they do invest, it tends to be in goods which could be easily sold (such as trucks, motor cycles or gold) in an emergency. Many also strive, and even harder than before, to get a family member to Malaysia or Saudi Arabia. However, migration to Malaysia has become very difficult and many who have tried to migrate end up stuck in East Kalimantan and especially in the northern district of Nunukan. Overall, Madurese in Kalimantan remain 'small and lowly' (*di bawah angin*).

CHAPTER 8

Risk, Illegality and the State in Kalimantan[1]

This chapter focuses on one particular group of Madurese migrants, the entrepreneurs who make a living in East Kalimantan, and it concentrates on one specific topic, the ambiguous relationships that some of these entrepreneurs have with police officers and the illegal activities they jointly engage in. These relationships are key to understanding the establishment and survival of Madurese businesses in East Kalimantan. The analysis offers a view of the everyday interactions between police officers and Madurese migrants in East Kalimantan. This chapter does not deal with the Indonesian police or the state in a wider sense but focuses on the relationship between Madurese and the police in local settings. It provides a view of the state and illegality as seen from below by offering an account based on the perspectives of ordinary people, centring on their everyday life experiences. In so doing, the chapter shows how illegal activities are often essential in establishing business at the lower levels of society. Without illegality and social relationships with the police (*aparat*), life would be considerably more difficult for migrants.

In the previous chapter, I focused on Madurese migrants and entrepreneurs and the strategies they undertake under the threat of ethnic violence. When I was busy with that study, I soon added illegal activities and the relationships that migrants had with police to my research focus. It turned out that to understand the successes, failures and insecurities of Madurese migrant entrepreneurs in East Kalimantan it was also essential to understand their involvement in illicit and illegal activities. As we shall see, my investigations led to the conclusion that illegal activities and the relationships with the police benefit both migrants and the police in Samarinda. The police needs to tolerate a certain level of crime in order to keep criminality under control. Before reaching that conclusion, I will discuss the nature of Madurese businesses in East Kalimantan and their relationship with police officers.

Risky Business

Engaging in entrepreneurial activities is an inherently risky business, especially for immigrants who are poorly educated and originate from an ethnic

1 This chapter has been modified and rewritten to fit within the context of this book. It is based on a chapter published in Aspinall and Van Klinken in 2011.

 | DOI 10.1163/9789004282988_009

group that is unpopular in the recipient society. The obstacles for migrant entrepreneurs are numerous. They range from a lack of cash or credit, limited access to indigenous networks of information and support, and a general lack of insight into and access to local bureaucratic procedures. Discrimination and even threats of ethnic violence can be a problem. For low-skilled migrants, large parts of the host community are inaccessible and the better jobs are already taken and distributed among established groups. Apart from waged labour within the lowest echelons of society, taking up a trade or business is often the only option.

Being part of an ethnic minority group, apart from the disadvantages outlined above, also has the comparative advantage of being sufficiently distant from the local society and its governing norms to make it possible to engage in profitable, but illicit, activities. Hans Dieter Evers describes the trader's dilemma:

> ...of either being integrated into the moral economy of the host society, and consequently subjugated to the pressure of solidarity and sharing, or, on the other hand, of separating from the host society, facing discrimination but also being able to claim debts, to accumulate capital and to conduct business and trade successfully.
>
> EVERS 1990:11

Elsewhere, Evers emphasizes how traders tend to minimize risk and maximize trust in inter-ethnic relationships through engaging in many kinds of trading and other relationships (Evers and Schrader 1994; Evers and Mehmet 1994:1). Such considerations largely explain why large proportions of many immigrant minority groups over the world are entrepreneurs (Raillon 1994), and that they are often successful, especially in the informal sector.

The success of immigrant entrepreneurs seems to be the result of a combination of factors: their will (and need) to succeed, their strategic use of ethnic trading networks and inter-ethnic trust, their lack of assimilation and their willingness to take up any activity, no matter how dirty, difficult or unacceptable in local society. The last of these factors is behind why immigrant entrepreneurs are regularly reported as being involved in illegality.

This general picture applies to Madurese entrepreneurs in East Kalimantan. In Samarinda, the capital of the province, about 15% of Madurese migrants are involved in business or trade. Most of these businesses are small, but they offer work to about three-quarters of the approximately 15,000–20,000 Madurese in the city. Some of the early Madurese migrants (who arrived before the 1990s) are now well-off and own land, houses, cars, transport businesses, recycling firms, construction companies, gambling dens and brothels. They earned their 'fortunes' during the late 1980s and 1990s when the economy of Samarinda was booming as a result of logging and mining. A number of these businesses operate in the twilight zone between legality and illegality. A small number of them combine perfectly legal trade with activities such as theft, cheating, illegal logging or land occupation and running sex and gambling businesses. Many individual Madurese also work as security guards and assistants for the ethnic Chinese businessmen who organize large-scale gambling at malls, discotheques and bars. However, widespread violence against Madurese in other parts of Kalimantan in 1997–2001 damaged the image and self-esteem of Madurese migrants, making them less attractive as guards.[2] Some Madurese who had formerly worked as guards have started their own businesses, others have retreated into less risky businesses, or are no longer hired.

In the overal field of illegal economic activities in Samarinda, Madurese are only small players. Very few Madurese were involved in the massive illegal logging operations of the late 1990s and early 2000s. More recently, Madurese have also been little involved in the corruption associated with government projects, timber and plantation concessions, and with the embezzlement of royalties from mining activities.[3] Although Samarinda citizens often view criminality as a characteristic trait of the Madurese people, they are in fact no more engaged in illegal activities than other ethnic groups such as the Buginese, Banjarese, Javanese, Torajanese and Butonese.

According to a middle-ranking police officer in Samarinda, the Banjarese and Buginese are currently among the most criminally active ethnic groups in Samarinda. Buginese gangs dominate protection rackets, the lucrative harbour and market areas and large-scale illegal trades of all kinds, while Banjarese gangs are involved in petty crime such as burglary and pickpocketing. As long as criminality remains petty, and mobs of people are themselves able to punish some of the criminals through public lynching, the police seem not overly concerned.[4] In general, trust in the police in Indonesia is low and 'people feel that lynching makes the streets safer' (Colombijn 2002:302).

---

2 For an analysis of anti-Madurese violence elsewhere in Kalimantan see: Schiller and Garang 2002; Davidson and Kammen 2002; Peluso 2006; Peluso and Harwell 2001; Van Klinken 2002. I have discussed the loss of self-esteem and its impact in the previous chapter and also in De Jonge and Nooteboom 2006; Nooteboom 2005.

3 For illegal logging in East Kalimantan, see Casson and Obidzinski 2002.

4 In his discussion of public lynching across the country, Freek Colombijn gives several examples of lynching with the police standing by while the mobs act. He concludes: 'The response of the police to mob justice is in general half-hearted [...]. After the fact, however, the police accept the lynching as it is. They never try to investigate the matter' (2002:319). See also Welsh 2008.

There is much guessing but few hard facts based on research on the relationships between small entrepreneurs, illegal activities and the police in Indonesia. Adopting a micro-perspective, I have followed Madurese entrepreneurs who have been involved in legal as well as illegal activities in East Kalimantan. Some of the illegal activities are deemed acceptable by the police and yield mutual benefits, while others are clearly unacceptable and the police attempt to stamp them out. Also among Madurese themselves, there are different views on what constitutes acceptable behaviour. Further, it turns out that police officers often collaborate with, or help, Madurese in carrying out many illegal activities. Before discussing these activities in detail, I will first elaborate on the research methodology I used and then outline the background and structure of Madurese migration and entrepreneurship in East Kalimantan.

Researching Illegality

Studying the relationships between police and migrants in the context of illegality is not easy. By its nature, illegality concerns covert activities, sensitive topics, uneasy relationships, distrust and a shared interest in secrecy by all the actors involved. Both migrant groups and police networks are difficult to penetrate. Access to information and sites is often blocked by gatekeepers, including gang leaders and police officers, who tend to deny activities, prohibit access or frustrate interviews and observations. Outsiders, including researchers, represent a potential threat. Silence is essential to the smooth running of illegal activities.

Knowledge of illegal activities is not limited to their leaders. Many people know something about such activities, and even have crucial information about them because they usually take place through networks of social relationships which, in some cases, can involve huge numbers of actors. These actors usually do not know all the facts, but they can generally reveal some of the illegal practices concerned. In anthropological research, there are always ways to approach some of these people, gain access to their networks and gather insights without directly mentioning illegality as a research theme.

The study of illegality in daily life requires an unobtrusive and indirect approach. As part of a larger study on livelihood and social security styles, I used a bottom-up method to gather information about all sorts of economic activities engaged in by Madurese migrants in East Kalimantan. By studying the livelihood activities, insecurities and social networks of migrants, it proved possible, at the same time, to study, from the perspective of the Madurese migrants themselves, their illegal activities and their relationships with police officers. In carrying out this research it was crucial to develop good relationships with ordinary Madurese workers, migrants and entrepreneurs. Many such people were willing to tell me about their livelihood activities, including the 'less legal' ones, and take me to backstage areas at markets, wedding ceremonies and bars, as well as to cockfights, illegal brothels and gambling dens.

During the fieldwork, I became interested in the illegal activities in which people were involved and made further inquiries among brickmakers, and among people working in the quarries and brothels. I further investigated the key players among the brickmakers and brothel workers and carried out participant observation during cockfights, gambling and brickmaking activities. It was almost impossible to interview police officers, officials from the State Intelligence Agency (BIN, Badan Intelijen Negara) or politicians, but I managed to carry out a few informal interviews with such people without revealing the purpose of this study. In large part because of these limitations, this chapter mainly adopts a perspective on state and illegality from below, looking at the interactions through the eyes of Madurese migrants.

Many Madurese born in Kalimantan blame their negative image on newcomers, who they claim do not know how to behave, and on *preman* (thugs) who are members of criminal gangs and often involved in illegal logging, in running brothels and gambling dens and in smuggling consumer goods. According to those born in Kalimantan, these people cast a slur on the whole Madurese community.

Relationships with Police Officers

An element of the negative stereotyping of Madurese in Samarinda is that whenever a theft takes place, local Madurese are typically amongst the earliest to be blamed. This stereotyping makes it hard for Madurese to establish new businesses or to expand their existing ones. However, their disadvantaged status as migrants in the lower echelons of society also confers an advantage: they have more room to manoeuvre in the illegal sectors of the economy. To protect their position on the margins, many Madurese entrepreneurs maintain regular contacts with police officers, who protect their businesses and provide them with informal permission for illegal activities.

For the police, marginalized Madurese entrepreneurs are also attractive partners because, through them, the police gain access to lucrative illegal activities. Moreover, the entrepreneurs are willing to do the 'dirty' jobs which the police cannot do themselves. Examples include running semi-legal stone quarries and excavations of clay for the brick industry, running brothels, organizing cockfights and other forms of gambling, running protection rackets and even engaging in petty crime such as pickpocketing, organizing pyramid games and stealing. For such activities, the participants need to pay regular premiums to the police officers who routinely visit them. These premiums range from five to twenty per cent of the takings for brick, stone and transport businesses operating without licences, to over 50% for the most illegal and criminal activities such as running brothels or organizing large gambling games. According to some of my Madurese informants, at least when it comes to the small-scale activities, police officers tend to 'look after' specific sectors or businesses, which they do not always reveal to their colleagues, in order to secure a higher gain.

Moreover, Madurese, as a feared and reviled minority group, can be used by security personnel for dirty political games involving intimidation and competition between political rivals or interest groups. Many Madurese *preman* used to be involved in such activities in the 1980s and 1990s but the violence against Madurese in West and Central Kalimantan from 1997 on made the Madurese more politically vulnerable in East Kalimantan, weakening their role as a political tool to be used in gang fights and protection rackets. Active Madurese involvement in the intimidation of business or political groups has declined in recent years. Nevertheless, many Madurese are still employed as security guards including in gambling dens, bars, discotheques and brothels. Good relationships with the police are needed to maintain these positions since, if relations with the police are poor, the Madurese are the first to be punished.

By not engaging directly in illegal activities, the police remain removed from direct responsibility for those illegal activities, but can share in the profits they generate. The ordinary police officers who collect a share of the proceeds from petty illegality pay, in turn, part of these proceeds to their superiors within the police apparatus. The downside of this process for the Madurese population at large is that the Madurese who engage in these mutually beneficial relationships with the police, by participating in the visible elements of illegality, reproduce the negative public image of the Madurese as a group.

Community Ideas on Illegality

Internally, the Madurese community does not tolerate every activity. On the contrary, most Madurese are proud of their community and are religiously orthodox. They clearly distinguish between licit and illicit behaviour in business. For instance, 'bad' behaviour includes involvement in drinking, prostitution and gambling. Involving Madurese women in prostitution, no matter how bad their reputation may already be, is perceived as a humiliation for the community as a whole and is severely sanctioned.[5]

Stealing and cheating customers (for example by not repaying debts, delivering lower quantity or quality of goods than ordered, or taking cash advances and never delivering orders at all) are viewed less severely provided other Madurese are not the target and nobody gets hurt. Many Madurese men retell stories of their own feats in cheating and stealing over and over again, and doing so helps to build one's status as a 'daredevil', and shows one's strength and cleverness. Nevertheless, no matter how much money is earned by such activities, the profit is generally perceived as being '*haram*' (unclean, forbidden) and cannot be used for Islamic goals such as paying Islamic tax (*zakat*) and making donations to build mosques nor, at least according to some purists, for household needs. Many Madurese say such profits are *uang panas*, 'hot money' that will disappear as quickly as it came. Some women told me they would not accept money from their husbands that they knew to be *haram*, even if they badly needed it for the household. As a result, men often buy clothes, food or presents with such money, and give goods rather than money to their wives.

At *Idhul Fitri*, the festivities that follow the fasting month, I witnessed the youngest son of Haji Yusuf visiting his father's home.[6] Family members had seldom mentioned this son in my regular chats with them as he is a habitual gambler and works as a gaming organizer and security guard for a Chinese businessman in Balikpapan. I never gained a full picture of his activities, as his father and brothers did not want to talk much about him. At the visit, he offered his poor father a few Rp 50,000 notes. However, the father, quite embarrassingly for the son I thought, rejected the money and ignored his son completely. Later, Haji Yusuf explained to me that he did not want to take this money as it was probably earned from *haram* activities. Later, however, at the back of the house when I was collecting my motorbike to leave, Yusuf's wife

5 Remarkably, Madurese-speaking prostitutes from the island of Java, especially from the areas of Pasuruan, Lumayang, Besuki, Bondowoso, Jember and Sitobondo, are permitted to work in Madurese-run brothels in East Kalimantan. They are generally considered to be outsiders by members of the local Madurese community who come from the island of Madura. A rapid survey among owners of brothels shows that these Madurese-speaking women from East Java form the largest group of prostitutes in Samarinda.

6 Hajji Yusuf is a close friend of Hajji Romli, one of the cases presented later in this chapter. Hajji Yusuf used to work for Hajji Romli before they went to Mecca.

showed me proudly the money she had been given by her son. She had taken it gladly. Most likely, Haji Yusuf will never know how his wife paid for the kitchen supplies that month.

Illegality seems first and foremost to be a male matter, but women often condone their husbands' activities and play an important role in the background. They are often prominent, for instance, in money laundering, in sending profits for investing in Madura, in managing the girls in the brothels or in establishing legal enterprises to cover the illegal activities. Often they remain silent or let it pass when their husbands lose large sums of money due to gambling or fines that result from illegal activities if they have lost their police protection. The wives of men involved in illegal practices secretly save gold or cash for difficult times, act as moneylenders to other Madurese or invest in 'clean' businesses for themselves. Such side-businesses might involve investing in a local shop, trade, food stall (*warung*) or truck, or in cattle, land or a house on Madura. At the same time, women often try to encourage their husbands away from criminal activities and sometimes play a crucial role in eventually converting them to a more honest lifestyle.

After achieving success in the illegal sector during their younger years, many men, typically when in their mid-thirties or early forties, have a sort of mid-life crisis. They come to see the dirty and dangerous work they are involved in as emotionally exhausting or unsustainable. Gradually, or sometimes abruptly, many men abandon their criminal activities and invest their money in cleaner business activities. They often accompany this switch with a move towards a more religious life, which they often see as a form of repentance, and which is not infrequently followed by a pilgrimage to Mecca. Such transformations are usually celebrated by Madurese friends and relatives, who view it as a move towards a better life rather than as a sign of weakness or declining power. A 'life of sin' lived during one's younger years is almost viewed as a prerequisite for becoming a true man and a genuine Muslim later. Most entrepreneurs pay a high price for their conversion, most enterprises quickly lose customers and resources, and household incomes diminish sharply. As such, a certain degree of illegality facilitates economic success, and good relationships with the police are essential for even simple businesses to run successfully.

Three Life Stories

In the remainder of this chapter, I illustrate how relationships between Madurese entrepreneurs and police work by discussing three examples. They are presented in ascending order of closeness with the police and with illegality. Sudi, Romli and Tamim (not their real names) have worked themselves up to become independent entrepreneurs. Sudi is a brickmaker, but without proper rights to the land he uses. He receives protection from a police officer in return for bricks or money. His good relations with the police, although costly, ensure the survival of his enterprise. They save Sudi from time-consuming bureaucratic exercises and legitimize his excavation of fertile topsoil. Moreover, his connections with the police protect Sudi against competing land claims and hostility from his neighbours. Romli, a transporter and trader of building materials, used to make a living from smuggling, theft and extortion. After ceasing these activities under police pressure, Romli fell on hard times but, through his wife and her brother, succeeded in transforming himself from a feared gang leader into a respectable community leader. Due to his good contacts with the police, he is often able to negotiate on behalf of Madurese arrested for petty crimes, reducing their fines or getting them released from police custody. In return, Romli provides intelligence to the police in cases of murder or ethnic violence. Finally, Tagil offers us a glimpse into the split life of many criminals in Indonesia: he is a gambling boss and pimp running his own illegal activities but, at the same time, he is an instrument in the hands of the police apparatus.

Seeking protection: Sudi

In 2003 and 2004, I met Sudi several times at his brick kiln, located on the back road to Bayur. When taking a rest, overseeing his workers or firing the bricks, he was always ready for long talks, and he openly shared the story of his life with me. Within five years of arriving in East Kalimantan from Madura in the mid-1980s, Sudi had become a successful organizer of cockfights and other gambling. He was feared for his aggressiveness and bad temper. Many people saw him as one of the most daring of the young Madurese 'madmen' roaming the area of Samarinda in the mid-1990s. 'Everyone was afraid of me', he told me during one of our conversations. 'I could beat anyone. Be it fighting, drinking or motorbike racing, I always wanted to win. Sometimes I had loads of money in those days, but sometimes I lost large amounts and did not come home for days. In the end, I had a debt of Rp 26 million.' In one of our interviews I ventured to ask his wife, sitting towards the back of the house, but listening carefully, if she had not become angry with his behaviour, or tried to prevent him from gambling. 'Angry? What do you think? I was mad with him. But, you know, it was better to remain silent with this man. I was at home with two small children. If you get mad with hot-headed people like he was, they get even more angry and rough. It's better to be careful.' Sudi nods. 'I was like that. When I came home late at night and my wife did not open the door fast enough, I kicked it in.'

After a violent fight with Buginese thugs, one of whom was reported to be severely wounded or even killed, Sudi ended up in a police cell.[7] One of his maternal uncles in East Kalimantan, Saïd, had good connections with the police and succeeded in buying him out, on the condition that Sudi would never again engage in crime. Saïd demanded that Sudi quit his 'bad' life of drinking, gambling and living with prostitutes, and offered him a job as foreman in his brickmaking enterprise. Saïd's good relations with the police protected Sudi from the revenge of the Bugis men and their networks. From that time onwards, life went better for Sudi.

Nine years later, Saïd sold some of his possessions in Kalimantan and went on the pilgrimage to Mecca. When he came back, he went bankrupt due to his own overspending and being cheated by his business partner. Sudi lost his job and started to gamble again. He lost millions of rupiah in the course of a few months. In an attempt to change his luck, he borrowed money from a friend and bought a cheap brick kiln in Bayur. This kiln had previously belonged to a Madurese who had been attacked and killed by an angry mob who had accused him of theft. To obtain clay, Sudi, with the help of a policeman who had been befriended by his uncle Saïd, rented land from villagers. The policeman gave money to one or two of the villagers and told them to refrain from further hostilities against Madurese. After Sudi made his first bricks, it turned out that there were multiple claims to the plot where his kiln was located and also where Sudi obtained his clay. Villagers from two neighbouring villages claimed it as their community land and protested against the commercial excavation of the soil. Moreover, they no longer wanted any Madurese living close.

Sudi called in the help of the policeman who visited regularly in that period. Word of Sudi's friendship with the policeman spread fast, and regular sightings of him at Sudi's kiln was enough to discourage villagers from protesting. According to Sudi, he also talked to the village heads. From that time on, his relations with his neighbours have been calm. 'I

7 Sudi did not tell me much about what happened to these Bugis men, and simply referred to them as 'wounded thugs'. I got some information about them from others, but the accounts were neither first hand nor unambiguous. Some spoke of one or more of Bugis thugs being killed, others of them being severely wounded.

even visited their mosque and donated 4,000 bricks for its renovation. But I do not fully trust them. I need my friend, the police officer. He also helped me when some Bugis men were looking for me in an attempt to reclaim a gambling debt. My friend [the police officer] gave them some of my money and told them to be silent. They never returned.' The help of the policeman-cum-friend is not without cost. At the start of their cooperation, the police officer asked for a percentage of the bricks that Sudi produced: 5,000 out of every 100,000 bricks produced. In Sudi's first year, when bricks were expensive and production still low, this amounted to 17,000 bricks, worth almost Rp 6 million. 'It was said he was busy building a house for himself.' Later, when the price of bricks fell, the police officer wanted to have Rp 500,000 for every 100,000 bricks produced. By the time of my research, Sudi had built up a large business producing about 250,000–300,000 bricks per year with about eight to ten people working for him. Still, when bricks are fired, about five or six times a year, the policeman visits Sudi and asks for money. 'I do not know where he lives, but if he comes, I give him Rp 100,000 or more if he keeps on asking. He's actually a poor guy', justifies Sudi to himself, 'He has got to give most of his money to his seniors.'

During my study of Madurese livelihoods in East Kalimantan, I encountered several enterprises such as Sudi's. The entrepreneurs involved gained access to land and sometimes even land titles by using close connections with the police. Some of them received direct police protection in the event of land conflicts, hostility or problems with creditors. In 7 cases out of 118 in my sample, entrepreneurs told me explicitly, and in detail and without prompting, about their relationships with the police: about the payments they made and the percentages taken. In another five cases businesspeople informed me about similar relationships but with less detail.[8] Two-thirds of these twelve cases were brickmaking enterprises, while most of the others were remote quarries where stones were cut for road construction.

The labourers in the quarries are predominantly workers from Sampang who, for one reason or another, prefer to work in faraway places. Some of them are refugees from ethnic violence in West and Central Kalimantan, others are migrants with a dubious legal status because they lack local identity permits

8 I could not inquire directly about relationships with the police in all the interviews with entrepreneurs. Sometimes, I thought that discussing these relationships would be considered inappropriate and, in some of my early interviews, the topic had yet to seem important.

(KTP). Others have problems such as unpaid debts, criminal charges or accusations of extra-marital relationships hanging over their heads. They often mention threats of a revenge killing (*carok*) as a reason for working in remote places. These quarries are located in the hills and in largely uninhabited areas 5–20 kilometres from the city. In the quarries, individual police officers provide protection in return for a percentage of the price earned for all the truckloads of stones that leave. They come to visit every week and sometimes bring basic supplies such as drinking water, salt, soap or rice. In the quarries, policemen are paid commissions of up to 15% of the value of the stone produced there. Percentages in the brick kilns seem to be generally lower and I did not hear of any 'commissions' higher than five percent in the brick industry. I suspect that percentages at the quarries are higher because the people there are more vulnerable and the money covers personal protection as well as business protection.

Nevertheless, it seems money well spent. In the case of Sudi, these premiums protected the enterprise against legal claims by neighbouring villagers and freed him from hassles with old enemies. Unlike in some other cases, where police officers turned out to be unreliable or incapable of helping out, his relationship with a specific police officer yielded results. It has ensured continued access to resources and the sustainability of the family business. Five to fifteen per cent seems a not unusual fee for a migrant to pay for success. Premiums depend on the kind of business, the level of illegality and the tolerance shown by senior police officers. Sometimes the control exerted and the demands of police officers are larger.

Squeezed loyalties: Romli

Hajji Romli lives on one of the main roads connecting Samarinda to the hinterland of East Kalimantan. With his white *peci* hat and grey beard, it is difficult to guess his age, but his black eyes stare with great intensity. He talks fast and asks direct questions. With his wife, he runs a successful distribution centre, crammed with building materials such as sand, bricks, stone, cement and timber. Since 2006, he has also operated as a subcontractor doing the rough construction work in large projects won by large contractors. In large projects tendered by other players, Romli takes care of the supplies, the groundwork, the foundations and sometimes the construction of brick walls, sewage systems and roads. Other subcontractors take care of the wood, metal and roofing work and other skilled tasks. Romli also tenders directly for smaller projects, such as public buildings, small roads, drains and the like. The trade and contracting business are essentially his, but his wife organizes the transportation side. She owns four trucks and an excavator. Romli usually uses two of these trucks if he has construction orders: 'I only take large orders such as for houses, blocks or shops, otherwise I do not make a profit. If there is a lot of work, I will send for more labourers from Java and use trucks from fellow Madurese businesses.'

As my research progressed, I slowly discovered how important Romli was as an informal leader in the Madurese community, and as a broker in relations with the police. He negotiates bribes when Madurese are arrested for petty crimes or taken into custody following traffic accidents. He supports Madurese who are occupying land that is claimed by others, and he mediates in property conflicts. He takes parts in tendering for projects. He was also involved in peace negotiations during ethnic tensions in 2005 and 2007.[9] In return for his loyalty to East Kalimantan's elites, he has been granted excavation concessions in the rocky hills of Batu Besaung and is able to acquire construction projects. Whenever ethnic tensions rise in Samarinda or its vicinity, he is called upon by the town mayor, members of the East Kalimantan parliament, or the head of the police or of the military to prevent Madurese from engaging in violence. He is regarded as influential among the Madurese and loyal to the interests of the ruling elites who prefer stability.[10] During our conversations, it seemed that Madurese people almost continuously entered the house to ask for advice, to borrow money or to discuss matters of political interest. The almost constant beeps and rings from his several cell phones also illustrated the extent of his social network.

Before all this, in the 1970s and 1980s, Romli used to be a notorious gang leader and gambler in Samarinda. His wife saved some of the profits and, at the end of the 1980s, she bought a truck to rent out and use to transport construction materials. In those years, Romli was involved both in simple theft and in swindles that involved goods that were never delivered and loans that were never paid back. He also organized large-scale

---

9 The 2005 negotiations, which were initiated by East Kalimantan's security forces, are briefly described in De Jonge and Nooteboom (2006: 470–471). At the end of 2005, tensions rose between Dayak and Madurese in Samarinda due to the stabbing of the son of a Dayak *adat* leader and the deaths of two Madurese. Romli was invited to the security meetings and was able to calm Madurese groups who called for revenge. This increased his political influence and improved his contacts with high-ranking security officials.

10 See: De Jonge and Nooteboom 2006 and Van Klinken 2002 for a description of these elite interests in East Kalimantan.

gambling frauds. However, he is quick to point out that 'we did not steal from our friends and fellow Madurese.' It is also said that he was involved in the killing of several Bugis rivals, but he always remains vague on this point. Nevertheless, these rumours add to his reputation for toughness. To this day, any Madurese who killed Bugis gang leaders in those diffiicult years still retain a lot of respect among members of the Madurese community.

'In the 1980s, it was not safe in Samarinda', Hajji Romli recalls quietly. Then he reached a turning point: 'I lived a bad life and almost daily we had fights at the market. I was clever enough never to be caught and I had many friends in the police who informed me when activities were getting too hot. One day, a high-ranking police officer came to my house and asked me to stop stealing and to help them fight criminality. If I declined, I would be the first Madurese to be taken to prison, they said. I could not do anything but obey. Moreover, deep inside of me, I already knew the things I was doing were wrong. I longed to live a better life.'

From that time onwards, Romli stepped down as a gang leader and ceased stealing. 'I also no longer fought, and tried to prevent my people from gambling', he adds. 'I was regularly asked by police officers to 'convert' certain hotheads and criminals who were fighting and making trouble at the market. I had to turn them into hardworking people, which I did through offering jobs. The police would allow me to continue to organize gambling, but they asked for some of the profit.'

It was only after Romli went on a pilgrimage to Mecca that his gambling activities stopped. Hajji Yusuf told me once that Hajji Romli had persuaded him to go to Mecca. 'He even provided part of the money for me', Yusuf said. 'However, we could not quit our habits at first. While waiting at the airport, we continued to gamble for money. Only after our return from the holy land, did we stop gambling for money. Now we use 'penalties' which do not involve money such as drawing something on someones face or hanging batteries at someone's ears.'

In the meantime, his wife bought a second truck and due to an increasing demand for construction materials, business expanded and Romli offered work to a number of his former gang members. Not everyone accepted his change to a regular lifestyle. Many of his former followers continued their previous criminal activities, others joined different gangs or started businesses of their own. 'The majority remained loyal to me and, after some time, I could persuade them to start working for me.' Eventually, the police caught most of the notorious thieves from his group. 'I was a good leader and bought them out of the prison.' He smiles self-confidently when he says this: 'it was a good investment. They are now my most loyal workers...And, I got some good friends in the police, which is important.'

Living dangerously: Tagil

Tagil's activities are much more dangerous. Tagil is a notorious gambler, and also a known *preman*, gang leader, organizer of cockfights and operator of a large bar-cum-brothel in Damanhuri, a prostitution compound on the edge of Samarinda. 30 to 40 women and girls work in this brothel. Most of them come from mainland East Java and roughly half speak Madurese. None of them originate from the island of Madura itself according to Tagil: 'We would never permit Madurese women to do this. It would make us ashamed. She would be killed.'

On Saturdays and Sundays, Tagil organizes cockfights on the outskirts of Samarinda. Two to three hundred people participate during these fights, and large bets are taken. Most are Madurese and Bugis, but also Chinese, Banjar, Javanese, Dayak and Butonese attend. The stakes are high. Especially the Chinese and Bugis, but also sometimes Madurese, can bet large amounts. On days like Christmas and New Year, stakes can amount to tens of millions of rupiah per fight. At the same time, spectators bet with smaller amounts ranging from Rp 50,000 to Rp 500,000. From each fight, the winner pays 10% to Tagil who, for his part, pays half of this to policemen who are unofficially present in the arena and to higher ranked police officers. Tagil also earns money from the entrance fee of Rp 5,000 paid by each spectator, and from other gambling activities that take place at the site, such as Cap Ceki, card and dice games, and from the rents collected from the dozens of ordinary vendors there. The rents range from Rp 10,000 per day for a cigarette seller to 50,000 for a fully equipped food stall offering several kinds of food and drinks.

Tensions around the cockfights get so heated that Tagil's gang members sometimes need to restore order. If they are unable to do so, the undercover policemen who are present intervene by shooting in the air, arresting people or even randomly shooting some of the fighters in the leg or knee. With payments, and mediation provided by Tagil, the arrested gamblers can be freed. The usual fees for the police in such a case depend on the status of the captured person and the severity of the offence, and range from Rp 5 million to Rp 15 million. The ties between Tagil and the police who attend his cockfights are close. They regularly visit each other at home, or go out to eat or drink together. Police officers are also said to visit his brothel.

In one of my visits, Tagil told me how, in the early 1980s, he was hunted by the police for having murdered a competing Bugis gang member. 'I fled to Madura to a place where they would never find me. After a few years, a distant relative of mine succeeded, after making large payments, to erase my name from the police archives. The police officer at that time urged me never to commit murder again and asked if I wanted to help with searching for criminals who had fled to Java. That's what I did and I still sometimes do. I have become quite good at it. Last year, we tracked down a lad in Malang who had raped a girl here and run away to Java.'

But things are not as secure as Tagil made out when I met him that time. 'The police are asking for more and more money all the time', he complained in a confident moment later in 2004. 'The work is dangerous and I cannot do business with the new chief commissioner. I would prefer to retire and move to Java. But I am obliged to keep in touch with them. It's like a forced marriage.' He hopes to be able to save enough money for a quiet retirement. In his home village in Madura, he is no longer welcome. 'They don't want to take my money there anymore. It's *haram*, they say, unclean.'

A few months after this talk, in early 2005, Tagil was sent to prison by the new chief of the police who accused him of verbally abusing the governor of East Kalimantan. At a meeting with high ranking officials, Tagil had argued against the closure of the Damanhuri complex during Ramadan and accused the governor of being inconsistent because some complexes remained open, while others had to close. The governor took offence. Other people subsequently told me that Tagil's business had in fact been declining for some time, as he had been unable to deliver sufficient funds to the police. The new chief of police demanded more money than Tagil wanted or could pay. Remarkably, the Damanhuri complex did not close during Ramadan that year and Tagil continued to run his activities from within prison.

Three months later, Tagil was freed after paying large sums of money. Some people say that one or two of his uncles, large entrepreneurs with good connections with the governor, paid to free him. The uncles told me that they helped Tagil a bit so that he could succeed in business. 'This is just a family obligation', they said. By 2006, Tagil had joined a new business of his uncles. They had just acquired a badly managed coal concession and started to excavate, with the backing of influential police officers and politicians, in areas contested by other claimants. In 2008, Tagil and his uncles were busy supporting candidates for the provincial elections. One uncle expressed an ambition of a political career for himself. The fact that their business is risky and legally dubious does not prevent them becoming involved in politics, in fact it makes political connections and protection all the more important.

Conclusions: Out of Wedlock

Migrant Madurese entrepreneurs in East Kalimantan face numerous obstacles in making their enterprises work. Brickmakers face difficulties in obtaining land rights and cheap firewood, transport entrepreneurs face insecurities in obtaining transport licences, and workers in stone quarries need protection against exploitative middlemen and insecure contracts. Moreover, Madurese migrants are not among the most favoured ethnic groups in East Kalimantan and sometimes face severe discrimination and hostility. This is not always for unjustifiable reasons, as some Madurese migrants are, or have been, involved in illegal and illicit activities such as organizing cockfights, gambling, theft, gang fights and running prostitution rackets. Madurese entrepreneurs and *preman* involved in such illegal activities find it essential to maintain good relationships with police officers, generally low-ranking ones, for protection and to keep their activities running. They maintain these relationships with police officers through regular visits and payments of either irregular sums or fixed shares of the profit from the businesses concerned.

If we invert our perspective for a moment, it becomes immediately apparent that the relationships with Madurese migrants are also beneficial for the police. Besides generating additional income, these relationships offer the police access to an otherwise closed migrant community and helps them to control that community.[11] In the event of increased ethnic tensions or unacceptable rises in crime, the police use their contacts with entrepreneurs, *preman* and ethnic leaders who depend on them for business success. These same contacts can then be used to help control their own community and fight criminality. These individuals might provide the police with information, they may utilize their own networks to try to calm social tensions, or to curb the activities of particular members of the community and, in extreme cases, they might even detain aberrant members of the community and hand them over to the police.

11 The strategy is similar to one used by the army's special forces (Kopassus) which frequently recruit criminals to use in counter-insurgency campaigns: Liem Soei Liong (2002: 202).

These examples show that the mutual dependence of Madurese entrepreneurs and police officers not only provides direct financial and other benefits to both parties involved, but also sometimes serves a higher goal of maintaining security and stability for society at large. It is ironic that this social control is only made possible by allowing criminality and instability to exist at an 'agreed' level.

In the illustrated cases of Sudi, Romli and Tagil it is difficult to demarcate precisely where the border between legality and illegality lies. However, doing so is also not necessary: the twilight zone between legal and illegal activities offers Madurese entrepreneurs and the policc many financial and political opportunities. The police offer migrants protection and, in return, get a share of the profits generated by illegal activities. At the same time, the police make no promises to tolerate *all* forms of criminality. On the contrary, they can use their connections with gang leaders to help fight crime. They get to control the underworld by a combination of taxation and repression. At the same time, they also get a steady income from illegal activities.

Bribes, commissions and the profits of illegal activities lower the transaction costs for disadvantaged groups who cannot, or do not know how to, navigate the road of formal and legal economic activities. Without the payments and commissions, it would probably be much more difficult for Madurese to sustain their economic activities. At the same time, one should not forget that the police are also dependent on the entrepreneurs. Police officers are poorly paid in Indonesia but face high expectations in their social environment (from friends, family members, neighbours and so on) that they will maintain a comfortable lifestyle and provide help when it is needed; they also face demands for payments from their superiors within the police apparatus. In short, there is a successful and mutually beneficial 'marriage' between entrepreneurs and police officers. The intimacy of the marriage makes it unlikely that there will be an early victory in Indonesia's repeatedly proclaimed war on corruption.

This marriage is, however, often not based on love. Just as some marriages involve a certain amount of discretion and even deliberate blindness, the relationship between the police and Madurese businesspeople and criminals in East Kalimantan is also based on a sort of paradox. The police in Samarinda need to permit a certain level of criminality in order to keep criminality under control. By permitting some forms of 'petty' criminality (such as pickpocketing, stealing, cheating, gambling, prostitution) – activities which are detested by the community, but which can be dealt with by mobs through lynching and public justice – they are able to gain access to and control over the worst forms of organized crime (such as killings, gang fights, gang rapes, car thefts) and even ethnic violence. They do this by mingling with and engaging in the networks of criminal groups.

This world of petty criminality, at least in East Kalimantan, involves collaboration between police and small entrepreneurs, and the regular payment of small fees (5–15% of turnover). The payments are essential to the smooth functioning of the system, a system that is based on personal contacts and offers an alternative to a properly functioning Weberian taxation and policing system. It can thus be argued that the state in Indonesia needs to be involved in illegality in order to be able to control criminality: and that state officials have been relatively successful in this. From a citizen's perspective, Indonesia is a relatively safe country. In most Indonesian cities, people are not in constant fear of being robbed, killed or raped. Where justice falls short, the police leaves the mob sufficient space to take revenge. A premium of 5 to 15% is a much lower sum for security than the taxes most people pay in countries relatively free of corruption. As such illegality is not only destructive, it can also help to sustain order in society.

CONCLUSION

Forgotten people?

Poverty, Risk and Social Security in Indonesia

Many of the people who are described in this book can be called poor – living below or close to the official Indonesian poverty line – and are living in a more-or-less continuous state of insecurity. Poor people however do not stand alone, but search out and receive – directly or indirectly – support from others. Moreover, they are not always 'frozen' below or close to the poverty line since poorer and richer periods might alternate as a result of seasonal fluctuations in income, lifecycles and alternating periods of misfortune and relative prosperity. Clearly, the poor described here are not living in isolation, but need and use other individuals and institutions to secure their living, access to resources, to gather wealth and status and to provide support in times of need. The book aims to understand these relational aspects of poverty and everyday responses of people living on the margins of society when they are confronted with misfortune and major and minor crises in their everyday lives. It deals with the many ways in which people try to secure their livelihoods over time, directly through their own efforts, or indirectly through support from others – often this locally organized social security is arranged in opposition to the state rather than with its support. In this way, it aims to overcome static approaches to poverty which tend to focus primarily on single and often individualistic elements such as income, poverty lines, material wealth and vulnerability.

A key feature of this book is its central aim to capture diversity. Diversity in poverty and livelihoods, in social security arrangements, in capabilities and networks, in risk-taking strategies among 'the poor', a category much more diverse than generalized statements would suggest. The actions and responses of poor people of different social economic backgrounds, occupations, ages and genders vary greatly. Central to this book is the idea that people follow diverse trajectories guided by individual and cultural preferences that are shaped within structural boundaries, which I call styles. As we have seen in Chapter 4, the concept of style offers an alternative to poverty studies focussed primarily on incomes and assets as well as to structural approaches which emphasise structural inequalities and the adverse consequences of capitalism and globalisation. Styles are both empirically recognizable as analytically distinct. By its focus on styles or pathways, this book offers a new conceptual way to deal with diversity in vulnerability and poverty. At the same time it criticises populist and neoliberal approaches to poverty which over-emphasise the capacity of poor people to change their lives on their own. The concept of style integrates strategic and structural dimensions of making a living and securing support at a daily basis.

This book thus takes the middle road between studies focussing on the agency, capabilities and opportunities of the poor and critical approaches which emphasise structural inequality, adverse incorporations into the capitalist system and the negative effects of structural power differences. First, it highlights the material basis of poverty and the resource base and livelihoods of peasants and migrants and the diversity found within the livelihoods and the reportoires of mutual help and social assistance. Second, it describes the different combinations people make in linking their livelihoods to mutual relationships of support, social security arrangements and institutions of mutual help to show opportunities for social protection and room to manoeuvre for poor people living under adverse conditions. And third, it describes and analyses the intricate interplay of structure and agency, individual survival and social protection, individuals *vis* à *vis* the state over time and space.

Forgotten People? The Case of the Madurese

The story of the Madurese in the new Indonesia is largely a story of a changing Indonesia seen from below. The Madurese, as an ethnic group, are socially, culturally and economically excluded from mainstream developments in Indonesia. The Madurese belong to the poorest ethnic groups in Indonesia; they are underrepresented in the government bureaucracy and the higher ranks of the army and the police, they are relatively poorly educated and often referred to in negative terms such as unrefined, unreliable and uncivilized and are to be found in low-paid, dirty and manual jobs (De Jonge 1995, 2012, Niehof et al. 2005, Retsikas 2007:187, Smith 2011, Stenross 2011). Investigating Madurese making a living in modern Indonesia largely means looking at Indonesia from its fringes.

The lives of Madurese described in this book are stories of people dealing with poverty, risk, social exclusion and threats of violence. It shows the intricacies, insecurities and ambiguities of people making a living through a turbulent decade (1997–2009). At the same time, it is a dynamic story of people taking chances, seeking and creating forms of social protection and of active engagement in new opportunities in the frontier areas.

During the last decade of Suharto's rule and the years of transition that followed, the relatively poor and lowly educated Madurese have not fared well. They have been confronted with ethnic violence (Davidson and Kammen 2002, Van Klinken 2006), social exclusion, increasingly negative stereotyping (De Jonge and Nooteboom 2006), a deteriorating rural resource base (Smith 2011, Stenross 2011:18–19) and a decrease in favourable migration opportunities (Nooteboom 2008, Wilson 2011:251).

The Madurese are among the least educated groups in Indonesian society with one of the highest illiteracy rates (BPS 2011, Jones 2001:70, Minza 2012:67–69). Increasingly, a good education is one of the major assets in the new Indonesia, and development plans are increasingly oriented towards rapid economic growth to be achieved through industrial and infrastructural, mostly urban, development, resource extraction in frontier areas, industrial agriculture, mining and palm oil development and boosting export sectors. If Madurese do work in these sectors, it tends to be in the lower and unregulated echelons of society and, as unskilled workers, they occupy low paid jobs. Moreover, as described in the first part of the book, Madurese living in rural East Java tend to have been left behind in this process. As a relatively neglected group, they represent other categories of rural poor people in Indonesia.

Changes such as decentralization, liberalization, increased natural resource extraction and a shift in the national development focus have led to major changes in agricultural policy (Fuady 2012, McCarthy et al. 2012). After the fall of Suharto, agricultural policies, previously oriented towards the rural masses in Java and Madura, disappeared from the political agenda, and rural policies have turned into schemes of social protection, consumption subsidies and poverty eradication. The slogan: 'Under Suharto, life was much better for us', often to be heard among Madurese small farmers in East Java and among poor migrants in Kalimantan, seems to be true for most Madurese. They lost their relatively privileged position and now, while others are able to prosper, Madurese livelihoods and poverty are stagnating, probably because they tend to live in rural areas (Suryadarma et al. 2006:20). It was also apparent that more research was needed to gain a better picture of this phenomenon and to gather comparable and quantitative data. Migrants with poor and less privileged backgrounds, such as Madurese and people from Eastern Indonesia (NTT) and Papua, face relative stagnation or even deteriorating positions as a direct or indirect effect of these changes (De Jonge 2012, Rachman et al. 2009, Suryahadi and Sumarto 2003, Vel 2001). Are these categories of people what Tania Li (2009) calls surplus people?

In an attempt to understand the socioeconomic position of Madurese in Indonesia today, as well as the diverse old and new forms of poverty and the possible pathways out of poverty, it is important to look at some plausible explanations for their relative exclusion, marginalization and distinctiveness. The answers lie in a combination of the analysis of structural processes of poverty and exclusion such as described in Hart et al. (1989), Hill et al. (2011) and as a consequence of the *Will to Improve* (Li 2006) and in studies on agency and creativity such as in many livelihood studies or actor-oriented approaches Long (2001). A close ethnographic look reveals both the power of structures of exclusion and the capability of individuals and groups to make a minor difference at a daily basis. It also helps to explain who some people are successful in coping with difficulties or as a migrant, while others fail and remain trapped in cylces of debt and poverty. Although socially excluded as a social group in the nation of Indonesia, often forgotten or overlooked, probably surplus to global capitalism (Li 2009), individual Madurese show a 'knack for life' (Scheper-Hughes 1992:446), creativity, endurance, and a persistent will to succeed.

How do the livelihoods of the Madurese in East Java and Samarinda appear and how do they compare with those of other ethnicities and classes? If we consider the mixed experiences of Madurese on leaving Madura as settlers (Krajan, Bondowoso), migrants (Samarinda) or seafarers (Stenross 2011), can we even speak of a shared Madurese culture? What is the role of the state and social safety nets in the new Indonesia? Given the absence of large state-organized welfare schemes, how do Madurese organize social security and welfare among themselves, sometimes stretching over long distances?

It is hard to distinguish a single distinct Madurese culture. Although the people in this book share similar cultural traits and a similar language, these break down into a large number of local variations. The language for instance divides into two language groups (West Madurese and East Madurese) and also has a large number of local dialects. The same is true with a number of visible cultural traits in which cattle play an important role, as well as the celurit, the crescent-shaped knife, local and religious (*kiai*) leadership, *pesantren* (Islamic boarding school) education and traditional Islam. The Madurese beyond Madura do not share a single culture, a single authority structure or a single indigenous legal system.

It are outsiders who identify them as a people with a strong perception of honour and pride, as hot-tempered, traditionally Islamic, but also as loyal, friendly and hospitable. Madurese themselves tend not to identify Madurese from mainland East Java as genuine Madurese, but rather as 'mixed' people (Retsikas 2007:189). Probably as a consequence of the widespread negative stereotyping and traumatic experiences in West and Central Kalimantan migration areas, they often prefer not to be identified as Madurese. Again, as this book shows, local variations dominate over universal traits. It is only in their homes, or back in East Java, where Madurese characteristics become visible and survive in music, arts, food habits, naval trade and agro-ecological and socio-cultural arrangements (Bouvier 2002, De Jonge 2012, Latief Wiyata 2002, Smith 2011, Stenross 2011). These cultural issues however were not the core focus of this study and have been studied extensively by others (Bouvier 2002, De Jonge 1990, 1993, 2012, Husson 1997b, Van Dijk et al. 1995).

Another pattern that emerges out of this book is that most Madurese have never established a constructive relationship with the state and largely miss out on its enormous powers of patronage. In the past, keeping the state at arm's length may have been a good strategy, but this may no longer be true in the new rapidly developing Indonesia. Among the existing relationships with the state are negative forms through corruption. The majority of the Madurese described in this book are disconnected from the bureaucratic and educational system, and lack the important connections that help access projects, income-earning opportunities and state-based social protection. This becomes especially clear when it comes to social welfare and social security. They have to organize their livelihood security and social welfare themselves through social means. Where is the Madurese middle class? Is that what is missing and does the lack of a brokering middleclass explain them seemingly forgotten or 'surplus' to the Indonesian economy?

Despite not faring as well as others, this does not mean that they have not benefited at all from the major developmental changes in Indonesia. Since 1997, large improvements have been made in Indonesia through road development, improved sanitation, electrification, credit opportunities (enabling the purchase of motorbikes), mobility and the introduction of village healthcare and education – albeit not always of good quality.

The Madurese in East Java have benefitted from these developments. Since the crisis years of 1997–2000, small rations of subsidized food for the poor (*sembako, raskin*) have become available to most poor villagers, as well as some financial support for disabled people. Access to medical care has improved through the introduction of basic health insurance, and emergency aid has become more available, as seen with the landslides in Krajan in 2003, a tornado in 2009 and the resettlement of Madurese displaced from Kalimantan between 2001 and 2005. Nevertheless, many of these interventions are incidental and focussed on minimal support for the poorest. They do not lead to social inclusion in the productive sectors of the mainstream economy.

Despite impressive national growth figures, making Indonesia a middle-income country, state social-security programmes are limited and unable to cover all the people in poor and remote villages such as Krajan in East Java and migrants in East Kalimantan. In the new Indonesia, the majority of Madurese, and the poor in general, have to rely on their own resources and on local forms of support.

The national developmental success of Indonesia has not led to continued rural development in the poor and remote villages of Java and Madura, in the sense of increased productive opportunities, higher incomes or the creation of wealth. On the contrary, the image from rural East Java is one of stagnation. In the villages, as described in Chapter 2, a process of ongoing differentiation is taking place with inequalities in social relations increasing among villagers. For many who stay put in the village, making a decent livelihood is impossible because land ownership is unequal and income-earning opportunities are few.

Migration opportunities offer a way out of poverty – although only a few Krajanese have ever been successful in the diaspora and returned with the hoped-for money. They seem to lack the skills, the capital and the networks to move to the more lucrative jobs in the Middle East or to Malaysia. Those who went to Malaysia could only travel the '*aspal* route' (Cribb 2000:58, Ford and Lyons 2011), or illegally, and ended up in low paid, problematic jobs or in countries like Yemen (De Regt and Moors 2008).

Over the years, hundreds of men and women from the village of Krajan have tried their luck elsewhere – sometimes enforced by debts from gambling or risky investments, maybe spurred on by death threats, or simply lured into disadvantageous labour arrangements by middlemen and recruiters who promise work and a good income by riding the waves of economic opportunity. The large majority of these migrants end up in Kalimantan's construction sector, informal economy, brick kilns or oil palm plantations. Some are successful and return home, the majority simply 'vanish' and never come back or send any money. Enthusiastic or not, migration is the only option for many, but chances on success are low. As a result of agrarian differentiation and migration, 'locally organized, village-based social security arrangements are coming under increasing pressure and are increasingly exclusivist' (Hüsken and Koning 2006:25).

Historic Parallels

For decades, Madurese have migrated in search of a better life. With improved transportation and communication, this migration has grown massively since 2001. Reliable figures on this undocumented migration between East Java and East Kalimantan is lacking and more research on this topic is needed. Contrary to many other migration waves in Indonesia, which flow to Indonesia's major cities and to the Middle East and Gulf countries, the poorly educated Madurese from mainland East Java head for rural areas in Kalimantan and to the unstable frontier areas that offer them a slightly better livelihood through access to low paid jobs in plantations, mines, quarries and in the construction industry. They are the labour force who occupy the ranks of a huge army of – often

ILLUSTRATION 14 *Successful farmer from Malang*

unnoticed – people who make the Indonesian economic growth model – still dependend on the production and export of minerals and raw resources – possible. The threats of ethnic violence in Kalimantan have clearly not ended the Madurese search for work and income in Kalimantan -probably because there is no other option.

A historical comparison shows parallels between migration to Krajan in the 19th century and the contemporary migration of Madurese and Krajan people who settle in the frontier areas of Kalimantan. Historically, three waves of Madurese migration can be distinguished. The first, in the 18th and 19th centuries, being the early migration of people looking for land to mainland East Java.

At the end of 19th century and the first half of the 20th century, a second wave of migrants mobilized themselves to work as labourers in the agricultural commodity production and plantation economy of East Java serving the needs of cheap workers to produce commodities for the global market. Finally, since the mid-1970s, there was a wave of Madurese migrants to Kalimantan, initially looking for land, work and a job and increasingly to work as labourers in the oil palm plantations. Again to serve the needs of cheap commodity production for the global market.

Today's patterns of Madurese migration to rural Kalimantan are thus somewhat similar to the earlier waves of migration to East Java. Whereas East Java can be characterized as the Madurese homeland complete with established social and cultural agrarian practices (although the social life is not at all static and isolated); East Kalimatan is a dynamic frontier area directly connected to global commodity markets. In both places, if they are noticed at all, Madurese are seen as somewhat of a nuisance and their poverty as a threat to national security and the established livelihoods of urban middle classes and elites. Their role as reliable and cheap workers, who serve the production of global commodities, is largely left out of public discourse.

Due to difficulties in making a living and low education, since colonial times, many Madurese juggle their livelihoods in the grey area between legal and illegal, licit and illicit activities as described in the last chapter. Studying these activities and the relationships with the police or other state representatives in detail, it becomes clear that the state is as much dependent on them to secure income, order and security as migrants depend on the state for protection and recognition. It is maintaining these ambigious and intricate patrimonial relationships with lower ranked state officials which turn out crucial.

The history of Madurese migration to the uplands of East Java, of 'land-poor marginalized people creeping into upland spaces beyond control of valley states and lowland people' (Scott 2009:179), would be repeated in the 20th century by Madurese occupying the frontier areas of Kalimantan. Whereas Scott interprets these processes as state evasion and as 'designed to position themselves vis-à-vis the valley states' (Scott 2009:179), the migration histories and interviews with recent settlers show rather that these processes are often driven by a thirst for empty land – although much of the land was probably never empty – and a hope of a better future. These processes cannot be understood as protests against the state, or as a reaction on processes of state making and cultural dominance in East Java. Rather, Madurese migration takes place despite the state and in accordance to long established nation state ideologies about nation making and unity in diversity. Thus, the waves of Madurese coming to Kalimantan today to work at the oil palm and rubber estates of the newly colonized plains of Kalimantan resemble the earlier waves which were enabled by the colonial government in the late 19th century and early 20th century. Plantation owners continue to favour Madurese labourers, just as they did during colonial times: seeing them as cheap, hardworking, honest, disciplined, loyal and strong (De Jonge 1995:15).

Poverty and Social Security

People in rural East Java often told that social isolation was the largest problem of poverty. Isolated people have less access to information, employment, networks and systems of support and redistribution, all of which have the potential to offer some access to resources. A lack of resources, or access to resources, and being excluded from redistribution mechanisms such as social security arrangements make people much more vulnerable to contingencies in life than simply a lack of income. Being poor means being restricted and vulnerable in many respects: poor people face a wide range of limitations, and have fewer options and abilities for strategic action than their more prosperous fellow villagers.

The examples of people and families in this book show that the lives and living conditions of poor people are not stable, incomes cannot be taken for granted and social security entitlements can change relatively quickly. Over the course of one generation, families have fallen from relative wealth into poverty, while others were able to escape poverty. Class does not determine someone's future. Poverty and affluence are not fixed categories, and nor are kinship and other social ties that might offer protection. Wealth can diminish over the years, and friends or relatives can disappear or turn out to be unreliable partners. Sometimes only minor events or misfortunes are enough to trigger the downfall of a family, while others would receive support in similar circumstances. Conversely, with some luck, hard work and favourable conditions, some manage to rise above others, and establish a stronger livelihood or better support relationships. This book describes many such stories. Moreover, these stories are not unique, they could be the life histories of poor families all over Indonesia, families who are slowly rising, declining or cyclically crossing the poverty line.

The Satrawi family offers a good example of villagers who have invested in social relationships and mutual help, but who then failed to get back what they had invested (see Chapter 3). Organizing large weddings and rituals proved not to be a reliable strategy for insuring against severe livelihood setbacks. The problem is that, given their present poverty, people calculate that providing large contributions is not worthwhile as even the Satrawi children will probably never be in a position to repay them. As such, this reflects a situation where investments in local forms of social security tend to be 'upward looking' rather than 'downwardly protective'.

Many years ago, James Scott argued in his book 'The Moral Economy of the Peasant' (1976), that peasant societies in South East Asia can be characterized by two principles: (1) that peasants are risk-averse and oriented towards subsistence and reciprocity; and (2) that inequalities between peasants are not extreme and the 'moral economy' offers its members a certain 'right of subsistence' based on 'the norm of reciprocity' (Scott 1976:30). He argues that peasants have collectively developed risk-insurance subsistence mechanisms out of a shared moral norm which enable them survive the most difficult times and which provide the basis of local social security. This book shows that the relationships of mutual help and village social security are seldom enough to protect against the negative impact of poverty, social exclusion and the shocks and stresses in livelihoods.

A significant number of the population are effectively excluded from most exchanges and forms of support, and these are the people who most need support. It seems that those who need the most receive the least: the poorest villagers receive insufficient support and are unable to secure their welfare. These poor, who make up one-third of the Krajan population, need the support of village institutions but because they cannot contribute to them, and have poor networks, they face social exclusion from them. Moreover, even if they do manage to meet some of the social expectations, they pay relatively more than their richer neighbours and certainly more than they will ever receive back. The mid-level and richer categories of the local population get more out of village social welfare than they put in.

These paradoxes of local social security can be summarized as follows. Firstly, poorer villagers are more vulnerable to insecurities than richer villagers, and they have fewer means of protection. Poorer villagers pay relatively more (as a proportion of total income) for their funerals, rituals (*selamatan*) and weddings, while receiving less support and gifts (*sumbangan*) on these occasions because their networks are smaller and their friends and relatives are generally poorer. Secondly, poorer villagers who are engaged in mutual help and mutual labour groups generally donate more labour to their richer neighbours, due to their larger plots, than is reciprocated. Labour services given to richer village members, politicians, relatives and patrons are often seen as investments and premiums but, again, these generally cost more than the social security ever provided by these politicians, patrons and relatives. Moreover, their labour contributes to the prosperity of such patrons and thus sustains or increases the gap between rich and poor in rural Java. Those who most need credit can borrow least, and pay the highest interest rates. Clearly, the institutions, arrangements and social relationships in rural East Java are inadequate to overcome the 'insecurity trap' and it seems likely that this will remain the situation. These arrangements are even becoming more exclusionist: it is now the 'little-less-poor' who are excluding the 'poor'.

Even if such a subsistence ethic and its related village-levelling mechanisms, or collective support systems, did once exist – which is strongly doubted by several historians and anthropologists (Abdullah and White 2006, Hüsken and Koning 2006:18, Hüsken and White 1989, Popkin 1979, White 1983, 2000) – it seems highly unlikely that they would remain strong in present-day peasant societies which are increasingly incorporated into the global economy and closely linked to urban centres and national policies. This book concurs with the view that strong collective support systems in rural Indonesia are largely a myth (see Chapter 3). Rather, such ideas romanticize local communities as harmonious and sharing – and the question can be asked as to who is interested in maintaining these images and why are they maintained? The image of the romantic village also contributes to the blindly accepted beliefs of policy-makers who often assume rural societies to be harmonious. It might serve to legitimize economic development policies which do not invest in peasant livelihoods and strengthening social safety nets. Maybe it also explains why the Indonesian government's social protection schemes in general still fail to reach the majority of the poor.

Poverty and Risk

From this study, one cannot conclude, as others have done, that poor people and poor migrants are inherently risk averse. On the contrary, many of the poor people described in this book consciously take huge risks, and also sometimes unconsciously. As described in Chapter 5, deliberate risk-taking by the very poor seems to be a reaction to their limited prospects and dull and tied village lives. Some people no longer accept working every day for a small wage with no prospect of improvement and a better livelihood with fewer difficulties. Instead, some opt for thrills and the chance of success, even if this loses them their entitlement to minimum subsistence and involves a break with family members. However, maybe for some, this lifestyle is less risky than it first appears because gendered structures in the household and societal social relations will sometimes offer a minimal safety net as can be seen in Chapter 8.

In looking at the examples in this book, and those who are taking risks in East Java and East Kalimantan, we see an association between certain people, households and risk-taking activities. Those willing to take huge risks in gambling, often also adopt a chancy style in their farming or trading, and they show great machismo. For this group of people, called *orang nakal* in East Java and in East Kalimantan, risk-taking is more than a livelihood strategy, it is rather a lifestyle in itself. In Kalimantan, taking huge risks might be the only way out for migrants. While it is generally held that people only take risks when their basic means are secured, and that people seek a favourable mix of security and risk, many of the *orang nakal* are poor and combine risks with other risks. Combining gambling and illicit sexual affairs is not uncommon; although not all gamblers are promiscuous, and not all womanizers are gamblers or take huge risks in other aspects of their lives. Other combinations are also frequent, such as gambling and sudden migration, reckless business investments and heavy borrowing.

Madurese migrant entrepreneurs in East Kalimantan face numerous obstacles in making their enterprises work. Brickmakers face difficulties in obtaining land rights and cheap firewood. Transport entrepreneurs face insecurities in obtaining transport licences. Workers in the stone quarries need protection against exploitative middlemen and insecure contracts. Moreover, Madurese migrants are not among the most-favoured ethnic groups in East Kalimantan and sometimes face discrimination and severe hostility. This is not always without good reason as some Madurese migrants are, or have been, involved in illegal and illicit activities such as organizing cockfights, gambling, theft, gang fights and running prostitution rackets. Madurese entrepreneurs and *preman* involved in such illegal activities find it essential to maintain good relationships with police officers, and generally with low-ranking ones, for protection and to keep their activities running. They maintain these relationships with police officers through regular visits and payments of either irregular sums or fixed shares of the profits generated from the business.

Social Security in the Migration Areas

Many of the village-based forms of social security, described in the first part of the book, that are to be found in the villages of East Java do not exist in the migration areas studied. In these locations, the Madurese live among other ethnic groups and do not form or maintain the community- and membership-based arrangements seen in East Java. Neither do they create new forms that cross ethnic lines. Arrangements that I did not find in East Kalimantan include collective house-building (*gotong royong*), massive funerals attended by the full neighbourhood, large *selamatan* – and thus also no systems of reciprocal gift giving (*sumbangan*), rotating labour groups and assistance (*giliran* and *keajegan* Mad.), *arisan*, share-raising of cattle (*oanan* Mad., *mengubu* Mad.) and harvest shares (*babun* Mad.). These arrangements are very dependent on community solidarity and specific modes of production that do not exist in the migration areas.

This does not mean that there is no social safety net among Madurese migrants. Ones found are much more based on kinship and ethnicity. Social security in migration areas is limited to close kin (siblings, uncles and aunts, and nephews and nieces), to among neighbours who left together and now live close by and to fellow workers, for instance in brick kilns. Kinship is the prime locus of support, and even more important than in East Java. Relatives help each other out with small loans to provide care and protection, for business development, in the event of hospitalization, when in trouble with authorities or neighbours and with coping with all kind of daily troubles. However, with the exception of brickmaking entrepreneurs, this help is not extended beyond kin. These entrepreneurs almost all come from the village of Geger, in Bangkalan Madura, and they are prepared to help non-kin with business loans, loans in the event of an emergency, with labour when firing bricks and collecting firewood, and when political tensions occur.

In all the migrants groups studied, patronage was to be found within employer – labourer relationships and sometimes among creditors and borrowers, within family clans and also among religious and strong leaders, such as *kiai* and gang leaders, and their followers. Occasionally, non-Madurese people would act as a patron, such as in the described cases of policemen offering business protection, Chinese employers who employ Madurese as security guards, and rich neighbours who provide land and protection in return for a large share of the business profit.

From this, one can conclude that, contrary to a persistent stereotype, Madurese do not form close communities offering support and protection to each other. In reality, the perceived Madurese society in Samarinda is actually several highly stratified clusters based on kinship and/or shared roots that often compete with each other. When a crisis occurs, it is everyman for himself.

When it comes to sending remittances home, two patterns can be seen. In the case of migrants from Bangkalan, money was regularly sent home to support parents, children and close relatives for purposes such as care, house construction and the education of siblings, nephews and nieces. This seldom occurred In the case of migrants from mainland East Java and specifically

Krajan. This might be linked to the relatively prosperous position of the Bangkalan migrants, and the fact that they migrated earlier and were able to establish a more stable business or enterprise. Generally, poor labourers seldom send money home, they can only aim to save a little from their meagre incomes and return with some money to be spent on household needs or specific purposes such as paying off debts or contributing to a marriage or a *selamatan*. Only those few migrants who have been able to establish a stable livelihood, a business or good trade with regular incomes are able to regularly send money home to support parents, siblings or children. To date few Krajanese migrants have been able to establish such a stable livelihood.

If local social security institutions and arrangements work at all, they generally seem to only cover specific risks and uncertainties, to be accessible only to certain groups and categories of people, and only to be tapped in specific circumstances or periods (Hüsken and Koning 2006:18). In Chapter 3 of this book, the scope and limitations of local forms of social security are described in detail. These limits mean that people are often excluded from such collective or communal provisions and that, therefore, they have to rely on their own devices, relations and inventiveness. Essentially, the poorer you are and the most support you need, the less you are protected. Will this remain reality for the majority of the poor and the Madurese in the new Indonesia?

Bibliography

Abdullah, Irwan and Ben White 2006. 'Harvesting and Housebuilding: Decline and Persistence of Reciprocal Labour in a Javanese Village, 1973–2000', in: Koning, Juliette and Frans Hüsken (eds), *Ropewalking and Safetynets: Local Ways of Managing Insecurities in Indonesia*, pp. 55–78. Leiden: Brill.

Acciaioli, Greg 1999. 'Principles and Strategies of Bugis Migration: Some Contextual Factors Relating to Ethnic Conflict', *Masyarakat Indonesia* XXV(2):239–263.

Ahmad, Etisham, Jean Dreze and John Hills 1991. *Social Security in Developing Countries*, edited by Sen, Amartya. Oxford: Clarendon Press.

Akram-Lodhi, A. Haroon and Saturnino M. Borras 2007. *Land, Poverty and Livelihoods in an Era of Globalization: Perspectives from Developing and Transition Countries*. Vol. 1, Routledge ISS Studies in Rural Livelihoods London: Routledge.

Alatas, Vivi, Abhijit Banerjee, Rema Hanna, Benjamin A. Olken and Julia Tobias 2012. 'Targeting the Poor: Evidence from a Field Experiment in Indonesia', *The American Economic Review* 102(4):1206–1240.

Alexander, Jennifer and Paul Alexander 1979. 'Labour Demands and the "involution" of Javanese Agriculture', *Social Analysis* 3:22–44.

——. 1982. 'Shared Poverty as Ideology: Agrarian Relationships in Colonial Java', *Man* 17(4):597–619.

Antlöv, Hans 1999. 'The New Rich and Cultural Tensions in Rural Indonesia', *Pinches*:188–207.

Antlöv, Hans and Sven Cederroth, (eds.) 1994. *Leadership on Java: Gentle Hints, Authoritarian Rule*. Vol. 16, Studies in Asian Topics. Richmond: Curzon Press/Nordic Institute of Asian Studies.

Aspinall, Ed and Gerry van Klinken 2011. *State and Illegality in Indonesia*. Leiden: KITLV Press.

Ave, Jan 2003. 'West Kalimantan, een analyse van etnische conflicten', in: Holtzappel, Coen (ed.), *Eenheid in verscheidenheid. Droom of werkelijkheid? Een inleiding tot de culturele en etnische verscheidenheid van Indonesië*, pp. 299–315. Amsterdam: Rozenberg Publishers.

Bankoff, Greg 2009. 'Cultures of Disaster, Cultures of Coping; Hazard as a Frequent Life Experience in the Philippines, 1600–2000', in: Mauch, Christof and Christian Pfister (eds), *Natural Disasters, Cultural Responses: Case Studies toward a Global Environmental History*, pp. 265–284. Lanham: Lexington Books.

Barlocco, Fausto 2010. 'The Village as a "Community of Practice": Constitution of Village Belonging through Leisure Sociality', *Bijdragen tot de Taal-, Land- en Volkenkunde* 166 (4):404–425.

Bebington, Anthony 1999. 'Capitals and Capabilities: A Framework for Analyzing Peasant Viability, Rural Livelihoods and Poverty', *World Development* 27(12):2021–2044.

Bedner, Adriaan 2007. 'Access to Environmental Justice in Indonesia', in: Harding, Andrew (ed.), *Access to Environmental Justice: A Comparative Study*, pp. 89–123. Leiden/Boston: Martinus Nijhoff Publishers.

Bertrand, Jacques 2004. *Nationalism and Ethnic Conflict in Indonesia*. Cambridge: Cambridge University Press.

Best, Jacqueline 2012. 'Bureaucratic Ambiguity', *Economy and Society* 41(1):84–106.

Biezeveld, Renske 2002. *Between Individualism and Mutual Help; Social Security in a Minangkabau Village*. Delft: Eburon. Published PhD thesis, Erasmus University, Rotterdam.

Blaikie, Piers, Terry Cannon, Ian Davis and Ben Wisner, (eds.) 1994. *At Risk; Natural Hazards, People's Vulnerability and Disasters*. London and New York: Routledge.

Boomgaard, Peter 1988. *Between Sovereign Domain and Servile Tenure; The Development of Rights to Land in Java, 1795–1880*, CAS 4. Dordrecht, Netherlands: Foris Publications.

—— 1999. 'Maize and Tobacco in Upland Indonesia, 1600–1940', in: Murray-Li, Tania (ed.), *Transforming the Indonesian Uplands*, pp. 45–78. Amsterdam: Overseas Publishers Association.

Bottema, Taco 1995. Market Formation and Agriculture in Indonesia from the Mid 19th Century to 1990. PhD thesis, Department of Antropology, University of Nijmegen, Nijmegen.

Bouman, F.J.A. 1983. 'Indigenous Savings and Credit Societies in the Developing World', in: Von Pischke, J.D., D.W. Adams and G. Donald (eds), *Rural Financial Markets in Developing Countries: Their Use and Abuse*, pp. 262–268. Baltimore: Johns Hopkins University Press.

——. 1995. 'ROSCA: On the Origin of the Species', *Savings and Development* XIX(2):117–148.

Bourdieu, Piere 1989. 'Economisch kapitaal, cultureel kapitaal, sociaal kapitaal', in: Pels, Dick (ed.), *Opstellen over smaak, habitus en het veldbegrip*, pp. 120–141. Amsterdam: Van Gennep. Original edition, The Forms of Capital. In J.G. Richardson (Ed.), Handbook of Theory and Research for the Sociology of Education, pp. 241–258. New York: Greenwood, 1986.

Bouvier, Helene 2002. *Lèbur; Seni musik dan pertunjukan dalam masyarakat Madura*, Seri tradisi lisan nusantara 14. Jakarta: Yayasan Obor Indonesia.

Bouvier, Hélène, Huub de Jonge and Glenn Smith 2006. 'Special Issue on Violence in Southeast Asia', *Asian Journal of Social Science* 34(3):357–491.

Bouvier, Hélène and Glenn Smith 2006. 'Of Spontaneity and Conspiracy Theories: Explaining Violence in Central Kalimantan', *Asian Journal of Social Science* 34(3):475–491.

Bowen, J.R. 1986. 'On the Political Construction of Tradition: Gotong Royong in Indonesia', *Journal of Asian Studies* XLV(3):545–559.

BPS 2001. *Population of Indonesia: Results of the 2000 Population Census*. Jakarta: Badan Pusat Statistik (BPS go.id).

——. 2011. *Persentase penduduk buta huruf 2003–2011: Badan Pusat Statistik Republik Indonesia* (BPS.go.id).

Breman, Jan 1980. *The Village on Java and the Early-Colonial State*. Vol. 1, Comparative Asian Studies Programme. Rotterdam: Erasmus University.

——. 1994. *Wage Hunters and Gatherers: Search for Work in the Urban and Rural Economy of South Gujarat*. Delhi [etc.]: Oxford University Press.

——. 2000. *The Impact of the Asian Economic Crisis on Work and Welfare in Village Java*, ISS Lecture Series 1. The Hague: Institute of Social Studies.

Brusset, Emery, Birthe Nautrup, Yulia Immajati and Susanne B. Pedersen 2004. 'Assistance to Internally Displaced Persons (IDPS) in Indonesia', Sida Evaluations 04/27. Stockholm: Sida, Swedisch Development Institution.

Burawoy, Michael 2009. *The Extended Case Method: Four Countries, Four Decades, Four Great Transformations and One Theoretical Tradition*. Berkeley: University of California Press.

Burke, Paul J. and Budy P. Resosudarmo 2012. 'Survey of Recent Developments', *Bulletin of Indonesian Economic Studies* 48(3):299–324.

Cashdan, E. 1985. 'Coping with Risk; Reciprocity among the Basarwa of Northern Botswana', *Man* 20(3):454–474.

Casson, Anne and Krystof Obidzinski 2002. 'From New Order to Regional Autonomy: Shifting Dynamics of 'Illegal' Logging in Kalimantan, Indonesia', *World Development* 30(12):2133–2151.

Cederroth, Sven 1995. *Survival and Profit in Rural Java: The Case of an East Javanese Village*, Nordic Institute of Asian Studies. Richmond: Curzon Press.

Chambers, Robert 1989. 'Vulnerability; How the Poor Cope?', *IDS Bulletin* 20(2):1–7.

Chambers, Robert and G. Conway 1992. 'Sustainable Rural Livelihoods: Practical Concepts for the 21st Century', IDS Discussion Paper 296. Brighton: IDS.

Chambers, Robert, A. Pacey and Lory Ann Trupp, (eds.) 1990. *Farmer First, Farmer Innovation and Agricultural Research*. London: Intermediate Technology Publications.

Chandrasekaran, Rajiv 2004. Savage Attacks Terrorize Migrants on Borneo February 24, 2001 February 2004]. Available from Washington Post Foreign Service. On website: http://www.genocidewatch.org/borneo.htm.

CNN Violence Sweeps Northern Indonesia. Dozens Killed [Newsreport on the Internet] March 19,1999. Available from http://cnn.com./WORLD/asiapcf/9903/19/indonesia.01/index.htm.

——. Borneo Riots Marked by Grisly Ritual Killings [internet] March 21,1999. Available from http://cnn.com./WORLD/asiapcf/9903/21/indonesia.borneo/index.htm.

Collier, William 1981. 'Declining Labour Absorption (1878–1980) in Javanese Rice Production', *Kajian Ekonomi Malaysia* 17:102–136.

Collins, Elizabeth Fuller 2007. *Indonesia Betrayed: How Development Fails*. Honolulu: University of Hawai'i Press.

Colombijn, Freek 2002. 'Explaining the Violent Solution in Indonesia', *The Brown Journal of World Affairs* IX(1):49–56.

Coppel, Charles A., (ed.) 2006. *Violenct Conflicts in Indonesia: Analysis, Representation, Resolution.* Routledge Contemporary Southeast Asia Series. London: Routledge.

Cribb, Robert, (ed.) 1990. *The Indonesian Killings of 1965–1966; Studies from Java and Bali*, edited by Cribb, Robert. Vol. 21, Monash Papers on Southeast Asia. Clayton Victory: Centre of Southeast Asian Studies, Monash University.

——. 2000. *Historical Atlas of Indonesia*. London: NIAS/Turton Press.

——. 2010. *Digital Atlas of Indonesian History*. Copenhagen: NIAS.

Dahles, Heidi and Karin Bras 1999. *Tourism and Small Entrepreneurs: Development, National Policy, and Entrepreneurial Culture: Indonesian Cases*. New York: Cognizant Communication Corporation.

Davidson, Jamie S. 2003. 'The Politics of Violence on an Indonesian Periphery', *South East Asia Research* 11(1):59–89.

Davidson, Jamie S. and Douglas Kammen 2002. 'Indonesia's Unknown War and the Lineages of Violence in West Kalimantan', *Indonesia* 73:53–87.

De Bruijn, Mirjam and Han van Dijk 1994. Arid Ways: Cultural Understandings of Insecurity in Fulbe Society, Central Mali. PhD thesis, Department of Social Geography, University of Amsterdam, Amsterdam.

De Haan, Leo J. and Annelies Zoomers 2005. 'Exploring the Frontier of Livelihoods Research', *Development and Change* 36(1):27–47.

De Jong, E.B.P. 2006. 'Reshaping Tana Toraja: A Century of Decentralisation and Power Politics in the Highlands of South Sulawesi, Indonesia', in: Holtzappel, Coen and Martin Ramstedt (eds), *Decentralisation and Regional Autonomy in Indonesia: Implementation and Challenge*, pp. 256–292. Singapore: ISEAS-Press.

De Jonge Huub 1990. 'Of bulls and men; The Madurese aduan sapi [bull fight]', *Bijdragen tot de Taal-, Land-, en Volkenkunde* 146:423–447.

——. 1993. 'Credit, Trust and Knowledge; Middlemen and Commercialization on the Island of Madura', in: Jonge, Huub de and Willem Wolters (eds), *Commercialization and Market Formation in Developing Countries*, pp. 116–139. Saarbrücken and Fort Lauderdale: Breitenbach.

——. 1994. 'Spel en ernst in het Madurese stierengevecht', in: Jonge, Huub de and Henk Driesen (eds), *In de ban van betekenis: Proeven van symbolische antropologie*, pp. 267–294. Nijmegen: SUN.

——. 1995. 'Stereotypes of the Madurese', in: Van Dijk, Kees, Huub de Jonge and Elly Touwen-Bouwsma (eds), *Across Madura Strait: The Dynamics of an Insular Society*, pp. 7–25. Leiden, Netherlands: KITLV Press.

——. 2002. 'Rather White Bones than White Eyes; Violent Self-help among the Madurese', in: Hüsken, Frans and Huub de Jonge (eds), *Violence and Vengeance: Discontent and Conflict in New Order Indonesia*, pp. 143–156. Nijmegen, Saarbrücken: Verlag für Entwicklungspolitik Saarbrücken GmbH.

——. 2004. Beyond despair: The Madurese in West Kalimantan. Paper read at the Asian-Seminar Penang, Malaysia, May 2004, Penang.

——. 2012. *Garam, kekerasan dan aduan sapi: Esai-esai tentang orang Madura dan kebudayaan Madura*. Yogyakarta: LKIS.

De Jonge, Huub and Gerben Nooteboom 2006. 'Why the Madurese? Ethnic Conflict in West and East Kalimantan Compared', *Asian Journal of Social Science* 34 (3):456–474.

De Regt, Marina and Annelies Moors 2008. 'Migrant Domestic Workers in the Middle East', in: Schrover, Marlou, Joanne van der Leun, Leo Lucassen and Chris Quispel (eds), *Illegal Migration and Gender in a Global and Historical Perspective*, pp. 151–170. Amsterdam: IMISCOE.

Den Ouden, Jan H.B. 1989. *A Three Generation Perspective. Its Importance for Ethnographic Research in Development Studies: Case Studies from Cameroon and Benin*. Wageningen: Agricultural University.

Dietz, Ton, R. Bymolt, A. Bélemvire, K. van der Geest, D. de Groot, D. Millar, F. Obeng, N. Pouw, W. Rijneveld and F. Zaal 2013. *PADev Guidebook Participatory Assessment of Development*. Amsterdam: AISSR.

Dixon, John 1985. *Social Welfare in Asia*. London: Croom Helm.

Dixon, John and David Macarov, (eds.) 1998. *Poverty: A Persistent Global Reality*. London and New York: Routledge.

Dove, Michael 1997. 'Dayak Anger Ignored', *Inside Indonesia* (51):13–14.

Edmunson, Wade C. 1994. 'Do the Rich Get Richer, Do the Poor Get Poorer? East Java, Two Decades, Three Villages, 46 People', *Bulletin of Indonesian Economic Studies* 30(2):133–148.

Ellis, Frank 1989. *Peasant Economics: Farm Household and Agrarian Development*. Cambridge: Cambridge University Press.

——. 2000. *Rural Livelihoods and Diversity in Developing Countries*. Oxford: Oxford University Press.

Elmhirst, Rebecca 1999. 'Space, Identity Politics and Resource Control in Indonesia's Transmigration Programme', *Political Geography* 18:813–835.

Evers, H.D. and S. Gerke 1992. 'The Culture of Planning: Transmigration Area Development in East Kalimantan, Indonesia', *International Sociology* 7:141–151.

Farrington, John, Diana Carney, Caroline Ashley and Cathryn Turton 1999. *Sustainable Livelihood in Practice: Early Application of Concepts in Rural Areas*. Vol. 42, ODI Natural Resource Perspectives: Overseas Development Institute (ODI), Sussex.

Feeny, D. 1983. 'The Moral or the Rational Peasant? Competing Hypotheses of Collective Action', *Journal of Asian Studies* 27(4):769–789.

Ford, Michele and Lenore Lyons 2006. 'The Borders within: Mobility and Enclosure in the Riau Islands', *Asia Pacific Viewpoint* 47(2):257–271.

——. 2007. *Making the Most of What You've Got: Sex Work and Class Mobility in the Riau Islands*, Indonesian Studies Working Papers. Sydney: University of Sydney, May 2007.

——. 2011. 'Travelling the *Aspal* Route: Grey Labour Migration through an Indonesian Border Town', in: Aspinall, Edward and Gerry Van Klinken (eds), *The State and Illegality in Indonesia*, pp. 107–122. Leiden: KITLV Press.

Fuady, Ahmad Helmy 2012. *Elites and Economic Policies in Indonesia and Nigeria, 1966–1998*. PhD thesis, Amsterdam Institute for Social Science Research (AISSR), Universtiy of Amsterdam, Amsterdam.

Geertz, Clifford 1962. 'The Rotating Credit Association: A 'Middle Rung' in Development', *Economic Development and Cultural Change* 10(3):241–263.

——. 1963. *Agricultural Involution. The Process of Ecological Change in Indonesia*. Berkeley: University of California Press.

——. 1973. 'Deep Play: Notes on the Balinese Cockfight', in: Clifford Geertz (ed.), *The Interpretation of Cultures: Selected Essays*, pp. 412–453. New York: Basic Books.

——. 1983. *Local Knowledge: Further Essays in Interpretative Anthropology*. New York: Basic Books.

Gennep, J.L. van 1895. *De hoogvlakte van het Jang-gebergte op Java; De meest geschikte plaats voor de oprichting van een sanatorium, een krankzinnigengesticht en een Europese landbouwkolonie*. Semarang and Amsterdam: Van Dorp, Scheltema & Holkema's Boekhandel.

Hall, Derek, Philip Hirsch and Tania Murray Li 2011. *Powers of Exclusion: Land Dilemmas in Southeast Asia*. Hawai'i: University of Hawai'i Press.

Harjono, J.M. 1977. *Transmigration in Indonesia*. Kuala Lumpur [etc.]: Oxford University Press.

——. 1988. 'The Indonesian Transmigration Program in Historical Perspective', *International Migration* 26:427–439.

Hart, Gillian, Andrew Turton and Benjamin White, (eds.) 1989. *Agrarian Transformations: Local Processes and the State in Southeast Asia*. Berkeley, CA: University of California Press.

Hartveld, Aart 1996. Raising Cane: Linkages, Organizations and Negotiations in Malang's Sugar Industry, East Java. PhD thesis, Agricultural University, Wageningen.

Hefner, Robert W. 1990. *The Political Economy of Mountain Java, an Interpretive History*. Berkeley, CA: University of California Press.

Hendro, Suroyo Sudagung 2001. *Mengurai pertikaian etnis; Migrasi Swakarsa etnis Madura ke Kalimantan Barat*. Jakarta: Institut Studi Arus Informasi.

Herlijanto, Johanes 2013. *Emulating China: Representation of China and the Contemporary Critique of Indonesia*. PhD thesis, Vrije Universiteit, Amsterdam.

Hilhorst, Dorothea and Greg Bankhoff 2004. 'Introduction: Mapping Vulnerability', in: Bankhoff, Greg, Georg Frerks and Dorothea Hilhorst (eds), *Mapping Vulnerability: Disasters, Development and People*, pp. 1–9. London: Earthscan.

Hill, Hall 1999. *The Indonesian Economy in Crisis: Causes, Consequences and Lessons.* Singapore: Institute of Southeast Asian Studies.

Hirtz, Frank 1995. *Managing Insecurity, State Social Policy and Family Networks in the Rural Philippines*, edited by Elwert, G., V. Luhr and M. Schulz. Vol. 42, Spectrum: Berliner Reihe zu Geschellschaft, Wirtschaft und Politik in Entwicklungslandern. Saarbrücken: Verlag für Entwicklungspolitik.

Hornby, A.S. 1990. *Oxford Advanced Learner's Dictionary of Current English*, edited by Cowie, A.P. 4 ed. Oxford: Oxford University Press.

Horne, Elinor Clark 1974. *Javanese – English Dictionary.* New Haven and London: Yale University Press.

Hospes, Otto 1995. 'Women's Differential Use of ROSCA's in Indonesia', in: Ardener, S. and S. Burman (eds), *Money-Go-Rounds: The Importance of Rotating Savings and Credit Associations for Women*, pp. 127–148. Oxford: Berg.

HRW 1997. 'West Kalimantan; Communal Violence in West Kalimantan'. New York: Human Rights Watch, December.

Huijsman, Abraham 1986. *Choice and Uncertainty in a Semi-Subsistence Economy: A Study of Decision Making in a Philippine Village.* PhD Thesis, Dept. of Development Economy, Wageningen. Amsterdam: Koninklijk Instituut voor de Tropen. Original edition, PhD Thesis University of Wageningen.

Hull, Terence and Tukiran 1976. 'Regional Variations in the Prevalence of Childlessness in Indonesia', *Indonesian Journal of Geography* 32:1–25.

Hüsken, Frans 1988. *Een dorp op Java: Sociale differentiatie in een boerengemeenschap, 1850–1980.* 2nd ed. Overveen: ACASEA. Published PhD thesis, University of Amsterdam, Amsterdam.

——. 1989. 'Cycles of Commercialization and Accumulation in a Central Javanese Village', in: Hart, Gillian, Andrew Turton and Benjamin White (eds), *Agrarian Transformations*, pp. 303–331. Berkeley, CA: University of California Press.

—— 1999. Crisis, What Crisis? The Village Community of Gondosari during the Krismon. Paper read at Workshop on The Economic Crisis and Social Security in Indonesia, at Berg en Dal, Netherlands.

Hüsken, Frans and Huub de Jonge, (eds.) 2002. *Violence and Vengeance: Discontent and Conflict in New Order Indonesia.* Nijmegen, Saarbrücken: Verlag für Entwicklungspolitik Saarbrücken GmbH.

Hüsken, Frans and Jeremy Kemp 1992. *Cognation and Social Organisation in Southeast Asia.* Leiden: KITLV Press.

Hüsken, Frans and Julliette Koning 2006. 'Between Two Worlds: Social Security in Indonesia', in: Koning, Juliette and Frans Hüsken (eds), *Ropewalking and Safety Nets: Local Ways of Managing Insecurities in Indonesia*, pp. 1–26. Leiden: Brill.

Hüsken, Frans and Benjamin White 1989. 'Java; Social Differentiation, Food Production and Agrarian Control', in: Hart, Gillian, Andrew Turton and Benjamin White (eds), *Agrarian Transformations: Local Processes and the State in Southeast Asia*, pp. 235–265. Berkeley, CA: University of California Press.

Husson, Laurence 1997a 'Eight Centuries of Madurese Migration to East Java', *Asian and Pacific Migration Journal* 6(1):77–102.

——. 1997b. 'Portraits and Strategies of Madurese Migrants in Surabaya, Indonesia', *Asian Migrant* 10(4):122–129.

ICG 2001 *Communal Violence in Indonesia; Lessons from Kalimantan*. Jakarta/Brussels: International Crisis Group, June 27, retrieved from internet June 2003.

Indiyanto, Agus, Edwin de Jong, Gerben Nooteboom and Benjamin White 2006 'Close Encounters and Distant Violence: Local Experiences of Indonesia's "Total Crisis"', in: Schulte Nordholt, Henk and Ireen Hoogenboom (eds), *Indonesian Transitions*, pp. 23–74. Yogyakarta: Pustaka Pelajar.

Ingleson, J. 1996. 'Mutual Benefit Societies in Indonesia', in: Linden, M. van der (ed.), *Social Security Mutualism*, pp. 577–588. Bern: Peter lang.

Jackson, Karl D. 1974. *Urbanization and the Rise of Patron-Client Relations: The Changing Quality of Interpersonal Communications in the Neighborhoods of Bandung and the Villages of West Java*. Vol. C/74-26, Working Paper. Cambridge, MA: Center for International Studies, Massachusetts Institute of Technology.

Jakarta Post 2001. Online Special: Human tragedy in Sampit [Online Newspaper]. Jakarta Post 2001 April 12 2001]. Available from http://www.thejakartapost.com/special/.

Jay, Robert 1969. *Javanese Villagers: Social Relations in Rural Modjokuto*. Cambridge, CA: Massachusetts Institute of Technology Press.

Jellinek, Lea 1991. *The Wheel of Fortune: The History of a Poor Community in Jakarta*. Honolulu: University of Hawai'i Press.

Jellinek, Lea and Bambang Rustanto 1999. *Survival Strategies of the Javanese During the Economic Crisis*. Jakarta: World Bank.

Jones, Gavin W. 2001. 'Which Indonesian Women Marry Youngest, and Why?', *Journal of Southeast Asian Studies* 32(1):67–78.

Kaag, Mayke, Johan Brons, Mirjam De Bruijn, Leo J. De Haan, Gerben Nooteboom, Rik Van Berkel, Han Van Dijk and Annelies Zoomers 2004. 'Ways Forward in Livelihood Research', in: Kalb, Don, Wil Pansters and Hans Siebers (eds), *Globalization and Development: Themes and Concepts in Current Research*, pp. 50–74. Dordrecht, Boston, London: Kluwer Academic Publishers.

Kanó, Hiroyoshi 1980. 'The Economic History of Javanese Rural Society: A Reinterpretation', *Developing Economies* 18(5):3–22.

Kawagoe, T., K. Ohkama and A. Bagyo 1992. 'Collective Actions and Rural Organization in a Peasant Economy in Indonesia', *The Developing Economies* XXX-3:215–235.

Kelly, P.F. 2002. 'Spaces of Labour Control: Comparative Perspectives from Southeast Asia', *Transactions of the Institute of British Geographers* 27 (4):395–411.

Keyes, C.F. 1983. 'Peasant Strategies in Asian Societies: Moral and Rational Economic Approaches – A Symposium', *Journal of Asian Studies* 42(4):753–768.

Koentjaraningrat 1967a *Beberapa pokok antropologi social*. Jakarta: Dian Rakyat.

—— 1967b. *The Village in Indonesia Today*, edited by Koentjaraningrat, A. Villages in Indonesia, Ithaca: Cornell University Press.

Koning, Juliette 1997. Generations of Change: A Javanese Village in the 1990s. PhD thesis, Amsterdam School voor Social Science Studies, University of Amsterdam, Amsterdam.

——. 2001. Rural Java and the Crisis: A Rice-cultivating Village and a Fishing Community Compared. In *EUROSEAS Conference*. London.

Koning, Juliet 2006. 'Exclusion, Inclusion and Social Security in Central Java', in: Koning, J. and F. Hüsken (eds), *Ropewalking and Safetynets; Local Ways of Managing Insecurities in Indonesia*, pp. 27–54. Leiden: Brill.

Koning, Juliette and Frans Hüsken 2005. 'Managing Risks and Resources along the South Coast of Java', in: Koning, J. and F. Hüsken (eds), *Ropewalking and Safetynets: Local Ways of Managing Insecurity*. Leiden, Singapore: Brill & Times Academic Publishers.

Koning, Juliet and Frans Hüsken 2006. *Ropewalking and Safetynets: Local Ways of Managing Insecurities in Indonesia*. Leiden: Brill.

Kreager, Philip and Elisabeth Schröder-Butterfill 2005. *Gaps in the Family Networks of Older People in Three Indonesian Communities*. Oxford: Oxford Institute of Ageing.

Kumar, Ann 1979. 'Javanese Historiography in and of the 'Colonial Period': A Case Study', in: Reid, Anthony and D. Marr (eds), *Perceptions of the Past in Southeast Asia*, pp. 187–206. Singapore: Heinemann.

Kuntowijoyo 1980. Social Change in an Agrarian Society; Madura, 1850–1940, Columbia University, Ann Arbor: UMI.

Kutanegara, Pande Made and Gerben Nooteboom 2000. 'Forgotten Villages: The Effects of the Crisis and the Role of the Government in Rural Java', *Populasi* 11(2):23–60.

Kwee, Hui Kian 2006. The Political Economy of Java's Northeast Coast, c. 1740–1800: Elite Synergy, Brill, Leiden, Boston. Blussé, Leonard and Hendrik E. Niemeijer (eds). TANAP Monographs on the History of the Asian-European Interaction, Vol. 3.

Latief Wiyata, A. 2002. *Carok. Konflik kekerasan dan harga diri orang Madura*. Yogyakarta: LKIS.

Leliveld, Andre 1994. *Social Security in Developing Countries: Operation and Dynamics of Social Security Mechanisms in Rural Swaziland*. Vol. 85, Tinbergen Institute Research Series. Amsterdam: Thesis Publishers.

Leunissen, J.A.C.M. 1982. Landbouwen op Madura; Een ecologisch-antropologische beschrijving. PhD thesis, Department of Anthropology, University of Nijmegen, Nijmegen.

Levinsohn, James, Steven Berry and Jed Friendman 1999. *Impacts of the Indonesian Economic Crisis: Price Changes and the Poor*. Vol. 7194, NBER Working Paper Series. Cambridge: National Bureau of Economic Research.

Lewis, Martin W. 1992. *Wagering the Land: Ritual Capital and Environmental Degradation in the Cordillera of Northern Luzon, 1900–1986*. Berkeley, CA: University of California Press.

Li, Tania Murray, (ed.) 1999. *Transforming the Indonesian Uplands: Marginality, Power and Production*, Studies in Environmental Anthropology. Amsterdam: Harwood Academic Publishers.

——. 2007. The Will to Improve: Governmentality, Development and the Practice of Politics. Durham & London: Duke University Press.

——. 2009. 'To Make Live or Let Die? Rural Dispossession and the Protection of Surplus Populations', *Antipode* 14(6):6693.

——. 2014. Land's End: Capitalist Relations on an Indigenous Frontier [Submitted manuscript May 2013]. Durham & London: Duke University Press.

Liem, Soei Liong 2002. 'It's the military stupid!', in: Freek Colombijn and Thomas Lindblad (eds), *Roots of Violence in Indonesia: Contemporary Violence in Historical Perspective*, pp. 197–225. Leiden: KITLV Press. [Verhandelingen 194.]

Linder, Dianne Ethnic Conflict in Kalimantan 1999. Available from The Trade and Environment Database (TED): http://www.american.edu/projects/mandala/TED/ice/kalimantan.htm.

Lont, Hotze 2000. 'More Money, More Autonomy? Women and Credit in a Javanese Urban Community', *Indonesia* 70:83–100.

——. 2002. Juggling Money in Yogyakarta; Financial Self-help Organisations and the Quest for Security. PhD thesis, Amsterdam School of Social Science Research, University of Amsterdam, Amsterdam.

——. 2005. *Jugling Money: Financial Self-Help Organizations and Social Security in Yogyakarta*. Vol. 221, Verhandelingen Van Het Koninklijk Instituut Voor Taal-, Land - En Volkenkunde. Leiden: KITLV.

Lont, Hotze and Ben White 2003. 'Critical Review of Crisis Studies, 1998–2002; Debates on Poverty, Employment and Solidarity in Indonesia', in: Schulte-Nordholt, Henk and Gusti Asnan (eds), *Indonesia in Transition; Work in Progress*, pp. 125–160. Yogyakarta: Pustaka Pelajar.

Macarov, D. 1995. *Social Welfare: Structure and Practice*. London: Sage Publications.

Madurese Refugees get Relief from WVI. 1999 *Jakarta Post*, April 1.

Mansurnoor, Iik Arifin 1990. *Islam in an Indonesian World: Ulama of Madura*. Yogyakarta: Gajah Mada University Press.

Marcus, Anthony and Sulikah Asmorowati 2006. 'Urban Poverty and the Rural Development Bias: Some Notes from Indonesia', *Journal of Development Societies* 22(2):145–168.

Marianti, Ruli 2002. Surviving Spouses: Support for Widows in Malang, East Java. PhD thesis, Amsterdam School of Social Science Research, University of Amsterdam, Amsterdam.

McCarthy, John F., Piers Gillespie and Zahari Zen 2012. 'Swimming Upstream: Local Indonesian Production Networks in 'Globalized' Palm Oil Production', *World Development* 40(3):555–569.

McGoey, Linsey 2012. 'Strategic Unknowns: Toward a Sociology of Ignorance', *Economy and Society* 41(1):1–16.

Melvill van Carnbée, P. and W.F. Versteeg 1853–1862 *Atlas van Nederlandsch Indië*. Batavia: Van Haren, Norman & Kolff.

Midgley, James 1994. 'Social Security Policy in Developing Countries; Integrating State and Traditional Systems', *Focaal* 22(23):219–229.

Minza, Wenty Marina 2012. 'Young Migrants and Education-to-Work Transitions in Pontianak, West Kalimantan', *The Asia Pacific Journal of Anthropology* 13(1):64–75.

Mishra, Satish Chandra, B. Bawono Kristiaji and Ricardo G. Perkasa 2009. *Economic Inequality in Indonesia: Trends, Causes, and Policy Response, Strategic Asia*. Colombo: UNDP Regional Office Colombo.

Moser, C. and A. Norton 2001. *To Claim our Rights: Livelihood Security, Human Rights and Sustainable Development*. London: Overseas Development Institute.

Nawiyanto, S. 2003. *Agricultural Development in a Frontier Region of Java; Besuki, 1870 – Early 1990s*. Yogyakarta: Galang Press.

New York Times Indonesian gangs slaughter foes [The New York Times on the Web] March 21, 1999. Available from http://www.nytimes.com/aponline/i/AP-Indonesia-Village-Army.htm.

Niehof, Anke 1985. Women and Fertility in Madura (Indonesia). PhD thesis, Instituut voor Culturele Antropologie en Sociologie der Niet-Westerse Volken, Leiden University, Leiden.

Niehof, Anke, Roy Jordaan and Affandy Santoso 2005. 'Technological and Social Change in a Madurese Fishing Village (1978–2004)', *Bijdragen tot de Taal- Land- en Volkenkunde* 161(4):397–432.

Nooteboom, Gerben 2001. 'Kerja terus: Realitas kerja sehari-hari dan akses pada sumber daya di Krajan, Jawa Timur [Work and work; The reality of everyday work and access to resources in Krajan village, East Java]', in: Benda-Beckmann, F. von, K. von Benda-Beckmann and J. Koning (eds), *Sumber Daya Alam dan Jaminan Social di Indonesia* [*Natural Resources and Social Security in Indonesia*], pp. 345–378. Yogyakarta: Pustaka Pelajar.

——. 2003. A Matter of Style: Social Security and Livelihood in Upland East Java. PhD thesis, Dept. of Anthropology, Radboud University Nijmegen, Nijmegen http://webdoc.ubn.kun.nl/mono/n/nooteboom_g/mattofst.pdf.

——. 2005. 'Ondernemers en politie', in: Hüsken, Frans and Huub de Jonge (eds), *Schemerzones & Schaduwzijden: Opstellen over Ambiguïteit in Samenlevingen*, pp. 168–173. Nijmegen: Roelants.

——. 2008. 'Through Turbulent Times: Diversity, Vulnerability and Resilience of Madurese Livelihoods in East Kalimantan', in: Titus, M.J. and Paul P.M. Burgers (eds), *Rural Livelihoods, Resources and Coping with Crisis in Indonesia*, pp. 43–70. Amsterdam: Amsterdam University Press.

Nooteboom, Gerben and Laurens Bakker 2013. 'Beyond the Gulf State Investment Hype: The Case of Indonesia and the Philippines', in: Kaag, Mayke and Annelies Zoomers (eds), *Beyond the Land Grab Hype*, Chapter 10. London: Zed Books.

Nooteboom, Gerben and Pande Made Kutanegara 2003. 'The Storm Will Soon Be Over? Winners and Losers during the Economic Crisis in Java', *Moussons* 6:3–36.

Olivier de Sardan, Jean-Pierre 2005. *Anthropology and Development: Understanding Contemporary Social Change*. Translated by Alou, Antoinette Tidjani. London & New York: Zed Books.

PADev 2012. *Website: Participatory Assessment of Development (PADev)*. Amsterdam: University of Amsterdam: padev.nl.

Palte, G.L. 1989. *Upland Farming on Java, Indonesia: A Socio-Economic Study of Upland Agriculture and Subsistence under Population Pressure*. Vol. 97, Nederlandse Geografische Studies. Amsterdam: Koninklijk Nederlands Aardrijkskundig Genootschap. Original edition, thesis.

Peluso, Nancy Lee 2006. 'Passing the Red Bowl: Creating Community Identity through Violence in West Kalimantan, 1967–1997', in: Coppel, Charles (ed.), *Violent Conflicts in Indonesia: Analysis, Representation, Resolution*, pp. 106–128. London: Routledge.

Peluso, Nancy Lee and Emily Harwell 2001. 'Territory, Custom, and the Cultural Politics of Ethnic War in West Kalimantan, Indonesia', in: Peluso, Nancy Lee and Michael Watts (eds), *Violent Environments*, pp. 83–116. Ithaca and London: Cornell University Press.

Platteau, Jean-Philippe 1991. 'Traditional Systems of Social Security and Hunger Insurance: Past Achievements and Modern Challenges', in: Ahmad, E., J. Drèze and J. Hills (eds), *Social Security in Developing Countries*, pp. 112–163. Oxford: Clarendon Press.

——. 1995. 'A Framework for the Analysis of Evolving Patron-Client Ties in Agrarian Economics', *World Development* 23(5):767–786.

Popkin, Samuel L. 1979. *The Rational Peasant, the Political Economy of Rural Society in Vietnam*. Berkely: University of Calefornia Press.

Putra, R. Masri Sareb. 1999. *The Solution to the Sambas Riots. The Jakarta Post*, April 20.

Rachman, Noer Fauzi, Laksmi A. Savitri and Mohamad Shohibuddin 2009. 'Questioning Pathways Out of Poverty: Indonesia as an Illustrative Case for the World Bank's Transforming Countries', *Journal of Peasant Studies* 36(3):621–627.

Rankin, K.N. 2001. 'Governing Development: Neoliberalism, Microcredit, and Rational Economic Women', *Economy and Society* 30(1):18–37.

Retsikas, Konstantinos 2007. 'The Power of the Senses: Ethnicity, History, and Embodiment in East Java, Indonesia', *Indonesia and the Malay World* 35(102):183–210.

Richards, Paul 1985. *Indigenous Agricultural Revolution: Ecology and Food Production in West Africa*. Boulder, CO: Westview Press.

Ricklefs, M.C. 1991. *A History of Modern Indonesia Since c. 1300*. 2nd ed. London: Macmillan Press.

Robinson, Kathryn 2000. 'Economy as a Cultural System: The Economic Anthropology of Paul Alexander', *The Asia Pacific Journal of Anthropology* 1(1):3–13.

Rutten, Mario 2005. Differentiation and Labour Relations: Entrepreneurs and Labourers in Iron Foundries. Paper read at the Seminar Crisis and Social Change in Indonesia: Local, Comparative and Historical Dimensions, 6–7 January 2005, Yogyakarta.

Saptari, Ratna 1995. Rural Women to the Factories: Continuity and Change in East Java's kretek Cigarette Industry. PhD thesis, University of Amsterdam, Amsterdam.

Scheper-Hughes, Nancy 1992. *Death without Weeping: The Violence of Everyday Life in Brazil*. Berkeley, Los Angeles, London: University of California Press.

Schiller, Anne and Bambang Garang 2002. 'Religion and Inter-ethnic Violence in Indonesia', *Journal of Contemporary Asia* 32(2):244–254.

Schmit, Leo 1994. 'A History of the Volkscredietwezen (Popular Credit System) in Indonesia (1895–1935)', edited by Kuiper, Klaas. The Hague: Development Cooperation Information Department of the Ministry of Foreign Affairs.

Schröder-Butterfill, Elisabeth 2004. 'Adoption, Patronage and Charity: Arrangements for the Elderly without Children in East Java', in: Kreager, Philip and Elisabeth Schröder-Butterfill (eds), *Ageing without Children: European and Asian Perspectives*, pp. 106–146. New York: Blackwell.

Schröder-Butterfill, Elisabeth and Philip Kreager. 2001. Actual and de facto Childlessness in East Java: A Preliminary Analysis. *Paper read at the 3rd EUROSEAS Conference*, 6–8 December 2001, London.

Schulte Nordholt, Henk 1991. 'The Jago in the Shadow: Crime and 'Order' in the Colonial State in Java', *RIMA* 25(1):74–91.

Scoones, Ian 2009. 'Livelihoods Perspectives and Rural Development', *Journal of Peasant Studies* 36(1):171–196.

Scoones, I. and J. Thompson, (eds.) 1994. *Beyond Farmers First: Rural People's Knowledge, Agricultural Research and Extension Practice*. London: Intermediate Technology Publications.

Scoones, Ian and William Wolmer 2003. 'Introduction: Livelihoods in Crisis. Challenges for Rural Development in Southern Africa', *IDS Bulletin* 34(3):1–115.

Scott, James C. 1972. 'The Erosion of Patron-Client Bonds and Social Change in Rural Southeast Asia', *Journal of Asian Studies* 32(1):6–37.

——. 1976. *The Moral Economy of the Peasant: Rebellion and Subsistence in Southeast Asia*. New Haven and London: Yale University Press.

Scott, James 2009. *The Art of Not Being Governed: An Anarchist History of Upland Southeast Asia*. New Haven & London: Yale University Press.

Shakya, Yogendra B. and K.N. Rankin 2008. 'The Politics of Subversion in Development Practice: Microfinance in Nepal and Vietnam', *Journal of Development Studies* 44(8):1214–1235.

Singarimbun, Masri, (ed.) 1996. *Peluang Kerja dan Kemiskinan di Miri Sriharjo*, Penduduk dan Perubahan. Yogyakarta: Pustaka Pelajar.

Singarimbun, Masri and David Penny 1973. *Population and Poverty in Rural Java: Some Economic Arithmetic from Sriharjo*. New York: Ithaca, Cornell University Press.

Smith, Glen 1997. 'Carok Violence in Madura: From Historical Conditions to Contemporary Manifestations', *Folk: Journal of the Danish Ethnographic Society* 39:57–75.

——. 2011. Ecological Anthropology of Households in East Madura, Indonesia. PhD thesis, Department of Sociology of Consumers and Households, Wageningen University, Wageningen.

Stenross, Kurt 2011. *Madurese Seafarers: Prahus, Timber and Illegality on the Margins of the Indonesian State*. Honolulu: University of Hawai'i Press.

Streefland, P.H. 1996. 'Armoede en onderlinge hulp in Zuid-Azie', in: Linden, M. van der and J. Sluijs (eds), *Onderlinge hulpfondsen*, pp. 81–97. Amsterdam: International Institute of Social History.

Strout, Alan 1974. 'Population and Rural Poverty', *Bulletin of Indonesian Economic Studies* 10:125–136.

Sukma, Rizal 2005. 'Ethnic Conflict in Indonesia: Causes and the Quest for Solution', in: Snitwongse, Kusuma and W. Scott Thompson (eds), *Ethnic Conflicts in Southeast Asia*, pp. 1–41. Singapore: ISIS/ISEAS Press.

Suryadarma, Daniel, Wenefrida Widyanti, Asep Suryahadi and Sudarno Sumarto 2006. 'From Access to Income: Regional and Ethnic Inequality in Indonesia', Smeru Working Papers. Jakarta: Smeru Research Institute.

Suryadinata, Leo, Evi Nurvidya Arifin and Aris Ananta 2003. *Indonesia's Population: Ethnicity and Religion in a Changing Political Landscape*. Indonesian's Population Series No. 1. Singapore: Institute of Southeast Asian Studies.

Suryahadi, Asep and Sudarno Sumarto 2003. *Poverty Mapping Efforts in Indonesia*. Jakarta: SMERU.

Susanto, Andreas 2005. Crisis and Resilience among the Ethnic Chinese of Yogyakarta. Paper read at the seminar Crisis and Social Change in Indonesia; Local, comparative and historical dimensions, 6–7 January 2005, Yogyakarta.

——. 2006. 'Safety First: Strategies of Managing Insecurity among Chinese Indonesians in Yogyakarta', in: Koning, Julliette and Frans Hüsken (eds), *Ropewalking and*

Safetynets: Local Ways of Managing Insecurities in Indonesia, pp. 107–125. Leiden, Boston: Brill.

Tennekens, J. 1963. 'De bevolkingsspreiding der residentie Besoeki in 1930', *Tijdschrift van het Koninklijk Nederlandsch Aardrijkskundig Genootschap*, 80:309–423.

Townsend, Peter 1993. *The International Analysis of Poverty*. New York and London: Harvester Wheatsheaf.

Tsing, Anna Lowenhaupt 1999. 'Becoming a Tribal Elder, and Other Green Development Fantasies', in: Li, Tania Murray (ed.), *Transforming the Indonesian Uplands: Marginality, Power and Production*, pp. 159–202. Amsterdam: Harwood Academic Publishers.

——. 2005. *Friction: An Ethnography of Global Connection*. Princeton: Princeton University Press.

Van de Koppel, C. and C. Van Hall 1946–1950 *De landbouw in den Indischen archipel*. Vol. 1, 2a, 2b, & 3. The Hague: Van Hoeve.

Van der Kolff, G.H. 1937. *The Historical Development of the Labour Relationships in a Remote Corner of Java as They Apply to the Cultivation of Rice: Provisional Results of Local Investigations*. Batavia: Institute of Pacific Relations.

Van der Ploeg, Jan Douwe 1990. *Labor, Markets, and Agricultural Production*. Translated by Long, Ann. Boulder, CO: Westview Press.

——. 1999. *De virtuele boer*. Assen: Van Gorcum.

Van der Ploeg, Jan Douwe 2008. *The New Peasantries: Struggles for Autonomy and Sustainability in an Era of Empire and Globalization*. London: Earthscan.

——. 2010. 'The Peasantries of the Twenty-First Century: The Commoditisation Debate Revisited', *Journal of Peasant Studies* 37(1):1–30.

Van Dijk, Han 1994. 'Livestock Transfers and Social Security in Fulbe Society in the Hayre, Central Mali', *Focaal* 22–23:85–96.

Van Dijk, Kees, Huub de Jonge and Elly Touwen-Bouwsma, (eds.) 1995. *Across Madura strait: The Dynamics of an Insular Society, Proceedings/Koninklijk Insituut voor Taal-, Land- en Volkenkunde; 2*. Leiden: KITLV Press.

Van Ginneken, Wouter 1999. *Social Security for the Excluded Majority: Case Studies of Developing Countries*, edited by Ginneken, Wouter van. Geneva: International Labour Office.

Van Klinken, Gerry 2002. 'Indonesia's New Ethnic Elites', in: Schulte-Nordholt, Henk and Irwan Abdullah (eds), *Indonesia: In Search of Transition*, pp. 67–105. Yogyakarta: Pustaka Pelajar.

——. 2006. 'The Forest, the State, and Communal Conflict in West Kalimantan, Indonesia', in: Schulte Nordholt, Henk and Ireen Hoogenboom (eds), *Indonesian Transitions*, pp. 163–204. Yogyakarta: Pustaka Pelajar.

Van Schaik, Arthur 1986. Colonial Control and Peasant Resources in Java: Agricultural Involution Reconsidered. PhD thesis, Instituut voor Sociale Geografie, University of Amsterdam, Amsterdam.

Van Velsen, J. 1967. 'The Extended-Case Method and Situational Analysis', in: Epstein, A.L. (ed.), *The Craft of Social Anthropology*, pp. 129–149. London: Tavistock.

Van Voorst, Roanne 2014. Get Ready for the Flood: Risk-Handling Styles in Jakarta, Indonesia. PhD thesis Department of Anthropology and Sociology, AISSR, University of Amsterdam, Amsterdam.

Van Voorst, Roanne and M.J.J. Handgraaf. 2012. *Coping with Floods in a Riverbank-Settlement in Jakarta, Indonesia. The Influence of Material and Cognitive Indicators on Human Actor's Coping Behaviour. In the International Disaster and Risk Conference* (*IDRC*). Davos, Switzerland: IDRC.

Vel, Jacqueline 2000. 'Manu Wolu and the Birds' Nests: The Consequences of a Deviant Way to Cope with Insecurity', *Focaal* 22(23):35–46. Special issue: Coping with Insecurity; An 'Underall' Perspective on Social Security in the Third World, edited by Franz von Benda-Beckmann, Keebet von Benda- Beckmann and Hans Marks.

Vel, Jacqueline A.C. 2001. 'Tribal Battle in a Remote Island: Crisis and Violence in Sumba (Eastern Indonesia)', *Indonesia* 72:141–158.

——. 2008. *Uma Politics: An Ethnography of Democratization in West Sumba, Indonesia, 1986–2006*. Vol. 260, Verhandelingen. Leiden: KITLV Press.

Veth, P.J. 1903. 'Argopoera', in: Veth, P.J., Joh. F. Snelleman and J.F. Niermeyer (eds), *Java, Geographisch, Ethnologisch, Historisch*, pp. 564–75. Batavia: G. Kolff.

Von Benda-Beckmann, Franz 1990. 'Sago, Law and Food Security on Ambon', in: Bakker, J.I. Hans (ed.), *The World Food Crisis: Food Security in Comparative Perspective*, pp. 157–201. Toronto, ON: Canadian Scholars' Press.

Von Benda-Beckmann, Franz and Keebet Von Benda-Beckmann 1998. 'Where Structures Merge: State and Off-State Involvement in Rural Social Security on Ambon, Indonesia', in: Pannell, S. and F. von Benda-Beckmann (eds), *Old World Places, New World Problems: Exploring Resource Management Issues in Eastern Indonesia*, pp. 143–180. Canberra: The Australian National University, Centre for Resource and Environmental Studies.

Von Benda-Beckmann, Franz, Keebet Von Benda-Beckmann, E. Casino, Frank Hirtz, G.R. Woodman and H.F. Zacher, (eds) 1988. *Between Kinship and the State: Social Security and Law in Developing Countries*. Dordrecht, Netherlands: Foris Publications.

Von Benda-Beckmann, Franz, Keebet Von Benda-Beckmann and Juliette Koning (eds) 2001. *Sumber daya alam dan jaminan social di Indonesia* [*Natural Resources and Social Security in Indonesia*]. Yogyakarta: Pustaka Pelajar.

Von Benda-Beckmann, Franz, Keebet Von Benda-Beckmann and Hans Marks, (eds) 1994. *Special Issue: Coping with Insecurity: An 'Underall' Perspective on Social Security in the Third World*, Focaal. Focaal: 22/23.

White, Benjamin 1983. 'Agricultural Involution and Its Critics; Twenty Years after', *Bulletin of Concerned Asian Scholars* 15(2):18–31.

——. 2000. 'Rice Harvesting and Social Change in Java: An Unfinished Debate', *The Asia Pacific Journal of Anthropology* 1(1):79–102.

——. 2012. 'Changing Childhoods: Javanese Village Children in Three Generations', *Journal of Agrarian Change* 12(1):81–97.

White, Benjamin and Gunawan Wiradi 1989. 'Agrarian and Non-agrarian Bases of Inequality in Nine Javanese Villages', in: Hart, Gillian, Andrew Tarton and Benjamin White, et al. (eds), *Agrarian Transformations, Local Processes and the State in Southeast Asia*, pp. 266–302. Berkeley, CA: University of California Press.

Wiessner, P. 1982. 'Risk, Reciprocity and Social Influences on! Kung San Economics', in: Leacock, E. and R.B. Lee (eds), *Politics and History in Band Societies.* Cambridge: Cambridge University Press.

Wilson, Ian 2011. 'Reconfiguring Rackets: Racket Regimes, Protection and the State in Post-new Order Jakarta', in: Aspinall, Edward and Gerry Van Klinken (eds), *The State and Illegality in Indonesia*, pp. 239–259. Leiden: KITLV Press.

Wiradi, Gunawan 1984. 'Pola penguasaan tanah dan reforma agraria', in: Tjondronegoro, S.M.P. and Gunawan Wiradi (eds), *Dua abad penguasaan tanah; Pola penguasaan tanah pertanian di Jawa dar masa ke masa*, Jakarta: PT Gramedia.

Wisner, Ben, J.C. Gaillard and I. Kelman, (eds.) 2012. *The Routledge Handbook of Hazards and Disaster Risk Reduction.* London: Routledge.

Wolf, Eric R. 1966. 'Kinship, Friendship and Patron-Client Relations', in: Banton, M. (ed.), *The Social Anthropology of Complex Societies.* New York: Frederick A. Praeger.

World Bank 2012a. 'Protecting Poor and Vulnerable Households in Indonesia'. Jakarta: The World Bank.

——. 2012b. 'Targetting Poor and Vulnerable Housholds in Indonesia'. Jakarta: The World Bank.

Index